Richard Claverhouse Jebb

Attic Orators from Antiphon to Isaeus,

Volume 1

Richard Claverhouse Jebb

Attic Orators from Antiphon to Isaeus,
Volume 1

ISBN/EAN: 9783744738187

Printed in Europe, USA, Canada, Australia, Japan

Cover: Foto ©ninafisch / pixelio.de

More available books at **www.hansebooks.com**

THE ATTIC ORATORS

FROM ANTIPHON TO ISAEUS

THE ATTIC ORATORS

FROM

ANTIPHON TO ISAEUS

BY

R. C. JEBB, Litt.D.

REGIUS PROFESSOR OF GREEK AND FELLOW OF TRINITY COLLEGE, CAMBRIDGE
AND M.P. FOR THE UNIVERSITY

HON. D.C.L. OXON.; HON. LL.D. EDINBURGH, HARVARD, DUBLIN, AND GLASGOW
HON. DOCT. PHILOS. BOLOGNA

VOL. I

London
MACMILLAN AND CO.
AND NEW YORK
1893

First Edition printed 1876
Second Edition 1893

TO

THE REVEREND J. B. LIGHTFOOT, D.D.

CANON OF ST. PAUL'S,

LADY MARGARET PROFESSOR OF DIVINITY IN THE UNIVERSITY OF CAMBRIDGE,

HONORARY FELLOW AND LATE TUTOR OF TRINITY COLLEGE,

THESE PAGES ARE INSCRIBED

IN ADMIRATION OF HIS SERVICES TO THE CAUSE OF TRUE LEARNING,
AND IN AFFECTIONATE REMEMBRANCE OF CONSTANT KINDNESS,

BY HIS FORMER PUPIL

THE AUTHOR

1876

ὡς ἀνὴρ ἔκδαμος ὁδοιπορέων ἀυγάζεται   στρ.
γλυπτοὺς τεχνιτῶν τῶν πάρος ἔργα κολοσσούς,
ἀσύχοις μορφαῖσι νόον φθιμένων ἐξαγγελλομένους ἔτ' ἐοῦσιν,
οὐδὲ φρεσὶν δύναταί πω συμμαθεῖν
οἷος ἄρ' ἦν ὁ βίος
ὁπόθεν θ' αἱ φροντίδες
τῶν τάδ' ἐξειργασμένων·

ἀλλὰ λεύσσων θέλγεται ἐς τέλος ἐν θυμῷ λαβὼν   ἀντ.
κάλλος τι πάνταρχον, σκοπέει δὲ πανῆμαρ
τὰν προσώποις φαιδρὸν ἐφεζομέναν τοῖς ἡμιθέοισι γαλάναν
καὶ μελέων ἁβρὸν εὐρύθμων σθένος,
ἐκ δ' ὀλόλυξε χαρείς,
μακρός, ὦ κλεινοί, χρόνος
ὔμμε μὴ κάμνοι σέβων·

ὧδ', ἀείμναστοι στομάτων Διῒ τερπνῶν ῥήσιες,   ἐπ.
ἷς μένει ὑμετέρα, θαῦμ' ἀνδράσιν ἀλλοδαποῖς
οἳ σέλας οὐκ ἴδομεν χρυσανίου
τᾷ πρὶν ἐφ' Ἑλλάδι Φοίβου,
οὐδὲ πάτραν ἀνακαρῦξαί κεν ἔχοιμεν Ἀθάνας.
ὔμμι γὰρ ἀέλιον μέν φαμι δεδυκέναι, οὐδ' ἔμμεν σκότον,
ἀλλὰ λάμπους' ἀθάνατοι χάριτες
λευκὰν πρὸς ἀκτῖν' Ἑσπέρου.

PREFACE TO THE FIRST EDITION

THE first object of this book is to offer a contribution to a chapter in the history of Greek Literature which has perhaps received less attention than its importance deserves. The oratorical branch of Attic prose has a more direct and more fruitful relation to the general development than modern analogies would suggest. To trace the course of Athenian oratory from its beginnings as an art to the days of its decline is, necessarily, to sketch the history of Greek prose expression in its most widely influential form, and to show how this form was affected by a series of causes, political or social.

The second object of the book is to supply an aid to the particular study of the Attic orators before Demosthenes. The artistic development of Attic oratory is sketched as a whole. But a separate and minute treatment is given only to Antiphon, Andocides, Lysias, Isocrates and Isaeus. The period thus specially determined has more than a correspondence with a practical need: it has an inner unity, resting on grounds which are stated in the

Introduction and which are illustrated at each stage of the subsequent inquiry.

As regards the former and larger of these two purposes, the writer may venture to hope that his attempt, however imperfect, will be recognised at least as one for which, in this country, there is room. The History of Greek Literature by Otfried Müller —translated and continued by Donaldson—had been carried only to Isocrates when the author died, at the early age of forty-three, in 1840. Müller's chapters on "The beginnings of regular Political and Forensic Oratory among the Athenians" (XXXIII), on "The new cultivation of Oratory by Lysias" (XXXV), and on "Isocrates" (XXXVI), are, relatively to the plan of his work, very good: that is, they state clearly the chief characteristics of each writer separately. But this very plan precluded a full examination of each writer's works, and even a full discussion of his style. Nor does Müller appear to have regarded Oratory otherwise than as strictly a department, or adequately to have conceived its relation to the universal prose literature. The materials for a more comprehensive estimate had already been brought together in Westermann's *Geschichte der Beredsamkeit*, which carries the chronicle of technical rhetoric and of eloquence to the days of Chrysostom. But this great work is rather a storehouse of references than properly a history; and, owing to its vast compass and its annalistic method, gives too little space, proportionally, to the best period of Athens. Westermann's thesaurus and Müller's sketch have recently been supplemented by the excellent works of Dr. F. Blass: (1) "Die Attische Beredsamkeit von Gorgias bis zu Lysias," 1868: (2) "Isokrates und Isaios," 1874—of which the latter came into my hands only after my own chapters on Isocrates were almost wholly printed. I desire here to record in general terms my obligations to both these works. Particular debts are in every case, so far as I know, acknowledged on the page where they occur.

For the analyses of the orations it seemed best to adopt no uniform scale, but to make them more or less full according to the interest of the subject-matter or the nature of its difficulties. In analysing the works of Isocrates, which abound in matter of literary or historical value, I have endeavoured to give the whole of the contents in a form easy of access, and, at the same time, to preserve the most characteristic features of expression. A careful analysis, whether copious or not, is necessarily to some extent a commentary, since the analyst must exhibit his view of the relation in which each part of the writer's meaning stands to the rest.

In this sense, I hope that the analyses will serve my second and more special purpose—to help students of these five orators who have nothing but a Greek text before them. Critical scholarship in

England has done some of its best work on the orators before Demosthenes. The names of John Taylor, Markland, Robert Tyrwhitt, Dobree, Dobson, Churchill Babington — to mention only a few — are proof enough. But it is long since the orators before Demosthenes have been taken into the ordinary course of reading at our schools and universities. The commentary of Mr. Sandys on Isocrates *Ad Demonicum* and *Panegyricus* is (so far as I know) alone in this country. Frohberger's selections from Lysias, Schneider's selections from Isocrates, Rauchenstein's selections from Lysias and from Isocrates, Bremi's selections from Lysias and from Aeschines, are representative of the German feeling that these Greek orators should be read by ordinary students. The principal reason why they have dropped out of school and university favour among ourselves is perhaps not difficult to assign. Demosthenes and (in his measure) Aeschines have a political and historical interest of a kind which every one recognises, and which lends dignity to ancient prose in the eyes of a public that is rather political than philological. Many speeches which Demosthenes did not write have long been studied among us in the belief that they were composed by that statesman : while, on the other hand, comparatively few know, or comprehend, the conjecture of Mr. Freeman that every Athenian ecclesiast was equal in political intelligence to an average Member of Parliament.

In truth, an oration taken at hazard from Antiphon, Andocides, Lysias, Isocrates or Isaeus, will often be poor food for the mind if it is read alone. What is necessary to make it profitable is some idea of the world in which it was spoken. These orators who were not conspicuous actors in history must be read, not fragmentarily or in the light of notes which confine themselves to explaining what are termed "allusions," but more systematically, and with some general comprehension of the author and the age. Brougham, one of the best and most diligent critics of ancient oratory, himself tells us that he could not read Isaeus:—"the total want of interest in the subject, and the minuteness of the topics, has always made a perusal of them so tedious as to prevent us from being duly sensible of the force and keenness with which they are said to abound." If, however, Brougham had considered Isaeus, not as merely a writer on a series of will-cases, but as the oldest and most vivid witness for the working of inchoate testation in a primitive society, and, on the other hand, as the man who, alone, marks a critical phase in the growth of Attic prose, it is conceivable that Brougham should have thought Isaeus worthy of the most attentive perusal.

The present attempt to aid in giving Attic Oratory its due place in the history of Attic Prose was begun in the summer of 1870, and has since employed all the time that could be spared to it from the severe and almost incessant pressure of other occupations. In addition to the works of Dr. Blass, I would name the exhaustive work of Arnold Schäfer, *Demosthenes und seine Zeit*, as one which has been my constant help. M. Perrot's "L'Éloquence Politique et Judiciaire à Athènes: 1ʳᵉ Partie, Les Précurseurs de Démosthène," and Mr. Forsyth's *Hortensius*, also claim my gratitude. Among particular aids, I must mention the Essay on Isocrates, by M. Havet, prefixed to M. Cartelier's translation of the περὶ ἀντιδόσεως,—an acknowledgment which is the more due since, by an inadvertence for which I would fain atone, the essay is ascribed at p. 43 of my second volume, not to its true author, but to the scholar whose memory he has so loyally served. The article of Weissenborn on Isaeus in Ersch and Gruber's Encyclopaedia, the editions of Isaeus by Schömann and Scheibe, and the edition of the two Speeches On the Crown by MM. Simcox, must be added to the list. I am glad that my Introduction was not printed too soon to profit by some of Mr. Watkiss Lloyd's remarks on Pericles. The authorities, general or particular, not specified above will be found in a list which is subjoined. If an obligation anywhere remains unacknowledged, I would beg my readers to believe that it is by an oversight which I should rejoice to have the opportunity of repairing.

Last, though not least, I have to thank my

friend Mr. Sandys for his help in revising some of
the earlier sheets of the book for the press, as well
as for several valuable suggestions.

It seems probable that the study of antiquity,
especially of the Greek and Latin languages and
literatures, so far from declining, is about to enter
on a larger and a more truly vigorous life than it
has had since the Revival of Letters. That study
has become, in a new and fuller sense, scientific.
The Comparative Method, in its application to
Language, to Literature, to Mythology, to Political
or Constitutional History, has given to the classics
a general interest and importance far greater than
they possessed in the days when the devotion
which they attracted was most exclusive. For the
present, indeed, during a time of transition, the
very breadth of the view thus opened is apt to be
attended by a disadvantage of its own. So long as
the study given to ancient Greece or Rome was
practically confined to the short periods during
which the literature of either was most brilliant,
this study was often narrow, perhaps, but it was
usually searching and sympathetic. The great
masters in each kind were known at close quarters.
Their excellence was not something taken on credit,
as giving them their claim to a place in a rapid
survey. It was apprehended and felt. Paradoxes
as to their relative merits were, therefore, not so
easily commended to educated opinion in the name

of a revolt from academical prescription. I remember to have seen an ingenious travesty of "The Last Days of Pompeii," in which the sorcerer Arbaces had occasion to recite the praises of his countrymen, the Egyptians. "The Greeks," Arbaces sang, "are wonderfully clever; but *we* have invented the Greeks." Goethe said that Winckelmann had "found" the antique; but it appears sometimes to be forgotten that this merit is essentially distinct from that intimated by the Egyptian. In the meantime, I am persuaded that any one will be doing useful work who makes a contribution, however slight, to that close study of the *best* Greek literature which ought ever to be united with attention to the place of Greece in the universal history of the mind. In these things, as in greater still, the words are true, "Securus iudicat orbis terrarum."

THE UNIVERSITY, GLASGOW,
November 1875.

EDITIONS AND AUTHORITIES

I. CLASSICAL TEXTS

1. *Greek*

Oratores Attici.	J. G. Baiter and Hermann Sauppe, 1850. Vol. I.: Antiphon, Andocides, Lysias, Isocrates, Isaeus, Lycurgus, Aeschines, Deinarchus, Demosthenes. Vol. II.: Scholia to Isocrates, Aeschines, Demosthenes, and the Fragments of the Orators, from Gorgias to Demetrius Phalereus, arranged, with comments, by Sauppe. Hypereides, ed. F. Blass, 1869 (Teubner).—For the text, I have consulted also :—1. *Oratores Attici*, ed. Imm. Bekker, 1828. —2. *Oratores Attici*, ed. G. S. Dobson, with notes by H. Stephens, J. J. Scaliger, J. Taylor, J. Markland, J. J. Reiske, A. Auger, etc., 1828.— 3. Antiphon, Andocides, Deinarchus, ed. F. Blass, and Isaeus, ed. C. Scheibe, in Teubner's series.
Aristotle.	Imm. Bekker, edition of the Imperial Academy of Berlin, 1831–1870. The *Rhetoric*, with Commentary, L. Spengel, 1867.
Athenaeus.	J. Schweighauser, 1801–1804.
Comicorum Fragmenta.	F. H. Bothe, 1855 (Didot).
Diodorus.	L. Dindorf and C. Müller (Didot).
Diogenes Laertius.	C. G. Cobet, 1862 (Didot).
Dionysius of Halicarnassus.	J. J. Reiske, 1774. (Also text in the series of C. Tauchnitz, 1829.)
Eunapius.	Βίοι φιλοσόφων καὶ σοφιστῶν. J. F. Boissonade, Amsterdam, 1822.
Harpocration.	W. Dindorf, 1850.
Hesychius.	J. Alberti, 1746.
Lucian.	Imm. Bekker, 1853.
Pausanias.	L. Dindorf (Didot), 1845.
Philostratus.	C. L. Kayser, 1844.
Photius.	Imm. Bekker, 1824.

Plato.	J. G. Baiter, J. C. Orelli, and A. G. Winckelmann, 1842.
Plutarch, *Parallel Lives*.	Imm. Bekker, 1855.
[Plutarch] *Lives of the Ten Orators*.	In Plutarchi *Moralia*, ed. F. Dübner (Didot), 1868.
Pollux.	Imm. Bekker, 1846.
Rhetores Graeci.	(1) For Anaximenes, Aphthonius, Aristeides *Rhetoric*, Demetrius περὶ ἑρμηνείας, Hermogenes, Longinus, Theon, and the writer περὶ ὕψους:—*Rhetores Graeci*, ed. L. Spengel, 3 vols., 1853. (2) For the scholia, and for the lesser writers generally:—*Rhetores Graeci*, ed. C. Walz, 9 vols., 1832.
Sextus Empiricus.	πρὸς τοὺς μαθηματικοὺς ἀντιρρητικοί. J. A. Fabricius, Leipzig, 1718.
Stobaeus.	*Anthology*, 4 vols. ; *Eclogues*, 2 vols., ed. A. Meineke (Teubner), 1860.
Strabo.	C. Müller and F. Dübner (Didot), 1853.
Suidas.	G. Bernhardy, 1853.
Thucydides.	Imm. Bekker, 2nd ed., 1868.
Xenophon.	G. Sauppe, 1865.

2. Latin

Cicero.	*Opera omnia* (with the incerti *Rhet. ad Herennium*), C. F. A. Nobbe, Leipzig, 1869.
„	*Rhetorica* (*De Inventione*, l. II.), with the *Rhet. ad Her.*, F. Lindemann, Leipzig, 1828.
„	*De Oratore*, l. III. C. W. Piderit, Leipzig, 4th ed., 1873.
„	*Brutus de claris oratoribus*, C. W. Piderit, Leipzig, 2nd ed., 1875.
„	*Partitiones Oratoriae*, C. W. Piderit, Leipzig, 1867.
„	*De Optimo Genere Oratorum* (with *Orator*), O. Jahn, Berlin, 3rd ed., 1869.
Gellius.	Mart. Hertz (Teubner), 1853.
Lucilius, Fragments of.	In L. Müller's *Saturarum Reliquiae*, 1872.
Quintilian.	E. Bonnell (Teubner), 1868 ; commentary—Spalding, Buttmann, Bonnell, and Zumpt ; bks. I.-VI. Leipzig, 1798–1834.
Rhetorica ad Herennium.	F. Lindemann (see above), Leipzig, 1828.
De Oratoribus Dialogus.	In Tacitus, ed. J. G. Orelli, 1846.

II. OTHER AUTHORITIES[1]

Belin de Ballu, J. N.	*Histoire Critique de l'Éloquence chez les Grecs.* Paris, 1813.
Barthélemy, J. J.	*Voyage du jeune Anacharsis en Grèce.* Paris, 1788.
Becker, A. G.	*Andokides, übersetzt und erläutert.* 1832.
Beckhaus, H.	*Xenophon der jüngere und Isokrates.* Posen, 1872.
Benseler, G. E.	*De Hiatu in Oratoribus Atticis et Historicis Graecis.* 1841.
Berbig, F.	*Ueber das genus dicendi tenue des Redners Lysias.* Cüstrin, 1871.
,,	*Isokrates Werke, Griechisch und Deutsch.* 1854.
Blair, H.	*Lectures on Rhetoric and Belles Lettres.* London, 1783.
Blass, F.	*Die Attische Beredsamkeit von Gorgias bis zu Lysias.* Leipzig, 1868.
,,	*Isokrates und Isaios.* 1874.
,,	*Die Griechische Beredsamkeit in dem Zeitraum von Alexander bis auf Augustus.* 1865.
Boeckh, A.	*Die Staatshaushaltung der Athener.* 2nd ed., 1851.
Boehnecke, G.	*Demosthenes, Lykurgos, Hyperides und ihr Zeitalter.* 1864.
Brause, R. T.	*De aliquot locis Isocratis.* Freiburg, 1843.
Bremi, J. H.	*Lysiae et Aeschinis Orationes selectae.* 1826.
Brougham, Lord.	*Rhetorical and Literary Dissertations and Addresses.* 1856.
Campbell, G.	*The Philosophy of Rhetoric.* 7th ed., 1823.
Cartelier, A.	*Le Discours d'Isocrate sur lui-même* (with Introduction by E. Havet), 1862.
Clinton, H. Fynes.	*Fasti Hellenici.* 3 vols., 1834-1851.
Cobet, C. G.	*Novae Lectiones.* 1858.—*Variae Lectiones.* 1873.
Cope, E. M.	*The Sophists*, in Journ. of Class. and Sacred Philology, I. 145 : *On the Sophistical Rhetoric*, ib. II. 129, III. 253.
,,	*Introduction to Aristotle's Rhetoric.* 1867.
,,	*Plato's Gorgias, literally translated, with an Introductory Essay.* 1864.
Cowell, Herbert.	*Tagore Law Lectures for 1870.* Calcutta, 1870.
Cox, G. W.	*History of Greece.* Vols. I. and II., 1874.
Curtius, E.	*History of Greece*, translated by A. W. Ward. 5 vols., 1868-1872.
Dobree, P. P.	*Adversaria.* 2 vols., 1831.
Dyer, T. H.	*Ancient Athens.* 1873.
Eckert, H.	*De Epitaphio Lysiae falso tributo.* Berlin, 1865 (?).
Ernesti, J. C. T.	*Lexicon Technologiae Graecorum Rhetoricae.* 1795.
Finlay, G.	*Greece under the Romans*, B.C. 146–A.D. 716. 2nd ed., 1857.

---

[1] The following list does not claim to represent the literature of the subject. My purpose has been to set down every book—whether it has been expressly quoted or not—to which I am conscious of having owed help.

Forsyth, W.	*Hortensius: an Historical Essay on the Office and Duties of an Advocate.* 1874.
Francken, C. M.	*Commentationes Lysiacae.* Utrecht, 1865.
Franz, J.	*Dissertatio de locis quibusdam Lysiae arte critica persanandis.* Munich, 1830.
Freeman, E. A.	*Historical Essays.* Second Series, 1873.
„	*History of Federal Government.* Vol. I., *The Greek Federations*, 1863.
Frohberger, H.	*Lysias ausgewählte Reden.* 1868.
Gladstone, W. E.	*Studies on Homer.* 1858.
Grote, G.	*History of Greece*, ed. 1870.
Hager, Herman.	*Quaestionum Hyperidearum capita duo.* Leipzig, 1870.
„	*De Graecitate Hyperidea.*
Hecker, A.	*De Oratione in Eratosthenem XXXvirum Lysiae falso tributa.* 1847–8.
Henn, P.	*De Isocrate rhetore.* Köln, 1861.
Holmes, A.	*Demosthenes De Corona.* 1871.
Hölscher, L.	*Quaestiunculae Lysiacae.* Herford, 1857.
Hume, D.	*Essay XII., Of Eloquence.*
Jones, Sir W.	*The Speeches of Isaeus, with a Prefatory Discourse*, etc. 1779.
Jowett, B.	*The Dialogues of Plato, translated into English, with Analyses and Introduction.* 1st ed. 1871, and 2nd ed. 1875.
Kirchhoff, A.	*Andocidea,* in Hermes, I. 1–20.
Kyprianos, A.	Τὰ Ἀπόρρητα τοῦ Ἰσοκράτους. Athens, 1871.
Le Beau, A.	*Lysias Epitaphios als echt erwiesen.* Stuttgart, 1863.
Leloup, P. J.	*Prolegomena in Isocratis Philippicum.* 1825.
Liebmann, J. A.	*De Isaei Vita et Scriptis.* Halle, 1831.
Lightfoot, J. B.	On *Hyperides,* in Journ. of Class. and Sacred Philology, IV. p. 318. 1859.
Ljungdahl, S.	*De transeundi generibus quibus utitur Isocrates commentatio.* Upsala, 1871.
Lloyd, W. W.	*The Age of Pericles.* 1874.
Macaulay, Lord.	*On the Athenian Orators* (in *Miscellaneous Writings.* Vol. I.) 1860.
Madvig, J. N.	*Adversaria,* Vol. I.
Maine, H. S.	*Ancient Law.* 5th ed., 1874.
Meier and Schömann.	*Der Attische Process.* 1824.
Mitchell, T.	*Indices Graecitatis Oratorum Graecorum* (after Reiske). 1828.
Müller, K. O.	*History of the Literature of Ancient Greece*, translated and continued by J. W. Donaldson. 1858.
Mure, W.	*A Critical History of the Language and Literature of Ancient Greece.* 1857.
Oncken, W.	*Isokrates und Athen.* Heidelberg, 1862.
Ottsen, P. G.	*De rerum inventione ac dispositione quae est in Lysiae atque Antiphontis orationibus.* Flensburg, 1847.

EDITIONS AND AUTHORITIES

Overbeck, J.	*Geschichte der Griechischen Plastik.* 1869.
,,	*Die Antiken Schriftquellen zur Gesch. der Bildenden Künste bei den Griechen.* 1868.
Paley, F. A., and J. E. Sandys.	{ *Select Private Orations of Demosthenes.* Part I. Cambridge, 1874.
Pater, W. H.	*Studies in the History of the Renaissance.* 1873.
Perrot, G.	*L'Éloquence Politique et Judiciaire à Athènes : Première Partie, Les Précurseurs de Démosthène.* 1873.
,,	*Démosthène et ses Contemporains* (Revue des Deux Mondes, June 15, 1873).
Pfund, J. G.	*De Isocratis Vita et Scriptis.* Berlin, 1833.
Philippi, A.	*Beiträge zu einer Geschichte des Attischen Bürgerrechtes.* Berlin, 1870.
Rauchenstein, R.	*Ausgewählte Reden des Lysias.* 1864.
,,	*Isokrates, Panegyricus, Areopagiticus.* 1864.
Roelfzema, C. H. B. H.	*Annotationes in Isocratis Evagoram.* Gröningen, 1837.
Ruhnken, D.	*Historia Critica Oratorum Graecorum*, in his Opuscula.
,,	*Disputatio de Antiphonte*, ib.
Sandys, J. E.	*Isocrates. Ad Demonicum et Panegyricus.* 1868.
Sanneg, P.	*De Schola Isocratea.* Halle, 1867.
Schäfer, A.	*Demosthenes und seine Zeit.* 1856.
Schirach, G. B.	*De vita et genere scribendi Isocratis.* 1766.
Schmitz, P. J. A.	*Animadversiones in Isocratis Panathenaicum.* Marburg, 1835.
Schneider, O.	*Isokrates ausgewählte Reden.* 1860.
Schömann, G. F.	*Commentarii in Isaeum* (appended to an edit. of the text). Greisswald, 1831.
Schröder, H. P.	*Quaestiones Isocrateae duae.* Utrecht, 1859.
Sidgwick, H.	*The Sophists:* in Journal of Philology, IV. p. 288. 1872.
Simcox, G. A. Simcox, W. H.	{ *The Orations of Demosthenes and Aeschines On the Crown, with Introductory Essays and Notes.* 1872.
Sluiter, J. O.	*Lectiones Andocideae* (with C. Schiller's notes). 1834.
Spengel, L.	Συναγωγὴ Τεχνῶν, *sive Artium Scriptores.* 1828.
Stallbaum, G.	*Lysiaca ad illustrandas Phaedri Platonici origines.* 1851.
Starke, F. A. H.	*De Isocratis Orationibus Forensibus Commentationis Specimen.* 1845.
Strang, J. G.	*Kritische Bemerkungen zu den Reden des Isokrates.* 1831.
Symonds, J. A.	*Studies of the Greek Poets.* 1873.
,,	*Renaissance in Italy: Age of the Despots.* 1875.
Taylor, John.	*Lectiones Lysiacae* (in Dobson's *Oratores Attici*, Vol. II. pp. 94–158. 1828).
Télfy, J. B.	Συναγωγὴ τῶν Ἀττικῶν νόμων. Pesth, 1868.
Thirlwall, C.	*History of Greece*, ed. of 1855.
Thompson, W. H.	*On the Philosophy of Isocrates, and his Relation to the Socratic Schools.* Appendix II. to edition of

	Plato's *Phaedrus*, 1868. Also the Introductions to the *Phaedrus* and the *Gorgias* (1871), and the Commentary on both Dialogues.
Volkmann, R.	*Die Rhetorik der Griechen und Römer.* Berlin, 1872.
Wackernagel, W.	*Poetik, Rhetorik und Stilistik.* Halle, 1873.
Weijers, F. V.	*Diatribe in Lysiae Orationem in Nicomachum.* Leyden, 1839.
Weil, H.	*Les Harangues de Démosthène* (with Introd. and Commentary). 1873.
Weissenborn, H.	*Isäus*, in Ersch and Gruber's Encyclopaedia, Section II., Part 38, pp. 286–310.
Westermann, A.	*Geschichte der Griechischen Beredsamkeit.* 1835.
Whately, R.	*Elements of Rhetoric.* 7th ed., 1866.
Wilkins, A. S.	*National Education in Greece.* 1873.

CONTENTS

	PAGE
ANNALS	xxxv

INTRODUCTION

The Augustan Atticism	lxi
Caecilius and Dionysius	lxii
Caecilius on the Attic Orators	lxiii
The decade	ib.
Dionysius on the Attic Orators	lxiv
His classification—the εὑρεταί and the τελειωταί	lxvi
Plan of this book	ib.
The English word "orator" compared with the Latin, and with the Greek word ῥήτωρ	lxvii
Significance of the term "rhetor"	lxviii
Relation between ancient oratory and ancient prose	ib.
Relation between ancient and modern oratory	lxix
Ancient oratory is a fine art	ib.
I. Internal Evidence: 1. Finish of form; 2. Repetitions; 3. Speakers criticise each other's style	ib.
II. External evidence: 1. Training of speakers: 2. Appreciation shown by hearers; 3. Pamphlets in the oratorical form; 4. Collections of commonplaces; 5. Ancient critics compare oratory with sculpture or painting	lxxi
This conception is originally Greek	lxxv
Its basis—the idealisation of man	ib.
Its secondary motives: (1) the oral tradition of poetry; (2) the civil importance of speech; (3) competition	lxxvi
Characteristics of modern oratory	ib.

Aristotle on the three instruments of rhetorical proof (πίστις)	lxxvii
His estimate is that of the modern world : modern Oratory puts the logical proof first	ib.
The modern speaker has no distinct acceptance as an artist	lxxviii
The ancients were less strict about *logical* relevance	ib.
Influence of perfect reporting for the Press	lxxix
The modern feeling that a great speech must be extemporary	ib.
Sources of this feeling : 1. the failures of premeditation ; 2. the Hebraic basis of Christian education	ib.
Modern approximations to the theory of ancient Oratory : influence of debate	lxxxi
Finished rhetorical prose—Canning	ib.
Union of rhythmical finish with passion : Grattan—Erskine—Burke	lxxxii
Brougham on Burke compared with Demosthenes	lxxxvi
Modern eloquence of the pulpit	lxxxvii
Modern Oratory—its greatest triumphs won by sudden bursts	lxxxviii
Use of quotation	lxxxix
Special characteristics of Greek Oratory	xc
All Greek art has the plastic character	ib.
Popular misconception of what is meant by "plastic"	xci
A result of this misconception	ib.
Consequent danger to the whole study of the antique	xcii
Character of Greek thought in the best days of Greek art, compared with the oriental and with the mediaeval	ib.
Greek reflection was at a happy pause, and the Greeks were beautiful	xciv
Why Greek art became plastic rather than picturesque	ib.
Series of the arts — Sculpture comes between Architecture and the romantic group (Painting, Music, Poetry) — The limit of expression in Sculpture — not irksome, but congenial to the Greek	ib.
The best Sculpture is not cold nor vague	xcvi
Mistake of conceiving Greek Tragedy as the daughter of Sculpture	ib.
They are sister forms of that one tendency which we call "plastic"	ib.

	PAGE
Greek Tragedy has an alloy of trouble, but is still typical	xcvi
The true greatness of Euripides	xcvii
Fallacy involved in calling Euripides the most "human" of the Greek Dramatists	ib.
Sophocles is the most human	xcviii
Sophocles is the most perfect type of the Greek intellect	ib.
The plastic character as manifested in Greek Oratory	xcix
A series of types is developed by a series of artists	ib.
In the individual oration, the main lines of the theme are unperplexed, and the unity is sealed by a final calm	ci
Attic perorations in Cicero and in Erskine	cii
The personalities of ancient oratory	ib.
Superiority of Greek to Roman Oratory	ciii
Brougham on Cicero	ib.
Cicero's orations utterly unfit for the modern Senate or Bar; whereas almost all the Greek orations could be adapted	civ
Reasons of this superiority: 1. Greek Oratory is always to the point; 2. The political inspirations of Greek Oratory are nobler, and the forensic motive is more genuine	ib.
Early History of Greek Oratory—two conditions for the possibility of any such history	cvi
Late appearance of Greek Oratory as an art—brilliancy of the pre-theoretic Oratory	ib.
Homeric estimate and illustrations of eloquence	cvii
Modern character of the great Homeric speeches	ib.
Their historical significance	cviii
The Homeric eloquence is still aristocratic, not civil	ib.
First conditions of civil eloquence (1) ἰσηγορία, and (2) popular culture	ib.
The faculty of speech—its place in early Greek Democracy	cix
The intellectual turning-point—first conception of a literary prose	ib.
The political turning-point—opening of secure intercourse between the cities, and the new primacy of Athens	cx
External influences which prepared Attic oratory—I. The Practical Culture of Ionia	ib.

	PAGE
Protagoras	cxi
Prodicus	cxii
Hippias	cxiii
Summary: Influence of the Ionian practical culture	cxiv
II. The Sicilian Rhetoric	ib.
Character of the Sicilian Greeks	ib.
Political development of the Sicilian cities	cxv
The Age of the Tyrants—the Democratic Revolution	ib.
Character of Sicilian Democracy	ib.
Circumstances under which Rhetoric became an art:— Derangement of civil life by the Tyrants	ib.
Claims thence arising	cxvi
General features of such claims	cxvii
Best aids for such claimants,—1. skill in marshalling facts, 2. skill in arguing probabilities	ib.
Empedocles	ib.
Corax	cxviii
The treatise of Corax on Rhetoric—Arrangement, and the topic of εἰκός	ib.
Tisias and his Rhetoric	cxix
The topic of εἰκός further developed	cxx
Real meaning of the lawsuit story	ib.
Gorgias	ib.
His province neither Dialectic nor Rhetoric, but Oratory	cxxi
His first visit to Athens	cxxii
τὸ ξενίζον in his speaking	cxxiii
Its poetical character	ib.
Specimen from his Funeral Oration	cxxiv
His great popularity at Athens—how it is to be understood	ib.
Pericles: was his oratory artistic in form?	cxxv
Statement of Plutarch	cxxvi
Thucydidean speeches of Pericles	ib.
Notices of his oratory	ib.
Its distinctive conditions	cxxvii
History of Athenian oratory begins with Antiphon—a disciple not of Gorgias but of the Sicilian Rhetoric	ib.

	PAGE
Rhetoric and Popular Dialectic at Athens from 450 B.C.—Tragedy	cxxviii
Forensic Advocacy	ib.
Athens the chief seat of Civil Oratory	ib
Political morality of the Greeks—This morality most practical at Athens	cxxix
Relation of Athenian to Greek Oratory	ib.
Political aspect of Athenian Oratory	cxxxi
Political training of the Greek citizen, and especially of the Athenian	ib.
Civic sentiment in the Greek and in the Italian Republics—Athens and Florence	cxxxii
Civil Oratory defined—Attic Oratory fulfils this definition	cxxxiii

CHAPTER I

ANTIPHON.—LIFE

Birth of Antiphon	2
Antiphon the first λογογράφος	3
Antiphon and Thucydides	4
Antiphon's life to 411 B.C.	5
The Revolution	7
The two parties in the Council	9
Fall of the Four Hundred	11
Trial and Condemnation of Antiphon	12
Character of Antiphon's political life	14
Character of his ability	15
His ἀρετή	16
The new power of Rhetoric	17

CHAPTER II

ANTIPHON.—STYLE

Antiphon the most antique of the orators	18
The beginnings of Greek Prose	ib.
Character of the early Prose	20

	PAGE
Dionysius on the "austere" style .	21
Antiphon's style—its dignity	24
Reliance on single words . . .	25
Antiphon is imaginative, but not florid .	27
Pathos and êthos in Antiphon . .	29
The style of Antiphon—how far periodic	31
Antiphon's treatment of subject-matter .	36
Religious feeling of Antiphon	39
His Aeschylean tone	41
Relation of Antiphon to the elder democracy .	43

CHAPTER III

ANTIPHON.—WORKS

The φονικοὶ λόγοι alone extant	44
The Tetralogies .	ib.
First Tetralogy .	46
Second Tetralogy	51
Third Tetralogy . .	53
Speech on the Murder of Herodes	55
Speech on the Choreutes .	61
Speech Against a Stepmother	64
Lost Works: Authorship of the treatises On Truth, On Concord, On Statesmanship . . .	67
The Rhetoric—the Proems and Epilogues	69

CHAPTER IV

ANDOCIDES.—LIFE

Birth of Andocides	70
Affair of the Hermae .	71
Decree of Isotimides . .	74
The Speech On the Mysteries .	75
Life of Andocides from 415 to 402 B.C.	77
Life after 402 . .	80
Character of Andocides	83

CHAPTER V

ANDOCIDES.—STYLE

	PAGE
Andocides not an artist	87
Comparative neglect of him by the ancient critics	ib.
General tendency of ancient criticism upon oratory—unjust to Andocides	93
Four epithets given to his style in the Plutarchic Life	95
The diction of Andocides is "plain" (ἀφελής)	ib.
And "sparing of figures" (ἀσχημάτιστος)	96
His method is "simple" (ἁπλοῦς) and "inartificial" (ἀκατάσκευος)	98
Andocides has little skill in commonplaces of argument	100
His strength is in narrative	101
His references to the early history of Attica	103
Love of Andocides for gossip	104
His proneness to low comedy	105
Summary	ib.

CHAPTER VI

ANDOCIDES.—WORKS

Speech On his Return	107
Speech On the Mysteries	112
Historical matter in the Speech	118
Its arrangement and style	124
Speech On the Peace with the Lacedaemonians	125
Question of authenticity	127
Historical difficulties	ib.
Passage common to Andocides and Aeschines	130
Speech Against Alcibiades	131
Not by Andocides	132
Was Phaeax the author?	133
Ostracism misconceived	134
Particular errors in the speech	136
Lost works of Andocides	ib.
Doubtful Fragments	138

CHAPTER VII

LYSIAS.—LIFE

	PAGE
Birth of Lysias—doubt about the date	141
Lysias at Thurii	144
His life at Athens from 412 to 405 B.C.	145
The Anarchy	146
Lysias aids the Exiles	148
His professional life	149
The impeachment of Eratosthenes	150
Lysias and Socrates	*ib.*
Lysias at Olympia	151
Chronological limit of his known work	152
Character of Lysias	153

CHAPTER VIII

LYSIAS.—STYLE

It is easier for us to appreciate Lysias as a writer than as an orator; reason of this	155
Lysias the representative of the Plain Style	157
Its general characteristics	158
Originality of Lysias	159
Had his style been florid before it became plain?	161
His Composition	163
His diction—its purity	164
simplicity	166
clearness	167
conciseness, vividness	168
His ethopoiïa	169
The "propriety" of Lysias. His "charm"	172
His treatment of subject-matter	174
Invention. Arrangement	175
Proem	177
Narrative. Proof	178
Epilogue	179

The tact of Lysias	179
His humour	180
His sarcasm.—Defects of Lysias as an orator	181
The limits of pathos in Lysias	*ib.*
His eloquence rarely passionate	183
Exceptions	184
Place of Lysias in the history of Rhetoric	188
The ancient critics upon Lysias	189
Lysias and his successors	192
His services to the prose idiom	193

CHAPTER IX

LYSIAS.—WORKS

THE EXTANT COLLECTION.—EPIDEICTIC AND DELIBERATIVE SPEECHES

Proportion of extant to lost works	195
Condition of the extant speeches	*ib.*
Arrangement in the MSS.	196
Oratory at the Panhellenic festivals	198
The Olympiacus	199
Compared with the Panegyricus	201
The Epitaphius	*ib.*
Its character and authorship	203
Oration XXXIV., a Plea for the Constitution	206

CHAPTER X

LYSIAS.—WORKS

FORENSIC SPEECHES IN PUBLIC CAUSES

Principle of distinction between "public" and "private" law-speeches	208
I. Causes relating to offences directly against the State: (γραφαὶ δημοσίων ἀδικημάτων):	
1. Oration XX., For Polystratus	211
2. Oration XXI., Defence on a Charge of taking Bribes	214

	PAGE
3. Oration xxviii., Against Ergocles	215
4. Oration xxvii., Against Epicrates	217
5. Oration xxx., Against Nicomachus	218
6. Oration xxii., Against the Corndealers	221

II. Indictment for proposing an Unconstitutional Measure (γραφὴ παρανόμων)—Oration xviii., On the Property of the Brother of Nicias . . . 223

III. Claims for Moneys withheld from the State (ἀπογραφαί):
1. Oration ix., For the Soldier . 227
  The speech spurious . . 230
2. Oration xix., On the property of Aristophanes *ib.*
3. Oration xxix., Against Philocrates 235

IV. Causes relating to a Scrutiny (δοκιμασία) before the Senate; especially of Officials-designate :
1. Oration xxiv., Against Evandrus . 237
2. Oration xvi., For Mantitheus 240
3. Oration xxxi., Against Philon . 243
4. Oration xxv. (So-called) Defence on a Charge of seeking to abolish the Democracy 245
5. Oration xxiv., For the Invalid . 249

V. Causes relating to Military Offences (λιποταξίου—ἀστρατείας): 1. Oration xiv., Against Alcibiades, on a Charge of Desertion; 2. Oration xv., Against Alcibiades, on a Charge of Failure to Serve 251

VI. Causes relating to Murder or Intent to Murder (γραφαὶ φόνου — τραύματος ἐκ προνοίας) : 1. Oration xii., Against Eratosthenes . . . 256
2. Oration xiii., Against Agoratus . 265
3. Oration i., On the Death of Eratosthenes 271
4. Oration iii., Defence against Simon 272
5. Oration iv., On Wounding with Intent . 274

VII. Causes relating to Impiety (γραφαὶ ἀσεβείας, ἱεροσυλίας, κ.τ.λ.): 1. Oration vi., Against Andocides 277
  The speech not by Lysias 280
2. Oration v., For Callias . 283
3. Oration vii., On the Sacred Olive . 284

CHAPTER XI

LYSIAS.—WORKS

FORENSIC SPEECHES IN PRIVATE CAUSES—MISCELLANEOUS
WRITINGS—FRAGMENTS

	PAGE
I. Action for Defamation (δίκη κακηγορίας): Oration X., Against Theomnestus	289
II. Action by a Ward against a Guardian (δίκη ἐπιτροπῆς): Oration XXXII., Against Diogeiton . . .	293
III. Trial of a Claim to Property (διαδικασία): Oration XVII., On the Property of Eraton	296
IV. Answer to a Special Plea (πρὸς παραγραφήν): Oration XXIII., Against Pancleon	298
Miscellaneous Writings: 1. Oration VIII., To his Companions.—Not by Lysias . . .	300
2. The Eroticus in Plato's Phaedrus .	301
Preparation for a verbally exact recital	302
Character of the Criticism on the Speech	303
The ἐρωτικός is really by Lysias	305
Fragments	306
1. Against Cinesias . . .	307
2. Against Tisis. 3. For Pherenicus	308
4. Against the Sons of Hippocrates	309
5. Against Archebiades	*ib.*
6. Against Aeschines	310
Letters	311

VOL. I   *c*

ANNALS

Olympiads and Archons.	B.C.		
72. Diognetus	492		Fleet of Mardonius destroyed off Athos.
2. Hybrilides	491		Persian heralds sent by Dareius to demand earth and water from the Greek cities.
3. Phaenippus	490	Pindar Πυθ. 7 and (?) 12. Aeschylus fights at Marathon.	Persians, under Artaphernes and Datis, invade Greece: Hippias lands with them at Marathon. Athenian victory.
4. Aristides	489		Expedition of Miltiades to Paros: his disgrace and death.
73. Anchises	488	Pheidias born?	
2.	487	Simonides of Ceos flourishes.	
3.	486	Pindar Πυθ. 3.	Death of Dareius: Xerxes king of Persia.
4. Philocrates	485	Gorgias, Protagoras and Tisias born about this time.	Gelon becomes tyrant of Syracuse.
74. Leostratus	484	Pindar 'Ολυμπ. 10 and 11. Epicharmus writes Comedy at Syracuse. Aeschylus begins to be eminent in Tragedy. Herodotus born.	
2. Nicodemus	483		Aristeides ostracised.
3.	482		
4. Themistocles	481		
75. Calliades	480	Antiphon born. Pindar 'Ισθμ. 7. Euripides born. (Aeschylus was now 45, and Sophocles 15.)	Amnesty at Athens before Salamis I. 123. Second Persian invasion. Xerxes crosses Hellespont. Battles of Thermopylae, Artemisium and Salamis.
2. Xanthippus	479		Athenians reject the offers of Mardonius: he occupies Athens. Battles of Plataea and Mycale. Athenian ἀρχή founded. Athens rebuilt and Peiraeus fortified: Walls of Themistocles.

Olympiads and Archons	B.C.		
3. Timosthenes	478	History of Herodotus ends at siege of Sestus (spring).	Hieron succeeds Gelon as tyrant of Syracuse: Corax flourishes in his reign (cf. 466 B.C.). Pausanias recalled from Byzantium to Sparta.
4. Adeimantus	477		Formation of Delian Confederacy under headship of Athens: tribute assessed on members by Aristeides. Treason of Pausanias.—Cleisthenean constitution begins to be developed through the ναυτικὸς ὄχλος: Fourth Class made eligible for archonship: boards for internal administration multiplied (ἀγοράνομοι, ἀστύνομοι, etc.)
76. Phaedon	476	Phrynichus tragicus victor with Φοίνισσαι.	Athenians take Eion, reconquer Lemnos, reduce Scyros and Carystus.
2. Dromocleides	475		
3. Acestorides	474		
4. Menon	473		
77. Chares	472	Pindar Ὀλυμπ. 1 and 12. Death of Pythagoras act. 99. Aeschylus Πέρσαι.	Thrasydaeus, tyrant of Agrigentum, expelled: Empedocles opposes the restoration of the tyranny, I. cxviii.
2. Praxiergus	471	Thucydides born.	
3. Demotion	470		
4. Apsephion	469		
78. Theagenides	468	Pindar Ὀλυμπ. 6. Sophocles gains his first tragic victory, aet. 28. Socrates born.	Death of Aristeides.
2. Lysistratus	467		Thrasybulus succeeds Hieron as tyrant of Syracuse.
3. Lysanias	466	Corax begins to teach Rhetoric at Syracuse: I. cxviii.—Pindar Πυθ. 4 and 5.	Thrasybulus expelled from Syracuse: Gelonian dynasty overthrown and a democracy established. Naxos revolts from Athens and is subjugated.
4. Lysitheus	465	Bacchylides flor.	Athenian colonists destroyed by Thracians near Ennea Hodoi: II. 189. Thasos revolts from Athens: is reduced 463 B.C. Death of Xerxes: Artaxerxes I. (Μακρόχειρ) king (—425 B.C.)
79. Archidemides	464	Pindar Ὀλυμπ. 7 and 13.	Helots rise against Spartans (—455 B.C.): quarrel between Athens and Sparta: alliance between Athens and Argos.
2. Tlepolemus	463		
3. Conon	462		
4. Evippus	461		Megara joins Athenian alliance: Long Walls of Megara built.

ANNALS

Olympiads and Archons.	B.C.		
80. Phrasiclei-des	460	Parmenides visits Athens. Zenon of Elea ("inventor of Dialectic," Arist.) flor. Hippocrates the physician born. Democritus born. Calamis, sculptor, flor. Polygnotus, painter, flor.	Cephalus, father of Lysias, invited to settle at Athens by Pericles ? I. 140. Revolt of Egypt from Persia (—455 B.C.)
2. Philocles	459	Lysias born, acc. to [Plut.] and Dionys. (cf. 444 B.C.) I. 141. — Thrasymachus of Chalcedon born ?	Reforms of Ephialtes II. 209.
3. Bion	458	Aeschylus 'Ορεστεία.	Cimon ostracised ?
4. Mnesithei-des	457		Long Walls of Athens begun. Embitterment of the conservative party: murder of Ephialtes.—Athenians defeated at Tanagra by Lacedaemonians and allies. — Athenians defeat Boeotians at Oenophyta. Athenian empire at its greatest extent.
81. Callias	456	Pindar 'Ολυμπ. 9. Death of Aeschylus aet. 69.	Cimon recalled from exile. Completion of two Long Walls, viz. (1) that from Athens to Phaleron, τὸ Φαληρικὸν τεῖχος, and (2) that from Athens to the Peiraeus, afterwards known as τὸ Βόρειον τεῖχος. A third wall, between these two (τὸ διὰ μέσου, or τὸ νότιον), was built some years later.
2. Sosistratus	455	First tragedy, Πελιάδες, of Euripides, aet. 36.	Destruction of Athenian armament sent to help Inaros II. 188. Persians reduce all Egypt except the fens held by Amyrtaeus.—Ithome surrenders to Sparta (cf. 464 B.C.): Tolmides, στρατηγός, settles expelled Helots at Naupactus.—Athens conquers Aegina.
3. Ariston	454		Death of Alexander I. (φιλέλ-λην) of Macedon (498 B.C.—): accession of Perdiccas.
4. Lysicrates	453		
82. Chaerepha-nes	452	Pindar 'Ολυμπ. 4 and 5.	
2. Antidotus	451	Ion of Chios, tragic poet, begins to exhibit.	
3. Euthyde-mus	450	Crates comicus. Anaxagoras aet. 50 withdraws from Athens: he had taught Pericles and Euripides.	Five Years' Truce between Athens and Sparta I. 129. Athens sends 60 ships to help Amyrtaeus in Egypt.
4. Pedieus	449		Siege of Citium in Cyprus by Cimon: cf. II. 188. His death. Athenian victory at

Olympiads and Archons.	B.C.		
83. Philiscus 2. Timarchides	448 447	Cratinus comicus flor.	the Cyprian Salamis. Alleged treaty ("of Callias") between Athens and Persia, II. 156. Alcibiades born? Death of Themistocles.—Athenians under Tolmides defeated by Boeotians at Coronea. Athenians evacuate Boeotia: their ἀρχή begins to break up.
3. Callimachus 4. Lysimachides	446 445	Ictinus and Callicrates, architects, flor.	Euboea and Megara revolt from Athens. Lacedaemonians under Pleistonnax invade Attica. Thirty Years' Truce between Athens and Sparta: Andocides, grandfather of the orator, an envoy, I. 130.
84. Praxiteles	444	Date for birth of Lysias placed between this year and 436 by C. F. Hermann and Blass, I. 142 (cf. 459 B.C.). Pheidias act. 44 has superintendence of the public art-works of Athens.	
2. Lysanias	443	Death of Pindar act. 79. Herod. act. 43 goes to Thurii: Lysias either now or later.	Foundation of Thurii (I. 141), by Athenian colonists, on the site of Sybaris. Thucydides, son of Melesias, ostracised: aristocratic party broken up.
3. Diphilus	442	Euripides act. 49 gains, for the first time, the first prize in tragedy.	
4. Timocles 85. Myrochides	441 440	Andocides born, I. 70. Decree to put down Comedy (ψήφισμα τοῦ μὴ κωμῳδεῖν). Sophocles 'Αντιγόνη (in the year of his στρατηγία).	Revolt of Samos from Athens: Andocides avus and Sophocles command with Pericles against Samos, I. 71. Samos surrenders in 9th month. Appeal of Samians to Lacedaemonians: congress at Sparta: Corinthians insist on the principle of non-interference with an autonomous city.
2. Glaucines 3. Theodorus	439 438	Parthenon completed and dedicated: Pheidias act. 50. — Euripides Ἄλκηστις.	
4. Euthymenes	437	Pheidias goes to Elis. Decree against Comedy repealed.	
86. Lysimachus	436	Isocrates born, II. 2. The Zeus at Olympia completed by Pheidias.	The people of Epidamnus apply to their metropolis Corcyra:

Olympiads and Archons.	B.C.		
2. Antilochides	435	Propylaea of Athens begun. Phrynichus comicus begins to write.	help is refused, and they apply to Corinth. Corinthian army admitted into Epidamnus: sea-fight between Corinthians and Corcyraeans: Epidamnus capitulates to Corcyraeans.
3. Chares	434		
4. Apseudes	433		Embassies to Athens from Corcyra and from Corinth: Athens makes a *defensive* alliance with Corcyra: 10 Athenian ships sent to Corcyra under Lacedaemonius son of Cimon.
87. Pythodorus	432	Pheidias and Aspasia prosecuted. ἀσεβείας: Pheidias dies in prison—Anaxagoras also prosecuted: he withdraws to Lampsacus.	Corcyraeans, supported by Athenians, defeated in a sea-fight by Corinthians (spring).—Athenians blockade Pydna and Potidaea.—Congress at Sparta (autumn): a large majority of the allies vote for war with Athens.
2. Euthydemus	431	Pericles speaks the ἐπιτάφιος of those who had fallen in the first year of the war. Euripides Μήδεια. Xenophon born.	Peloponnesian demands rejected by Athens.—*Beginning of Peloponnesian War.*—Theban attempt on Plataea.—First invasion of Attica under Archidamus.—Brasidas, now first heard of, rescues Methone from Athenians.
3. Apollodorus	430	Polycleitus, sculptor, flor.	*Year 2 of War.*—Second invasion of Attica.—Plague at Athens.—Pericles unpopular: he is fined, but re-elected strategus.
4. Epameinon	429	Damon, musician, flor. II. 143. Plato born (May).—Death of Pericles (autumn). Eupolis writes Comedy.	*Year 3 of War.*—Potidaea surrenders on conditions (cf. 332 B.C.)—Phormion, commanding Athenian fleet, gains two victories in Corinthian gulf.
88. Diotimus	428		*Year 4 of War.*—Lesbos, except Methymna, revolts: Athenians besiege Mytilene.—Third invasion of Attica, led by Cleomenes.
2. Eucleides	427	Gorgias visits Athens as chief envoy of Leontini, I. cxxiii. Tisias accompanies him, acc. to Paus. Aristophanes begins to satirise the New Culture in his Δαιταλεῖς—a contrast between the old school and the new.	*Year 5 of War.*—Plataea destroyed by Sparta, II. 175.—Fourth invasion of Attica, led by Cleomenes.—Mytilene taken by Athenians, I. 55: massacre proposed by Cleon and averted by Diodotus.—Strife at Corcyra between oligarchs and demos (summer). Athens sends help to Leontini.
3. Euthynus	426	Aristophanes Βαβυλώνιοι—	*Year 6 of War.*—Athenians

Olympiads and Archons.	B.C.		
4. Stratocles	425	a plea for the allies against Cleon, etc. Aristophanes 'Αχαρνεῖς. Zeuxis, painter, flor.	purify Delos and restore the Panionic festival, to be held there every 4 years. Year 7 of War.—Corcyraean demos, helped by Eurymedon and Athenians, storm Istone: massacre of oligarchs.—Fifth invasion of Attica led by Agis II.—Demosthenes occupies Pylos. Spartan hoplites blockaded in Sphacteria: Cleon takes the island, and brings Spartan prisoners to Athens.—Death of Artaxerxes I. (465 B.C.—See next year.)
89. Isarchus	424	Aristophanes Ἱππεῖς.	Year 8 of War.—Defeat of Athenians by Thebans at Delium.—Brasidas in Thrace: he gains Acanthus, Amphipolis, Stageirus, Torone.—Congress of Sicilian Greeks at Gela: Hermocrates denounces Athenian aggression. Accession of Dareius II. (Νόθος—405 B.C.) after a contest.
2. Ameinias	423	Thucydides, the historian, is banished, or withdraws from Athens, in consequence of his failure to save Amphipolis (January?). Returns to Athens in 403. Aristophanes Νεφέλαι (1st edit.)	Year 9 of War.—Brasidas in Thrace: Scione and Mende revolt from Athens.—Truce for a year.
3. Alcaeus	422	Aristophanes Σφῆκες.	Year 10 of War.—Torone recovered by Cleon. Battle of Amphipolis: Cleon and Brasidas killed.—Number of Athenian males above the age of 20 was at this time about 20,000: total civic population (excluding μέτοικοι and slaves) about 82,000: average attendance in Ecclesia, about 5000.
4. Aristion	421	Eupolis in his Κόλακες brings in Protagoras as then living at Athens.	Year 11 of War.—Peace " of Nicias," for 50 years, nominally valid down to 414, but not accepted by Boeotians, Corinthians or Megarians.
90. Astyphilus	420	Isaeus born II. 264. Plato comicus flor.	Year 12 of War.—Separate treaty of Sparta with (1) Boeotians, (2) Argives.—Alcibiades contrives to alienate the Argives from Sparta: defensive alliance between Athens, Argos, Elis and Mantineia.

ANNALS

Olympiads and Archons.	B.C.		
2. Archias	419		Year 13 of War.—Alcibiades στρατηγός: he makes a progress through Achaia.—Invasion of Epidaurus by Argives.
3. Antiphon	418		Year 14 of War.—Spartans invade Argos. Argives, with Alcibiades, attack Orchomenus: Spartans come to the defence of Tegea. Battle of Mantineia (cf. 362 B.C.): Complete victory of Spartans over Argives and Athenians. Oligarchical conspiracy of the Thousand at Argos.
4. Euphemus	417	Antiphon or. 5 περὶ τοῦ Ἡρώδου φόνου, I. 58.	Year 15 of War.—Rising of Argive demos against oligarchs. —Athenian expedition to get back Amphipolis: Perdiccas of Macedon breaks faith, and the plan fails.—Ostracism of Hyperbolus, I. 131—the tenth, and last, recorded exercise of ostracism since its institution by Cleisthenes about 509 B.C. (Cf. I. 134.)
91. Arimnestus	416	Agathon tragicus flor.	Year 16 of War.—Athenians take Melos, II. 154. Victories of Alcibiades at Olympia! II. 228.—Embassy to Athens from Egesta, asking help against Selinus. Athenian envoys sent to Egesta.
2. Chabrias	415	Andocides banished, under the decree of Isotimides, I. 74. Fictitious date of [Andoc.] or. 4 κατὰ Ἀλκιβιάδου, I. 131. Socrates flor., aet. 53: Plato is now 14: Alcibiades circ. 34, Xenophon circ. 16.—Euripides Τρωάδες.	Year 17 of War.—Envoys return from Egesta: Sicilian Expedition voted.—Mutilation of the Hermae, just as fleet is going to sail for Sicily (May), I. 71—(Athenian ambitions in 415: II. 187.)—Alcibiades accused of profaning Mysteries.—Expedition sails for Sicily under Nicias, Lamachus and Alcibiades. — Excitement caused at Athens by disclosures of Diocleides and Andocides. Alcibiades condemned to death in his absence. Nicias misses his chance of investing Syracuse.
3. Peisander	414	Aristophanes Ὄρνιθες.	Year 18 of War.—Second campaign in Sicily. Lamachus killed. Gylippus enters Syracuse. Nicias writes to Athens for help.
4. Cleocritus	413		Year 19 of War.—Decelcia in Attica fortified by Lacedaemonians, II. 188, who ravage Attica. Formal end to the truce of 421. Beginning of

Olympiads and Archons.	B.C.		
			the second chapter of the War, called the Δεκελεικὸς or Ἰώνιος πόλεμος (—404 B.C.)—*Third campaign in Sicily.* Sea-fight at Syracuse: Athenian fleet destroyed. Death of Nicias and of Demosthenes. Death of Perdiccas, King of Macedon (454 B.C.—): accession of Archelaus (—399 B.C.)
92. Callias	412	Antiphon or. 6 περὶ τοῦ χορευτοῦ? I. 61.—Lysias and his brother Polemarchus, driven from Thurii, come to Athens. —Euripides Ἑλένη, Ἀνδρομέδα. Callimachus, sculptor, flor.	*Year* 20 *of War.* — Revolt of Lesbos from Athens, I. 58. Revolt of Euboea, II. 265. Revolt of Chios, II. 158. Pedaritus commands there for Sparta, II. 198. Revolt of Miletus. Oropus seized by Boeotians, II. 178. Athenians lose a sea-fight off Cnidus, II. 351. — Samian demos, true to Athens, rises against the oligarchs. Athenian fleet musters at Samos: Spartan Astyochus defeats Charminus. Alcibiades takes refuge from Spartans with Tissaphernes: his overtures to the Athenian leaders.
2. Theopompus	411	First return of Andocides to Athens, I. 78. Antiphon dies, I. 13. Xenophon begins his Ἑλληνικά with the manœuvres at the Hellespont just after the battle of Cynossema: cf. 362 B.C. Aristophanes Λυσιστράτη, Θεσμοφοριάζουσαι.	*Year* 21 *of War.*—Government of the Four Hundred, I. 7: (March — June.) — Eratosthenes (Lys. or. 12) active at the Hellespont for the oligarchs: I. 261. — Athenian victory at Cynossema.—Evagoras begins to reign? II. 106.
3. Glaucippus	410	Second return of Andocides to Athens: or. 2. περὶ τῆς ἑαυτοῦ καθόδου, I. 107.—Dramatic date of Plato Φαῖδρος? II. 3.—History of Thucydides breaks off after the battle of Cyzicus.	*Year* 22 *of War.*—Thrasyllus commands on coast of Asia Minor, I. 294.—Second form of the Trierarchy brought in — συντριηραρχία: cf. 357, 340 B.C.—Athenians attack and recover Cyzicus: death of Spartan admiral Mindarus. — Cleophon δημαγωγός: Athens rejects Spartan offers of peace.
4. Diocles	409	Sophocles Φιλοκτήτης.	*Year* 23 *of War.* — Athenian campaign under Thrasyllus in Lydia. — Messenians in Pylus surrender to Sparta — Megara recovers Nisaea.
93. Euctemon	408	Euripides Ὀρέστης. Aristophanes Πλοῦτος (1st edit.: cf. 388 B.C.)	*Year* 24 *of War.*—Alcibiades recovers Selymbria and Byzantium for Athens. — Troops under Thrasyllus defeated at Ephesus, I. 294.

ANNALS

Olympiads and Archons.	B.C.		
2. Antigenes	407	Lysias or. 20 ὑπὲρ Πολυστράτου? I. 211.	*Year 25 of War.*—Alcibiades returns to Athens, is chosen στρατηγός and leads the procession to Eleusis. — Antiochus, the pilot of Alcibiades, defeated by Lysander off Notion. Alcibiades plunders Cyme. He is deposed from his στρατηγία: ten new Generals are chosen.
3. Callias	406	Death of Euripides.	*Year 26 of War.*—Dionysius I. becomes tyrant of Syracuse, II. 170. —Callicratidas (successor of Lysander) storms Methymna and blockades Conon in Mytilene. Complete victory of Athenians at Arginusae: death of Callicratidas.—Theramenes accuses the Generals: six are put to death, Socrates protesting.
4. Alexias	405	Death of Sophocles. Aristophanes Βάτραχοι. Dramatic date of Plato Γοργίας.	*Year 27 of War.* — Battle of Aegospotami (late autumn). The Areiopagus takes measures for public safety, II. 212. Conon escapes to Evagoras. Death of Darieus II. (424 B.C.—): Artaxerxes II. (Μνήμων—359 B.C.) succeeds him.
94. Pythodorus	404	Polemarchus, brother of Lysias, put to death by the Thirty (May); Lysias escapes to Megara, I. 148: cf. 263.—Isocrates leaves Athens for Chios, II. 6.	Theramenes brings the terms of peace from Sparta. Agoratus informs, I. 265. Athens surrenders to Lysander. Critias and Eratosthenes are among the five ἔφοροι, and then among the Thirty, I. 261. Tyranny of the Thirty begins (April). Thrasybulus advances from Phyle to Peiraeus. The Thirty deposed in 8th month (Dec.). Theramenes put to death in autumn, II. 6.— Death of Alcibiades *aet. circ.* 45.
2. Eucleides	403	Proposal to give Lysias the citizenship defeated by Archinus, I. 149. Lysias or. 12 κατὰ Ἐρατοσθένους, I. 256.—Lysias or. 34 περὶ τοῦ μὴ καταλῦσαι τὴν πολιτείαν, I. 206. Isocrates returns to Athens, II. 6. Isocrates or. 21 πρὸς Εὐθύνουν, II. 221.	Thrasybulus and the exiles in the Peiraeus are at war with the Ten; but are in possession of Athens before the end of July. — Democracy formally restored in September.—Law of Aristophon, II. 329. — Knights who had served under the Thirty are required to refund their κατάστασις, I. 242. —Expedition from Athens to Eleusis, to dislodge the Thirty, I. 247.
3. Micon	402	Third and final return of Andocides to Athens.	

Olympiads and Archons.	B.C.		
4. Xenaenetus	401	Lysias or. 21 δωροδοκίας ἀπολογία, I. 214. Lysias or. 24 ὑπὲρ τοῦ ἀδυνάτου? I. 249. Isocrates or. 18 πρὸς Καλλίμαχον, II. 233. Lysias or. 25 δήμου καταλύσεως ἀπολογία, I. 245. Sophocles Οἰδίπους ἐπὶ Κολωνῷ: brought out by Sophocles nepos.	Expedition of Cyrus the younger, II. 159,171. Battle of Cynaxa and death of Cyrus (autumn). —Retreat of the Greeks: they reach Armenia in the winter. —War between Lacedaemon and Elis.
95. Laches	400	Parrhasius, painter, flor.	Campaign of Thimbron in Asia Minor, II. 159. The Greeks in their retreat reach Cotyora on the Euxine eight months after battle of Cynaxa.
2. Aristocrates	399	Andocides or. 1 περὶ τῶν μυστηρίων, I. 112.—Death of Socrates, I. 150.— Lysias or. 30 κατὰ Νικομάχου, I. 218.—[Lys.] or. 6 κατὰ 'Ανδοκίδου, I. 277. — Plato withdraws to Megara. — Lys. or. 13 κατὰ 'Αγοράτου. I. 265.	Proceedings before the Areiopagus against men formerly of the XXX., I. 292. Dercyllidas supersedes Thimbron in Asia Minor, II. 159. —Death of Archelaus of Macedon (413 B.C.—) ; his son Orestes succeeds, but is dispossessed (396 B.C.) by his guardian Aeropus. See 394.
3. Ithycles	398	Ctesias brought his Περσικά to this year.	Second campaign of Dercyllidas in Asia Minor.
4. Suniades	397	Lysias or. 17 περὶ δημοσίων χρημάτων [better περὶ τῶν 'Εράτωνος χρημάτων], I. 296. Isocrates or. 17 περὶ τοῦ ζεύγους, II. 228.	Third campaign of Dercyllidas in Asia Minor: he is about to invade Caria when he meets the satraps and makes an armistice with Tissaphernes.
96. Phormion	396		Beginning of ὁ περὶ 'Ρόδον πόλεμος between Persia and Sparta (—394 B.C.), II. 159. First campaign of Agesilaus in Asia Minor, II. 160.
2. Diophantus	395	Lysias or. 18 περὶ δημεύσεως τῶν τοῦ Νικίου ἀδελφοῦ, I. 223. Plato act. 34 returns to Athens. His Γοργίας written between this year and 389. Lysias or. 7 περὶ τοῦ σηκοῦ? I. 284.	Athenian expedition to relieve Haliartus, I. 242. Alcibiades the younger takes part, I. 253. and Lysander is killed.— Second campaign of Agesilaus.
3. Eubulides	394	[Lysias] or. 9 ὑπὲρ τοῦ στρατιωτοῦ, I. 227. Isocrates or. 20 κατὰ Λοχίτου, II. 215. — (or 393) or. 19 Αἰγινητικός, II. 218: or. 17 Τραπεζιτικός, II. 223.	Beginning of Corinthian War (—390 B.C.), II. 159. Naval campaigns of Conon (Lys. or. 19),I.230.—Battle of Corinth. Agesilaus in Boeotia (autumn), I. 242. Battle of Cnidus, ii. 159. — Dionysius I. hard pressed by Carthaginians, ii.

Olympiads and Archons.	B.C.		
4. Demostratus	393	Lysias or. 3 κατὰ Σίμωνος, I. 272. Polycrates κατηγορία Σωκράτους, II. 90. (—391) Isaeus the pupil of Isocrates, II. 266.	198.—Amyntas II. of Macedon begins to reign, II. 156. Long Walls of Athens restored by Conon, I. 82. Lechaeum, western port of Corinth, taken by Lacedaemonians, II. 352.
97. Philocles	392	Lysias or. 16 ὑπὲρ Μαντιθέου? I. 240. Isocrates begins to teach. First period of his School, 392–378 B.C.: II. 9.— Aristophanes Ἐκκλησιάζουσαι.	
2. Nicoteles	391	(—390 B.C.) Isocrates or. 11 Βούσιρις, II. 91: or. 13 κατὰ σοφιστῶν, II. 124.	Plenipotentiaries sent by Athens to treat for peace at Sparta, I. 82 (winter 391–390).
3. Demostratus	390	Andocides or. 1 περὶ τῆς πρὸς Λακεδαιμονίους εἰρήνης (spring), I. 125.—Isocrates visits Gorgias in Thessaly, II. 5. Isaeus or. 5 περὶ τοῦ Δικαιογένους κλήρου, II. 349. Scopas, sculptor, and Theopompus, last poet of Old Comedy, flor.	Thrasybulus the Steirian receives Amadocus I. and Seuthes into the alliance of Athens, II. 166: descends the coast of Asia Minor, II. 346.
4. Antipater	389	Lysias or. 28 κατὰ Ἐργοκλέους, I. 215. Lysias or. 27 κατὰ Ἐπικράτους? I. 217. Lysias or. 29 κατὰ Φιλοκράτους, I. 235. Aeschines born. Plato act. 40 first visits Sicily. His Πολιτεία was begun before this year.	Death of Thrasybulus the Steirian, I. 241. Athenian expedition to aid Evagoras, I. 231.—Conquests of Dionysius I. in Sicily and Magna Graecia, II. 161 (389–387 B.C.).
98. Pyrrhion	388	Lysias or. 33 Ὀλυμπιακός, I. 199. Aristophanes Πλοῦτος—second (the extant) edition, marking the transition to Middle Comedy; cf. 408 B.C. Polycrates eminent as a teacher of Rhetoric, II. 91.	388–387 B.C., Diotimus commands in Hellespont, I. 232. Dionysius I. of Syracuse sends an embassy to Olympia: I. 152.
2. Theodotus	387	Lysias or. 19 περὶ τῶν Ἀριστοφάνους χρημάτων, I. 230.	Eight triremes under Thrasybulus the Collytean taken by Antalcidas, near Abydus, I. 238. —Peace of Antalcidas, II. 149.
3. Mystichides	386	Lysias or. 22 κατὰ τῶν σιτοπωλῶν? I. 221. Plato act. 43 begins to teach in the Academy?	Plataea rebuilt by Sparta as a stronghold against Thebes, II. 175.
4. Dexitheus	385		Mantineia destroyed by Lacedaemonians, II. 150.—Beginning of war between Evagoras and Artaxerxes II., II. 157.

Olympiads and Archons.	B.C.		
99. Diotrephes	384	(—383 B.C.) Lys. or. 10 κατὰ Θεομνήστου, I. 289. Demosthenes born (Schäfer). Aristotle born: Plato aet. 45.	
2. Phanostratus	383		Olynthus besieged by Lacedaemonians, II. 148.—Beginning of Olynthian War (—379), II. 156. Cotys becomes King of Thracian Odrysae. Iphicrates goes against him with Athenian force: then makes peace with him, II. 338.
3. Evandrus	382	Lysias or. 26 κατὰ Εὐάνδρου, I. 237.	The Cadmeia seized by Lacedaemonians, II. 150.—Philip of Macedon, son of Amyntas II., born: cf. 359 B.C.
4. Demophilus	381	(—380 B.C.) Lysias frag. cxx. f. (Sauppe) ὑπὲρ Φερενίκου, I. 308.	
100. Pytheas	380	Lysias (I. 152).	Phlius besieged by Lacedaemonians, II. 148.
2. Nicon	379	Gorgias and Aristophanes die about this time.	End of Olynthian War, II. 156.
3. Nausinicus	378	(—376 B.C.) Isocrates companion and secretary of Timotheus, II. 9. These orators flourish:— Callistratus, Leodamas, Thrasybulus and Cephalus of Collytus, II. 372.	Athens at the head of a new Naval Confederacy, II. 9.— Financial reform: establishment of the 20 συμμορίαι for payment of war-tax, II. 29. Θηβαϊκὸς πόλεμος (II. 331) begins (—371 B.C.). Invasions of Boeotia by Agesilaus and Cleombrotus, II. 175.
4. Callias	377	(—371 B.C.) Isaeus or. 10 περὶ τοῦ Ἀριστάρχου κλήρου, II. 333.	Agesilaus invades Boeotia.— Thebes begins to reorganise the Boeotian Confederacy, II. 175.
101. Charisandrus	376	—351, Second period of the school of Isocrates, II. 10. Death of Antisthenes, II. 99.	End of war (385—) between Evagoras and Artaxerxes II., II. 156. Cleombrotus invades Boeotia.
2. Hippodamus	375	Isaeus or. 8 περὶ τοῦ Κίρωνος κλήρου? II. 327. Ararôs (son of Aristophanes) and Eubulus, earliest poets of Middle Comedy.	Timotheus sails round Peloponnesus: Corcyra and other cities of the Ionian Sea join the Athenian League.
3. Socratides	374	Isocrates or. 2 πρὸς Νικοκλέα, II. 83.	—370 B.C., Jason of Pherae tagos of Thessaly, II. 18. Death of Evagoras king of the Cyprian Salamis, II. 103. Congress at Sparta. Peace between Athens and Sparta, II. 177: Thebes excluded from it, ib. 180.
4. Asteius	373	Isocrates or. 14 Πλαταϊκός, II. 175.	Plataea destroyed. Walls of Thespiae razed by Thebans, II. 177–8. At this time

Olympiads and Archons.	B.C.		
			Oropus belonged to Athens, 178: cf. 412 B.C.—Timotheus deposed from his στρατηγία and accused by Iphicrates and Callistratus.—Iphicrates, Chabrias, Callistratus chosen Generals.
102. Alcisthenes	372	Isocrates or. 1 πρὸς Δημόνικον? II. 80: or. 3 Νικοκλῆς ἢ Κύπριοι, II. 86.	
2. Phrasicleides	371		Battle of Leuctra, July 6. II. 195. General Peace (excluding the Thebans) concluded at Sparta ("Peace of Callias"), June 16. II. 138.—Jason of Pherae enters Greece as mediator.
3. Dysnicetus	370	Isocrates or. 10 Ἑλένης ἐγκώμιον, II. 96.	Jason assassinated, II. 18. First march of Epameinondas into Peloponnesus: invasion of Laconia: foundation of Megalopolis and of the new Messene, II. 193.
4. Lysistratus	369	Isaeus or. 9 περὶ τοῦ Ἀστυφίλου κλήρου, II. 330.	Second march of Epameinondas into Peloponnesus. First expedition sent by Dionysius I. of Syracuse to help the Corinthians and Spartans: Athens also forms friendly relations with him.—Death of Amyntas II. of Macedon: accession of his eldest son Alexander II. (brother of Philip).
103. Nausigenes	368	Isocrates Epist. I. Διονυσίῳ, II. 239.	Second expedition sent by Dionysius I. Pelopidas imprisoned by Alexander of Pherae: released by Epameinondas.—Philip (act. 14) sent by Ptolemaeus as a hostage to Thebes: lives there till 365 B.C.—Alexander II. of Macedon put to death by usurper Ptolemaeus (—365 B.C.)
2. Polyzelus	367	Dionysius I. gains tragic prize with Λύτρα "Εκτορος. Plato aet. 62 visits Sicily for second time. Aristotle aet. 17 comes to Athens, where he lives till Plato's death in 347.	Death of Dionysius I. of Syracuse, II. 18. His son Dionysius II. succeeds him. Third march of Epameinondas into Peloponnesus.—Timotheus again in command of Athenian fleet.
3. Cephisodorus	366	Isocrates or. 6 Ἀρχίδαμος, II. 193. Demosthenes comes of age: his studies with Isaeus probably begin, II. 268.	Sparta refuses to recognise Messene. Corinth. Epidaurus and Phlius make peace for themselves with Thebes. II. 194. Oropus revolts from Athens and is occupied by the Thebans.

Olympiads and Archons.	B.C.		
4. Chion	365	Isocrates or. 9 Εὐαγόρας II. 103.	Callistratus and Chabrias impeached for the Oropus affair by Leodamas, Philostratus Κολωνεύς, and (?) Hegesippus :—acquitted. Timotheus reduces Samos (where κληροῦχοι are established), Sestos and Crithote. —Perdiccas III. (second son of Amyntas II. and brother of Philip) King of Macedon (—359 B.C.)
104. Timocrates	364	(—363 B.C.) Isaeus or. 6 περὶ τοῦ Φιλοκτήμονος κλήρου, II. 343.	Timotheus succeeds to the command of Iphicrates in Thrace; takes Methone, Pydna, Potidaea, Torone. Expedition of Pelopidas into Thessaly: his death.
2. Charicleides	363	Demosthenes or. 27 κατὰ Ἀφόβου α΄, or 28 κατὰ Ἀφόβου β΄, II. 302.	Campaign of Timotheus against Cotys and Byzantines: his return to Athens.
3. Molon	362	Demosthenes or. 30 πρὸς Ὀνήτορα α΄, or 31 πρὸς Ὀνήτορα β΄, II. 302. Plato's third visit to Sicily. Xenophon closes his Ἑλληνικά (411 B.C.—) at the battle of Mantineia.	Fourth and last march of Epameinondas into Peloponnesus. Battle of Mantineia (July 3); death of Epameinondas. General peace, excluding Sparta. — Autocles Athenian commander at the Hellespont.
4. Nicophemus	361	Demosthenes or. 41, πρὸς Σπουδίαν, or. 55 πρὸς Καλλικλέα, II. 302. Deinarchus born.	Archidamus III. succeeds his father Agesilaus as a king of Sparta, II. 18.—Callistratus flies from Athens to Thasos: Thasians recolonise Datos, II. 185. Aristophon δημαγωγός.
105. Callimedes	360	(—353 B.C.) Isaeus or. 1 περὶ τοῦ Κλεωνύμου κλήρου, II. 319. Hypereides κατ' Αὐτοκλέους, II. 381. Praxiteles, sculptor, flor.	War between Artaxerxes II. and his satrap Orontes: Athens supports the latter, II. 185.
2. Eucharistus	359	Isaeus or. 11 περὶ τοῦ Ἁγνίου κλήρου, II. 355. Demosthenes trierarch. Isocrates *Epist.* VI. τοῖς Ἰάσονος παισίν, II. 242.	Death of Artaxerxes II. Μνήμων, 405 B.C.—Accession of Artaxerxes III. (Ὦχος—337 B.C.)—Perdiccas III. of Macedon killed in battle with Illyrians: contest for throne: accession of Philip (—336 B.C.) —Alexander of Pherae murdered by his wife Thebe's half-brothers, Tisiphonus, Peitholaus and Lycophron, II. 242. Cotys, king of Thracian Odrysae, murdered: his son Cersobleptes prevails, in a contest for the succession, over Berisades and Amadocus II., II. 184.

ANNALS

Olympiads and Archons.	B.C.		
3. Cephisodotus	358		
4. Agathocles	357		Chios, Cos, Rhodes, Byzantium revolt from Athens. Social War begins (—355 B.C.), II. 182. Philip takes Amphipolis, II. 184. Treaty between Chares and Cersobleptes: Thracian Chersonese (except Cardia) ceded to Athens, ib. Third form of the Trierarchy brought in by the συμμορίαι of Periander: cf. 410 B.C.
106. Elpines	356	Isaeus frag. XVI (Sauppe) ὑπὲρ Εὐμάθους, II. 367. Demosthenes or. 54 κατὰ Κόνωνος ? II. 302. Isocrates *Epist.* IX Ἀρχιδάμῳ, II. 244 Alexis writes Comedy.	Philip victor at Olympia: takes and destroys Potidaea: founds Philippi. Alexander the Great born. Chares defeats a Persian force, II. 206.
2. Callistratus	355	Isocrates or. 8 περὶ τῆς εἰρήνης (or συμμαχικός): or. 7 Ἀρεοπαγιτικός, II. 202. Demosthenes or. 22 κατὰ Ἀνδροτίωνος, II. 303. Aristotle may have taught Rhetoric as early as this year.	Social War ends (midsummer), II. 182.—Phocian (or Sacred) War begins (—346 B.C.).—Oligarchies set up at Corcyra, Chios, Mytilene, etc., II. 249.
3. Diotimus	354	Death of Xenophon? Isaeus or. 2 περὶ τοῦ Μενεκλέους κλήρου, II. 336. Dem. or. 14 περὶ τῶν συμμοριῶν, II. 302, 373, or. 20 πρὸς Λεπτίνην, II. 303.	Eubulus becomes financial minister of Athens (ταμίας τῆς κοινῆς προσόδου), II. 25: cf. 338 B.C.—Timotheus brought to trial: dies at Chalcis.—Callistratus returns to Athens (cf. 361 B.C.):—his death, II. 185.—The Generals Iphicrates, Menestheus and Timotheus arraigned by Aristophon and Chares.
4. Eudemus	353	Isocrates or. 15 περὶ τῆς ἀντιδόσεως, II. 131. Isaeus or. 7 περὶ τοῦ Ἀπολλοδώρου κλήρου, II. 325.	Philip marches along the Thracian coasts, and takes Abdera and Maroneia.—Philip takes Methone: is defeated in Thessaly by Onomarchus.
107. Aristodemus	352	Demosthenes or. 16 ὑπὲρ Μεγαλοπολιτῶν, or. 24 κατὰ Τιμοκράτους, or. 23 κατὰ Ἀριστοκράτους, or. 36 ὑπὲρ Φορμίωνος, II. 302. Theodectes tragicus flor. Theopompus, historian, flor.	Philip re-enters Thessaly: defeats Phocians under Onomarchus (who is killed), and advances to Thermopylae: finds it held by Athenians, and retires. He marches to Heraeon on Propontis: dictates peace to Cersobleptes, makes alliance with Cardia, Perinthus and Byzantium.—He frees Pherae from the Tyranny, II. 242.
2. Thessalus	351	Demosthenes or. 4 κατὰ Φιλίππου α΄, II. 303: or. 15 ὑπὲρ τῆς Ῥοδίων ἐλευθερίας.	Death of Mausolus. Artemisia proposes a contest of oratory: Theopompus the historian

Olympiads and Archons.	B.C.		
3. Apollodorus	350	(—338.) Third period of the school of Isocrates, II. 11. Demosthenes or. 39 πρὸς Βοιωτὸν περὶ τοῦ ὀνόματος, II. 302. Isocrates *Epist.* VIII τοῖς Μυτιληναίων ἄρχουσιν, II. 249. Death of Isaeus? II. 271.	gains the prize, II. 11. Idrieus, brother of Mausôlus, succeeds Artemisia as dynast of Caria, II. 171.—Philip marches against the Molossian Arybbas. Euboeans ally themselves with Athens. Phocion leads Athenians to support Plutarchus of Eretria: battle of Tamynae.—Apollodorus tried and condemned for proposing to apply the θεωρικὸν to the war.—First help sent by Athens to Olynthus.
4. Callimachus	349	Demosthenes or. 26 κατὰ Μειδίου, or. 1 Ὀλυνθιακὸς α΄, or. 2 Ὀλυνθιακὸς β΄.	Philip makes war on Olynthus and the Chalcidic towns. Alliance between Olynthians and Athens.—Second Athenian expedition, under Chares, to help them.
108. Theophilus	348	Demosthenes or. 3 Ὀλυνθιακὸς γ΄.	Philip besieges Olynthus—third Athenian expedition, under Chares, to help it:—Philip takes Olynthus: destroys it and the 32 Chalcidic towns of its Confederacy.
2. Themistocles	347	[Dem.] or. 40 πρὸς Βοιωτὸν περὶ προικός. Death of Plato aet. 82. Aristotle leaves Athens and goes to Hermeias of Atarneus.	Philip renews war with Cersobleptes (cf. 352)—which he ends in 346 by dictating a peace. Athenian troops under Chares sent to Thrace.—Mytilene returns into alliance with Athens.
3. Archias	346	Isocrates or. 5 Φίλιππος (April), II. 165. Demosthenes or. 5 περὶ εἰρήνης (August).	Envoys (Philocrates, Aeschines, Demosthenes, etc.) sent by Athens to Philip. — Philip goes to Thracian War.—Antipater and Parmenion negotiate with Athenian envoys. — Peace "of Philocrates" ratified on part of Athens and allies (April).—Second Athenian embassy to await Philip at Pella: he returns and takes the envoys to Pherae: ratifies peace there (end of June).—Philip occupies Phocis: end of Phocian War.
4. Eubulus	345	Demosthenes or. 37 πρὸς Παντaίνετον, or. 38 πρὸς Ναυσίμαχον, II. 302. Aeschines or. 1 κατὰ Τιμάρχου.	Philip becomes a member of Amphictyonic Council, and thereby a Greek Power. Philip marches against Illyrii, Dardani, Triballi.—Timoleon of Corinth goes against Dionysius II. of Syracuse.

ANNALS

Olympiads and Archons.	B.C.		
109. Lyciscus	344	Isocrates *Epist.* VII. Τιμοθέῳ, II. 247. The Δηλιακός of Hypereides (cf. II. 386 n.) earlier than 344: Sauppe II. 285 f. Demosthenes or. 6 κατὰ Φιλίππου β'. Aristotle removes from Atarneus to Mytilene. Ephorus, historian, flor.	Timoleon frees Sicily.—Philip begins to meddle in Peloponnesus. Demosthenes goes thither to counteract him. Embassy, in remonstrance, from Philip, Argos and Messene to Athens.
2. Pythodotus	343	Demosthenes or. 19, and Aeschines or. 2, περὶ τῆς παραπρεσβείας. Antiphanes still writing Comedy.	Philocrates is accused by Hypereides: goes into exile.—Aeschines is accused by Demosthenes of malversation in the embassy (346 B.C.), but is acquitted.
3. Sosigenes	342	Hegesippus ([Dem.] or. 7), περὶ Ἁλοννήσου. Isocrates *Epist.* II. Φιλίππῳ a', II. 251: *Epist.* v. Ἀλεξάνδρῳ, II. 253. Aristotle begins to teach Alexander. Menander born.	Philip sets up tetrarchies in Thessaly. — His letter to Athens about Halonnesus.—Alliance between Euboean Chalcis and Athens.—Beginning of Philip's Third Thracian War (—339 B.C.): cf. 352, 347 B.C.
4. Nicomachus	341	Demosthenes or. 8 περὶ τῶν ἐν Χερσοννήσῳ, or. 9 κατὰ Φιλίππου γ'. Aphareus tragicus flor. down to this time.	Feud between Cardia and Attic cleruchi of Chersonese.—Philip supports Cardia: Diopeithes, Athenian General, ravages Thracian seaboard. Letter of Philip to Athens about the Chersonese.—Philip approaches Perinthus. — Demosthenes envoy to Byzantium: its alliance with Athens.
110. Theophrastus	340	Isocrates *Epist.* IV. Ἀντιπάτρῳ, II. 254. Anaximenes Ῥητορικὴ [πρὸς Ἀλέξανδρον]?	Philip besieges Perinthus and Byzantium:—Athenians under Chares support Byzantines.—Philip's ultimatum: Athens, on proposal of Demosthenes, declares war.—Fourth form of the Trierarchy brought in by law of Demosthenes, equalising the burden on taxable capital: cf. 410, 357 B.C.
2. Lysimachides	339	Isocrates or. 12 Παναθηναϊκός, II. 110. Xenocrates begins to teach in the Academy.	Aeschines and Meidias go as πυλαγόραι to Amphictyonic Council: Amphictyons make war on Locrians of Amphissa.—Second Athenian force sent to help Byzantium: Philip raises the siege.—Amphictyons make Philip their General (Oct.). He returns to Greece, defeats mercenaries under Chares and Proxenus, and destroys Amphissa.

Olympiads and Archons.	B.C.		
3. Chaerondas	338	Isocrates *Epist.* III. Φιλίππῳ β', II. 256. Death of Isocrates, II. 30. (—326 B.C.) Lycurgus, the orator, is ταμίας τῆς κοινῆς προσόδου, II. 375.	Commissioners (including Demosthenes) appointed to restore fortifications of Athens: Demosthenes administers the θεωρικόν.—Immediately after destroying Amphissa, Philip hands over the Achaean Naupactus to the Aetolians: then enters Phocis, and occupies Cytinion and Elatcia (Feb. ?). Battle of Chaeroneia: μεταγειτνιῶνος ἑβδόμῃ (Aug. 2. ! Curt. v. 436 Eng. tr. *n.*). Peace "of Demades" between Philip and Athens. End of Athenian Naval Hegemony: Congress of Corinth: Hellenic League under Macedonian Hegemony: Philip Hellenic General against Persia. — Artaxerxes III. (Ὦχος) dies: Arses succeeds him.
4. Phrynichus	337	(Jan.?) At the annual winter Festival of the Dead in the outer Cerameicus, Demosthenes speaks the epitaph of those who fell at Chaeroneia. [Not extant: the Demosthenic or. 60 is spurious.]	
111. Pythodemus	336	Ctesiphon proposes (March) that Demosthenes should be crowned at the Great Dionysia. Aeschines gives notice of an action παρανόμων against Ctesiphon. Deinarchus begins his activity as λογογράφος.	Death of Arses: Darcius III. King of Persia (—330 B.C.). Parmenion and Attalus open the Persian War in Asia. Philip assassinated at Aegae (early in August). Alexander the Great becomes king of Macedon.—He enters Greece: Thessaly, Amphictyons, Athens and Congress of Corinth acknowledge his hegemony.
2. Evaenetus	335	The surrender of Demosthenes. Lycurgus, etc. is demanded from Athens by Alexander:—Demades helps to arrange a peace.	Parmenion repulsed in Asia by Memnon, who takes Ephesus. —Thebans rise against Macedon: Alexander takes and destroys Thebes (autumn).
3. Ctesicles	334	Aristotle settles at Athens and teaches in the Lyceum.—His Ῥητορική certainly later than 338 B.C.	Alexander sets out for Persian War, and crosses Hellespont: wins battle of Granicus (May: reduces Acolis and Ionia: takes Miletus and Halicarnassus: and advances to Gordion in Phrygia.
4. Nicocrates	333		Alexander routs Darcius III. at Issus (Oct.).
112. Nicetes	332		Alexander besieges Tyre; takes it (July): takes Gaza: occu-

Olympiads and Archons.	B.C.		
2. Aristophanes	331	Lysippus, sculptor, flor. With his school began a decline of Sculpture, parallel to that of Oratory. Cf. II. 447. Callisthenes of Stageirus, who went with Alexander to Asia, represents the decay of taste in oratorical prose.	pies Egypt: founds Alexandria: winters at Memphis. Alexander crosses Euphrates (July); routs Dareius at Arbela (Oct.); marches to Babylon, Susa and Persepolis.
3. Aristophon	330	(August?) Demosthenes or. 18 περὶ τοῦ στεφάνου, Aeschines or. 3 κατὰ Κτησιφῶντος, II. 399.—Aeschines leaves Athens. Lycurgus κατὰ Λεωκράτους, II. 377. Demades administers the θεωρικόν.—[Dem.] or. 17 περὶ τῶν πρὸς Ἀλέξανδρον συνθηκῶν (by Hegesippus?). Hypereides ὑπὲρ Εὐξενίππου? II. 388.	Spartans, under Agis III., rise against Macedon: are defeated at Megalopolis by Antipater; and accept Macedonian hegemony: death of Agis III. —Alexander pursues Dareius, who is murdered by Bessus in Parthia:—enters Hyrcania, Drangiana, and Aracosia: founds Alexandria ad Caucasum (Kandahar?).
4. Cephisophon	329		Alexander enters Bactria and Sogdiana; takes Maracanda (Samarcand): crosses the Oxus and advances to Jaxartes: founds Alexandria Eschate (Khojend?).—Returns to winter-quarters in Bactria.
113. Euthycritus	328	Between 330 and 326 B.C. (Schäfer) there was a great dearth at Athens, during which Demosthenes administered the σιτωνία.	Alexander subdues Sogdiana.— Slays Cleitus at Maracanda. —Harpalus sends supplies of corn to Athens, and receives the citizenship.
2. Hegemon	327		Alexander crosses the Indus and enters the Punjaub.
3. Chremes	326	End of financial administration of Lycurgus (338 B.C.—): Menesaechmus becomes ταμίας. Fictitious date of the speech περὶ τῆς δωδεκαετίας (i.c. 338–326 B.C.): not by Demades, Sauppe II. 312.	Alexander defeats Porus. — Begins his river-voyage southwards through India.
4. Anticles	325		Alexander reaches mouth of Indus about July.—Sets out on march westward in Aug., and reaches capital of Gedrosia in Oct.—Nearchus sails for Persian Gulf in Oct.— Harpalus, the profligate treasurer of Alexander, crosses from Asia to Attica:—is

Olympiads and Archons.	B.C.		
114. Hegesias	324	Deinarchus or. 1 κατὰ Δημοσθένους, or. 2 κατὰ Ἀριστογείτονος, or. 3 κατὰ Φιλοκλέους, II. 378. Hypereides κατὰ Δημοσθένους.—Death of Lycurgus (before midsummer).	warned from the Peiraeus, and goes to Taenaron. Alexander celebrates the Dionysia at Susa.—Death of Hephaestion at Ecbatana.—Athens decrees divine honours to Alexander.—Demosthenes ἀρχιθέωρος at Olympia (July).—Areiopagus directs that Demosthenes, Philocles, Demades, etc. be prosecuted for taking bribes from Harpalus.—Demosthenes is fined and imprisoned :—escapes to Aegina.
2. Cephisodorus	323	Epicurus aet. 18 comes to Athens.	Alexander holds court at Babylon and receives the embassies.—His death, June 8. Lamian War, promoted by Hypereides.—Leosthenes of Athens defeats Antipater at Heracleia and besieges him in Lamia.
3. Philocles	322	Hypereides ἐπιτάφιος, II. 390. Death of Hypereides (Oct. 5). Death of Demosthenes (Oct. 12). Aristotle retires to Chalcis, and dies there (Oct. ?). Theophrastus succeeds him in the Lyceum.	Leosthenes killed before Lamia. Antiphilus succeeds to command of the Greeks and defeats Leonnatus.—Decisive victory of Macedonians at Crannon (Aug. 5).—Hellenic League breaks up. Athens submits to Antipater. On proposal of Demades, the Ecclesia pronounces Demosthenes, Hypereides, and others, traitors.
4. Archippus	321	New Comedy beginning.—Menander aet. 21 Ὀργή (his first play).—Philemon, Diphilus comici flor.	Alexander's Empire divided among his Generals. Ptolemy founds a monarchy in Egypt (306 B.C.). The descendants of Seleucus found a kingdom in Asia, which afterwards shrinks up into Syria. In Macedonia there is confusion till about 272 B.C.: then the house of Antigonus reigns till 168 B.C., when Rome abolishes the kingdom.
115. Neaechmus	320		
2. Apollodorus	319		Death of Antipater.
3. Archippus	318	Death of Demades.—Demetrius Phalereus flor. Decline of Oratory begins.	
116. 4.	314	Death of Aeschines.	
120. 1.	300	Cleitarchus of Soli, representative of the florid Asianism.	
			306–285. Ptolemy Soter.
122. 3.	290	Hegesias of Magnesia, the so-called founder of Asianism, flor.	

Olympiads.	B.C.		
127. 3.	270	Theocritus, Bion, Moschus flor.	285-247. Ptolemy Philadelphus.
129. 1.	264	Timaeus of Tauromenium (now aet. circ. 70, resident at Athens since about 310 B.C.) brought his History down to this year. He represents the epigrammatic Asianism.	280-251. First period of Achaean League. 247-222. Ptolemy Euergetes.
130. 1.	260	Callimachus, the poet, librarian of Alexandria.	
132. 3.– 157. 3.	250– 150	A period of almost total darkness in the history of Greek Oratory. When light returns, Asianism is fully dominant, but a reaction to Atticism is just beginning.	205-181. Ptolemy Epiphanes. 197. Battle of Cynoscephalae. The Greek allies of Rome, though nominally free, are henceforth practically dependent.
145. 1.	200	Aristophanes librarian of Alexandria.	
146. 3.	194	Apollonius Rhodius librarian of Alexandria.	
156. 1.	156	Aristarchus librarian of Alexandria.	
158. 3.	146	Polybius brought his History from 264 B.C. (where Timaeus left off) to this year.	Corinth destroyed. The Achaean cities become formally subject to Rome. 145. Polybius legislates for the Achaean cities.
165. 1.	120	Hierocles and Menecles represent the epigrammatic Asianism in its maturity.	
166. 3.	114	Hortensius born.	
167. 3.	110	Approximate date for Hermagoras of Temnos [usually put much too late —by Clinton, about 62 B.C. See Cic. de Invent. I. 8, written about 84 B.C., which shows that Hermagoras was then long dead: Blass, die Griech. Ber. von Alex. bis zu Aug., pp. 84 f.] — Hermagoras founds the Scholastic Rhetoric, and thus prepares the way for Atticism. Apollonius ὁ μαλακός eminent as a teacher of Rhetoric at Rhodes.	
168. 3.	106	Cicero born.	
170. 1.	100	Established fame of the Rhodian eclectic school of Oratory,—Attic in basis, but with Asian elements. Julius Caesar born. Greek Rhetoric is already	

Olympiads.	B.C.		
		thoroughly fashionable at Rome.	
171. 2.	95	Apollonius, surnamed Molon (Cicero's master), eminent at Rhodes.	
172. 1.	92	L. Plotius and others open schools at Rome for the teaching of Rhetoric, no longer in Greek, but in Latin.	
173. 3.	86		Sulla takes Athens.
174. 1.	84	Cicero *De Inventione* ?	
3.	82	Caius Licinius Calvus born.	
175. 1.	80	The *Rhetorica ad Herennium* (incerti) not earlier than this year.—Aeschylus of Cnidus and Aeschines of Miletus represent the florid Asianism. Cf. 120 B.C.	
175. 2.	79	Cicero, *aet.* 27, at Athens.	
177. 4.	69	Hortensius, the Roman representative of Asianism, is Consul. After this time he comes little forward as a speaker; and leaves the field to Cicero, the representative of the Rhodian eclecticism.	
181. 2.	55	Cicero *De Oratore*. Calvus represents pure Atticism of the Lysian type.	
182. 3.	50	Apollodorus of Pergamus and Theodorus of Gadara are rival masters of Scholastic Rhetoric.	
183. 1.		Death of Calvus.	
2.	46	Cicero *Brutus*. Cicero *Orator*.	
4.	44	Cicero *De Optimo Genere Oratorum*.	Death of Caesar.
184. 1.	43	Death of Cicero.	
187. 3.	30	Didymus of Alexandria, grammarian and critic, flor.	Octavianus (Augustus Caesar) begins to govern the Republic as Emperor.
188. 4.	25	Dionysius of Halicarnassus and Caecilius of Calacte, a Sicilian Greek, flourish at Rome as scholars and critics. Victory of Atticism over Asianism complete and nearly universal.	
189. 4.	21		Athens deprived of its jurisdiction over Eretria and Aegina: Confederacy of the free Laconian cities formed by Augustus.

ANNALS

Olympiads.	A.D.		
198. 2.	14		Death of Augustus.
199. 2.	18	Strabo (born 66 B.C.) published his γεωγραφικά about this year.	
213. 2.	74	Tacitus *Dialogus De Oratoribus*.	69–79. Vespasian.
214. 4.	80	The βίοι τῶν δέκα ῥητόρων, wrongly ascribed to Plutarch, were perhaps compiled about this time, chiefly from Caecilius.	
217. 2.	90	Plutarch flor. Quintilian flor.	81–96. Domitian. 98–117. Trajan.
230. 3.	143	Herodes Atticus, the master in Greek oratory of Marcus Aurelius and Lucius Verus, is made consul *act*. 40, by Antoninus Pius. — Favorinus and Fronto flor.	117–138. Hadrian. His visits to Athens, 122–135. 138–161. Antoninus Pius.
234. 4.	160	Lucian, a Syrian of Samosata, writes the best Attic prose since Hypereides. — Aulus Gellius *Noctes Atticae*.—Pausanias the geographer, Ptolemy the astronomer, Polyaenus (Στρατηγήματα), and Galen flor.	161–180. Marcus Aurelius.
237. 2.	170	Publius Aelius Aristeides, of Mysia, in his Παναθηναικός and ἱεροὶ λόγοι, imitates the Attic models of ἐπίδειξις. Hermogenes makes a complete digest of the Scholastic Rhetoric since Hermagoras of Temnos (110 B.C.). It is contained in his περὶ στάσεων, περὶ ἰδεῶν, περὶ εὑρέσεως, περὶ μεθόδου δεινότητος, προγυμνάσματα (in *Rhetores Graeci*, II. Spengel). Hermog. was the chief authority on his subject till Aphthonius.	
242. 2.	190	Athenaeus Δειπνοσοφισταί. Dio Cassius flor.—The ὀνομαστικόν of Julius Pollux drawn up about this time.	
247. 2.	210	Tertullian flor.	
249. 4.	220	Origen flor.	
251. 1.	225	Sextus Empiricus πρὸς τοὺς μαθηματικοὺς ἀντιρρητικοί: a controversy with the professors of (1) grammar and history,	

Olympiads.	A.D.		
		(2) rhetoric, (3) geometry, (4) arithmetic, (5) astrology, (6) music.—Diogenes Laertius φιλόσοφοι βίοι.	
253. 3.	235	Philostratus βίοι σοφιστῶν. Aelian flor.	
259. 4.	260	Longinus (Διονύσιος Κάσσιος Λογγῖνος) flor. His τέχνη ῥητορική is printed in *Rhet. Graec.*, II. 298 f., ed. Spengel. [The treatise *On the Sublime* (περὶ ὕψους, *ib.* 245 f.) may be his, and is at least of about this date. The ground of the doubt is that the oldest MS. has Διονυσίου (certainly not the Halicarnassian) ἢ Λογγίνου: another, ἀνωνύμου.]	
264. 4.	280	Timaeus λέξεις Πλατωνικαί.	284–305. Diocletian. 306. Flavius Valerius Constantinus (the Great) begins to reign.
273. 3.	315	Aphthonius προγυμνάσματα (in *Rhet. Graec.* II. Spengel). This book superseded Hermogenes in the schools. At the Revival of Letters it again became a text-book of Rhetoric, saec. XVI. and XVII.	323–337. Constantine makes Christianity the religion of the Empire, and builds Constantinople as its new capital.
282. 2.	350	Libanius of Antioch ὑποθέσεις εἰς τοὺς Δημοσθένους λόγους, βίος Δημοσθένους: μελέται: προγυμνασμάτων παραδείγματα, etc.—Gregory of Nazianzus: Athanasius flor.	361–363. Julian Emperor. 379–395. Theodosius the Great.
289. 4.	380	Aelius Theon, of Alexandria, προγυμνάσματα (in *Rhet. Graec.* II. Speng.). [The only clue to his date is that he certainly used both Hermog. and Aphthonius, though he does not name them; and probably wrote while the popularity of the latter was fresh. Cf. Walz, *Rhet. Gracc.* vol. v. pp. 137 f.]. Eunapius of Sardis, βίοι φιλοσόφων καὶ σοφιστῶν.	390–420. The Pagan religion prohibited, and (except in the rural districts) extinguished.

ANNALS

Olympiads.	A.D.		
293. 2.	394		Olympic Games abolished under Theodosius I.
	395		The Empire divided between the Caesar of the West and the Caesar of the East.
	397	Ioannes, surnamed Χρυσόστομος, archbishop of Constantinople.	
	480	Ioannes Stobaeus, Ἀνθολόγιον Ἐκλογαί.	
	800		Charles, king of the Franks, crowned Emperor of Rome.
	858	Photius raised to the patriarchate, 25th Dec., βιβλιοθήκη, λεξέων συναγωγή.	
	988		Cherson, the last of the Greek Commonwealths, submits to Wladimir of Russia.
	1050	? Byzantine Ἐτυμολογικὸν μέγα.	
	1100	? Suidas λέξεις. Harpocration's Lexicon to the Ten Orators (λέξεις τῶν ι´ ῥητόρων) was used both by the compilers of the Etymologicum and by Suidas. Its author has been identified (1) with the Harpocration who taught Lucius Verus, about 150 A.D.: (2) with the poet and teacher praised by Libanius, about 350 A.D.: (3) with the Harpocration of Mendes mentioned by Athenaeus— whom Schweighäuser (ad XIV. 648 b) identifies with the friend of Julius Caesar.	

INTRODUCTION

In the reign of Augustus, when Rome had become the intellectual no less than the political centre of the earth, a controversy was drawing to a close for which the legionaries cared less than their master, but which for at least fifty years had been of some practical interest for the Forum and the Senate, and which for nearly three centuries had divided the schools of Athens, of Pergamus, of Antioch, of Alexandria, of all places where men spoke and wrote a language which, though changed from the glory of its prime, was still the idiom of philosophy and of art. This controversy involved principles by which every artistic creation must be judged; but, as it then came forward, it referred to the standard of merit in prose literature, and, first of all, in oratory. Are the true models those Attic writers of the fifth and fourth centuries, from Thucydides to Demosthenes, whose most general characteristics are, the subordination of the form to the thought, and the avoidance of such faults as come from a misuse of ornament? Or have these been surpassed in brilliancy, in freshness of fancy, in effective force, by those writers, belonging sometimes to the schools or cities of Asia Minor, sometimes to Athens itself or to Sicily, but collectively

The Augustan Atticism.

called "Asiatics," who flourished between Demosthenes and Cicero? This was the question of Atticism against Asianism. For a long time Asianism had been predominant. But, in the last century of the Republic, the contest had centred at Rome, at Rome it was fought out, and the voice that decided the strife of the schools was the same that commanded the nations. If the Roman genius for art had little in common with the Greek, if it was ill fitted to apprehend the Greek subtleties, it had pre-eminently that sound instinct in large art-questions which goes with directness of character, with the faculty of creating and maintaining order and with reverence for the majesty of law. A ruling race may not always produce the greatest artists or the finest critics. But in a broad issue between a pure and a false taste its collective opinion is almost sure to be found on the right side. Rome pronounced for Atticism.

<small>Caecilius and Dionysius.</small> Among the Greeks then living in the Imperial City were two men, united by friendship, by community of labours and by zeal for the Atticist revival; symbols, by birthplace, of influences which in the past had converged upon the Athens of Pericles from Sicily and the Ionian East,—Caecilius of Calacte and Dionysius of Halicarnassus, now met in that new capital of civilised mankind to which the arts, too, of Athens were passing. Both were scholars of manifold industry, in history, in archæology, in literary criticism, in technical rhetoric, and in a field which the catalogues of the libraries had left almost untouched—discrimination between the genuine and the spurious works of Attic writers. Both wrote upon the Attic

orators, but with a difference of plan which is instructive.

The lost work of Caecilius was entitled περὶ χαρακτῆρος τῶν δέκα ῥητόρων, *On the Style of the Ten Orators*. These ten were Antiphon, Andocides, Lysias, Isocrates, Isaeus, Lycurgus, Aeschines, Hypercides, Demosthenes, Deinarchus. Now, Caecilius, and his contemporary Didymus, the grammarian and critic of Alexandria, are the earliest writers who know this decade. Dionysius takes no notice whatever of the canon thus adopted by his friend. He seems never to have heard of the number "ten" in connection with the Attic orators. But from the first century A.D. onwards the decade is established. It is attested, for instance, by the Lives of the Ten Orators, wrongly ascribed to Plutarch, but probably composed about 80 A.D.; by Quintilian; by the neoplatonist Proclus, about 450 A.D.; and by Suidas, about 1100 A.D.—from whom it appears that, in his time, the grammarians had added a second list of ten to the first. The origin of the canon is unknown. It has been ascribed to Caecilius himself, mainly on the ground that it is not heard of before his time. It has been referred to Aristophanes the Byzantine, librarian at Alexandria about 200 B.C., or to his successor Aristarchus, about 156 B.C.,—by whom a canon of the poets, at least, was certainly framed. Another view is that it arose simply from the general tendency to reduce the number of distinguished names in any field to a definite number,—the tendency that gives the Seven Sages of Greece, the Seven Champions of Christendom, and the like. This last theory may safely be rejected.

<small>Caecilius on the Attic Orators.</small>

<small>The decade.</small>

The decade includes at least three names which this kind of halo can never have surrounded—Andocides, Isaeus and Deinarchus. It excludes other orators who, though inferior as artists, would have had a stronger popular claim, such as Callistratus of Aphidnae, the chief organiser of the Athenian Confederacy in 378, of whom Demosthenes said, when asked whether he or Callistratus were the better speaker, "I, on paper—Callistratus on the platform," —his opponents, Leodamas of Acharnae, Aristophon of Azenia, Thrasybulus and Cephalus of Collytus,—or that vigorous member of the anti-Macedonian party. Polyeuctus of Sphettus. Clearly, this canon was framed once for all by a critic or a school from whose decree contemporary opinion allowed no appeal, was adopted by successive generations, and ultimately secured the preservation of the writings which it contained, while others, not so privileged, were neglected, and at last suffered to perish. The decade was probably drawn up by Alexandrian grammarians in the course of the last two centuries before our era: but there is no warrant for connecting it with any particular name.[1]

Dionysius on the Attic Orators.

Dionysius, as has been said, altogether ignores the decade. If we supposed that Caecilius was its author, and that, when Dionysius wrote, Caecilius had not yet made his selection, the fact would be explained. But the double supposition involves the

---

[1] On the history of the decade, see Ruhnken, *Historia Critica Oratorum Graecorum*, who brings together the ancient authorities; Meier, *Comment. Andoc.* IV. 140; and the observations in Blass, *Die Griechische Beredsamkeit in dem Zeitraum von Alexander bis auf Augustus* (Berlin, 1865) p. 193.

strongest improbability. Even if Caecilius had been the framer of the decade, it can hardly be doubted that at least the idea must have been known through him to his intimate friend Dionysius before the latter had completed the series of works which we possess, and that we should find some trace of it in those long lists of orators which Dionysius frequently gives. The truth probably is that Dionysius was perfectly aware of this arbitrary canon, but disregarded it, because it was not a help, but a hindrance, to the purpose with which he studied the Attic orators.

Nothing is more characteristic of Dionysius as a critic than his resolution not to accept tradition as such, but to bring it to the test of reason. This comes out strikingly, for instance, in his distrust of merely prescriptive or titular authenticity when he is going through the list of an ancient writer's works. Now, his object in handling the Attic orators was not to complete a set of biographies or essays, but to establish a standard for Greek prose, applicable alike to oratory and to every other branch of composition. He considers the orators, accordingly, less as individual writers than as representatives of tendencies. He seeks to determine their mutual relations, and, with the aid of the results thus obtained, to trace a historical development. The orators whom he chose as, in this sense, representative were six in number— Lysias, Isocrates, Isaeus, Demosthenes, Hypereides, Aeschines. We have his treatises on Lysias, Isocrates, and Isaeus. We have also the first part of his treatise on Demosthenes—that part in which he discusses expression as managed by Demosthenes; the second

His object in handling them.

part, in which he discussed the Demosthenic handling of subject-matter, has perished with his discourses on Hypereides and Aeschines. The treatise on Deinarchus, it need hardly be said, is bibliographical, and has nothing to do with the other series. Dionysius considers his six orators as forming two classes. Between these classes the line is clearly drawn. Lysias, Isocrates, Isaeus are εὑρεταί, inventors,—differing indeed, in degree of originality, but alike in this, that each struck out a new line, each has a distinctive character of which the conception was his own. Demosthenes, Hypereides, Aeschines, are τελειωταί, perfecters,—men who, having regard to the historical growth of Attic prose, cannot be said to have revealed secrets of its capability, but who, using all that their predecessors had provided, wrought up the several elements in a richer synthesis or with a subtler finish.[1]

His classification—the εὑρεταί and the τελειωταί.

Plan of this book.

The task which I have set before me is to consider the lives, the styles and the writings of Antiphon, Andocides, Lysias, Isocrates and Isaeus, with a view to showing how Greek oratory was developed, and thereby how Greek prose was moulded, from the outset of its existence as an art down to the point at which the organic forces of Attic speech were matured, its leading tendencies determined, and its destinies committed, no longer to discoverers, but to those who should crown its perfection or initiate its decay. The men and the writings that mark this progress will need to be studied systematically and closely. It is hoped that much which is of historical, literary or social interest will be found by the way. But the

[1] Dionys. *De Deinarch.* c. 1 ; cf. c. 5.

great reward of the labour will be to get, if it may be,
a more complete and accurate notion of the way in
which Greek prose grew. It will not be enough, then,
if we break off when the study of Isaeus has been
finished. It will be necessary to look at the general
characteristics of the mature political oratory built
on those foundations at which Isaeus was the latest
worker. It will be necessary to conceive distinctly
how Isaeus and those before him were related to
Lycurgus, Hypereides, Aeschines, Demosthenes. Nor
must we stop here. The tendencies set in movement
during the fifth and fourth centuries B.C. were not
spent before they had passed into that life of the
Empire which sent them on into the modern world.
The inquiry which starts from the Athens of Pericles
has no proper goal but in the Rome of Augustus.

At the outset, it is well to clear away a verbal *The English word "orator"* hindrance to the comprehension of this subject in its
right bearings. The English term "orator," when
it is not used ironically, is reserved for one who, in
relation to speaking, has genius of an order analogous
to that which entitles a man to be seriously called a
poet. The term "oratory," though the exigencies
of the language lead to its often being used as a mere
synonym for "set speaking," is yet always inconveniently coloured with the same suggestion either
of irony or of superlative praise. The Roman term *compared with the Latin,* *orator*, "pleader," had this advantage over ours, that
it related, not to a faculty, but to a professional or
official attitude. It could therefore be applied to any
one who stood in that attitude, whether effectively
or otherwise. Thus the Romans could legitimately

say "mediocris" or "malus orator," whereas, in English, the corresponding phrases are either incorrect or sarcastic. Even the Romans, however, seem to have felt that their word was unsatisfactory, and to have confessed this sense by using "dicere," "ars dicendi," as much as possible. But the Greeks had a word which presented the man of eloquence, not, like the English word, as a man of genius, nor like the Roman word, as an official person, but simply as a *speaker*, ῥήτωρ. This designation was claimed by those Sicilian masters who taught men how to speak: at Athens it was given especially to the habitual speakers in the public assembly: in later times it was applied to students or theorists of Rhetoric. What, then, is the fact signified by this double phenomenon—that the Greeks had the word *rhetor*, and that they did not apply it to everybody? It is this: that, in the Greek view, a man who speaks may, without necessarily having first-rate natural gifts for eloquence, or being invested with office, yet deserve to be distinguished from his fellows by the name of a *speaker*. It attests the conception that speaking is potentially an *art*, and that one who speaks may, in speaking, be an *artist*.

This is the fundamental conception on which rests, first, the relation between ancient oratory and ancient prose; secondly, the relation between ancient and modern oratory.

The relation between ancient oratory and ancient prose, philosophical, historical or literary, is necessarily of the closest kind. Here our unfortunate word "oratory," with its arbitrary and perplexing associations, is a standing impediment to clearness of view. The proposition will be more evident if it is stated thus:—In Greek and Roman antiquity, that prose which was written with a view to being *spoken* stood in the closest relation with that prose which was written with a view to being *read*. Hence the historical study of ancient oratory has an interest wider and deeper than that which belongs to the study of modern oratory. It is that study by which the practical politics of antiquity are brought into immediate connexion with ancient literature.

The affinities between ancient and modern oratory have been more often assumed than examined. To discuss and illustrate them with any approach to completeness would be matter for a separate work. We must try, however, to apprehend the chief points. These shall be stated as concisely as possible, with such illustrations only as are indispensable for clearness. *Relation between Ancient and Modern Oratory.*

Ancient oratory is a fine art, an art regarded by its cultivators, and by the public, as analogous to sculpture, to poetry, to painting, to music and to acting. This character is common to Greek and Roman oratory; but it originated with the Greeks, and was only acquired by the Romans. The evidence for this character may be considered as internal and external.[1] The internal evidence is that which is afforded by the ancient orations themselves. First, we find in these, considered universally, a fastidious nicety of diction, of composition and of arrangement, which shows that the attention bestowed on their *Ancient Oratory a fine art.* *I. Internal evidence.* *1. Finish of form.*

---

[1] Some of the chief heads of the evidence are given by Brougham, *Dissertation on the Eloquence of the Ancients.*

2. Repetitions.

form, as distinguished from their matter, was both disciplined and minute. Secondly, we find the orator occasionally repeating shorter or longer passages—not always striking passages—from some other speech of his own, with or without verbal amendments; or we find him borrowing such passages from another orator. Thus Isocrates, in his *Panegyricus*, borrowed from the *Olympiacus* of Lysias, and from the so-called Lysian Epitaphius. Demosthenes, in the speech against Meidias, borrowed from speeches of Lysias, of Isaeus and of Lycurgus, in like cases of outrage. In many places Demosthenes borrowed from himself. This was done on the principle that τὸ καλῶς εἰπεῖν ἅπαξ περιγίγνεται, δὶς δὲ οὐκ ἐνδέχεται: *A thing can be well said once, but cannot be well said twice.*[1] That is, if a thought, however trivial, has once been perfectly expressed, it has, by that expression, become a morsel of the world's wealth of beauty. The doctrine might sometimes justify an artist in repeating *himself;* as an excuse for appropriation, it omits to distinguish the nature of the individual's property in a sunset and in a gem; but, among Greeks at least, it was probably not so much indolence as solicitude for the highest beauty, even in the least details, that prompted such occasional plagiarisms.

Speakers criticise each other's style.

Thirdly, we find that the orators, in addressing juries or assemblies, criticise each other's style. Aeschines, in a trial on which all his fortunes depended, quotes certain harsh or unpleasant figures of speech which, as he alleges, Demosthenes had used.

---

[1] Theon (who disputes the maxim) προγυμνάσματα c. 1 (*Rhet. Graec.* II. 62, ed. Spengel).

"How," he cries to the jurors, "how, men of iron, can you have supported them?" And then, turning in triumph to his rival, "What are these, knave ? ῥήματα ἢ θαύματα; metaphors or monsters ?"[1] When a poet, a painter or a musician thus scrutinises a brother artist's work, the modern world is not surprised. But a modern advocate or statesman would not expect to make a favourable impression by exposing in detail the stylistic shortcomings of an opponent.

The external evidence is supplied by what we know of the orators, of their hearers and of their critics. Already, before the art of Rhetoric had become an elaborate system, the orators were accustomed to prepare themselves for their task by laborious training, first in composition, then in delivery. They make no secret of this. They are not ashamed of it. On the contrary, they avow it and insist upon it. Demosthenes would never speak extemporarily when he could help it; he was unwilling to put his faculty at the mercy of fortune.[2] "Great is the labour of oratory," says Cicero, "as is its field, its dignity and its reward." Nor were the audiences less exacting than the speakers were painstaking. The hearers were attentive, not merely to the general drift or to the total effect, but to the

II. External evidence.

1. Training of speakers.

2. Appreciation shown by hearers.

---

[1] Aesch. *In Ctes.* §§ 166 f.
[2] ἐπὶ τύχῃ ποιεῖσθαι τὴν δύναμιν, Plut. *Demosth.* c. 9: who observes that this was certainly not from want of nerve, since, in the opinion of many contemporaries, Demosthenes showed *more τόλμα* and θάρσος when he spoke without premeditation. His habitual reluctance to do so is, however, well attested. See Plut. *l. c.* c. 8, and the story in

[Plut.] *Vitt. X. Oratt., Dem.* § 69. To the reproach, ὅτι ἀεὶ σκέπτοιτο, he answered:— αἰσχυνοίμην γὰρ ἂν εἰ τηλικούτῳ δήμῳ συμβουλεύων αὐτοσχεδιάζοιμι. The compiler naïvely adds, τοὺς δὲ πλείστους λόγους εἶπεν αὐτοσχεδιάσας, εὖ πρὸς αὐτὸ πεφυκώς, —a fact perfectly consistent with laborious preparation for all *grave* occasions.

particular elegance. Isocrates speaks of "the antitheses, the symmetrical clauses and other figures which lend brilliancy to oratorical displays, compelling the listeners to give clamorous applause."[1] Sentences, not especially striking or important in relation to the ideas which they convey, are praised by the ancient critics for their artistic excellence.[2] Further, when an orator, or a master of oratorical prose, wished to publish what we should now call a pamphlet, the form which he chose for it, as most likely to be effective, was that, not of an essay, but of a speech purporting to be delivered in certain circumstances which he imagined. Such are the *Archidamus*, the *Areopagiticus*, and the *Symmachicus* of Isocrates in the Deliberative form, and his speech *On the Antidosis* in the Forensic. Such again is the famous Second Philippic of Cicero. Then we know that orators compiled, for their own use, collections of exordia or of commonplaces, to be used as occasion might serve. Such was that *volumen prooemiorum* of Cicero's which betrayed him into a mistake which he has chronicled. He had sent Atticus his treatise "De Gloria" with the wrong exordium prefixed to it—one, namely, which he had already prefixed to the Third Book of the Academics. On discovering his mistake, he sends

3. Pamphlets in the oratorical form.

4. Collections of commonplaces.

---

[1] Isocr. *Panath.* (Or. XII.) § 2.

[2] *E.g.* Cic. *in Verr.* Act. II. Lib. v. c. xxxiii, *Stetit soleatus praetor populi Romani cum pallio purpureo tunicaque talari, muliercula nixus, in litore:* praised by Quint. VIII. 3 § 64 for ἐνάργεια, artistic *vividness*: (not, as Brougham says in alluding to it, *Dissert. on the Eloquence of the Ancients*, p. 42, for "fine and dignified composition").—Cic. *Orator*, c. 63 § 214, speaking of the rhythmical effect of the dichoreus, ‿‿‿, at the end of a sentence, quotes from the tribune Carbo, *Patris dictum sapiens temeritas filii comprobavit*: and adds, —"The applause drawn from the meeting by this dichoreus was positively astonishing."

Atticus a new exordium, begging him to "cut out the other, and substitute this."[1] Lastly, the ancient critics habitually compare the pains needful to produce a good speech with the pains needful to produce a good statue or picture. When Plato wishes to describe the finished smoothness of Lysias, he borrows his image from the sculptor, and says ἀποτετόρνευται. Theon says:—"Even as for him who would be a painter, it is unavailing to observe the works of Apelles and Protogenes and Antiphilus, unless he tries to paint with his own hand, so for him who would become a speaker there is no help in the speeches of the ancients, or in the copiousness of their thoughts, or in the purity of their diction, or in their harmonious composition, no, nor in lectures upon elegance, unless he disciplines himself by *writing* from day to day."[2] Lucilius, from whom Cicero borrows the simile, compares the phrases, *lexeis*, each fitted with nicety to its setting in a finished sentence, with the pieces, *tesserulae*, laid in a mosaic.[3] But among the passages, and they are innumerable, which express this view there is one in Dionysius that can never be too attentively considered by those who wish to under-

5. Ancient critics compare Oratory with Sculpture or Painting.

---

[1] Cic. *ad Att.* xvi. 6 § 4, quoted by Brougham, *Dissert.* p. 36. As to the "προοίμια of Demosthenes" there noticed, it is now well known that they were not drawn up by Demosthenes. The scholastic compiler, whoever he was, took some of them from Demosthenes, some from other orators, and probably wrote some himself: Schäfer, *Dem. u. seine Zeit*, iii. App. p. 129.

[2] Theon, προγυμνάσματα c. 1 (*Rhet. Graec.* i. p. 62 ed. Spengel).

[3] Lucilius *ap.* Cic. *De Oratore* iii. § 171:
*Quam lepide lexeis compostae! ut
  tesserulae omnes
arte pavimento atque emblemate vermiculato.*

The satirist was mocking T. Albucius, who wished himself to be thought "plane Graecus" (Cic. *De Fin.* i. 1 § 8), and was alluding especially to the Isocratics. No one, certainly, could say of Lucilius what he said of Albucius.

<small>Dionysius περὶ συνθέσεως, c. 25.</small> stand the real nature of ancient, and especially of Attic, oratory. He is explaining and defending—partly with a polemical purpose at which we shall have to glance by and by—that minute and incessant diligence which Demosthenes devoted to the perfecting of his orations. It is not strange, says the critic, "if a man who has won more glory for eloquence than any of those that were renowned before him, who is shaping works for all the future, who is offering himself to the scrutiny of all-testing Envy and Time, adopts no thought, no word, at random, but takes much care of both things, the arrangement of his ideas and the graciousness of his language: seeing, too, that the men of that day produced discourses which resembled no common scribblings, but rather were like to carved and chiselled forms,—I mean Isocrates and Plato, the Sophists. For Isocrates spent on the *Panegyricus*, to take the lowest traditional estimate, ten years; and Plato ceased not to smooth the locks, and adjust the tresses, or vary the braids, of his comely creations, even till he was eighty years old.[1] All lovers of literature are familiar, I suppose, with the stories of Plato's industry, especially the story about the tablet which, they say, was found after his death, with the first words of the *Republic* —κατέβην χθὲς εἰς Πειραιᾶ μετὰ Γλαύκωνος τοῦ Ἀρίστωνος—arranged in several different orders. What wonder, then, if Demosthenes also took pains to achieve euphony and harmony, and to avoid employ-

---

[1] The language here—τοὺς ἑαυτοῦ διαλόγους κτενίζων καὶ βοστρυχίζων καὶ πάντα τρόπον ἀναπλέκων—is not, perhaps, mere tautology. κτενίζων may be the general term; while βοστρυχίζων refers to the addition, and ἀναπλέκων to the retrenchment, of luxuriance.

ing a single word, or a single thought, which he had not weighed? *It seems to me far more natural that a man engaged in composing political discourses, imperishable memorials of his power, should neglect not even the smallest detail, than that the generation of painters and sculptors, who are darkly showing forth their manual tact and toil in a corruptible material, should exhaust the refinements of their art on the veins, on the feathers, on the down of the lip and the like niceties."*[1] Repeating this passage, slightly altered, in the essay on Demosthenes, Dionysius adds that we might indeed marvel if, while sculptors and painters are thus conscientious, "the artist in civil eloquence (πολιτικὸς δημιουργός) neglected the smallest aids to speaking well—*if indeed these be the smallest.*"[2]

It has already been observed that this feeling about speaking is originally Greek; and it is worth while to consider how it arose. That artistic sense which distinguished the Greeks above all races that the world has known was concentrated, in the happy pause of development to which we owe their supreme works, on the idealisation of man. Now, λόγος, speech, was recognised by the Greeks as the distinctive attribute of man.[3] It was necessary, therefore, that, at this stage, they should require in speech a clear-cut and typical beauty analogous to that of the

<small>This conception is originally Greek.</small>

<small>Its basis— the idealisation of man.</small>

---

[1] Dionys. περὶ συνθέσεως ὀνομάτων, c. 25.

[2] Id. *De Demosth.* c. 51.

[3] Aristotle uses this consideration to enforce the "defensive" use of Rhetoric :—πρὸς δὲ τούτοις ἄτοπον εἰ τῷ σώματι μὲν αἰσχρὸν μὴ δύνασθαι βοηθεῖν ἑαυτῷ, λόγῳ δ' οὐκ αἰσχρόν· ὃ μᾶλλον ἴδιόν ἐστιν ἀνθρώπου τῆς τοῦ σώματος χρείας, *Rhet.* I. 1. On λόγος as the distinction of man, see a splendid passage in Isocrates, *Antid.* (Or. xv.) §§ 252-257.

idealised human form. This was the central and primary motive, relatively to which all others were subsidiary or accidental. But, of these secondary motives, two at least demand a passing notice. First, the oral tradition of poetry and the habit of listening to poetical recitation furnished an analogy which was present to people's minds when they saw a man get up to make a set speech; they expected his words to have something like the coherence, something like the plastic outline, something even like the music of the verses which they were wont to hear flow from the lips of his counterpart, the rhapsode. Secondly, in the Greek cities, and especially at Athens, public speaking had, by 450 B.C., become so enormously important, opened so much to ambition, constituted a safeguard so essential for security of property and person, that not only was there the most various inducement to cultivate it, but it was positively dangerous to neglect it. Further, since in a law-court it was unavailing for the citizen that he could speak well unless the judges thought that he spoke better than his opponent, the art of persuasion was studied with a competitive zeal which wrought together with the whole bent of the Greek genius in securing attention to detail.

It will now be useful to look at some of the broad characteristics of modern oratory and of the modern feeling towards it; but only in so far as these will help our present purpose—namely, to elucidate the nature of ancient oratory. The first thing that strikes one is how completely modern life has redressed the complaint made by the earliest philosophical theorist of rhetoric. Aristotle opens his treatise with the observation that, whereas there are three instruments of rhetorical persuasion—the ethical, the pathetic and the logical—his predecessors have paid by far the most attention to the second, and have almost totally neglected the third, though this third is incomparably the most important,—indeed, the only one of the three which is truly scientific. The logical proof is the very body, σῶμα, of rhetorical persuasion,—everything else, appeal to feeling, attractive portrayal of character, and so forth, is, from the scientific point of view, only προσθήκη, appendage. This is essentially the modern, especially the modern Teutonic, theory of oratory, and the modern practice is in harmony with it. The broadest characteristic of modern oratory, as compared with ancient, is the predominance of a sustained appeal to the understanding. Hume, with general truth, declares the attributes of Greek oratory to be "rapid harmony, exactly adjusted to the sense," "vehement reasoning, without any appearance of art," "disdain, anger, boldness, freedom, involved in a continual stream of argument"[1]—a description, it must be observed, which should at all events be limited to the deliberative and forensic orators contemporary with Demosthenes. Brougham, however, states the case both more accurately and in terms of wider application, when he observes that in ancient oratory there are scarcely any long chains of elaborate reasoning; what was wanted to move, to rouse, and to please the hearers, was rather a copious stream of plain, intelligible observations upon their

[1] Essay XII., *Of Eloquence*.

interests, appeals to their feelings, reminiscences from the history, especially the recent history, of their city, expositions of the evils to be apprehended from inaction or from impolicy, vindications of the orator's own conduct, demonstrations of the folly which disobeys, or of the malice which assails him.[1] Aristotle himself, it may be observed, the very champion of the enthymeme, is the strongest witness to the truth of this. He impresses upon the student of Rhetoric that a speaker must ever remember that he is addressing the vulgar; he must not expect them to be capable of a far-reaching ratiocination, he must not string syllogism to syllogism, he must administer his logic temperately and discreetly.[2] Now, in contrast with this, long and elaborate chains of reasoning, or expositions of complicated facts, have been the very essence of the great efforts and triumphs of modern oratory; the imagery and the pathos heighten the effect, but would go only a very little way if the understandings of the hearers had not, in the first place, been convinced. We are here again reminded of the basis on which ancient oratory rested. The modern speaker comes before his audience with no *a priori* claim to be regarded as an artist whose display of his art may be commendable and interesting in itself. Cicero's speech for Archias, which is exquisitely composed, but of which not more than one-sixth is to the purpose, or his speech for Publius Sextus, in which the relevant part bears a yet smaller proportion to the whole, could

The modern speaker has no distinct acceptance as an artist.

The ancients less strict about logical relevance.

---

[1] *Dissertation on the Eloquence of the Ancients,* pp. 48, 58.
[2] See (*e.g.*) *Rhet.* I. 2 §§ 12, 13 (ὁ γὰρ κριτὴς ὑπόκειται εἶναι ἁπλοῦς, κ.τ.λ.): II. 22 §§ 2 ff., III. 17 § 6, etc.

not have been delivered in a British court of justice.[1]
There is usually, however, an important difference,
which will be noticed by and by, between the nature
of Greek and that of Roman irrelevance. On the
other hand, the modern exaction of consecutive and
intelligible reasoning becomes, of course, less severe
the more nearly the discourse approaches to the nature
of a display. Still, this logical vigilance, with a comparative indifference to form, is, on the whole, the
first great characteristic of modern oratory, and has,
of course, become more pronounced since the system
of reporting for the Press has been perfected, as it is *Influence of newspaper reporting.*
now, in many cases, far more important for the
speaker to convince readers than to fascinate hearers.
The characteristic which comes next in degree of significance for our present object is the habitual presumption that the speech is extempory. Even *Modern feeling that a great speech must be extemporary.*
where there has been the most laborious preparation,
even where the fact of such preparation is notorious,
it is generally felt to be essential to impressiveness
that the fact of *verbal* premeditation should be kept
out of sight, and on the part of the hearers it is considered more courteous to ignore it. A certain ridicule attaches to a speech which, not having been
delivered, is published, — the sense of something
ludicrous arising partly from the feeling, "What an
absurd disappointment," but also from the feeling,
"Here are the bursts which would have electrified the
audience." One thing which has helped to establish *Sources of this feeling: 1. The failures of Premeditation;*
this feeling is the frequent failure of those who have
attempted verbal premeditation; a failure probably

---

[1] Brougham, *l. c.* p. 46.

due less often to defective memory or nerve than to neglect of a department in which the ancient orators were most diligent, and in which, moreover, they were greatly assisted by the plastic forms among which they lived, by the share of musical training which they ordinarily possessed, and by the draping of the himation or the toga,—delivery, in respect both of voice and of action. When a premeditated speech is rendered lifeless or ludicrous by the manner in which it is pronounced, the modern mind at once recurs to its prejudice against Rhetoric—that is, against the Rhetoric of the later schools—and a contempt is generated for those who deign to labour beforehand on words that should come straight from the heart. There is, however, a much deeper cause than this for the popular modern notion that the greatest oratory must be extemporary, and it is one which, for the modern world, is analogous to the origin of the Greek requirement that speech should be artistic. This cause is the Hebraic basis of education in modern Christendom, especially in those countries which have been most influenced by the Reformation. It becomes a prepossession that the true adviser, the true warner, in all the gravest situations, on all the most momentous subjects, is one to whom it will in that hour be given what he shall speak, and whose inspiration, when it is loftiest, must be communicated to him at the moment by a Power external to himself. The ancient world compared the orator with the poet. The modern world compares the orator with the prophet.

2. The Hebraic basis of Christian education.

It is true, indeed, that the ancient theory has

often been partially applied in modern times, some- *Modern approximations to the theory of Ancient Oratory.*
times with great industry and with much success;
but modern conditions place necessary limits to the
application, and the great difference is this :—The
ancients required the speech to be an artistic whole;
the modern orator who composes, or verbally pre-
meditates, trusts chiefly, as a rule, to particular passages and is less solicitous for a total symmetry.
Debate, in our sense, is a modern institution; its *Influence of Debate.*
unforeseen exigencies claim a large margin in the most
careful premeditation; and hence, in the principal
field of oratory, an insurmountable barrier is at once
placed to any real assimilation between the ancient
and the modern modes. Just so much the more, if
only for contrast, is it interesting to contemplate
those modern orators who have approximated to the
classical theory in such measure as their genius and
their opportunities allowed. In an inquiry of the
present scope, it might be presumptuous to select
living illustrations of the Pulpit, the Senate, or the
Bar. It would not, indeed, be needful to go far back;
but it may be better, for our purpose, to seek
examples where the natural partialities of a recent
memory no longer refract the steady rays of fame.
In respect of finished rhetorical prose, which is not, *Finished Rhetorical Prose:*
either in the ancient or in the modern sense, great
oratory, but which bears to it the same kind of
relation that the Panegyricus of Isocrates bears to
the speech On the Crown, no one, perhaps, has
excelled Canning. The well-known passage of his *Canning's Plymouth speech.*
speech at Plymouth in 1823 will serve as an
illustration :—

"The resources created by peace are means of war. In cherishing those resources, we but accumulate those means. Our present repose is no more a proof of inability to act, than the state of inertness and inactivity in which I see those mighty masses that float in the waters above your town is a proof that they are devoid of strength and incapable of being fitted out for action. You well know, gentlemen, how soon one of those stupendous masses now reposing on their shadows in perfect stillness—how soon, upon any call of patriotism or of necessity, it would assume the likeness of an animated thing, instinct with life and motion—how soon would it ruffle, as it were, its swelling plumage—how quickly it would put forth all its beauty and its bravery, collect its scattered elements of strength, and awaken its dormant thunder. Such as is one of those magnificent machines when springing from inaction into a display of its might—such is England herself, while, apparently passive and motionless, she silently concentrates the power to be put forth on an adequate occasion."

His analogue—Isocrates.

The ancient parallel for this is such a passage as that in the Panegyricus, describing the irresistible and awe-inspiring might in which the Panhellenic invasion will move through Asia—$\theta\epsilon\omega\rho\iota\alpha$

Union of rhythmical finish with passion:

$\mu\hat{a}\lambda\lambda o\nu\ \hat{\eta}\ \sigma\tau\rho\alpha\tau\epsilon\iota\alpha\ \pi\rho o\sigma\epsilon o\iota\kappa\omega\varsigma$.[1] But a nearer resemblance to the classical union of rhythmical finish with living passion is afforded, in deliberative oratory, by Grattan, in forensic, by Erskine. Take the per-

Grattan.

oration of Grattan's speech in the Irish Parliament on the Declaration of Irish Rights:[2]—

"Do not suffer the arrogance of England to imagine a surviving hope in the fears of Ireland; do not send the people to their own resolves for liberty, passing by the

---

[1] Isocr. Or. IV. § 182.   [2] *Speeches*, Vol. I. pp. 52 f.

tribunals of justice and the high court of Parliament; neither imagine that, by any formation of apology, you can palliate such a commission to your hearts, still less to your children, who will sting you with their curses in your graves, for having interposed between them and their Maker, robbing them of an immense occasion, and losing an opportunity which you did not create and never can restore.

" Hereafter, when these things shall be history, your age of thraldom and poverty, your sudden resurrection, commercial redress, and miraculous armament, shall the historian stop at liberty, and observe—that here the principal men among us fell into mimic trances of gratitude; that they were awed by a weak ministry, and bribed by an empty treasury; and, when liberty was within their grasp, and the temple opened her folding doors, and the arms of the people clanged, and the zeal of the nation urged and encouraged them on,—that they fell down and were prostituted at the threshold.

" I might, as a constituent, come to your bar and demand my liberty,—I do call upon you, by the laws of the land and their violation, by the instruction of eighteen counties, by the arms, inspiration, and providence of the present moment, tell us the rule by which we shall go—assert the law of Ireland—declare the liberty of the land.

" I will not be answered by a public lie in the shape of an amendment; neither, speaking for the subject's freedom, am I to hear of faction. I wish for nothing but to breathe, in this our island, in common with my fellow-subjects, the air of liberty. I have no ambition, unless it be the ambition to break your chain and contemplate your glory. I never will be satisfied so long as the meanest cottager in Ireland has a link of the British chain clanking to his rags; he may be naked, he shall not be in iron; and I do see the time is at hand, the spirit is gone forth, the declaration is planted; and though great men should apostatise, yet the cause will live; and though the public speaker should die, yet the immortal fire shall outlast the organ which conveyed it, and the breath of liberty, like the word of the holy man, will not die with the prophet, but survive him."

Erskine.

Erskine's defence of Stockdale, the publisher of a pamphlet in defence of Warren Hastings, containing certain reflections on the Managers which the House of Commons pronounced libellous, contains a passage of which the ingenuity, no less than the finished art, recalls the best efforts of ancient forensic oratory: though this ingenuity cannot be fully appreciated without the context. At first, Erskine studiously keeps his defence of Stockdale separate from his defence of Hastings; then he gradually suggests that Hastings is entitled to indulgence on account (1) of his instructions, (2) of his situation, (3) of English and European policy abroad, (4) of the depravity to which, universally, men are liable who have vast power over a subject race,—and the last topic is illustrated thus:—

"Gentlemen, I think that I can observe that you are touched by this way of considering the subject; and I can account for it. I have not been considering it through the cold medium of books, but have been speaking of man and his nature, and of human dominion, from what I have seen of them myself among reluctant nations submitting to our authority. I know what they feel, and how such feelings can alone be repressed. I have heard them in my youth from a naked savage, in the indignant character of a prince surrounded by his subjects, addressing the governor of a British colony, holding a bundle of sticks in his hand as the notes of his unlettered eloquence; 'Who is it,' said the jealous ruler over the desert encroached upon by the restless foot of English adventure—' who is it that causes this river to rise in the high mountains and to empty itself into the ocean ? Who is it that causes to blow the loud winds of winter, and that calms them again in summer ? Who is it that rears up the shade of those lofty forests, and blasts them with the quick lightning at his pleasure ? The same Being who gave to you a country on the other side of the waters, and gave ours to us; and by this title we will defend it !' said the warrior, throwing down his tomahawk on the ground, and raising the war-sound of his nation. These are the feelings of subjugated men all round the globe ; and, depend upon it, nothing but fear will control where it is vain to look for affection." [1]

But no speaker, probably, of modern times has come nearer to the classical type than Burke ; and this because his reasonings, his passion, his imagery, are sustained by a consummate and unfailing beauty of language. The passage in which he describes the descent of Hyder Ali upon the Carnatic is supposed to owe the suggestion of its great image, not to Demosthenes, but to Livy's picture of Fabius hovering over Hannibal ; the whole passage is infinitely more Roman, more Verrine, if the phrase may be permitted, than Greek ; but it is anything rather than diffuse :— *Burke.*

" Having terminated his disputes with every enemy and every rival, who buried their mutual animosities in their common detestation against the creditors of the Nabob of Arcot, he drew from every quarter whatever a savage ferocity

---

[1] From a longer extract given by Brougham in his Essay on Erskine, reprinted from the *Edinburgh Review* in the volume of his " Rhetorical and Literary Dissertations and Addresses," p. 225.

could add to his new rudiments in the arts of destruction; and compounding all the materials of fury, havoc, and desolation into one black cloud, he hung for a while on the declivity of the mountains. Whilst the authors of all these evils were idly and stupidly gazing on this menacing meteor, which darkened all their horizon, it suddenly burst, and poured down the whole of its contents upon the plains of the Carnatic. Then ensued a scene of woe, the like of which no eye had seen, no heart conceived, and which no tongue can adequately tell. All the horrors of war before known or heard of were mercy to that new havoc. A storm of universal fire blasted every field, consumed every house, destroyed every temple. The miserable inhabitants, flying from their flaming villages, in part were slaughtered; others, without regard to sex, to age, to the respect of rank, or sacredness of function, fathers torn from children, husbands from wives, enveloped in a whirlwind of cavalry, and amidst the goading spears of drivers and the trampling of pursuing horses, were swept into captivity in an unknown and hostile land. Those who were able to evade this tempest fled to the walled cities. But, escaping from fire, sword and exile, they fell into the jaws of famine. For months together these creatures of sufferance, whose very excess and luxury in their most plenteous days had fallen short of the allowance of our austerest fasts, silent, patient, resigned, without sedition or disturbance, almost without complaint, perished by a hundred a day in the streets of Madras or on the glacis of Tangore, and expired of famine in the granary of India."

Brougham on Burke compared with Demosthenes. Brougham[1] contrasts this passage with that in which Demosthenes says that a danger "went by like a cloud," with that where he says, "If the Thebans had not joined us, all this trouble would have rushed like a mountain-torrent on the city," and

[1] In his *Inaugural Discourse* before the University of Glasgow.

with that where he asks, "If the thunderbolt which has fallen has overpowered, not us alone, but all the Greeks, what is to be done?"[1] Brougham contends that Burke has marred the sublimity of the "black cloud" and "the whirlwind of cavalry" by developing and amplifying both. This, surely, is to confound the plastic with the picturesque—a point which will presently claim our attention. Demosthenes is a sculptor, Burke a painter.

It might, however, have been anticipated that modern oratory would have most resembled the ancient in that branch where the conditions are most nearly similar. If Isocrates could have foreseen the splendid, the unique opportunities which in later ages would be enjoyed by the Christian preacher, what expectations would he not have formed, not merely of the heights that would be attained—past and living instances remind us that, in this respect, no estimate could well have been too sanguine—but of the average abundance in which compositions of merit would be produced! It will, of course, be recollected that no quality is here in question except that of an eloquence which, regarded as literary prose, has the finish which deserves to be called artistic. If the test, thus defined, be applied, it will be found to afford a striking confirmation of what has already been observed in regard to the effect upon oratory of that especially Protestant conception according to which the orator's function is prophetic. In the combination of argumentative power with lofty earnestness and with eloquence of

Modern Eloquence of the Pulpit.

---

[1] Dem. *de Corona* § 188 (νέφος), § 153 (χειμάρρους), § 194 (σκηπτός).

the Hebraic type,[1] none have surpassed, or perhaps equalled, those divines whose discourses are among the chief glories of the English language. In respect, however, of complete artistic form, of classical finish, a nearer resemblance to the antique has been presented by the great preachers of Catholic France.[2]

Modern Oratory—its greatest triumphs won by sudden bursts.

The most memorable triumphs of modern oratory are connected with the tradition of thrills, of electrical shocks, given to the hearers at the moment by bursts which were extemporary, not necessarily as regards the thought, but necessarily as regards the form. It was for such bursts that the eloquence of the elder Pitt was famous; that of Mirabeau, and of Patrick Henry, owed its highest renown to the same cause. Sheil's retort, in the debate on the Irish Municipal Bill in 1837, to Lord Lyndhurst's description of the Irish (in a phrase borrowed from O'Connell), as "aliens in blood, language and religion," was of this kind.[3] Erskine, in his defence of Lord George Gordon, produced an astonishing effect by a protestation,—which would have been violent if it had not been solemn,—of personal belief in his client's innocence; a daring transgression of the advocate's province which was paralleled, with some momentary success, in a celebrated criminal case about twenty

---

[1] Chatham prescribed a study of Barrow as the best foundation of a good style in speaking.

[2] In his Essay on "Pulpit Eloquence" Brougham seems hardly to do justice to Bossuet — the more florid Isocrates of the group. Bourdaloue, with his abundant resource, his temperate pathos and his frequent harshness, may perhaps be compared with Lycurgus: Massillon, Voltaire's favourite, with his severity, rapidity and lofty fervour, was probably the most Demosthenic.

[3] It is quoted in the excellent article on "The British Parliament; its History and Eloquence," Quarterly Review of April 1872, No. cxxxii. p. 480.

years ago. Now these sudden bursts, and the shock
or the transport which they may cause, were forbidden
to ancient oratory by the principal law of its being.
In nothing is the contrast more striking than in this—
that the greatest oratorical reputations of the ancient
world were chiefly made, and those of the modern
world have sometimes been endangered, by prepared works of art. Pericles and Hypereides were
renowned for no efforts of their eloquence more than
for their funeral orations. Fox's carefully composed
speech in honour of the Duke of Bedford, Chatham's
elaborate eulogy of Wolfe, were accounted among
the least happy of their respective performances.
There is, however, at least one instrument of sudden effect which Greek oratory and British Parliamentary oratory once had in common, but which the latter has now almost abandoned—poetical quotation. A quotation may, of course, be highly effective even for those to whom it is new. But the genuine oratorical force of quotation depends on the hearers knowing the context, having previous associations with the passage, and thus feeling the whole felicity of the application as, at the instant, it is flashed upon the mind. In this respect, the opportunities of the Greek orator were perfect. His hearers were universally and thoroughly familiar with the great poets. When Aeschines applies the lines from Hesiod to Demosthenes, it is as if Digby, addressing Puritans, had attempted to sum up Strafford in a verse of Isaiah. In the days when all educated Englishmen knew a good deal of Virgil and Horace, and something of the best English poets, quotation was not merely a keen,

Use of quotation.

but, in skilful hands, a really powerful weapon of parliamentary debate; and its almost total disuse, however unavoidable, is perhaps a more serious deduction than is generally perceived from the rather slender resources of modern English oratory for creating a glow. Pitt's speech on the Slave Trade concluded with the expression of this hope—that "Africa, though last of all the quarters of the globe, shall enjoy at length, in the evening of her days, those blessings which have descended so plentifully upon us in a much earlier period of the world": the first beams of the rising sun were just entering the windows of the House, and he looked upward as he said—

    Nos......primus equis Oriens afflavit anhelis;
    Illic sera rubens accendit lumina Vesper.

Special characteristics of Greek oratory:

Hitherto we have been seeking to bring into relief, against the modern conception, that character which is common to Greek and to Roman oratory. But Greek oratory, as compared with Roman, has a stamp of its own. It is separated from the Roman, not, indeed, by so wide an interval, yet by a line as firm as that which separates both from the modern.

all Greek art has the plastic character.

That character which, with special modifications, belongs to every artistic creation of the Greek mind, whether this be a statue, a temple, a poem, a speech, or an individual's conception of his own place in life, is usually, and rightly, called the plastic. When it is desired to describe the primary artistic aspect of Greek Tragedy, this is commonly and justly done by a comparison with Sculpture. But it is certain that comparatively few understand the real meaning of "plastic," "sculpturesque," in these relations; and that to a vast majority of even cultivated persons, the statement of this affinity conveys an altogether erroneous notion. The reason of this is that the place held in antiquity by Sculpture is now held jointly by Painting, Music and certain forms of Poetry; that the modern mind instinctively refers the sculptural to the standard of the picturesque; and that, consequently, while the positive and essential characteristics of Sculpture are lost sight of, its negative qualities, relatively to Painting, become most prominent. These are, the absence of colour and the exclusion of tumultuous or complex action. Hence to the popular modern conception of Sculpture there usually attaches the notion of coldness and of rigidity. When people are told that Greek Tragedy (for example) is sculpturesque, they form this idea of it—that it has grandeur, but that it is cold and rather stiff. Then, if they are convinced that somehow the Greeks really were a race with the very highest genius for art, they begin to feel a secret wish that this alleged analogy between Greek Tragedy and sculpture might turn out to be a mistake. Here is an opportunity. The ingenious step in and say, "It *is* a mistake. It is pedantry and sentiment. For our part, we have always felt that Sophocles was frigid, and that Euripides, with his pathetic humanity, his tender women, his heroes who are not ashamed to display their emotions, was the better artist; now, dismiss the prepossessions created by students who are in no sympathy with nature or men, look at the facts

Popular misconception of what is meant by "plastic":

A result of this misconception.

as they are, deign to take homely views, and say, Is it not so?"

Consequent danger to the whole study of the antique.

The question at issue here happens to be vital to the immediate subject of these pages, viz. the development, through Attic oratory, of Attic prose. It is, however, just as vital for every other department whatsoever in the study of ancient art, literature and thought, for it involves nothing less than our fundamental conception of the antique. Unless that conception is true, everything will be seen in a distorted light, and the best things that the ancient world has to teach will be neglected for the second best.

Character of Greek thought in the best days of Greek art;

Let us take a moment of the period when, as a matter of fact, the creative activity of Greek art was abundant—say 440 B.C.—and consider what, at that moment, was the principal characteristic of Greek reflection.[1] This will be best understood by a comparison with two other characters of thought: that which has belonged, though in a multitude of special shapes, to the East, and that of mediæval Europe. Oriental thought, as interpreted by Oriental

compared with the Oriental;

art, fails to define humanity or to give a clear-cut form to any material which the senses offer to it. Life is conceived only generally, as pervading men, animals and vegetables, but the distinctive attributes of human life, physical or spiritual, are not pondered or appreciated. The human form, the human soul,

---

[1] The essay on Winckelmann, in Mr. W. H. Pater's "Studies in the History of the Renaissance," is the most perfect interpretation of the Greek spirit in art that I know. If the restatement of some of its points should gain for it fresh students, such a separation of its teaching from its beauty may deserve to be forgiven.

are not, to this Eastern thought, the objects of an absorbing and analysing contemplation. To European mediævalism, they are so; but the body is regarded as the prison and the shame of the soul; and mediæval art expresses the burning eagerness of the soul to escape from this prison to a higher communion. The three marks of mediæval art are individualism, desire, and ecstasy: individualism, since the artist is struggling to interpret a personal intensity, and goes to grotesqueness in the effort; desire, since the perpetual longing of the Church on earth for her Master is the type of the artist's passion; ecstasy, since this passion demands the surrender of reason and has its climax in the adoration of a mystery revealed.[1] Between the Oriental and the Mediæval art stands the Greek. Greek art defines humanity, the body and the soul of man. But it has not reached the mediæval point; it has not learned to feel that the body is the prison and the shame of the soul. Rather, it regards the soul as reflecting its own divinity upon the body. "What a piece of work is man! how noble in reason! how infinite in faculty! in form and moving how express and admirable! in action how like an angel! in apprehension how like a god! the beauty of the world! the paragon of animals!" If Hamlet could have stopped there, he would have been a Greek; but he could not, he was sick with a modern distemper, abandonment to the brooding thought that sapped his will.[2] The Greek of the days when

and with the Mediæval.

---

[1] I have not at hand an article on (I think) Mr. Rossetti's poems, which appeared some years ago in the *Westminster Review*, and in which these traits of mediævalism were very finely delineated.

[2] Dowden, "Shakspere's Mind and Art," p. 47.

Greek reflection was at a happy pause: art was supreme could and did stop there; he was Narcissus, standing on the river-bank, looking into the deep, clear waters where the mirror of his image shows the soul, too, through the eyes, Narcissus in love with the image that he beholds,—but Narcissus as yet master of himself,—as yet with a firm foothold upon the bank, not as yet possessed by the delirious impulse to plunge into the depths. Here, then, was the first condition for the possibility of a great art. Reflection had taken the right direction, had got far enough, but had not got too far; it was a pause. But, in order that this pause should be joyous, and that the mind should not, from weariness or disappointment, hasten forward, another thing was necessary—*and the Greeks were beautiful.* that men and women should be beautiful. By some divine chance, the pause in reflection coincided with the physical perfection of a race; and the result was Greek art.

Why Greek art became plastic rather than picturesque. Why, however, should this art have expressed itself in Sculpture rather than, for instance, in Painting? Art gives pleasure by form, by colour, by sound, or, as in poetry, by the reminiscence of all these combined with the delight of motion. But the mind has had a history; and the very degree in *Series of the arts:* which the resources of a particular art are limited or ample may give it a special affinity with an earlier *Architecture:* or a later stage of the mind. Architecture corresponds with the phase when man's thoughts about himself are still indistinct; the building may hint, but it cannot express, the artist's personality: Egyptian art *Painting, Music, Poetry;* has been called a Memnon waiting for the day. Painting, Music and Poetry are the modern and romantic arts, with a range of expression adequate to every subtlety and intricacy of self-analysis. Between this group and Architecture comes Sculpture, the art kindred with that phase in the mind's history when man has just attained to recognition of himself and is observing his own typical characteristics of form and spirit with wonder and with joy, but, as yet, without the impulse towards analysis. In all the greatest sculpture there breathes the unshamed and innocent surprise of a child just waked from sleep. But this of itself implies renouncement; the limits of possible expression in Sculpture are severe. If, then, the Greek was contemplating his own soul as well as his own body, why, it might be asked, had he recourse to a medium of interpretation for which the spiritual subtleties of painting and poetry are impossible? The answer is,—Because he was not observing the soul apart from the body, but as one with the body in a godlike union; and because, to him, any expression of spiritual subtleties was not a gain but a loss, if it was effected at the expense of that in which he was absorbed—the contemplation of man as man, in his totality, as the paragon of animals. Sculpture cannot express a complex or refined situation; but its very limitations on that side make it the clearest interpretation of a character or a type. The Greek's attention was fixed on the typical, unchanging, divine lineaments of man, as he stood forth under the blue heaven, his outlines clear against the sunlit sea; and, for the Greek's purpose, sculpture was the more fitting just because it eliminates what is restless or accidental. But he did not

Sculpture.

The limit of expression in Sculpture not irksome, but congenial, to the Greek.

mean sculpture to be cold or rigid; he did not mean it to be blank or vague; and assuredly he made it none of these things. The "Adorante" lifting up his hands in praise for victory, the cousinship of Love with Death hinted in the Genius of Eternal Slumber,—let these works and such as these be witnesses.

<small>The best sculpture is not cold nor vague.</small>

This character of Sculpture belongs also to Greek Tragedy. But this is not, as seems sometimes to be imagined, because the Greeks sought to make Tragedy like Sculpture. It is because that tendency of intellect and feeling, for which Sculpture happened to be a peculiarly apt expression, set its necessary stamp equally on everything else that the Greek mind created. In naming this stamp "plastic" we borrow our term from the arts of modelling; but to conceive the form of Greek Tragedy as derived from Sculpture is like conceiving the Greek language to be derived from Sanskrit. It is true that, in reference to the history of Greek thought, Tragedy is a later manifestation than Sculpture; the perfect repose is already troubled, an element of conflict has entered. man is in the presence of Nemesis, and the δράσαντι παθεῖν, the law that sin shall entail suffering, is the theme. But the typical character is not lost: those unchanging attributes which, on the one hand, bring man near to the gods or, on the other, mark his brotherhood with the dust and the limits of his mortal destiny, are presented in emphatic, untroubled lines; and, when Retributive Justice has done its work, that blitheness out of which the passions rose into a storm returns subdued to the graver and

<small>Mistake of conceiving Greek Tragedy as the daughter of Sculpture:</small>

<small>They are sister forms of one tendency,</small>

<small>which we call "plastic."</small>

<small>Greek Tragedy has an alloy of trouble,</small>

<small>but is typical still.</small>

deeper calm that follows a transcendent contemplation. All honour to those sublime voices of Titanic pain or victory that roll, like dirges or paeans, along the spacious music of Aeschylus; all honour to Euripides also, for no one is capable of feeling that Sophocles is supreme who does not feel that Euripides is admirable. Euripides is a great emotional dramatist; a master of the picturesque; the only Greek, except Aristophanes, who set foot in the charmed woodlands of fancy.[1] That special claim, however, which has in recent times been made for Euripides, and on the strength of which he has by some been preferred to his predecessors, involves a fallacy which it is important to observe, since what is at issue is much more than our judgment on the relative merits of two poets: it is the principle of appreciation relatively to all the best Greek work in every kind. Euripides has been regarded as distinctively the human. Now if by this were meant only that he is great in dramatising the accidents of life, in portraying the more obvious phenomena of character, in exciting compassion for such troubles, or sympathy with such joys, as come home to us all, in establishing between the poet and the spectator not merely a vivid intelligence but something like a personal friendship, then the epithet would be per-

The true greatness of Euripides.

Fallacy involved in calling Euripides the most "human" of the Greek Tragedians.

---

[1] "An admirer of Aeschylus or Sophocles might affirm that neither Aeschylus nor Sophocles chose to use their art for the display of thrilling splendour. However that may be, Euripides, alone of Greeks, with the exception of Aristophanes, entered the fairyland of dazzling fancy which Calderon and Shakspere and Fletcher trod." Symonds, *The Greek Poets*, p. 230. This seems to me exactly to define one of the most attractive poetical distinctions of Euripides. Compare the same writer's remarks on the lyrics of Aristophanes, p. 250.

fectly just. If, however—and this is the popular notion—Euripides is to be called the "human" poet in contrast with, for instance, Sophocles; if it is meant that Sophocles is comparatively cold, pompous, stiff, while Euripides is in a warm, flexible, fruitful sympathy with humanity—then the epithet involves a confusion of ideas than which nothing could be more fatal. Euripides is human, but Sophocles is more human; Sophocles is so in the only way in which a Greek could be so, by being more Greek. When the best Greek mind was truest to the law of its own nature, it looked at man and man's life in the manner of Sophocles—fixing its regard on the permanent, divine characteristics of the human type, and not suffering minor accidents or unrulinesses or griefs so to thrust themselves forward as to mar the symmetry of the larger view. True simplicity is not the avoidance, but the control, of detail. In Sophocles, as in great sculpture, a thousand fine touches go to that which, as the greatest living creator in fiction has proved, he can still help to teach—the delineation of the great primary emotions. Sophocles is the purest type of the Greek intellect at its best. Euripides is a very different thing, a highly gifted son of his day. Rhetorical Dialectic has broken into Tragedy, and the religious basis, the doctrine of Nemesis, has been abandoned in favour of such other interests as the poet can devise. Euripides was brilliantly fertile in plots. This is what Aristotle means by τραγικώτατος, alluding especially to sudden and pathetic reversals of situation; for, before Alexander's time, "tragic" had

Sophocles is the most human, because he is the most Greek.

Sophocles the most perfect type of the Greek intellect.

already come near to "sensational."[1] No woman in Greek Tragedy is either so human, or so true a woman, as the Antigone of Sophocles.[2]

Since, as has been seen, Oratory was for the Greeks a fine art, it follows that Greek Oratory must have, after its own kind, that same typical character which belongs to Greek Sculpture and to Greek Tragedy. Wherein, then, does it manifest this character? We must here be on our guard against the great stumbling-block of such inquiries, the attempt to find the analogy in the particulars and not in the whole. It might be possible to take a speech of Demosthenes and to work out the details of a correspondence with a tragedy of Sophocles or a work of Pheidias; but such refinements have usually a perilous neighbourhood to fantasy, and, even when they are legitimate, are apt to be more curious than instructive. How truly and universally Greek Oratory bears the plastic stamp, can be seen only when it is regarded in its largest aspects. The first point to be observed is that, in Greek Oratory, we have a series of types developed by a series of artists, each of whom seeks to give to his own type the utmost clearness and distinction that he is capable of reaching. The same thing is true of

The plastic character as manifested in Greek oratory.

A series of types is developed by a series of artists.

---

[1] The gradual degradation of the words τραγῳδεῖν, τραγῳδία, etc., is a painful hint of this. Perhaps the nadir has been reached when a contemporary of Aristotle's, a master, too, of all Attic refinements, can use τραγῳδίαι of the menaces with which a Macedonian queen intimidated Athens: Hypereides ὑπὲρ Εὐξενίππου col. 37, τὰς τραγῳδίας αὐτῆς (i.e. Ὀλυμπιάδος) καὶ τὰς κατηγορίας ἀφῃρηκότες ἐσόμεθα.

[2] To Sophocles, hardly less than to Plato, apply the words of Professor Jowett (Introduction to the *Phaedrus*. 2nd edit. II. 102), "We do not immediately recognise that under the marble exterior of Greek literature was concealed a soul thrilling with spiritual emotion."

Tragedy, but not in the same degree; for, in Tragedy, the element of consecrated convention was more persistent; and, besides, Oratory stood in such manifold and intimate relations with the practical life that the artist, in expressing his oratorical theory, could express his entire civic personality. Hence the men who moulded Attic Oratory, whether statesmen or not, are good examples of conscious obedience to that law of Greek nature which constrained every man to make himself a living work of art. "In its poets and orators," says Hegel,[1] "its historians and philosophers, Greece cannot be conceived from a central point unless one brings, as a key to the understanding of it, an insight into the ideal forms of sculpture, and regards the images of statesmen and philosophers as well as epic and dramatic heroes from the artistic point of view; for those who act, as well as those who create and think, have, in those beautiful days of Greece, this plastic character. They are great and free, and have grown up on the soil of their own individuality, creating themselves out of themselves, and moulding themselves to what they were and willed to be. The age of Pericles was rich in such characters: Pericles himself, Pheidias, Plato, above all Sophocles, Thucydides also, Xenophon and Socrates, each in his own order, without the perfection of one being diminished by that of the others. They are ideal artists of themselves, cast each in one flawless mould — works of art which stand before us as an immortal presentment of the gods."

[1] Aesthetik, Part III. Section 2, ch. 1, quoted by Pater, p. 192.

The plastic character of Greek oratory, — thus seen, first of all, in the finished distinction of successive types, clearly modelled as the nature that wrought them, — is further seen in the individual oration. Take it whence we will, from the age of Antiphon or of Demosthenes, from the forensic, from the deliberative or from the epideictic class, two great characteristics will be found. First, however little of sustained reasoning there may be, however much the argument may be mingled with appeals, reminiscences or invectives, everything bears on the matter in hand. It is an exertion of art, but of art strictly pertinent to its scope. No Greek orator could have written such a speech as that of Cicero For Archias or For Publius Sextus. In a Greek speech the main lines of the subject are ever firm; they are never lost amid the flowers of a picturesque luxuriance. Secondly, wherever pity, terror, anger, or any passionate feeling is uttered or invited, this tumult is resolved in a final calm; and where such tumult has place in the peroration, it subsides before the last sentences of all. The ending of the speech On the Crown—which will be noticed hereafter[1]—is exceptional and unique. As a rule, the very end is calm; not so much because the speaker feels this to be necessary if he is to leave an impression of personal dignity, but rather because the sense of an ideal beauty in humanity and in human speech governs his effort as a whole, and makes him desire that, where this effort is most distinctly viewed as a whole —namely, at the close—it should have the serenity

In the individual oration,

the main lines of the theme are unperplexed,

and the unity is sealed by a final calm.

---

[1] Vol. II. pp. 416–17.

<small>Attic perorations in Cicero and Erskine.</small>

of a completed harmony. Cicero has now and then an Attic peroration, as in the Second Philippic and the Pro Milone; more often he breaks off in a burst of eloquence—as in the First Catilinarian, the Pro Flacco and the Pro Cluentio. Erskine's concluding sentences in his defence of Lord George Gordon are Attic:—"Such topics might be useful in the balance of a doubtful case; yet, even then, I should have trusted to the honest hearts of Englishmen to have felt them without excitation. At present the plain and rigid rules of justice are sufficient to entitle me to your verdict."[1]

<small>The personalities of ancient oratory.</small>

This seems the fitting place to touch for a moment on a trait of ancient forensic oratory which has sometimes been noticed with rather exaggerated emphasis, and which, it might be objected, is strangely discordant with the character just described—the disposition of Greek as well as Roman orators to indulge in personalities of a nature which would be deemed highly indecorous in modern times. Their case is scarcely, perhaps, mended by the observation that the point of honour did not then exist. A more important circumstance to observe is that the language in question, however strong, is seldom redundant. It finds its place; but it does not overflow; nor does it destroy that self-mastery in the speaker on

---

[1] This calmness of the Greek peroration is noticed by Brougham in his *Dissertation* (p. 25), but is more fully discussed in his essay on *Demosthenes*, pp. 184 f. He does not, however, penetrate to the true Greek feeling when he says, "The same chastened sense of beauty *which forbade a statue to speak the language of the passions*, required that both the whole oration and each highly impassioned portion of it, should close *with a calmness approaching to indifference, and tameness.*" There comes in the popular modern notion of the sculpturesque.

which the unity of his utterance depends. From the artistic point of view—and from this alone it is now being regarded—it is a distressing blemish; yet not, even here, of the order to which it is referred by those whose estimate of it is purely modern, since it is not permitted to disturb the symmetry or the repose of the whole. Unquestionably, the scale of life in the Greek republics, and the dialect of the aristocracy at Rome, often imparted to the mutual criticisms of their orators a parochial character which is comparatively rare in the public discussions of the present day. Apart from this accident, however, modern analogies are, unfortunately, not wanting.[1] The speech against Ctesiphon and the speech against Piso certainly contain exceedingly strong phrases. Catullus, who used the ordinary language of society in his day,[2] is less euphemistic than Byron. But scurrility is not the measure of vituperation. Ancient invective concentrated the former. Modern invective prefers to diffuse, without diluting, the latter.

The superiority of Greek oratory to Roman, in the deliberative and forensic branches alike, has been recognised by the best critics as well as by the most competent practical judges. Brougham, who speaks with the authority of both characters, brings this out with great force and clearness. He says:—"In

Superiority of Greek to Roman oratory.

Brougham on Cicero.

---

[1] Specimens of the language addressed by Coke, then Attorney-General, to Raleigh, whose prosecution he was conducting, will be found in a note to Mr. Forsyth's *Hortensius*, p. 45. The phrases are surpassed by nothing in Aeschines. Chatham's most effective retorts were personalities which might have satisfied Cicero. One or two of them will be found in the *Quarterly Review*, No. 132, p. 470. Those who desire further illustrations may read, or recall, the debates in the House of Commons of May 15 and June 8, 1846.

[2] See H. A. J. Munro on Catullus's 29th Poem in the *Journal of Philology*, II. 1-34 (1869).

all his (Cicero's) orations that were spoken (for, singular as it may seem, the remark applies less to those which were only written, as all the Verrine, except the first, all the Philippics, except the first and ninth, and the Pro Milone), hardly two pages can be found which a modern assembly would bear. Some admirable arguments on evidence, and the credit of witnesses, might be urged to a jury; several passages, given by him on the merits of the case, and in defence against the charge, might be spoken in mitigation of punishment after a conviction or confession of guilt; but, whether we regard the political or forensic orations, the style, both in respect of the reasoning and the ornaments, is wholly unfit for the more severe and less trifling nature of modern affairs in the senate or at the bar. Now, it is altogether otherwise with the Greek masters; changing a few phrases, which the difference of religion and of manners might render objectionable, —moderating, in some degree, the virulence of invective, especially against private character, to suit the chivalrous courtesy of modern hostility,—there is hardly one of the political or forensic orations of the Greeks that might not be delivered in similar circumstances before our senate or tribunals."[1]

Cicero's orations utterly unfit for the modern Senate or Bar:

whereas almost all the Greek orations could be adapted.

Reasons of this superiority: Greek oratory is always to the point;

The main reason of this decided advantage on the part of Greek practical oratory—and the epideictic oratory has a corresponding excellence relatively to that of the French Pulpit—is the business-like

---

[1] *Inaugural Discourse*, pp. 122 f. Hume, again, observing that Cicero is "too florid and rhetorical," and that Greek oratory is "more chaste and austere," adds:—"could it be copied, its success would be infallible over a modern assembly." (Essay XII., *Of Eloquence*, p. 60.)

character already noticed. If everything is not logical, everything is at least relevant. Cicero, with all his ingenuity, brilliancy and wit, is so apt to wander into mere display, and this display is so openly artificial, that, as Brougham says, "nothing can be less adapted to the genius of modern elocution." The style of modern debate comes far nearer to the Greek than to the Latin. But there are two other causes which should be remarked, one especially influential in Deliberative, the other in Forensic, oratory. The first is that, in the days of the great Roman eloquence, Rome had no political rival. Her discipline and her manners contributed with her civic security to exempt her citizens from sudden or violent emotion. What Claudian[1] afterwards happily called the *vitae Romana quies* already prevailed. If the paradox of Quintilian[2] be true, that Demosthenes has *plus curae*, Cicero *plus naturae*, it is true in this sense alone, that Cicero is an inferior artist, and indulges more freely the taste of the natural man for ornament. But that Roman oratory should be on the whole more artificial than the Greek, and more limited in its range of subjects, was inevitable. Athens, the antagonist of Sparta or Thebes, Athens vigilant against Persia or threatened by Macedon, was a city in which the inspirations of eloquence were not only personal but national. Secondly: the Roman *patronus*, who pleaded his client's cause gratuitously, rewarded by the fact that all the higher paths of ambition opened directly from the forum, had, doubtless, an incentive to

the political inspirations of Greek oratory are nobler:

and the forensic motive is more genuine.

[1] *De sexto consulatu Honorii Augusti* (404 A.D.), v. 150. [2] x. 1 § 106.

eloquent declamation which his Attic brother, the professional *logographos*, did not possess. But he had not anything like the same inducement to handle his case scientifically. He was a political aspirant, not a man settled to a calling; and, from a forensic point of view, the element of unreality in his position had a strong tendency to vitiate his performance by making it, before all things, a display.

<small>Early History of Greek Oratory.</small>

The least gifted people, in the earliest stage of intellectual or political growth, will always or usually have the idea, however rude, of a natural oratory.

<small>Two conditions for the possibility of any such history.</small>

But oratory first begins to have a history, of which the development can be traced, when two conditions have been fulfilled. First, that oratory should be conceived, no longer subjectively, but objectively also, and from having been a mere faculty, should have become an art. Secondly, that an oration should have been written in accordance with the theory of that art. The history of Greek oratory begins with Gorgias. The history of Attic oratory, properly so called, begins with Antiphon.

The special attributes and endowments of the Greeks would lead us to expect, before the beginnings of an oratorical art, a singularly rich and various manifestation of natural eloquence, and also an early

<small>Late appearance of Greek oratory as an Art.</small>

moment of origin for the art itself. Now, as a matter of fact, the origin of the art was singularly late, relatively to the gifts and to the general artistic tendency of the race; but the causes of this delay were external and political. On the other hand, no documents of any early society can show an exuberance, a brilliancy, a diversified perfection of natural eloquence comparable to that which makes one of the chief glories of the Homeric poems. By "natural" is meant, not necessarily unstudied, but unsystematic, or antecedent to a theory of Rhetoric. The man to whom the gods had given ἀγορητύς, the power of discourse,—that which, with beautiful strength, φυή, and good sense, φρένες, makes the Homeric triad of human excellences,—might cultivate it; but so long as this cultivation is empirical, not theoretic, the eloquence which it achieves is still natural. From Achilles to Thersites, the orators of the Iliad and the Odyssey are individual. If Achilles alone is a Demosthenes, who had no defects to conquer and no mysteries to learn, Nestor is an Isocrates unaided or unembarrassed by his system, Telemachus an ingenuous youth who has no need of prompting by a Lysias, Odysseus a speaker in whom the logical terseness of Isaeus is joined to something like the unscrupulous smartness, though to nothing like the theatrical splendour, of Aeschines. Nor does any oratory that the ancient world has left approach so nearly as the Homeric to the modern ideal. The reason of this is that the great orations of the Iliad are made in debate, and the greatest of all are replies, —as the answer of Achilles to the envoys in the First Book. Condensed statement, lucid argument, repartee, sarcasm, irony, overwhelming invective, profound and irresistible pathos,—all these resources are absolutely commanded by the orators of the Iliad,

[margin: Extraordinary brilliancy of the pre-theoretic Oratory. Homeric estimate of Eloquence. Homeric illustrations of Eloquence. Modern character of the great Homeric speeches:]

and all these must have belonged to him, or to those, by whom the Iliad was created. As Mr. Gladstone has said,[1] "Paradise Lost" does not represent the time of Charles the Second, nor the "Excursion" the first decades of this century, but "as, when we find these speeches in Homer, we know that there must have been men who could speak them, so, from the existence of units who could speak them, we know that there must have been crowds who could feel them."

their historical significance.

The Homeric ideal, to shine in eloquence as in action, to be at once "a speaker of words and a doer of deeds," "good in counsel, and mighty in war," had ample scope, as far as kings and nobles were concerned, in the council and the agora. But the eloquence of the commons does not appear to have been particularly encouraged by the chiefs, and the consummate individuality of an Achilles or an Odysseus was no real step towards the development of a popular oratory based upon a theory communicable to all. In the presence of these great debaters of the Iliad, the Homeric *tis*, when present at all, is essentially a layman, confined strictly to the critical function, and uttering his criticisms, when they find utterance, in the fewest and plainest words. Democracy, with its principle of ἰσηγορία,—the principle that every citizen has an equal right to speak his mind about the concerns of the city,—was necessary before a truly civil eloquence could be even possible. But, after Democracy had arisen, a further condition was needed,—the cultivation of

The Homeric eloquence is still aristocratic, not civil.

First conditions of civil eloquence— ἰσηγορία,

and popular culture.

[1] *Studies on Homer*, III. 107.

the popular intelligence. What is so strikingly characteristic of Greek Democracy in the period before an artistic oratory is this,—that the power of public speaking now exists, indeed, as a political weapon, but, instead of being the great organ by which the people wield the commonwealth, is constantly used by designing individuals against the people. It is employed as a lever for changing the democracy into a tyranny. Such names as Aristagoras, Evagoras, Protagoras, Peisistratus, frequent especially in the Ionian colonies, indicate, not the growth of a popular oratory, but the ascendency which exceptionally gifted speakers were able to acquire, especially in democracies, before oratory was yet an accomplishment studied according to a method. *The faculty of speech—its place in early Greek Democracy.*

The intellectual turning-point came when Poetry ceased to have a sway of which the exclusiveness rested on the presumption that no thought can be expressed artistically which is not expressed metrically. So soon as it had been apprehended that to forsake poetical form was not necessarily to renounce beauty of expression, an obstacle to clear reflection had been overcome. Mythology and cosmical speculation began to have a rival,—a curiosity withdrawn from the cloud-regions of the past or of the infinite to the things of practical life. And this life itself was growing more complex. The present, with its problems which must be solved under penalties, was becoming ever more importunate, and would no longer suffer men's thoughts to wander in mazes where they could find no end:— *The intellectual turning-point—first conception of a literary Prose.*

> The riddling Sphinx put dim things from our minds,
> And set us to the questions at our doors.

Political turning-point—opening of secure intercourse between the cities: The political turning-point came with the Persian Wars. Greek freedom was secured against the barbarian. A maritime career was opened to commerce. The Greek cities everywhere came into more active intercourse; and the centre of the Greek world was *and the new primacy of Athens.* Athens. The Dorian States, Sparta and Argos, had never been favourable to the artistic treatment of language. This, like all art and science, was especially the province of the Ionians; and, for the future of oratory, it was of the highest importance that the central city of Hellas should be Ionian. But, though Athens perfected the art, and soon became almost its sole possessor, the first elements were prepared elsewhere. *External influences which prepared Attic Oratory.* The two principal forces which moulded Attic oratory came from the East and the West. One was the Practical Culture of Ionia; the other was the Rhetoric of Sicily.

I. The Practical culture of Ionia. The theories of the Ionian physicists had not been able to interest more than a few, still less had they been able to draw away the mass of the people from the old poetical faith; nor had the Ionian chroniclers made any but the rudest approaches to a written prose. But the national Wars of Liberation had quickened all the pulses of civic life. Freedom once secured, the new intellectual tendency took a definite shape. Men arose who, in contrast with the speculative philosophers, undertook to give a practical culture. This culture had representatives in every part of Greece. But, while in Sicily and Magna Graecia it was engrossed with Rhetoric, in Asiatic, and especially

Ionian, Hellas it was more comprehensive. There, its essence was Dialectic, in connexion with a training sometimes encyclopaedic, sometimes directed especially to grammar or to literary criticism. These more comprehensive teachers were known by the general name of Sophists.[1] Those who, like the Sicilians, had a narrower scope were sometimes called Sophists, but were especially and properly called Rhetors.

Protagoras of Abdera, the earliest of the Sophists proper, was born about 485 B.C., and travelled throughout Greece, teaching, for about 40 years, from 455 to 415. The two things by which he is significant for artistic oratory are, his Dialectic, and the Commonplaces which he made his pupils commit to memory. His Dialectic is famous for its undertaking to make the weaker cause the stronger. One of the uses of Rhetoric, as Aristotle says, is to succour truth when truth is imperilled by the weakness of its champion; but this is not the place to inquire whether Protagoras intended, or how far he was bound to foresee, an immoral application. As a mental discipline, his Dialectic was important to oratory, not merely by its subtlety, but by its treatment of the rhetorical syllogism. The prepared topics which his pupils

Protagoras.

---

[1] It does not fall within my province to enter on the "Sophist" controversy, to which, in this country, eminent scholars have lately given a new life. But I would invite the reader's attention to a note, on p. 127 of my second volume, as to the use of the word by Isocrates. And I would record my general agreement with the reasoned development of Grote's view by Mr. H. Sidgwick, in the *Journal of Philology*, Vol. IV. No. 8 (1872).

For the details given here respecting particular Sophists or Rhetors, I have used chiefly:—(1) Cope's papers on the Sophists and the Sophistical Rhetoric, in the *Journal of Classical and Sacred Philology*, I. 145–188, II. 129–169, III. 34–80: (2) Westermann. *Gesch. der Beredsamkeit*, pp. 36–48: (3) Blass, *die Attische Beredsamkeit von Gorgias bis zu Lysias*, pp. 1–78.

learned seem to mark a stage when public speaking in general was no longer purely extemporary, but when, on the other hand, the speech was not, as in Antiphon's time, wholly written. In regard to language, Protagoras insisted on ὀρθοέπεια—*i.e.* a correct accidence: but there is no proof that he sought to make a style; both the Ionic fragment in Plutarch [1] and the myth in Plato [2] are, for the prose of the time, simple, and they are free from the Gorgian figures.

<small>Prodicus.</small>

Prodicus of Ceos—the junior by many years of Protagoras—was neither, like the latter, a dialectician nor a rhetor of the Siceliot type, but rather, like Hippias, the teacher of an encyclopaedic culture. There is no reason to think that he, any more than Protagoras or Hippias, concerned himself with the artistic oratory of Gorgias. Xenophon gives in the *Memorabilia* [3] a paraphrase of the "Choice of Heracles" as related by Prodicus in his fable called Ὧραι. When Philostratus [4] says that he need not describe the style of Prodicus because Xenophon has sketched it, he is refuted by Xenophon himself, who observes that the diction of Prodicus was more ambitious than that of his paraphrase.[5] There are certainly confusions of synonyms which the Platonic Prodicus distinguishes;[6] and the only safe inference appears to

---

[1] Plut. παραμυθητικὸς πρὸς Ἀπολλώνιον, c. 33 (*Moral.* p. 118), τῶν γὰρ ἱέων νεηνιῶν—ἀμηχανίην.

[2] Plat. *Protag.* pp. 320 D–328 c.

[3] II. i. §§ 21–33. Xen. calls it τὸ σύγγραμμα τὸ περὶ Ἡρακλέους.

[4] *Vit. Sophist.* p. 16 (Kayser), καὶ τί ἂν χαρακτηρίζοιμεν τὴν τοῦ Προδίκου γλῶτταν, Ξενοφῶντος αὐτὴν ἱκανῶς ὑπογράφοντος;

[5] *Mem.* II. i. § 34, οὕτω πως διώκει (διώκει?) Πρόδικος τὴν ὑπ' Ἀρετῆς Ἡρακλέους παίδευσιν, ἐκόσμησε μέντοι τὰς γνώμας ἔτι μεγαλειοτέροις ῥήμασιν ἢ ἐγὼ νῦν.

[6] As Blass points out (*l. c.*), Xenophon (*Mem.* II. i. § 24) makes Prodicus use τέρπεσθαι, ἥδεσθαι, εὐφραίνεσθαι, indistinguishably: whereas Plato (*Prot.* 337 c) makes Prodicus appropriate εὐφραίνεσθαι to intellectual, ἥδεσθαι to sensuous pleasure.

be that, however faithful Xenophon may have been to the matter of the fable, he is a witness of no authority for its form. The true point of contact between Prodicus and the early Rhetoric is his effort to discriminate words which express slight modifications of the same idea, and which, therefore, were not ordinarily distinguished by poets or in the idiom of daily life. However unscientific his effort may have been, it at least represented a scientific tendency, which soon set its mark on literature as well as on thought. Two men who are said to have been pupils of Prodicus—Euripides and Isocrates—show clear traces of it; but, for reasons which will appear further on, it is especially distinct in the earliest phase of artistic oratory — in Antiphon, and above all in Thucydides.

Hippias of Elis is of no immediate significance for our subject. Neither Dialectic nor Rhetoric was included, or at least prominent, in the large circle of arts and sciences which he professed to teach. Economics, Ethics and Politics—"the faculty of managing public affairs along with his own"[1]—formed his especial province. Like all the other Sophists, he touched, of course, the domain of grammar and prosody; his Τρωικὸς λόγος,[2] a dialogue between Nestor and Neoptolemus, made pretensions to elegance of style, but probably not of a poetical or Gorgian cast;[3] and, in Plato, Hippias assigns, not his oratory, but

Hippias.

---

[1] Plat. *Hipp. Mai.* 282 B, τὸ καὶ τὰ δημόσια πράττειν δύνασθαι μετὰ τῶν ἰδίων. Cf. Cope in *Journ. Class. and Sacr. Phil.* III. 63.

[2] Plat. *l. c.* p. 286 A.

[3] Philostratus, at least, says of Hippias that he wrote "powerfully and naturally," εἰς ὀλίγα καταφεύγων τῶν ἐκ ποιητικῆς ὀνόματα, *Vit. Sophist.* p. 15 (Kayser).

his political insight, as the ground of his selection as an ambassador by the Eleans.¹

Thrasymachus of Chalcedon stands in a far riper and more definite relation to Attic rhetorical prose, and will more properly be noticed in connexion with the progress from Antiphon to Lysias, when we come to look back on the development as a whole.²

<small>Summary: influence of the Ionian Practical culture.</small>

These, then, were the two things by which the Eastern or Ionian school of practical culture prepared the ground for Attic oratory: first and chiefly, popular Dialectic; secondly, in the phrase of Protagoras, orthoepy — attention to correctness in speaking or writing. In contrast with the Eastern Dialectic stands the Western Rhetoric. In contrast with the Ionian study of correct diction, ὀρθοέπεια, stands the Sicilian study of beautiful diction, εὐέπεια.

<small>II. The Sicilian Rhetoric.</small>

Deeper causes than a political crisis fitted Sicily to become the birthplace of Rhetoric. The first cause was the general character of the Sicilian Greeks.

<small>Character of the Sicilian Greeks.</small>

Thucydides remarks that the quick and adventurous Athenians, who were often benefited by Lacedaemonian slowness or caution, found most formidable adversaries in the Syracusans just because the Syracusans were so like themselves;³ and this resemblance, we have good reason to suppose, included the taste for lively controversy and the passion for lawsuits described by Aristophanes in the *Wasps*. "An acute people, with an inborn love of disputation," is the description of the Sicilians which Cicero quotes from

---

¹ Plat. *l. c.* p. 281 (*ad init.*). He is a δικαστὴς καὶ ἄγγελος τῶν λόγων οἳ ἂν παρὰ τῶν πόλεων ἑκάστων λέγωνται.

² See Vol. II. ch. xxiii.

³ μάλιστα ὁμοιότροποι, Thuc. VIII. 96.

Aristotle:[1] "Sicilians are never so miserable," he says in one of the Verrine speeches, "that they cannot make a happy joke."[2] The population thus gifted had, further, gone through the same political phases as Athens: through aristocracy they had arrived at tyranny, and through tyranny at a democracy. The flourishing age of the Sicilian Tyrants—the early part of the fifth century B.C.—was illustrated by art and literature, by the lyric poetry which, native to Ionia, found its most splendid theme in the glory of these Dorian princes of the West, and by a home-growth of Comedy, the creation of Phormis and Epicharmus. It was in 466 that Thrasybulus, last of the Gelonian dynasty, was expelled and that a democracy was established at Syracuse. Somewhat later, a democracy arose at Agrigentum also. Popular life was now as exuberant in Sicily as it was at Athens after the Persian Wars; but, with its mixture of races, it was less fortunately tempered; its vigour, instead of glowing with the sense of national welfare secured against aliens, had the feverish vehemence of a domestic reaction; and hence we should be prepared to find these younger democracies showing almost at once some features which do not appear in the elder Athenian democracy until the time of the Peloponnesian War. But it was neither by the turbulent rivalries of the popular assembly, nor by the natural growth of συκοφαντική or pettifogging, that the formulation of Rhetoric as an Art was immediately caused. The absolute princes of Sicily had done as they listed.

Political development of the Sicilian cities.

The Age of the Sicilian Tyrants.

The Democratic Revolution.

Character of Sicilian Democracy.

Circumstances under which Rhetoric became an Art.

---

[1] Cic. *Brut.* xii. § 46.
[2] Cic. *In Verr.* IV. 43 *ad fin.* Cf. Quint. VI. 3 § 41.

They had banished, they had confiscated,—like Dionysius I. in later times, they had effaced towns and transferred populations,—they had turned all things upside-down. When they were driven out, and when governments arose based on the equality of citizens before the law, a crowd of aggrieved claimants presented themselves wherever that law had a seat. "Ten years ago," this one would say, "Hieron banished me from Syracuse because I was too much a democrat, and gave my house on the Epipolae to Agathocles, who still lives among you; I ask the people to restore it to me." "When Gelon razed our city," another would say, "and divided the lands among his friends, we were commanded to dwell at Selinus, where I have lived many years; my father's land was given to a favourite of the tyrant's, whose first cousin still holds it; I ask you to insist on this man making restitution." Claims of this kind would be innumerable. And, besides those which were founded in justice, a vast number of false claims would be encouraged by the general presumption that the rights of property had been universally deranged. If, twenty years after the Cromwellian Settlement of Ireland, a government had arisen of such a nature as to make it worth people's while to dispute every possession taken under that settlement in the Ten Counties, the state of things which would have ensued would have borne some resemblance to that which prevailed throughout Sicily, but especially at Syracuse, in 466 B.C.[1]

Now, if we consider what would be, as a rule, the

---

[1] Those who wish to test the accuracy of this illustration are referred to the History of the Cromwellian Settlement by Mr. J. P. Prendergast. (Longmans, 1865.)

characteristics of claims to property made under such conditions, we shall find that they throw a significant light on the little which is expressly recorded in regard to the first artists of Rhetoric. First, such claims would, as a rule, go several years back, and would often require for their elucidation that a complicated mass of details should be stated or arranged. Secondly, such claims would often lack documentary support; the tablets proving a purchase, a sale, or a contract, would, in many or most cases, have been lost or destroyed, and the claimant would have to rely chiefly on inferences from other facts which he could substantiate. If, then, we imagine a man conceiving the idea that these innumerable claimants want help, and that the occupation of helping them may be a way to notoriety or gain, in what particular forms is it probable that he would have tried to render this help? He would have seen, first, that people must be assisted to deal with an array of complex facts; they must be taught method. He would have seen, secondly, that they must be assisted to dispense with documentary or circumstantial evidence; they must be given hints as to the best mode of arguing from general probabilities.

Diogenes Laertius quotes a statement of Aristotle that Empedocles was the inventor of Rhetoric, as Zenon of Dialectic.[1] The more cautious phrase of

---

[1] Diog. VIII. 57, Ἀριστοτέλης δ' ἐν τῷ σοφιστῇ φησι πρῶτον Ἐμπεδοκλέα ῥητορικὴν εὑρεῖν, Ζήνωνα δὲ διαλεκτικήν. In his lost work περὶ ποιητῶν, Arist. (as quoted by Diog. l. c.) said that Empedocles was δεινὸς περὶ τὴν φράσιν and μεταφορικός, as well as generally Ὁμηρικός. Twining notices (Vol. I. p. 249) the apparent discrepancy between this statement and that in the *Poetics* c. 1.—that Empedocles and Homer have οὐδὲν κοινὸν πλὴν τὸ μέτρον.

Sextus Empiricus [1] (also from Aristotle), which Quintilian translates, is that Empedocles *broke ground* (κεκινηκέναι, *aliqua movisse*) in Rhetoric. Assuredly the poet and philosopher of Agrigentum created, at least, no rhetorical system. His oratory—which, after the fall of Thrasydaeus in 472, found political scope in resistance to a restoration of the tyranny—however brilliant, was practical only; and his analogy—so far as the wanderings of his later years and the union of care for studied expression with a doctrine give the semblance of such—is, at least, more with the Sophists of proper Greece than with the Sicilian Rhetors.

<small>Corax.</small>

The founder of Rhetoric as an Art was Corax of Syracuse. He had enjoyed some political consideration in the reign of Hieron (478–467 B.C.), and was probably several years older than Empedocles. The lawsuits which followed the establishment of the democracy are said to have given him the idea of drawing up, and committing to writing, a system of rules for forensic speaking. This was his τέχνη or Art of Rhetoric—the earliest theoretical Greek book, not merely on Rhetoric, but in any branch of art. There is no mention of speeches composed by him either for himself or for others. Nor, except the story of his lawsuit with Tisias, is there any evidence that he

<small>Treatise of Corax on Rhetoric:</small>

taught Rhetoric for pay. In regard to the contents of his "Art," two facts are known which are of interest. They are precisely those which, as has been shown, we should have expected to find. First, he gave rules for *arrangement*—dividing the speech

---

[1] VII. 6: Quint. III. 1 § 8.

into five parts—proem, narrative, arguments (ἀγῶνες), subsidiary remarks (παρέκβασις) and peroration.[1] Secondly, he illustrated the topic of *general probability*, bringing out its two-edged application: e.g. if a physically weak man is accused of an assault, he is to ask, "Is it probable that *I* should have attacked him?" if a strong man is accused, he is to ask, "Is it probable that I should have committed an assault in a case where there was sure to be a presumption against me?" Nothing could be more suggestive of the special circumstances in which the art of Rhetoric had its birth. The same topic of Probability holds its place in the Tetralogies of Antiphon.[2] But its original prominence was, in truth, a Sicilian accident.[3]

Arrangement.

The topic of εἰκός.

Tisias, the pupil of Corax, must have been born about 485 B.C. We hear that he was the master of Lysias at the colony of Thurii (founded in 443 B.C.), and of the young Isocrates at Athens—about 418 B.C.; Pausanias makes him accompany Gorgias to Athens in 427 B.C.; and speaks of him as having been banished from Syracuse.[4] Whatever may be the worth of these details, the main facts about Tisias are clear. He led the wandering life of a Sophist.

Tisias.

[1] The ἀγῶνες and παρέκβασις are thus explained in the Greek prolegomena to Hermogenes, Spengel, συναγωγὴ τεχνῶν, p. 25.
[2] See below, pp. 46 ff.
[3] This topic of εἰκός—the great weapon of the early Rhetoric—stands ninth among those topics of the fallacious enthymeme which Aristotle enumerates in *Rhet.* II. 24—a chapter which, for his *Rhetoric*, is what the περὶ σοφιστικῶν ἐλέγχων is for the *Topica*. The fallacy arises from the omission to distinguish between abstract and particular probability. Arist. illustrates it by the verses of Agathon:—"Perhaps one might call this very thing a probability,—that many improbable things will happen to men." "Of this topic," says Aristotle (*Rh.* II. 24 § 9) "the Treatise of Corax is made up." Cf. Spengel, συναγωγὴ τεχνῶν, pp. 30 f.
[4] Pausan. VI. 17 § 8.

And in his Art of Rhetoric—the only work of his which antiquity possessed—he followed his master in further developing the topic of Probability.[1]

The "Rhetoric" of Tisias.
The topic of εἰκός further developed.

Those who bring a scientific spirit to the study of Attic oratory need not be cautioned against allowing what is ignoble, puerile, or even immoral in the earliest Greek Rhetoric to prejudice their estimate of the real services afterwards rendered both to language and to thought by the conception of expression as an art. Popular sentiment is universally against new subtleties. To gauge the morality of the early Rhetoric by the feeling of the people would be as unreasonable as to judge Socrates on the testimony of the *Clouds*. The real meaning of the story about the lawsuit between Corax and Tisias lies in its illustration of the people's feeling. Corax, suing Tisias for a fee, argued that it must be paid whether he gained or lost his cause; if he gained, under the verdict; if he lost, because the success of his pupil proved the fee to have been earned; Tisias inverted the dilemma; and the judges dismissed them both with the comment, "bad crow, bad eggs." What this really expresses is not the character of the earliest Rhetoric, but its grotesque unpopularity.

Real meaning of the lawsuit story.

Gorgias is a man of whose powers and merits it is extremely difficult for us now to form a clear or impartial notion. This is not, however, because the portrait of him in Plato is so vivid. Nothing more distinguishes Plato from later satirists of like keenness than his manner of hinting the redeeming points of the person under dissection; and, whenever

Gorgias.

---

[1] Plat. *Phaedr.* 267 A, 273 A–C.

Gorgias comes in—whether in the dialogue that bears his name or elsewhere—it may be discerned (I venture to think) that Plato's purpose was to bring out an aspect of the man—that aspect which he considered most important—but that he allowed, and was writing for those who knew, that there was another side to the picture. This other side is suggested by the fact that Gorgias had at least some influence on a man of such intellectual power as Thucydides, on one so highly cultivated as the tragic poet Agathon, and on so shrewd a judge of practical ability as Jason of Pherae. The difficulty of now estimating Gorgias comes from this,—that he was an inventor whose originality it is hard for us to realise, but an artist whose faults are to us peculiarly glaring. Gorgias of Leontini was born about 485 B.C. Tradition made him the pupil of Empedocles; but their nearness in age makes this unlikely. That they knew each other is probable enough. Gorgias, like Protagoras, began with natural philosophy; and, after employing Eleatic methods to combat Eleatic conclusions, turned from a field of which he held himself to have proved the barrenness. The practical culture to which he next addressed himself differed both from that of the Eastern Sophists and from that of the Sicilian Rhetors. It was founded neither upon Dialectic nor upon a systematic Rhetoric. Its basis was Oratory considered as a faculty to be developed empirically. Whether Gorgias left a written Art or not, is doubtful; it seems more probable that he did not;[1] and his method of teaching—which reappears

The province of Gorgias, neither Dialectic nor Rhetoric, but Oratory.

---

[1] On this point see Blass, p. 53.

a century and a half later with the beginnings of Asianism[1]—rested on the commission to memory of prepared passages. These passages were especially such as might serve to magnify the speaker's theme (αὔξησις) or to bring out the enormity of a wrong (δείνωσις). Beautiful and effective expression (λέξις) was the one great object. Gorgias seems to have given little or no heed to the treatment of subject-matter,—to invention or management; or even to that special topic of Probability which was already engaging so much of the attention of Rhetoric. He was himself a man with a brilliant gift for language. His general conception was simple enough, but, for his own day and world, both bold and original. If the faculty of expression is cultivated to the right point, and is combined with a certain amount of general information, it will carry all before it. Just in the spirit in which Vivian Grey is described as saying to himself "knowledge is power," Gorgias said to himself, "expression is power." He considered the gift in its relation to victory, and this victory not to be such narrow and painful success as was prepared by the pedantries of the rhetors, but dazzling and world-wide. Everything recorded of the man suggests his immense self-confidence, his capacity for sustained work, his exuberant vitality, and, above all, his power of doing what a new style would not have done without other gifts—setting the fashion to the ambitious among the rising generation, or even excit-

His first visit to Athens.

ing a popular enthusiasm. In 427 B.C. the Leontines sent an embassy to Athens, praying for help in their

[1] See Vol. II. ch. xxiv.

war with Syracuse. "At the head of the envoys," says Diodorus,[1] "was Gorgias the rhetor, a man who far surpassed all his contemporaries in oratorical force. He astonished the Athenians, with their quick minds and their love of eloquence, by the foreign fashion (τῷ ξενίζοντι) of his language"—and by figures which the historian proceeds to enumerate. Now Gorgias appears to have always spoken and written in the Attic dialect—not in the ordinary Sicilian Doric, nor in the Ionic of Leontini.[2] The τὸ ξενίζον of Diodorus is that "foreign" air which Aristotle in his Rhetoric calls τὸ ξενικόν,[3] and which, for Athenians at least, was capable, when rightly used, of being a charm in oratory. There is no word which will exactly translate it, but it is nearly akin to what we mean by "distinction." That which was, to the Athenians, τὸ ξενίζον, or the element of distinction, in the Sicilian's speaking, was its poetical character; and this depended on two things—the use of poetical words, and the use of symmetry or assonance between clauses in such a way as to give a strongly marked prose-rhythm and to reproduce, as far as possible, the metres of verse. The only considerable fragment of Gorgias extant is that from the Funeral Oration—for the *Palamedes* and the *Helen* are now generally admitted to be later imitations. A few sentences from this will give the best idea of his manner:—

to ξενίζον in his speaking,

its poetical character.

---

[1] XII. 53, τῷ ξενίζοντι τῆς λέξεως ἐξέπληξε τοὺς Ἀθηναίους ὄντας εὐφυεῖς καὶ φιλολόγους, διαφέρουσιν ἀντιθέτοις καὶ ἰσοκώλοις καὶ παρίσοις καὶ ὁμοιοτελεύτοις καὶ ἑτέροις τοιούτοις. On these, see Vol. II. pp. 61 f.

[2] Blass, p. 52.

[3] (*e.g.*) Arist. *Rhet.* III. 2 § 3, διὸ

δεῖ ποιεῖν ξένην τὴν διάλεκτον· θαυμασταὶ γὰρ τῶν ἀπόντων εἰσίν· ἡδὺ δὲ τὸ θαυμαστόν. So *ib.* § 8, τὸ σαφὲς καὶ τὸ ἡδὺ καὶ τὸ ξενικὸν ἔχει μάλιστα ἡ μεταφορά. And III. 7 § 11, τὰ ξένα μάλιστα ἁρμόττει λέγοντι παθητικῶς.

Specimen from his Epitaphius

μαρτυρίας δὲ τούτων τρόπαια ἐστήσαντο τῶν πολεμίων, Διὸς μὲν ἀγάλματα, τούτων δὲ ἀναθήματα, οὐκ ἄπειροι οὔτε ἐμφύτου Ἄρεος οὔτε νομίμων ἐρώτων οὔτε ἐνοπλίου ἔριδος οὔτε φιλοκάλου εἰρήνης, σεμνοὶ μὲν πρὸς τοὺς θεοὺς τῷ δικαίῳ, ὅσιοι δὲ πρὸς τοὺς τοκέας τῇ θεραπείᾳ, δίκαιοι πρὸς τοὺς ἀστοὺς τῷ ἴσῳ, εὐσεβεῖς δὲ πρὸς τοὺς φίλους τῇ πίστει. τοιγαροῦν αὐτῶν ἀποθανόντων ὁ πόθος οὐ συναπέθανεν, ἀλλ' ἀθάνατος ἐν οὐκ ἀσωμάτοις σώμασι ζῇ οὐ ζώντων.[1]

His great popularity at Athens—how it is to be understood.

It may be hard now to understand how such a style can have moved to transports of delight men who lived among the works of Pheidias and Ictinus, who knew the prose of Herodotus, and whose ears were familiar with Homer, with Aeschylus and with Sophocles. It is more difficult still, perhaps, to realise that the invention of this style was a proof of genius. Gorgias was the first man who definitely conceived how literary prose might be artistic. That he should instinctively compare it with the only other form of literature which was already artistic, namely poetry, was inevitable. Early prose necessarily begins by comparing itself with poetry. Gorgias was a man of glowing and eager power; he carried the assimilation to a length which seems incredibly tasteless now. But let it be remembered that the interval between Gorgias and Thucydides, in some passages of the historian's speeches, is not so very wide. And if the enthusiasm of the Ecclesia still seems incomprehensible, let it be remembered that they felt vividly the whole originality of the man, and did not at all see that his particular tendency was mistaken. It

---

[1] Sauppe, *Or. Att.* II. 130.

was only by and by, and after several compromises,
that men found out the difference between τὸ ἔρρυθμον
and τὸ εὔρυθμον, between verse and rhythmical prose:
namely, that rhythm is the framework of the former
but only the fluent outline of the latter. If a style is
new and forcible, extravagances will not hinder it
from being received with immense applause at its
first appearance. Then it is imitated until its originality is forgotten and its defects brought into relief.
In the maturity of his genius, Lord Macaulay pronounced the Essay on Milton to be "disfigured by
much gaudy and ungraceful ornament." Gorgias
was the founder of artistic prose; and his faults are
the more excusable because they were extravagant.
Granting the natural assumption that prose was to be
a kind of poetry, then Gorgias was brilliantly logical;
and, as the event proved, his excesses did good
service by calling earlier attention to the fallacy in
his theory. Allowing, however, all that has been
advanced above, it might still seem strange that
Gorgias should have had this reception from the
Assembly which, within three years, had been listening to Pericles. But the true question is whether
Pericles had aimed at giving to his eloquence the
finish of a literary form. Suidas says that Pericles
was the first who composed a forensic speech before
delivering it; his predecessors had extemporised.[1]
Cicero says that Pericles and Alcibiades are the most
ancient authors who have left authentic writings.[2]

Pericles.
Was his oratory artistic in form?

[1] Suidas *s. v.* Περικλῆς; ῥήτωρ καὶ δημαγωγός, ὅστις πρῶτος γραπτὸν λόγον ἐν δικαστηρίῳ εἶπε, τῶν πρὸ αὐτοῦ σχεδιαζόντων.

[2] Cic. *De Orat.* II. § 93, *antiquissimi fere sunt, quorum quidem scripta constent:* where the "constent" seems to imply that the

Quintilian, however, thinks that the compositions extant under the name of Pericles are not worthy of his reputation, and that, as others had conjectured, they were spurious.[1] Plutarch says positively that Pericles has left nothing written (ἔγγραφον) except decrees.[2] The antithesis meant by ἔγγραφον is with those sayings of Pericles which tradition had preserved; especially those bold similes from nature and life to which reference will be made in considering the style of Antiphon.[3] The speeches in Thucydides doubtless give the general ideas of Pericles with essential fidelity; it is possible, further, that they may contain recorded sayings of his like those in Aristotle: but it is certain that they cannot be taken as giving the form of the statesman's oratory. Like the other speeches, they bear the stamp of a manner which was not so fully developed until after his death. Pericles as an orator is best known to us from the brief but emphatic notices of the impression which he made. "This man," says Eupolis, "whenever he came forward, proved himself the greatest orator among men: like a good runner, he could give the other speakers ten feet start, and win.......Rapid you call him; but, besides his swiftness, a certain persuasion sat upon his lips—such was his spell: and, alone of the speakers, he ever left his sting in the

Statement of Plutarch.

Thucydidean Speeches of Pericles.

Notices of his oratory.

question of authenticity had been examined. But in *Brut.* § 27 he says, more doubtfully, *Ante Periclem, cuius scripta quaedam feruntur, littera nulla est quae quidem ornatum aliquem habeat.*

[1] Quint. III. 1 § 12, *Equidem non reperio quicquam tanta eloquentiae fama dignum; ideoque minus miror*

esse qui nihil ab eo scriptum putent, haec autem quae feruntur ab aliis esse composita.

[2] Plut. *Pericl.* c. 8, ἔγγραφον μὲν οὐδὲν ἀπολέλοιπε πλὴν τῶν ψηφισμάτων· ἀπομνημονεύεται δὲ ὀλίγα παντάπασιν.

[3] Below, pp. 27 f.

hearers."[1] When Aristophanes is describing the outbreak of the Peloponnesian War, "Pericles the Olympian," he says, "was thundering and lightening and putting Greece in a tumult."[2] Unique as an Athenian statesman, Pericles must have been in two respects unique also as an Athenian orator:—first, because he occupied such a position of personal ascendency as no man before or after him attained; secondly, because his thoughts and his moral force won him such renown for eloquence as no one else ever got from Athenians without the further aid of artistic expression. His manner of speaking seems to have been tranquil, stately to a degree which Plutarch seems inclined to satirise,[3] but varied by occasional bursts having the character of lofty poetry.[4]

Its distinctive conditions.

The earliest of those Athenian orators who have left writings is not the disciple of him who most represented the new art of oratory. Antiphon was chiefly formed, not by the new Oratory, but by the

History of Athenian oratory begins with Antiphon:

[1] A. κράτιστος οὗτος ἐγένετ' ἀνθρώπων λέγειν | ὁπότε παρέλθοι, χὤσπερ ἀγαθοὶ δρομῆς | ἐκ δέκα ποδῶν ἥρει λέγων τοὺς ῥήτορας. Β. ταχὺν λέγεις μέν· πρὸς δέ γ' αὐτοῦ τῷ τάχει | πειθώ τις ἐπεκάθιζεν ἐπὶ τοῖς χείλεσιν· οὕτως ἐκήλει· καὶ μόνος τῶν ῥητόρων | τὸ κέντρον ἐγκατέλειπε τοῖς ἀκροωμένοις. Eupolis, Δῆμοι, Bothe *Frag. Com.* I. 162, where the ancient citations of this famous passage are brought together. See (*e.g.*) Cic. Quint. XII. 10. *Brut.* § 38.

[2] Ar. *Ach.* 530. [3] Plut. *Per.* c. 5.

[4] Cf. Mr. Watkiss Lloyd's "Age of Pericles" I. 159 (speaking of the sweetness of voice and facile swiftness which distinguished the elocution of Pericles):—"The combination of power, rapidity, and fascination that is thus avouched is probably not so much explained by, as it explains, the tradition of his obligations to such varied instructors as Anaxagoras, Damon, and Aspasia... To Plato, Pericles was still, though only by traditional reputation, the most accomplished of all orators" (*Phaedr.* p. 269 E, πάντων τελεώτατος εἰς τὴν ῥητορικήν).—As Mr. Lloyd says, Plato seems inclined *there* to connect this excellence of Pericles with a study of psychology under Anaxagoras: though the *Phaedo* p. 97 B implies that Anaxagoras did not enter on such inquiries. Undoubtedly *psychology* is what Plato in the *Phaedrus* is recommending, first of all, to Isocrates; see on this, Blass, *Isocrates und Isaios*, p. 29.

a disciple, not of Gorgias, but of the Sicilian Rhetoric.

Rhetoric and Popular Dialectic at Athens from 450 B.C.

Tragedy.

Forensic Advocacy.

Athens the chief seat of Civil Oratory.

new Rhetoric, not by Gorgias but by Tisias. The influence of Gorgias meets us somewhat, of course, even in Antiphon, but far more decidedly in Thucydides, and then, chastened to a form of which its beginnings had little promise, in Isocrates. The second half of the fifth century at Athens had already given a place in the popular life to the new culture. While Comedy set itself against that culture, Tragedy had been more compliant. No contrast could be more significant than that between the singular barrenness of the trial-scene in the *Eumenides*, or the measured controversies of the *Ajax*, and the truly forensic subtleties of the *Orestes*. Nor was the exercise only mimic. Already the public advocates (συνηγόροι) formed a class. The private advocate was forbidden to take money. Hence he usually begins by defining the personal interest which has led him to appear. In the next century, at least, the law was not strictly observed;[1] private advocacy was often paid; and it is not rash to suppose that this practice was as old as the frequency of litigation.

But while literary fashion or private need thus lent their aid, greater and older causes than these had prepared Athens to be the home of Civil Oratory.

---

[1] Lycurgus thus speaks of the mercenary advocacy which in his time had become a tolerated practice, κατὰ Λεωκράτους § 138 (circ. 330 B.C.):— "I am astonished if you do not see that your extreme indignation is well deserved by men who, *although they have no tie whatever either of kinship or of friendship with the accused persons, continually help in defending* them for pay"—μισθοῦ συναπολογουμένοις ἀεὶ τοῖς κρινομένοις.—But the real error both of Greece and of Rome (until, at some time before Justinian, Trajan's renewal of the Lex Cincia was repealed) lay in their refusal to recognise Advocacy as a profession. See, on the theory, Forsyth, *Hortensius*, pp. 377 ff.

The chief importance of Grecian history depends on this, that the Greeks are the first people from whom we can learn any lessons in the art of ruling men according to law.¹ While all the nations with which the Greeks came in contact were governed more or less despotically, the Greek cities alone were governed politically. No Persian or Egyptian had any conception of the principle that both sides of a public question should be fairly heard, that it should be decided by the opinion of the civic majority, and that the minority should be bound by this decision. Every Greek city, be it planted where it might, at the Pillars of Heracles or on the shores of the Inhospitable Sea, was perfectly familiar with this doctrine. Sometimes a tyrant forcibly suspended its operation, sometimes an oligarchy capriciously narrowed its scope, but it was known wherever the Greek tongue was spoken. In democratic Athens, more than in any other Greek city, this doctrine was no speculative opinion, no occasional motive, but the present and perpetual spring of public action; nor did any goddess of the pantheon receive a tribute more fitting or more sincere than that which Athenians annually laid on the altar of Persuasion.² It has sometimes been said that Greek Oratory means Athenian Oratory. This is far from being true in the sense that all the considerable masters of oratorical prose were either natives of Attica or permanent residents at Athens.

Political morality of the Greeks.

This morality most practical at Athens.

Relation of Athenian to Greek Oratory.

---

¹ Freeman, "General Sketch of European History," ch. II. § 3: and the essay on "The Athenian Democracy" (Second Series, no. IV.).

² Isocr. *Antid.* (Or. XV.) § 249, τὴν μὲν γὰρ Πειθὼ μίαν τῶν θεῶν νομίζουσιν εἶναι, καὶ τὴν πόλιν ὁρῶσι καθ' ἕκαστον τὸν ἐνιαυτὸν θυσίαν αὐτῇ ποιουμένην.

Gorgias of Leontini, Theodorus of Byzantium, Thrasymachus of Chalcedon, Anaximenes of Lampsacus. Naucrates of Erythrae, Philiscus of Miletus, Ephorus of Cumae, Theopompus of Chios, Theodectes of Phaselis, and many more, might be adduced. But there is another sense in which the statement is true. Athens was the home, though Attica was not the birthplace, of all the very greatest men in this branch of art, of all the men whose works had wide and lasting acceptance as canons. Athens was, further, the educator of all those men, whether first-rate or not, who, after about 400 B.C., won a Panhellenic name for eloquence. The relation of Athenian to Greek oratory is accurately stated by Isocrates when, in 353 B.C., he is defending his theory of culture against supposed objections—objections which, as the very history of his school shows, had never really taken hold of the Athenian mind, but were restricted to a much narrower circle than his rather morbid sensibility imagined.[1] "You must not forget that our city is regarded as the established[2] teacher of all who can speak or teach others to speak. And naturally so, since men see that our city offers the greatest prizes to those who possess this faculty,—provides the most numerous and most various schools for those who, having resolved to enter the real contests, desire a preparatory discipline,—and, further, affords to all men that experience which is the main secret of success in speaking. Besides, men hold

---

[1] Isocr. *Antid.* (Or. xv.) §§ 295–298.
[2] δοκεῖ γεγενῆσθαι διδάσκαλος: note the tense,—expressing a position thoroughly won and generally recognised.

that the general diffusion and the happy temperament of Attic speech, the Attic flexibility of intelligence and taste for letters, contribute not a little to literary culture; and hence they not unjustly deem that all masters of expression are disciples of Athens. See, then, lest it be folly indeed to cast a slur on this name which you have among the Greeks...; that unjust judgment will be nothing else than your open condemnation of yourselves. You will have done as the Lacedaemonians would do if they introduced a penalty for attention to military exercises, or the Thessalians, if they instituted proceedings at law against men who seek to make themselves good riders."

Athenian oratory has two great aspects, the artistic and the political. The artistic aspect will necessarily be most prominent in the following pages, since their special object is to trace the development of Attic oratory in relation to the development of Attic prose. When, however, Attic oratory is considered, not relatively to Attic prose, but in itself, the artistic aspect is not more important than the political; and, if even the literary value of the Attic orations is to be fully understood, their political significance must not for a moment be left out of sight. This significance resides not merely in the matter or form of each discourse, but also in the training which had been received by the public to which it is addressed. We must ask ourselves, not merely, "Is this subject well treated?" but also, "What manner of a multitude can it have been for which the speaker thought this treatment adapted?" *Political aspect of Athenian Oratory.*

Political training of the Greek citizen,

The common life of every Greek city, not suppressed by tyranny or too much warped by oligarchy, was a political education for the citizens. The reason is manifest from the very fact that the society *was* a city, and neither a village nor a nation. On the one hand, there was the instinct which demanded the highest attainable organisation under laws. On the other, there was the inability to conceive parliament except as a primary assembly. At Athens this political education of the citizens was more thorough than elsewhere, because at Athens the tendency of a commonwealth to deposit all power in an assembly was worked out with most logical completeness.[1] All the powers of the State, legislative, executive and judicial, were concentrated in the absolute Demos: the law-courts were committees of the Ecclesia, as the archons or generals were its officers. The world has seen nothing like this. The Italian Republics of the middle age were fragments of the Roman Empire and the Kingdom of Italy. It was from their prosperity as municipalities that they had derived their independence as States. They grew up among traditions of feudal privilege, represented here and there by a noble who could openly violate the order of the city within whose walls he lived.[2] A Florentine, like an Athenian, was a citizen with his share in the government of the city: Florence, like Athens, recognised the right of the assembled People to decide questions of State. But Florence, until its latest days, had

and especially of the Athenian.

Civic sentiment in the Greek and in the Italian Republics.

Athens and Florence.

---

[1] Freeman, *Historical Essays* (Second Series), pp. 128 f.

[2] In the Essay on "Ancient Greece and Mediæval Italy" (*Historical Essays*, Second Series), Mr. Freeman has worked out the likeness and unlikeness which here are barely touched on.

nothing truly corresponding to the Ecclesia. The citizens were occasionally called together, but there was no popular Assembly with an organised and continual superintendence of all affairs. Nor was the civic sentiment so vivid or so direct for the Florentine as for the Athenian. The Florentine acted in politics primarily as member of a commercial guild[1] and only secondarily as a citizen. The Greek Republics far more than the Italian, Athens far more than Florence, afforded the proper atmosphere for such an oratory as alone, in strictness, can take the lofty name of Civil; that is, which is addressed by a citizen, educated both in ruling and in obeying, to the whole body of fellow-citizens who have had the same twofold training as himself. The glory of Attic oratory, as such, consists not solely in its intrinsic excellence, but also in its revelation of the corporate political intelligence to which it appealed: for it spoke sometimes to an Assembly debating an issue of peace or war, sometimes to a law-court occupied with a private plaint, sometimes to Athenians mingled with strangers at a festival, but everywhere and always to the Athenian Demos, everywhere and always to a paramount People, taught by life itself to reason and to judge.

Civil Oratory defined.

Attic Oratory fulfils this definition.

---

[1] The Florentine burgher was qualified for the franchise by belonging to one of the incorporated arts: Symonds, "Renaissance in Italy: Age of the Despots," p. 128. On the mercantile character of the Italian republics as influencing the political, *ib.* 173 f.

THE ATTIC ORATORS

CHAPTER I

ANTIPHON

LIFE

IN describing the Revolution of the Four Hundred at Athens, Thucydides lays stress upon the fact that the measures which had effected it owed their unity and their success to the control of a single mind. The figure of Peisander is most conspicuous in the foreground. "But he who contrived the whole matter, and the means by which it was brought to pass, and who had given his mind to it longest, was Antiphon; a man second to no Athenian of his day in virtue; a proved master of device and of expression; who did not come forward in the assembly, nor, by choice, in any scene of debate, since he lay under the suspicion of the people through a repute for cleverness; but who was better able than any other individual to assist, when consulted, those who were fighting a cause in a law-court or in the assembly. In his own case, too—when the Four Hundred in their later reverses were being roughly used by the people, and he was accused of having aided in setting up this same government—he is known to have delivered the greatest defence made in the memory of my age by a man on trial for his life."[1]

This passage gives in outline nearly all that is known of the life of Antiphon. Other sources supply details, and make it possible to work up the sketch into something like a picture; but they add nothing which enlarges its framework. The Revolution of the Four Hundred is still the one great scene presented to our view.

Birth of Antiphon

Antiphon was born about the year 480 B.C.,[2] being thus rather younger than Gorgias, and some eight or nine years older than the historian Thucydides. He was of the tribe of Aiantis and of the deme of Rhamnus;[3] of a family which cannot have been

---

[1] Thuc. VIII. 68.

[2] [Plut.] *Vitt. X. Oratt.* γέγονε κατὰ τὰ Περσικὰ καὶ Γοργίαν τὸν σοφιστήν, ὀλίγῳ νεώτερος αὐτοῦ. Gorgias can scarcely have been more than seventy in 411 B.C. Blass would place the birth of Gorgias "a few years" below 496 (*Att. Bereds.* p. 45). Clinton suggests 485 (sub ann. 427).

[3] He is often distinguished as the "Rhamnusian" from namesakes. Of these there are especially three with whom his ancient biographers—the pseudo-Plutarch, Philostratus, Photius (cod. 259), and the anonymous author of the γένος Ἀντιφῶντος—frequently confuse him. I. *The Antiphon who was put to death by the Thirty Tyrants*, seven years after the orator's death: Xen. *Hellen.* III. 40. He had furnished two triremes at his own cost during the war: and of him

Philostratus is probably thinking when he says of the *orator*, ἐστρατήγησε πλεῖστα, ἐνίκησε πλεῖστα, ἑξήκοντα τριήρεσι πεπληρωμέναις ηὔξησεν Ἀθηναίοις τὸ ναυτικόν. The speech of Lysias περὶ τῆς Ἀντιφῶντος θυγατρός (pseudo-Plut. *Vitt. X. Oratt.*) referred to his daughter. II. *Antiphon the tragedian*, put to death by Dionysius the elder, towards the end of his reign, i.e. about 370 B.C.: Arist. *Rhet.* II. 6. The anonymous biographer says of the *orator*, τραγῳδίας ἐποίει: and Philostratus describes him as put to death by Dionysius for criticising his tragedies. III. *Antiphon the Sophist*, introduced by Xenophon as disputing with Socrates, *Memor.* I. 6. 1. Diogenes calls him τερατοσκόπος (soothsayer), Suidas, ὀνειροκριτής—by which title he is often referred to. Hermogenes expressly distinguishes him from the

altogether obscure, since it was made a reproach to him on his trial that his grandfather had been a partisan of the Peisistratidae.[1] The tradition that his father Sophilus was a sophist antedates by a generation the appearance of that class of teachers,[2] and may have been suggested simply by the jingle of the words.[3] Antiphon himself, as the style of his composition indicates, must have felt the sophistic influence; but there is no evidence for his having been the pupil of any particular sophist. He is allowed by general consent to have been the first representative at Athens of a profession for which the new conditions of the time had just begun to make a place,—the first λογογράφος, or writer of speeches for money.[4] With the recent growth of Rhetoric as a definite art, the inequality, for purposes of pleading or debating, between men who had and who had not mastered the newly-invented weapons of speech had become seriously felt. A rogue skilled in the latest subtleties of argument and graces of style was now more than ever formidable to the plain man whom he chose to drag before a court or to attack in the ecclesia: and those who had no leisure or taste to become rhetoricians now began to find it worth while to buy their rhetoric ready-made. Forensic speeches were, no doubt, those with which Antiphon most frequently supplied his clients. But

Antiphon the first λογογράφος.

---

orator (περὶ ἰδεῶν, II. 497); but they are confused by the pseudo-Plut. and by Photius.

[1] Harpocration s. v. στασιώτης.
[2] K. O. Müller, *Hist. Gr. Lit.* c. XXXIII., Vol. II. p. 105, ed. Donaldson.
[3] Donalds., note, *ibid.*
[4] [Plut.] *Vitt. X. Oratt.* λόγους συνέγραψε πρῶτος ἐπὶ τοῦτο τραπεὶς, ὥσπερ τινές φασι. Diod. *ap.* Clem. Alex. *Strom.* I. 365, πρῶτον δικανικὸν λόγον εἰς ἔκδοσιν γραψάμενον.

Hermogenes[1] describes him as "the inventor and founder of the political style,"—a phrase including deliberative as well as forensic oratory: and this exactly agrees with the statement of Thucydides that Antiphon was practised in aiding, not only those who had lawsuits, but debaters in the ecclesia.[2] Besides being a speech-writer, he was also a teacher of rhetoric, and, as the allusion in the Menexenus[3] implies, the most fashionable master of Plato's time at Athens. The tradition that Thucydides was the pupil of Antiphon may have been suggested by the warmth and emphasis of the passage in which the orator is mentioned by the historian;[4] a passage which, in its sudden glow of a personal admiration, recalls two others in the History—the tribute to the genius of Themistocles, and the character of Pericles. In the tradition itself there is nothing improbable, but it wants the support of evidence. The special relation of master to pupil need not be assumed to account for a tone which congeniality of literary

Antiphon and Thucydides.

---

[1] Hermog. περὶ ἰδ. II. p. 415, λέγεται ... εὑρετὴς καὶ ἀρχηγὸς γενέσθαι τοῦ τύπου τοῦ πολιτικοῦ. By πολιτικοὶ λόγοι, as distinguished from διαλεκτική, were meant both συμβουλευτικοί and δικανικοί: see Isocr. κατὰ σοφ. § 20.

[2] Thuc. VIII. 68, τοὺς ἀγωνιζομένους καὶ ἐν δικαστηρίῳ καὶ ἐν δήμῳ ...δυνάμενος ὠφελεῖν.

[3] Plat. *Menex.* p. 236 A.

[4] [Plut.] *Vitt. X. Oratt.* Καικίλιος δὲ (Caecilius of Calacte, the Greek rhetorician of the time of Augustus) ἐν τῷ περὶ αὐτοῦ συντάγματι Θουκυδίδου τοῦ συγγραφέως (VIII. 68.) μαθητὴν τεκμαίρεται γεγονέναι, ἐξ ὧν ἐπαινεῖται παρ' αὐτῷ ὁ Ἀντιφῶν. Ruhnken (*Disp. de Ant.*) says that some mss. have διδάσκαλον instead of μαθητήν here: Blass suggests καθηγητήν. Hermogenes (περὶ ἰδ. II. 497) refers to the tradition as one which "many" receive; but rejects it for the inadequate reason that the style of Thucydides resembles that of Antiphon *the Sophist* (see note above) rather than that of Antiphon the orator. In Bishop Thirlwall's remarks (c. XXVIII. Vol. IV. p. 23 *note*, ed. 1855) I entirely concur. Ruhnken's "satis, ni fallor, *demonstravimus* Thucydidem ab Antiphonte esse eruditum," is surely not justified by his reasonings.

taste,[1] common sufferings at the hands of the democracy, or perhaps personal friendship, would sufficiently explain.

Nothing is directly known of Antiphon's political relations before the year 411 B.C.; but there are slight indications which agree well with his later hostility to the democracy. Harpocration has preserved the names of two speeches written by him, one for the people of Samothrace, on the subject of the tribute which they paid to Athens; another, on the same subject, for the people of Lindus in Rhodes.[2] The oppression of the subject-allies by the demagogues, who extorted from them large sums on any pretence or threat, was a commonplace of complaint with oligarchs.[3] The employment of Antiphon, afterwards so staunch an oligarch, by aggrieved allies, preparing to represent their grievances at the imperial city, was perhaps more than an accident of professional routine. The hostility of Antiphon to Alcibiades,[4] again, need not have had any political meaning; but it would have been especially natural

Antiphon's life to 411 B.C.

---

[1] See below, ch. II. pp. 23 ff., on the affinity between the styles of Antiphon and Thucydides.

[2] Harpocration quotes five times a speech of Antiphon περὶ τοῦ Σαμοθρᾴκων φόρου, spoken, as the fragments show, by their ambassador; and in ten places refers to another περὶ τοῦ Λινδίων φόρου.

[3] See, e.g., Ar. Vesp. 669 ff.

[4] Plutarch (Alc. c. 3) quotes Antiphon as the authority for a discreditable story about Alcibiades: and goes on to say that it must be received with caution, on account of Antiphon's avowed enmity towards him: ἐν δὲ ταῖς Ἀντιφῶντος λοιδορίαις γέγραπται. These λοιδορίαι would seem to have formed a sort of polemical pamphlet. But Athenaeus, on the other hand, quotes a statement made by Antiphon, ἐν τῷ κατ' Ἀλκιβιάδου λοιδορίας (Athen. XII. 525 B). This would seem to have been a speech in a δίκη κακηγορίας (Dem. Conon. § 18), for which λοιδορία is used as a convertible term: cf. Ar. Vesp. 1207, εἷλον διώκων λοιδορίας. Sauppe thinks that the mistake is with Athenaeus, not with Plutarch. See Blass, Att. Bereds. p. 95.

in one who had shared the views, and who mourned
the fate, of Nicias. At all events, the words of
Thucydides give a vivid idea of the position held at
Athens by Antiphon just before the Revolution of
the Four Hundred. His abilities were acknowledged,
but they were exerted only for others; he himself
came forward neither in the assembly, nor—"when
he could help it"[1]—in the law courts; he lay under
the suspicion of the people for "cleverness." The
nature of the "cleverness" (δεινότης) for which Antiphon was distrusted and disliked is sufficiently illustrated by his Tetralogies. It was the art of fighting
a cause which could hardly be defended on any broad
ground by raising in succession a number of more or
less fine points. The indignant bewilderment expressed by the imaginary prosecutor in the Second
Tetralogy[2] on finding the common-sense view of the
case turned upside-down represents what many a
citizen of the old school must have felt when he
encountered, in the ecclesia or the law-court, a client
of the ingenious "speech-writer." Antiphon was a
cautious, patient man. The comic poets could ridicule
him for his poverty or his avarice;[3] they could say
that the speeches which he sold for great sums were
"framed to defeat justice";[4] but a carefully obscure
life probably offered no hold to any more definite
attack. Meanwhile he was quietly at work with the

---

[1] Thuc. VIII. 68, οὐδ' ἐς ἄλλον
ἀγῶνα ἑκούσιος οὐδένα.
[2] Tetr. II. Γ ad init.
[3] [Plut.] Vitt. X. Oratt. κεκωμῴ-
δηται δ' εἰς φιλαργυρίαν ὑπὸ Πλάτωνος
ἐν Πεισάνδρῳ.

[4] Philostratus, p. 17, καθάπτεται ἡ
κωμῳδία τοῦ Ἀντιφῶντος ὡς δεινοῦ τὰ
δικανικὰ καὶ λόγους κατὰ τοῦ δικαίου
ξυγκειμένους ἀποδιδομένου πολλῶν
χρημάτων αὐτοῖς μάλιστα τοῖς κινδυ-
νεύουσιν.

oligarchic clubs. According to Thucydides he was not merely the arch-plotter of the Revolution. He was the man who "had thought about it longest."

In the spring of 411 B.C. the opportunity for which Antiphon had been waiting at last came. Alcibiades, by promises of Persian aid, induced the oligarchs in the army at Samos to commence a movement for the overthrow of the Athenian democracy. Peisander, as their representative, came to Athens, and, by insisting on the hopelessness of the war without such help as Alcibiades covenanted to bring, extorted from the ecclesia a vote for that change of constitution which the exile demanded. Having visited the various oligarchical clubs in the city and urged them to combine in favour of the project, Peisander went back to confer with Alcibiades. When he presently returned to Athens,—with the knowledge that his hopes from Persia were idle, but that, on the other hand, the Revolution must go on,—he found a state of things very different from that which he had left. He had left the people just conscious that an oligarchy was proposed, and consenting, in sheer despair, to entertain the idea; but, at the same time, openly and strongly averse to it, and in a temper which showed that the real difficulties of the undertaking were to come. He now finds that, in the brief interval of his absence, every difficulty has already vanished. Not a trace of open opposition remains in the senate or in the ecclesia; not a murmur is heard in the conversation of the citizens.[1] It is a fair inference from the words of

The Revolution.

---
[1] Thuc. VIII. 65, 66.

Thucydides that the principal agent in producing this rapid and wonderful change had been Antiphon.[1] A brief consideration of the task which he had to do, and of the manner in which it was done, will supply the best criterion of his capacity. He had, first, to bring into united and disciplined action those oligarchical clubs to which Peisander had appealed. These are described as "leagues with a view to lawsuits and to offices";[2] that is, associations of which the members were pledged by oath to support, personally and with funds, any one of their body who brought, or defended, a civil action, or who sought one of the offices of the State. When, with the steady advance of democracy from the Persian wars onwards, the oligarchs found themselves more and more in a minority, such associations became their means of concentrating and economising their one great power—wealth. The tone of such clubs would always be, in a general way, antipopular. But they were unaccustomed to systematic action for great ends; and, in regard to those smaller ends which they ordinarily pursued, their interests would, from the nature of the case, frequently conflict. Antiphon need not have had much difficulty in proving to them that, on this occasion, they had a common interest. But to make them effective as well as unanimous; to restrain, without discouraging, the zeal of novices in a political campaign, and to make of these a compact and temperate force, loyally taking the word from the best men among them, and so

---

[1] Cf. Grote, ch. LXII.; Curtius, *Hist. Gr.* Vol. III. p. 435 (Ward's transl.).

[2] ξυνωμοσίας ἐπὶ δίκαις καὶ ἀρχαῖς, Thuc. VIII. 54.

executing the prescribed manœuvres that in a short time they were completely ascendant over an enormous and hostile, but ill-organised majority,—this, assuredly, was the achievement of no ordinary leader. The absence of overt, and the skilful use of secret, violence was the characteristic of the Revolution. Adverse speakers were not menaced, but they disappeared; until apparent unanimity, and real terror, had silenced every objection. Antiphon had seen clearly how the Athenian instinct of reverence for constitutional forms might be used against the constitution. His too, on the showing of Thucydides, must have been that clever invention, the imaginary body of Five Thousand to whom the franchise was to be left; a fiction which, to the end, did service to the oligarchs by giving them a vague prestige for strength.

The Council of the Four Hundred comprised two distinct elements, — those thorough oligarchs who had been the core of the conspiracy; and a number of other men, more or less indifferent to the ideas of oligarchy, who had accepted the Revolution because they believed that it alone could save Athens. Had the new Government been able to conciliate or to frighten the army at Samos, both sorts of men would have been satisfied, and the Council would have gone on working, for a time at least, as a seemingly harmonious whole. But the resolute hostility of the army, which at once made the case of the Four Hundred really hopeless, brought the discord to light forthwith. The Council was thenceforth divided into an Extreme and a

The two parties in the Council.

Moderate party. Among the leaders of the Extreme party were Peisander, Phrynichus, Aristarchus, Archeptolemus, Onomacles and Antiphon. The Moderates were led by Theramenes and Aristocrates. Two chief questions were in dispute between the parties. The Moderates wished to call into political life the nominal civic body of Five Thousand; the ultra-oligarchs objected that it was better, at such a crisis, to avoid all chance of a popular rising. The ultra-oligarchs were fortifying Eëtioneia, alleging the danger of an attack from Samos; the Moderates accused them of wishing to receive Peloponnesian troops.

The Extreme party was soon driven, in May 411 B.C., to the last resource of an embassy to Sparta. Phrynichus, Antiphon, Archeptolemus, Onomacles and eight others[1] were sent "to make terms with the Lacedaemonians in any way that could at all be borne."[2] Thucydides does not say what the envoys offered at Sparta or what answer they got; but he states plainly the length which he conceives that their party was ready to go. "They wished, if possible, having their oligarchy, at the same time to rule the allies; if that could not be, to keep their ships, their walls, and their independence; or, if shut out even from this, at all events not to have their own lives taken first and foremost by the people on its restoration;

---

[1] Thuc. VIII. 90, Ἀντιφῶντα καὶ Φρύνιχον καὶ ἄλλους δέκα. That Archeptolemus and Onomacles were on the embassy appears from [Plut.] *Vitt. X. Oratt.*

[2] Thuc. *ib.* παντὶ τρόπῳ ὅστις καὶ ὁπωσοῦν ἀνεκτὸς ξυναλλαγῆναι πρὸς τοὺς Λακεδαιμονίους.

sooner would they bring in the enemy and covenant to keep the city on any terms, without wall or ships, if only their persons should be safe."[1]

This embassy brought the unpopularity of the Extreme party to a crisis. Immediately upon his return Phrynichus was assassinated. The revolt of the citizens employed in fortifying Eëtioneia quickly followed. The assembly in the Anakeion, broken up by the sudden appearance of the Peloponnesian fleet, met again on the Pnyx soon after the Peloponnesian victory at Oropus; and the Four Hundred, who had taken office in March, were deposed about the middle of June.

Fall of the Four Hundred.

The leading ultra-oligarchs hastened to save themselves by flight. Peisander, Alexicles and others went to Deceleia; Aristarchus, taking with him a body of bowmen, contrived to betray Oenoe on the Athenian frontier into the hands of the Boeotians who were besieging it. But, of the twelve who had formed the embassy, and who now, before all others, were in peril, three remained at Athens — Antiphon, Archeptolemus and Onomacles. An information against these three men was laid before the ecclesia by the Generals. The eisangelia charged them with having gone on an embassy to Sparta for mischief to Athens, sailing, on their way thither, in an enemy's ship, and traversing the enemy's camp at Decelcia. A psephism was passed by the ecclesia directing the arrest of the accused that they might be tried by a dicastery, and instructing the Thesmothetae to serve each of

[1] Thuc. VIII. 91.

them, on the day following the issue of the decree, with a formal summons. On the day fixed by the summons the Thesmothetae were to bring the cases into court; and the Generals, assisted by such Synegori, not more than ten in number, as they might choose from the Council of the Five Hundred, were to prosecute for treason.[1]

Trial and condemnation of Antiphon.

Onomacles seems to have escaped or died before the day. Archeptolemus and Antiphon were brought to trial. The scanty fragments of the speech made by Antiphon in his own defence reveal only one item of its contents. One of the prosecutors, Apolexis, having asserted that Antiphon's grandfather had been a partisan of the Peisistratidae, Antiphon replied that his grandfather had not been punished after the expulsion of the tyrants, and could scarcely, therefore, have been one of their "body-guard."[2] The other special topics are unknown; but their range, at least, is shown by the title under which the speech was extant. It was inscribed περὶ μετα-

---

[1] [Plut.] *Vitt. X. Oratt.*

[2] Harpocr. s.v. στασιώτης (Sauppe, *Or. Att.* II. p. 138). Ἀντιφῶν ἐν τῷ περὶ τῆς μεταστάσεως· περὶ τοίνυν ὧν Ἀπόληξις κατηγόρηκεν ὡς στασιώτης ἦν ἐγὼ καὶ ὁ πάππος ὁ ἐμός· ἔοικε νῦν ὁ ῥήτωρ ἰδίως ἐπὶ τοῦ δορυφόρου κεχρῆσθαι τῷ ὀνόματι· ἐν γοῦν τοῖς ἑξῆς φησιν ὅτι· οὐκ ἂν τοὺς μὲν τυραννοῦντας ἠδυνήθησαν οἱ πρόγονοι κολάσαι, τοὺς δὲ δορυφόρους ἠδυνάτησαν.

Curtius (*Hist. Gr.* Vol. III. p. 460, transl. Ward) infers from this fragment that Antiphon in his speech argued "that the Four Hundred had acted as one equally responsible body, and that, therefore, either all ought to be punished or all acquitted." He observes that "reference seems to be made to an unjustifiable separation of the parties involved: this is indicated by the distinction drawn between the τύραννοι and the δορυφόροι." It is very likely that Antiphon may have used this argument: but I do not see how it is to be inferred from the fragments of the speech περὶ τῆς μεταστάσεως that he used it. The distinction between the τύραννοι and the δορυφόροι is made, as a perusal of the fragment will show, solely in reference to the Peisistratidae.

στάσεως, On the Change of Government. It dealt, then, not merely with the matter specified in the eisangelia — the embassy to Sparta — but with the whole question of the Revolution. It is described by Thucydides as the greatest defence made in the memory of that age by a man on trial for his life. The story in the Eudemian Ethics,[1] whether true or not, seems at any rate characteristic. Agathon, the tragic poet, praised the speech; and Antiphon—on whom sentence of death had passed—answered that a man who respects himself must care more what one good man thinks than what is thought by many nobodies.

The sentence ran thus:—

"Found guilty of treason—Archeptolemus son of Hippodamus, of Agryle, being present: Antiphon son of Sophilus, of Rhamnus, being present. The award on these two men was—That they be delivered to the Eleven: that their property be confiscated and the goddess have the tithe: that their houses be razed and boundary-stones put on the sites, with the inscription, 'the houses of Archeptolemus and Antiphon the traitors:' that the two demarchs [of Agryle and Rhamnus] shall point out their houses. That it shall not be lawful to bury Archeptolemus and Antiphon at Athens or in any land of which the Athenians are masters. That Archeptolemus and Antiphon and their descendants, bastard or true-born, shall be infamous; and if a man adopt any

---

[1] *Eth. Eudem.* III. 5, καὶ μᾶλλον ἂν φροντίσειεν ἀνὴρ μεγαλόψυχος τί δοκεῖ ἑνὶ σπουδαίῳ ἢ πολλοῖς τοῖς τυγχάνουσιν, ὥσπερ Ἀντιφῶν ἔφη πρὸς Ἀγάθωνα κατεψηφισμένος τὴν ἀπολογίαν ἐπαινέσαντα.

one of the race of Archeptolemus or Antiphon, let the adopter be infamous. That this decree be written on a brazen column and put in the same place where the decrees about Phrynichus are set up."[1]

Character of Antiphon's political life.

The distinctive feature in the life of Antiphon is the suddenness of his appearance, at an advanced age, in the very front of Athenian politics. Unlike nearly all the men associated with him, he had neither made his mark in the public service nor come forward in the ecclesia; yet all at once he becomes the chief, though not the most conspicuous, organiser of an enterprise requiring in the highest degree trained political tact; does more than any other individual to set up a new government; and acts to the last as one of its foremost members. The reputation and the power which enabled him to take this part were mainly literary. Yet it would not probably be accurate to conceive Antiphon as a merely literary man who suddenly emerged and succeeded as a politician. It would have been a marvel, indeed, if any one had become a leader on the popular side in Athenian politics who had not already been prominent in the ecclesia. But the accomplishments most needed in a leader of the oligarchic party might be learned elsewhere than in the ecclesia. The member of a ἑταιρεία, though a stranger to the bema, might gain practice in the working of those secret and rapid combinations upon which his party had come to rely most in its unequal struggle with democracy. As fame and years by

[1] [Plut.] *Vitt. X. Oratt.*

degrees brought Antiphon more and more weight in the internal management of the oligarchic clubs, he would acquire more and more insight into the tactics of which at last he proved himself a master.[1] He need not, then, be taken as an example of instinct supplying the want of training: he had probably had precisely the training which could serve him best. The real significance of his late and sudden prominence lies in its suggestion of previous self-control. No desire of place, no consciousness of growing power, had tempted him to stir until in his old age he knew that the time had come and that all the threads were in his hand.

The ability which Antiphon brought to the service of his party is defined as the power ἐνθυμηθῆναι καὶ ἃ γνοίη εἰπεῖν. It was the power of a subtle and quick mind backed by a thorough command of the new rhetoric. He was masterly in device and in utterance. Fertility of expedient, ingenuity in making points in debate, were the qualities which the oligarchs most needed; and it was in these that the strength of Antiphon lay. In promptness of invention where difficulties were to be met on the instant he probably bore some likeness to Themistocles; but

Character of his ability.

---

[1] "By far the larger number of the members of the party belonged to the sophistically-trained younger generation...who greedily imbibed the political teaching communicated to them at the meetings of the party by Antiphon, *the Nestor of his party, as it was the fashion to call him.*" (Curtius, *Hist. Gr.* III. p. 435, transl. Ward.)

The only authority for this "fashion" which I have been able to find is [Plut.] *Vitt. X. Oratt.*: πρῶτος δὲ καὶ ῥητορικὰς τέχνας ἐξήνεγκε, γενόμενος ἀγχίνους· διὸ καὶ Νέστωρ ἐπεκαλεῖτο. As this notice makes the name "Nestor" refer simply to rhetorical skill, not to political sagacity, I have hesitated to follow Curtius in his picturesque application of it.

there is no reason for crediting him with that largeness of view, or with any share of that wonderful foresight, which made Themistocles a statesman as well as a diplomatist.

His ἀρετή.   Thucydides praises Antiphon not only for his ability but, with equal emphasis, for his ἀρετή, his virtue. The praise may be interpreted by what Thucydides himself says elsewhere about the moral results of the intense conflicts between oligarchy and democracy.[1] The ἀρετή, precious as rare, of a public man was to be a loyal partisan; to postpone personal selfishness to the selfishness of party; to be proof against bribes; and at the worst not to flinch, or at least not to desert. Thucydides means that of the men who brought about the Revolution Antiphon was perhaps the most disinterested and the most constant. He had taken previously no active part in public affairs, and was therefore less involved than such men as Peisander and Phrynichus in personal relations: his life had been to some extent that of a student: he had never put himself forward for office: he seems, to judge from his writings, to have really believed and felt that old Attic religion which at least the older school of oligarchs professed to cherish: and thus altogether might be considered as the most unselfishly earnest member of his party, the man who cared most for its ideas. In this measure he was disinterested: he was also constant. When the Council fell, he could, no doubt, have escaped with Peisander and the rest. Considering his long unpopularity, and the fact that he would

[1] Thuc. III. 82.

be assumed to have been the chief spokesman of the odious embassy to Sparta, his condemnation was perhaps more certain than that of any other person. But he stood his ground: and for the last time put out all his strength in a great defence of the fallen Government.

In a general view of Antiphon's career there is one aspect which ought not to be missed—that aspect in which it bears striking evidence to the growing importance in Athenian public life of the newly-developed art of Rhetoric. Antiphon's first and strongest claim to eminence was his mastery over the weapons now indispensable in the ecclesia and the law-courts; it was this accomplishment, no less fashionable than useful, which recommended him to the young men of his party whom he had no other pretension to influence; it was this rhetorical δεινότης to which he owed his efficiency in the Revolution. In his person the practical branch of the new culture for the first time takes a distinct place among the qualifications for political rank. The Art of Words had its definite share in bringing in the Four Hundred: it was a curious nemesis when seven years later it was banished from Athens by the Thirty.

The new power of Rhetoric.

CHAPTER II

ANTIPHON

STYLE

Antiphon the most antique of the orators.

ANTIPHON stands first among the orators of the Attic canon; and he claims this place not merely because he was born a few years earlier than any one of the rest. A broad difference separates him from those who were nearly his contemporaries hardly less than from men of the next century, from Andocides and Lysias as well as from Demosthenes and Hypereides. He represents older ideas and an older conception of the manner in which these ideas are to find expression. His successors, taken collectively, are moderns; compared with them, he is ancient.

The beginnings of Greek Prose.

The outburst of intellectual life in Hellas during the fifth century before Christ had for one of its results the creation of Greek prose. Before that age no Greek had conceived artistic composition except in the form of poetry. The Ionians who had already recorded myths or stated philosophies in prose had either made no effort to rise above the ease of daily talk, or had clothed their meaning in a poetical diction of the most ambitious kind. As the mental horizon of Greece was widened, as subtler ideas and more various combinations began to ask for closer and more flexible expression, the desire grew for something more precise than poetry, firmer and more compact than the idiom of conversation. Two special causes aided this general tendency. The development of democratic life, making the faculty of speech before popular assemblies and popular law-courts a necessity, hastened the formation of an oratorical prose. The Persian Wars, by changing Hellenic unity from a sentiment into a fact, and reminding men that there was a corporate life, higher and grander than that of the individual city, of which the story might be told, supplied a new motive to historical prose. Athens under Pericles became the focus of all the feelings which demanded this new utterance, and of all the capabilities which could make the utterance artistic. The Athenian mind, with its vigour, its sense of measure, its desire for clearness, was fitted to achieve the special excellences of prose,[1] and moulded that Attic dialect in which the prose-writer at last found his most perfect instrument. But the process of maturing the new kind of composition was necessarily slow; for it required, as its first condition, little less than the creation of a new language, of an idiom neither poetical nor mean. Herodotus, at the middle point of the fifth century, shows the poetical element still preponderant. The close of that century may be taken as the end of the first great stage in the growth of a prose literature. If a line is drawn there, Lysias will be perhaps the first representative

[1] See Curtius, *Hist. Gr.* Vol. II. p. 517, transl. Ward.

name below it: Antiphon and Thucydides will be among the last names above it.

<small>Character of the early Prose.</small> The leading characteristic of the earlier prose is dignity. The newly created art has the continual consciousness of being an art. It is always on its guard against sliding into the levity of a conversational style. The composer feels above all things that his written language must be so chosen as to produce a greater effect than would be produced by an equivalent amount of extemporary speaking. Every word is to be pointed and pregnant; every phrase is to be the condensed expression of his thought in its ultimate shape, however difficult this may be to the reader or hearer who meets it in that shape for the first time; the movement of the whole is to be slow and majestic, impressing by its weight and grandeur, not charming by its life and flow. The prose-writer of this epoch instinctively compares himself with the poet. The poet is a craftsman, the possessor of a mystery revealed to the many only in the spell which it exerts over their fancies; just so, in the beginnings of a literary prose, its shaper likes to think that he belongs to a guild. He does not care to be simply right and clear: rather he desires to have the whole advantage which his skill gives him over ordinary men; he is eager to bring his thoughts down upon them with a splendid and irresistible force. In Greece this character, natural to immature prose, was intensified by a special cause —the influence of the Sophists. In so far as these teachers dealt with the form of language, they tended to confirm that view of the prose-writer in which he

is a professional expert dazzling and overawing laymen. The Sophists of Hellas Proper dwelt especially on the minute proprieties of language, as Protagoras on correct grammatical forms[1] and Prodicus on the accurate use of synonyms;[2] the Sophists of Sicily taught its technical graces.[3] In this last respect the teaching of Gorgias was thoroughly reactionary, and was calculated to hinder the growth of a good prose just at the critical point. At the moment when prose was striving to disengage itself from the diction of poetry, Gorgias gave currency to the notion that poetical ornament of the most florid type was its true charm. When, indeed, he went further, and sought to imitate the rhythm as well as the phrase of poetry, this very extravagance had a useful result. Prose has a rhythm, though not of the kind at which Gorgias aimed; and the mere fact of the Greek ear becoming accustomed to look for a certain proportion between the parts of a sentence hastened the transition from the old running style to the periodic.

Dionysius has described vividly the characteristics of that elder school of composition to which Antiphon belonged. He distinguishes three principal styles, the austere, the smooth and the middle.[4] He cites poets,

Dionysius on the "austere" style.

---

[1] ὀρθοέπεια, Plat. *Phaedr.* p. 267 c.
[2] ὀρθότης ὀνομάτων, Plat. *Euthyd.* p. 277 E. On the work of Protagoras and Prodicus in these departments, see Mr. Cope in the *Journal of Classical and Sacred Philology,* vol. III. pp. 48–57.
[3] Spengel, Συναγ. τεχνῶν, p. 63: "Omnino Graeci sophistae, et quos diximus, et alii minus noti, recte et dilucide eloqui studebant; et si uno vocabulo omnia comprehendamus, Graeci ὀρθοέπειαν, Siculi εὐέπειαν elaborabant."
[4] αὐστηρά, γλαφυρά and κοινή (or μέση) ἁρμονία: Dionys. περὶ συνθ. ὀνομ. cc. 22, 23, 24. The three ἁρμονίαι, or styles of *compositio*, distinguished by Dionysius, must not be confused with the three λέξεις, or styles of *diction*, which he distinguishes in his essay on Demosthenes, cc. 1–3. The ἁρμονίαι refer, of course, to the putting together of

historians and orators who are examples of each. Among orators Antiphon is his representative of the austere style, Isocrates of the smooth, Demosthenes of the middle. The austere style is thus described :[1]

"It wishes its separate words to be planted firmly and to have strong positions, so that each word may be seen conspicuously; it wishes its several clauses to be well divided from each other by sensible pauses. It is willing to admit frequently rough and direct clashings of sounds, meeting like the bases of stones in loose wall-work, which have not been squared or smoothed to fit each other, but which show a certain negligence and absence of forethought. It loves, as a rule, to prolong itself by large words of portly breadth. Compression by short syllables is a thing which it shuns when not absolutely driven to it.

"As regards separate words, these are the objects of its pursuit and craving. In whole clauses it shows these tendencies no less strongly; especially it chooses the most dignified and majestic rhythms. It does not wish the clauses to be like each other in length of structure, or enslaved to a severe syntax, but noble, simple, free. It wishes them to bear the stamp of nature rather than that of art, and to stir feeling rather than to reflect character. It does not usually aim at com-

---

words; the λέξεις, to the choice of words. As to λέξεις, Dionysius recognises (1) an *elaborate diction*, which employs farfetched and unusual words, ἐξηλλαγμένη, περιττὴ λέξις, of which Thucydides is the great example: (2) a *smooth and plain diction*, λιτή, ἀφελὴς λέξις, best represented by Lysias: (3) a *mixed diction*, μικτὴ καὶ σύνθετος λέξις, of which the type is Isocrates. Of Antiphon and Isaeus, in respect to λέξις, he says merely that there was nothing "novel" or "striking" in their choice of words. (*Demosth.* c. 8.) Probably he would have regarded them as intermediate in λέξις between Thucydides and Lysias, but as representing the compromise in a less mature and finished form than Isocrates.

[1] Dionys. περὶ συνθ. ὀνομ. c. 22.

posing periods as a compact framework for its thought; but, if it should ever drift undesignedly into the periodic style, it desires to set on this the mark of spontaneity and plainness. It does not employ, in order to round a sentence, supplementary words which do not help the sense; it does not care that the march of its phrase should have stage-glitter or an artificial smoothness; nor that the clauses should be separately adapted to the length of the speaker's breath. No indeed. Of all such industry it is innocent... It is fanciful in imagery, sparing of copulas, anything but florid; it is haughty, straightforward, disdainful of prettiness, with its antique air and its negligence for its beauty."

It is important to remember that this description is applied to a certain kind of poetry as well as of prose, to Pindar and Aeschylus as well as to Thucydides and Antiphon; and that, taken in reference to prose alone, it needs modification. It is not true, for instance, of the older prose that it always shrank from the *display* of artificialism. Negligent it often was; but at other times it was consciously, ostentatiously artificial. Its general characteristics, however, are admirably given by Dionysius. It is dignified; it relies much on the weight of single words; it is bold but not florid; it aims at moving the hearer rather than at reflecting the character of the speaker. Antiphon, his representative orator, exemplifies these points clearly,—as will be seen better if he is compared from time to time with the critic's representative historian, Thucydides.

In the first place, then, Antiphon is pre-eminently

Antiphon's style—its dignity. dignified and noble. He is to his successors generally as Aeschylus to Euripides. The elder tragedy held its gods and heroes above the level of men by a colossal majesty of repose, by the passionless utterance of kingly thoughts; and the same feeling to which these things seemed divine conceived its ideal orator as one who controls a restless crowd by the royalty of his calm power, by a temperate and stately eloquence. The speaker who wins his hearers by blandishments, who surprises them by adroit turns, who hurries them away on a torrent of declamation, belonged to a generation for which gods also and heroes declaimed or quibbled on the stage. Plutarch has described, not without a tinge of sarcasm, the language and demeanour by which Pericles commanded the veneration of his age.[1] "His thoughts were awe-inspiring,[2] his language lofty, untainted by the ribaldry of the rascal crowd. His calm features, never breaking into laughter; his measured step; the ample robe which flowed around him and which nothing deranged; his moving eloquence; the tranquil modulation of his voice; these things, and such as these, had over all men a marvellous spell." The biographer goes on to relate how Pericles was once abused by a coarse fellow in the market-place, bore it in silence until he had finished his business there, and when his persecutor followed him home, merely desired a slave to take a lantern and see the man home.[3] It is not probable that

---

[1] Plut. *Per.* c. 5.
[2] σοβαρόν. The word is openly sarcastic, and is meant by Plutarch to describe a pompous tone which Pericles took from "his sublime speculations" (μετεωρολογία) and "supramundane talk" (μεταρσιολεσχία) with Anaxagoras.
[3] *loc. cit.*

the receiver of the escort felt all the severity of the moral defeat which he had sustained; and he is perhaps no bad representative of the Athenian democracy in its relations to the superb decorum[1] of the old school. Much of this decorum survives in Antiphon, who, in a literary as in a political sense, clung to traditions which were fading. Yet even in him the influence of the age is seen. The Tetralogies, written for practice, and in which he had to please no one but himself, are the most stately of his compositions. The speech On the Murder of Herodes is less so, even in its elaborate proem; while part of the speech On the Choreutes, doubtless the latest of his extant works, shows a marked advance towards the freedom and vivacity of a newer style. It was in the hands of Antiphon that rhetoric first became thoroughly practical; and for this very reason, conservative as he was, he could not maintain a rigid conservatism. The public position which he had taken for his art could be held only by concessions to the public taste.

Antiphon relies much on the full, intense significance of single words. This is, indeed, a cardinal point in the older prose. Its movement was slow; each word was dropped with deliberation; and now and then some important word, heavy with concentrated meaning, came down like a sledge-hammer. Take, for instance, the chapter in which Thucydides shows how party strife, like that in Corcyra, had the effect

Reliance on single words.

---

[1] εὐκοσμία. Aeschines says that Solon made regulations περὶ τῆς τῶν ῥητόρων εὐκοσμίας. The oldest citizen was to speak first in the assembly— σωφρόνως ἐπὶ τὸ βῆμα παρελθὼν ἄνευ θορύβου καὶ ταραχῆς. (In Ctes. § 2.) Cf. Dem. de F. L. § 251: "He said that the *sobriety* (σωφροσύνη) of the popular speakers of that day is illustrated by the statue of Solon with his cloak drawn round him and his hand within the folds."

of confusing moral distinctions. Blow on blow the nicely-balanced terms beat out the contrasts, until the ear is weary as with the clangour of an anvil. "Reckless daring was esteemed loyal courage, —prudent delay, specious cowardice; temperance seemed a cloak for pusillanimity; comprehensive sagacity was called universal indifference."[1] "Remonstrance is for friends who err; accusation for enemies who have done wrong."[2] In Antiphon's speech On the Murder of Herodes, the accused says (reminding the court that his case ought not to be decided until it has been heard before the Areiopagus) :—"Be now, therefore, surveyors of the cause, but then, judges of the evidence,—now surmisers, but then deciders, of the truth."[3] And in the Second Tetralogy :—"Those who fail to do what they mean are agents of a mischance; those who hurt, or are hurt, voluntarily, are authors of suffering."[4] Examples of this eagerness to press the exact meaning of words are frequent in Antiphon, though far less frequent than in Thucydides. It is evidently natural to that early phase of prose composition in which, newly conscious of itself as an art, it struggles to wring out

[1] Thuc. III. 82. Hermogenes (περὶ ἰδεῶν, I. cap. VI.) remarks that σεμνὴ λέξις depends more on ὀνόματα, substantives and adjectives, than on ῥήματα, verbs. Thus, he says, in this sentence of Thucydides, the whole effect is wrought by the ὀνόματα. And so verbal adjectives (ἀπὸ ῥημάτων εἰς ὄνομα πεποιημένα) are preferred to relative clauses with the verb. (E.g. τόλμα ἀλόγιστος is σεμνότερον than ὅστις τολμῶν οὐ λογίζεται.)

[2] Thuc. I. 69. Another good instance is II. 62, αὔχημα μὲν γὰρ καὶ ἀπὸ ἀμαθίας εὐτυχοῦς καὶ δειλῷ τινὶ ἐγγίγνεται, καταφρόνησις δὲ ὃς ἂν καὶ γνώμῃ πιστεύῃ τῶν ἐναντίων προέχειν.

[3] de caed. Herod. § 94, νῦν μὲν οὖν γνωρισταὶ γίνεσθε τῆς δίκης, τότε δὲ δικασταὶ τῶν μαρτύρων· νῦν μὲν δοξασταί, τότε δὲ κριταὶ τῶν ἀληθῶν.

[4] Tetral. II. B. § 6, οἵ τε γὰρ ἁμαρτάνοντες ὧν ἂν ἐπινοήσωσί τι δρᾶσαι, οὗτοι πράκτορες τῶν ἀκουσίων εἰσίν· οἱ δὲ ἑκούσιόν τι δρῶντες ἢ πάσχοντες, οὗτοι τῶν παθημάτων αἴτιοι γίγνονται.

of language a force strange to the ordinary idiom; and in Greece this tendency must have been further strengthened by the stress which Gorgias laid on antithesis, and Prodicus on the discriminating of terms nearly synonymous. Only so long as slow and measured declamation remained in fashion could the orator attempt thus to put a whole train of thought into a single weighty word. What the old school sought to effect by one powerful word, the later school did by the free, rapid, brilliant development of a thought in all its fulness and with all the variety of contrasts which it pressed upon the mind.

A further characteristic of the older style—that it is "fanciful in imagery, but by no means florid"—is exemplified in Antiphon. The meaning of the antithesis is sufficiently clear in reference to Aeschylus and Pindar, the poets chosen by Dionysius as his instances. In reference to prose also it means a choice of images like theirs, bold, rugged, grand; and a scorn, on the other hand, for small prettinesses, for showy colouring, for maudlin sentiment. The great representative in oratory of this special trait must have been Pericles. A few of his recorded expressions bear just this stamp of a vigorous and daring fancy;—his description of Aegina as the "eyesore" of the Peiraeus;[1] his saying that, in the slain youth of Athens, the year had lost its spring;[2] his declaration, over the bodies of those who fell at Samos, that they had become even as the gods; "for the gods themselves we see not, but infer their immortality from the honours paid to them and from the blessings

Antiphon is imaginative but not florid.

[1] Arist. *Rhet.* III. 10.   [2] *Ib.*, and I. 7.

which they bestow."[1] The same imaginative boldness is found in Antiphon, though but rarely, and under severe control. "Adversity herself is wronged by the accused," he makes a prosecutor exclaim, "when he puts her forward to screen a crime and to withdraw his own villainy from view."[2] A father, threatened with the condemnation of his son, cries to the judges:—"I shall be buried with my son—in the living tomb of my childlessness."[3] But in Antiphon, as in Thucydides, the haughty,[4] careless freedom of the old style is shown oftener in the employment of new or unusual words or phrases.[5] The orator could not, indeed, go so far as the historian, who is expressly censured on this score by his Greek critic;[6] but they have some expressions of the same character in common.[7] While Antiphon is sparing of imagery, he is equally moderate in the use of the technical figures of rhetoric. These have been well distinguished as "figures of language" (σχήματα λέξεως) and "figures of thought" (σχήματα διανοίας)—the first class including various forms of assonance and of artificial symmetry between clauses; the second including irony, abrupt pauses, feigned perplexity, rhetorical question and so forth. Caecilius

---

[1] Plut. *Per.* c. 8.
[2] *Tetr.* I. Γ. § 1.
[3] *Tetr.* II. B. § 10: cf. II. Γ. § 12.
[4] μεγαλόφρων—αὐθέκαστος: Dionys. περὶ συνθ. ὀνομ. c. 22.
[5] E.g. *Tetr.* I. Γ. § 10, τὰ ἴχνη τῆς ὑποψίας: *Tetr.* I. Δ. § 10, τὰ ἴχνη τοῦ φόνου: *Tetr.* II. B. § 2, ἀνατροπεὺς τοῦ οἴκου ἐγένετο: *Tetr.* IV. Γ. § 2, φιλοθύτης: *Herod.* § 78, χωροφιλεῖν (= φιλοχωρεῖν).
[6] Dionysius speaks of τὸ κατάγλωσσον τῆς λέξεως καὶ ξένον in Thucydides (*de Thuc.* c. 53), and

remarks (*ib.* 51) that it was not a general fashion of the time, but a characteristic distinctive of him.
[7] The Thucydidean style may be recognised, for instance, in *Tetr.* I. Γ. § 3, ἡ αἰσχύνη—ἀρκοῦσα ἦν σωφρονίσαι τὸ θυμούμενον τῆς γνώμης: *Herod.* § 73, κρεῖσσον δὲ χρὴ ἀεὶ γίγνεσθαι τὸ ὑμέτερον δυνάμενον ἐμὲ δικαίως σώζειν ἢ τὸ τῶν ἐχθρῶν βουλόμενον ἀδίκως με ἀπολλύναι: *ib.* § 84. οἱ μὲν ἄλλοι ἄνθρωποι τοῖς ἔργοις τοὺς λόγοις ἐλέγχουσιν, οὗτοι δὲ τοῖς λόγοις ζητοῦσι τὰ ἔργα ἄπιστα καθιστάναι.

of Calacte, the author of this distinction, was a student of Antiphon, and observed that the "figures of thought" are seldom or never used by him.[1] The figures of language all occur, but rarely.[2] Blass[3] and K. O. Müller[4] agree in referring this marked difference between the older and later schools of oratory—the absence, in the former, of those lively figures so abundant in the latter—to an essential change which passed upon Greek character in the interval. It was only when fierce passion and dishonesty had become strong traits of a degenerate national character that vehemence and trickiness came into oratory. This seems a harsh and scarcely accurate judgment. It appears simpler to suppose that the conventional stateliness of the old eloquence altogether precluded such vivacity as marked the later; and that the mainspring of this new vivacity was merely the natural impulse, set free from the restraints of the older style, to give arguments their most spirited and effective form.

Nothing in the criticism of Dionysius on the "austere" style is more appreciative than his remark, that it aims rather at pathos than at êthos. That is, it addresses itself directly to the feelings; but does not care to give a subtle persuasiveness to its words by artistically adjusting them to the character and position of the person who is supposed to speak them. It is tragic; yet it is not dramatic. There has never, perhaps, been a greater master of stern

Pathos and Ethos in Antiphon.

---

[1] Caecilius *ap.* Phot. *Cod.* 259, p. 485, Bekker.
[2] See Blass, *Att. Bereds.* pp. 130–134.
[3] *Att. Bereds.* p. 134.
[4] *Hist. Gk. Lit.* c. XXXIII. § 5.

and solemn pathos than Thucydides. The pleading of the Plataeans before their Theban judges, the dialogue between the Athenians and the Melians, the whole history of the Sicilian Expedition, and especially its terrible closing scene, have a wonderful power over the feelings; and this power is in a great degree due to a certain irony. The reader feels throughout the restrained emotion of the historian; he is conscious that the crisis described was an agonising one, and that he is hearing the least that could be said of it from one who felt, and could have said, far more. On the other hand, a characteristic colouring, in the literary sense, is scarcely attempted by Thucydides. No writer is more consummate in making personal or national character appear in the history of actions. And when his characters speak, they always speak from the general point of view which he conceived to be appropriate to them. But in the form and language of their speeches there is little discrimination. Athenians and Lacedaemonians, Pericles and Brasidas, Cleon and Diodotus [1] speak much in the same style; it is the ideas which they represent by which alone they are broadly distinguished.[2] The case is nearly the same with Antiphon. His extant works present no subject so great as those of Thucydides, and his pathos is necessarily inferior in degree to that of the historian; but it resembles it in its stern solemnity,

---

[1] Thuc. III. 42.
[2] One exception may possibly be noted. It seems as if the unique personality of Alcibiades were sometimes indicated by a characteristic insolence and vehemence of language: c.g. VI. 18 § 3, καὶ οὐκ ἔστιν ἡμῖν ταμιεύεσθαι εἰς ὅσον βουλόμεθα ἄρχειν: ib. § 4. ἵνα Πελοποννησίων στορέσωμεν τὸ φρόνημα.

and also in this, that it owes much of its impressiveness to its self-control. The second[1] and fourth[2] speeches of the First Tetralogy, and the second[3] and third[4] of the Second, furnish perhaps the best examples. In êthos, on the contrary, Antiphon is weak; and this, in a writer of speeches for persons of all ages and conditions, must be considered a defect. In the Herodes case the defendant is a young Mytilenean, who frequently pleads his inexperience of affairs and his want of practice as a speaker. The speech On the Choreutes is delivered by an Athenian citizen of mature age and eminent public services. But the two persons speak nearly in the same strain and with the same measure of self-confidence. Had Lysias been the composer, greater deference to the judges and a more decided avoidance of rhetoric would have distinguished the appeal of the young alien to an unfriendly court from the address of the statesman to his fellow-citizens.

The place of Antiphon in the history of his art is further marked by the degree in which he had attained a periodic style. It is perhaps impossible to find English terms which shall give all the clearness of the Greek contrast between περιοδική and εἰρομένη λέξις.[5] The "running" style, as εἰρομένη expresses, is that in which the ideas are merely strung together,

The style of Antiphon how far periodic.

[1] Esp. §§ 1-4, 9.
[2] Esp. §§ 1-3.
[3] §§ 1-3, 10-12.
[4] §§ 3, 4.
[5] λέξις εἰρομένη (Arist. *Rhet.* III. 9). Demetrius (ἑρμ. περὶ περιόδων, § 12) calls it διηρημένη, "disjointed," διαλελυμένη, "loose," διερριμμένη, "sprawling"—in contrast to the close, compact system of the periodic style. It is also called by Dionysius *de Demosth.* c. 39, κομματική, "commatic," as consisting of short clauses (κόμματα) following each other without pause. Aristotle (l. c.) calls the periodic style κατεστραμμένη, "compact."

like beads, in the order in which they naturally present themselves to the mind. Its characteristic is simple continuity. The characteristic of the "periodic" style is that each sentence "comes round" upon itself, so as to form a separate, symmetrical whole.[1] The running style may be represented by a straight line which may be cut short at any point or prolonged to any point: the periodic style is a system of independent circles. The period may be formed either, so to say, in one piece, or of several members ($\kappa\hat{\omega}\lambda a$, *membra*), as a hoop may be made either of a single lath bent round, or of segments fitted together. It was a maxim of the later Greek rhetoric that, for the sake of simplicity and strength, a period should not consist of more than four[2] of these members or segments; Roman rhetoric allowed a greater number.[3]

Aristotle[4] takes as his example of the "running" style the opening words of the History of Herodotus; and, speaking generally, it may be said that this was the style in which Herodotus and the earlier Ionian logographers wrote. But it ought to be remembered that neither Herodotus, nor any writer in a language which has passed beyond the rudest stage, exhibits the "running" style in an ideal simplicity. In its purest and simplest form, the running style is incompatible with the very idea of a literature.[5] Wherever a literature exists, it contains the germ, however imma-

---

[1] Cicero calls the period *circuitum et quasi orbem verborum* (*de Orat.* III. 51. 198).

[2] Hermogenes, περὶ εὑρεσ. II. p. 240, Spengel.

[3] Quint. IX. 4. 124.

[4] *Rhet.* III. 9.

[5] Blass, *Att. Bereds.* p. 124: Eine gewisse Periodik hat natürlich die griechische und jede Litteratur von Anfang an gehabt: eine ganz reine λέξις εἰρομένη ist in der Wirklichkeit nie vorhanden.

ture, of the periodic style ; which, if the literature is developed, is necessarily developed along with it. For every effort to grasp and limit an idea naturally finds expression more or less in the periodic manner, the very nature of a period being to comprehend and define. In Herodotus, the running style, so congenial to his direct narrative, is dominant; but when he pauses and braces himself to state some theory, some general result of his observations, he tends to become periodic just because he is striving to be precise.[1] From the time of Herodotus onward the periodic style is seen gradually more and more matured, according as men felt more and more the stimulus to find vigorous utterance for clear conceptions. Antiphon represents a moment at which this stimulus had become stronger than it had ever before been in the Greek world. His activity as a writer of speeches may be placed between the years 421 and 411 B.C.[2] The effects of the Peloponnesian war in sharpening political animosities had made themselves fully felt; that phase of Athenian democracy in which the contests of the ecclesia and of the lawcourts were keenest and most frequent had set in ; the teaching of the Sophists had thrown a new light upon language considered as a weapon. Every man felt the desire, the urgent necessity, of being able in all cases to express his opinions with the most

---

[1] See (for instance) the passage in which Herodotus speculates on the causes of the overflowing of the Nile, II. 24, 25. It begins in a thoroughly periodic style:— εἰ δὲ δεῖ, | μεμψάμενον γνώμας τὰς προκειμένας, | αὐτὸν περὶ τῶν ἀ- φανέων ἀποδέξασθαι, | φράσω διότι μοι δοκέει πληθύεσθαι ὁ Νεῖλος τοῦ θέρεος.

[2] The speech On the Murder of Herodes must probably be placed between 421 and 416 B.C. ; the speech On the Choreutes about 413.

trenchant force; at any moment his life might depend upon it. The new intensity of the age is reflected in the speeches of Antiphon. Wherever the feeling rises highest, as in the appeals to the judges, he strives to use a language which shall " pack the thoughts closely and bring them out roundly."[1] But it is striking to observe how far this periodic style still is from the ease of Lysias or the smooth completeness of Isocrates. The harshness of the old rugged writing refuses to blend with it harmoniously,—either taking it up with marked transitions, or suddenly breaking out in the midst of the most elaborate passages.[2] It is everywhere plain that the desire to be compact is greater than the power. Antitheses and parallelisms[3] are abundantly employed, giving a rigid and monotonous effect to the periods which they form. That more artistic period of which the several parts resemble the mutually-supporting stones of a vaulted roof,[4] and which leads the ear by a smooth curve to a happy finish, has not yet been found. An imperfect sense of rhythm, or a habit of composition to which rhythmical restraint is intolerable except for a very short space, is everywhere manifest. The vinegar and the oil refuse to mingle. Thucydides presents the same

---

[1] Dionys. *de Lys.* c. 6 (in reference to Lysias), ἡ συστρέφουσα τὰ νοήματα καὶ στρογγύλως ἐκφέρουσα λέξις,—a good description of the periodic style generally as opposed to the εἰρομένη.

[2] *E.g.*, in the speech On the Murder of Herodes, sections 1, 2 show thoroughly artistic periods: § 20, again, is almost pure εἰρομένη: in Tetral. II. I'. 7 (ἀξιῶν δὲ διὰ τὸ φανερὰν εἶναι τὴν ὑποψίαν...ἐπέθετο αὐτῷ) the κατεστραμμένη and εἰρομένη are combined.

[3] *E.g. Accus. Venen.* § 5, τοῦ μὲν ἐκ προβουλῆς ἀκουσίως ἀποθανόντος τῆς δὲ ἑκουσίως ἐκ προνοίας ἀποκτεινάσης.

[4] περιφερὴς στέγη, Demetrius περ. ἑρμ. § 12, where this comparison is made.

phenomenon, but with some curious differences. It may perhaps be said that, while Antiphon has more technical skill (incomplete as that skill is) in periodic writing, Thucydides has infinitely more of its spirit. He is always at high pressure, always nervous, intense. He struggles to bring a large, complex idea into a framework in which the whole can be seen at once. Aristotle says that a period must be of "a size to be taken in at a glance;"[1] and this is what Thucydides wishes the *thought* of each sentence to be, though he is sometimes clumsy in the mechanism of the sentence itself. Dionysius mentions among the excellences which Demosthenes borrowed from the historian, "his rapid movement, his terseness, his intensity, his sting;"[2] excellences, he adds, which neither Antiphon nor Lysias nor Isocrates possessed. This intensity, due primarily to genius, next to the absorbing interest of a great subject, does, in truth, place Thucydides, with all his roughness, far nearer than Antiphon to the ideal of a compact and masterly prose. Technically speaking, Thucydides as well as Antiphon must be placed in the border-land between the old running style and finished periodic writing. But the essential merits of the latter, though in a rude shape, have already been reached by the native vigour of the historian; while to the orator a period is still something which must be constructed with painful effort, and on a model admitting of little variety.

---

[1] μέγεθος εὐσύνοπτον: *Rhet.* III. 9.
[2] τὰ τάχη—τὰς συστροφάς—τοὺς τόνους—τὸ πικρόν: Dionys. *De Thuc.* 53. He adds τὸ στρυφνόν (which seems to be a metaphor of the same kind as αὐστηρόν, and to mean "his biting flavour"); and τὴν ἐξεγείρουσαν τὰ πάθη δεινότητα.

Antiphon's treatment of subject-matter.

These seem to be the leading characteristics of Antiphon as regards form : it remains to consider his treatment of subject-matter. The arrangement of his speeches, so far as the extant specimens warrant a judgment, was usually simple. First a proem (προοίμιον) explanatory or appealing; next an introduction (technically προκατασκευή) dealing with the circumstances under which the case had been brought into court, and noticing any informalities of procedure : then a narrative of the facts (διήγησις) : then arguments and proofs (πίστεις), the strongest first : finally an epilogue or peroration (ἐπίλογος). The Tetralogies, being merely sketches for practice, have only proem, arguments and epilogue, not the "introduction" or the narrative. The speech On the Murder of Herodes and the speech On the Choreutes (in the latter of which the epilogue seems to have been lost) are the best examples of Antiphon's method. It is noticeable that in neither of these are the facts of the particular case dealt with closely or searchingly; and consequently in both instances the narrative of the facts falls into the background. Narrative was the forte of Andocides and Lysias; it appears to have been the weak side of Antiphon, who was strongest in general argument. General presumptions,—those afforded, for instance, by the refusal of the prosecutors to give up their slaves for examination, or by the respective characters of prosecutor and prisoner and by their former relations—are most insisted upon. The First Tetralogy is a good example of Antiphon's ingenuity in dealing with abstract probabilities (εἰκότα); and the same preference for proofs external to the immediate circumstances of the case is traceable in all his extant work. The adroitness of the sophistical rhetoric shows itself, not merely in the variety of forms given to the same argument, but sometimes in sophistry of a more glaring kind.[1]

The rhetorician of the school is further seen in the great number of commonplaces, evidently elaborated beforehand and without reference to any special occasion, which are brought in as opportunity offers. The same panegyric on the laws for homicide occurs, in the same words, both in the speech On the Choreutes and in that On the Murder of Herodes. In the last-named speech the reflections on the strength of a good conscience,[2] and the defendant's contention that he deserves pity, not punishment,[3] are palpably commonplaces prepared for general use. Such patches, unless introduced with consummate skill, are doubly a blemish; they break the coherence of the argument and they destroy everything like fresh and uniform colouring; the speech becomes, as an old critic says, uneven.[4] But the crudities inseparable from a new art do not affect Antiphon's claim to be considered, for his day, a great and powerful orator. In two things, says Thucydides, he was masterly,—in power of conception and in power of expression.[5] These were the two supreme qualifications for a speaker at a time when the mere faculty of lucid and continuous exposition

---

[1] See c.g. the argument in a circle in Tetr. I. A. § 6.
[2] de Choreut. § 93.
[3] Ib. § 73.
[4] ἀνώμαλον: Alcidamas Περὶ Σοφιστ. §§ 24, 25.
[5] Thuc. VIII. 68: κράτιστος ἐνθυμηθῆναι γενόμενος καὶ ἃ γνοίη εἰπεῖν. Comp. [Plut.] Vitt. X. Oratt. 8: ἔστι δὲ ἐν τοῖς λόγοις ἀκριβὴς καὶ πιθανὸς καὶ δεινὸς περὶ τὴν εὕρεσιν.

was rare, and when the refinements of literary eloquence were as yet unknown. If the speaker could invent a sufficient number of telling points, and could put them clearly, this was everything. Antiphon, with his ingenuity in hypothesis and his stately rhetoric, fulfilled both requirements. Remembering the style of his oratory and his place in the history of the art, no one need be perplexed to reconcile the high praise of Thucydides with what is at first sight the startling judgment of Dionysius. That critic, speaking of the eloquence which aims at close reasoning and at victory in discussion, gives the foremost place in it to Lysias. He then mentions others who have practised it,—Antiphon among the rest. "Antiphon, however," he says, "has nothing but his antique and stern dignity; a fighter of causes (ἀγωνιστής) he is not, either in debate or in lawsuits."[1] If, as Thucydides tells us, no one could help so well as Antiphon those who were fighting causes (ἀγωνιζομένους)[2] in the ecclesia or the law-courts; if, on his own trial, he delivered a defence of unprecedented brilliancy; in what sense is Dionysius to be understood? The explanation lies probably in the notion which the critic attached to the word "agonist." He had before his mind the finished pleader or debater of a time when combative oratory considered as an art had reached its acme; when every discussion was a conflict in which the liveliest and supplest energy must be put forth in support of practised skill; when the successful speaker must grapple at close quarters with his

---

[1] Dionys. *de Isaeo*, c. 20: Ἀντιφῶν γε μὴν τὸ αὐστηρὸν ἔχει μόνον καὶ ἀρχαῖον, ἀγωνιστὴς δὲ λόγων οὔτε συμβουλευτικῶν οὔτε δικανικῶν ἐστί.

[2] Thuc. viii. 68.

adversary, and be in truth an "agonist," an athlete straining every nerve for victory. Already Cleon could describe the "agonistic" eloquence which was becoming the fashion in the ecclesia as characterized by swift surprises, by rapid thrust and parry;[1] already Strepsiades conceives the "agonist" of the law-courts as "bold, glib, audacious, headlong."[2] This was not the character of Antiphon. He was a subtle reasoner, a master of expression, and furnished others with arguments and words; but he was not himself a man of the arena. He never descended into it when he could help; he had nothing of its spirit. He did not grapple with his adversary, but in the statelier manner of the old orators attacked him (as it were) from an opposite platform. Opposed in court to such a speaker as Isaeus, he would have had as little chance with the judges as Burke with one of those juries which Curran used to take by storm. Perhaps it was precisely because he was not in this sense an "agonist" that he found his most congenial sphere in the calm and grave procedure of the Areiopagus.

Nor was it by the stamp of his eloquence alone that he was fitted to command the attention of that Court. In politics Antiphon was aristocratic; in religion, an upholder of those ancient ideas and conceptions, bound up with the primitive traditions of Attica, of which the Areiopagus was the

Religious feeling of Antiphon.

---

[1] It is remarkable how strongly this image of debate in the ecclesia as an ἀγών is brought out in Cleon's speech, Thuc. III. 37, 38: ἀγωνισταί —ξυνέσεως ἀγῶνι ἐπαιρομένοις — ὡς οὐκ ἔγνωσται ἀγωνίσαιτ' ἄν—ἐκ τῶν τοιῶνδε ἀγώνων—αἴτιοι δ' ὑμεῖς κα- κῶς ἀγωνοθετοῦντες — ἀνταγωνιζόμενοι. The characteristics of the ἀγωνιστής are τὸ εὐπρεπὲς τοῦ λόγου ἐκπονῆσαι—καινότης λόγου—ὀξέως λέγειν (ib.).

[2] Ar. Nub. 445. θρασύς, εὔγλωττος, τολμηρὸς, ἴτης.

embodiment and the guardian. For most minds of his day these ideas were losing their awful prestige,—fading, in the light of science, before newer beliefs, as oligarchy had yielded to democracy, as Cronus to the dynasty of Zeus. But, as Athena, speaking in the name of that dynasty, had reserved to the Eumenides a perpetual altar in her land,[1] so Antiphon had embraced the new culture without parting from a belief in gods who visit national defilement,[2] in spirits who hear the curse of dying men[3] and avenge blood crying from the ground. In the recent history of his own city he had seen a great impiety followed by a tremendous disaster.[4] The prominence which he always gives to the theological view of homicide means more than that this was the tone of the Court to which his speeches were most frequently addressed: it points to a real and earnest feeling in his own mind. There

---

[1] Aesch. *Eum.* 804.

[2] See, for instance, the close of the accuser's first speech in the First Tetralogy (I. A. § 10)..."It is also harmful for you that this man, vile and polluted as he is, should enter the precincts of the gods to defile them, or should poison with his infection the guiltless persons whom he meets at the same table. *From such causes spring plagues of barrenness* (αἱ ἀφορίαι) *and reverses in men's fortunes.* You must therefore remember that vengeance is yours: you must impute to this man his own crimes: you must bring their penalty home to him, and *purity back to Athens.*" Again, in *Tetr.* II. Γ. § 8, he speaks of θεία κηλίς. Compare the passage in which the Erinyes threaten Attica with λιχὴν ἄφυλλος, ἄτεκνος,

Eum. 815; and Soph. *O. T.* 25, 101.

[3] οἱ ἀλιτήριοι (which Antiphon uses in the sense of ἀλάστορες: and so Andoc. *de Myst.* § 131)—οἱ τῶν ἀποθανόντων προστρόπαιοι: *Tetr.* III. A. § 4. He uses ἐνθύμιος (*Tetr.* II. A. 2, etc.), just as the older poets do, of a sin which lies heavy on the soul, bringing a presage of avenging Furies; and the poetical ποινή (*Tetr.* I. Δ. § 11), of atonement for blood.

[4] Timaeus, writing early in the 3rd century B.C., directly connected the defeat of the Athenians in Sicily with the mutilation of the Hermae — noticing that the Syracusan Hermocrates was a descendant of the god Hermes: Tim. *frag.* 103-4, referred to by Grote, vol. VII. p. 230.

is no better instance of this feeling than the opening of the Third Tetralogy—a mere exercise, in which the elaborate simulation of a religious sentiment would have had no motive:—

"The god, when it was his will to create mankind, begat the earliest of our race and gave us for nourishers the earth and sea, that we might not die, for want of needful sustenance, before the term of old age. Whoever, then, having been deemed worthy of these things by the god, lawlessly robs any one among us of life, is impious towards heaven and confounds the ordinances of men. The dead man, robbed of the god's gift, necessarily bequeaths, as that god's punishment, the anger of avenging spirits —anger which unjust judges or false witnesses, becoming partners in the impiety of the murderer, bring, as a self-sought defilement, into their own houses. We, the champions of the murdered, if for any collateral enmity we prosecute innocent persons, shall find, by our failure to vindicate the dead, dread avengers in the spirits which hear his curse; while, by putting the pure to a wrongful death, we become liable to the penalties of murder, and, in persuading you to violate the law, responsible for your sin also."[1]

The analogy of Antiphon to Aeschylus in regard to general style has once already been noticed; it forces itself upon the mind in a special aspect here, where the threat of judgment from the grave on blood is wrapt round with the very terror and darkness of the *Eumenides*. In another place, where Antiphon is speaking of the signs by which the gods

Aeschylean tone in Antiphon.

---

[1] *Tetr.* III. A. §§ 2 f.

point out the guilty, the Aeschylean tone is still more striking. No passage, perhaps, in Aeschylus is more expressive of the poet's deepest feeling about life than that in which Eteocles forebodes that the personal goodness of Amphiaraus will not deliver him:—

> Alas that doom which mingles in the world
> A just man with the scorners of the gods!
> *   *
> Ay, for a pure man going on the sea
> With men fierce-blooded and their secret sin
> Dies in a moment with the loathed of heaven.[1]

In the Herodes trial the defendant appeals to the silent witness which the gods have borne in his behalf:—"You know doubtless that often ere now men red-handed or otherwise polluted have, by entering the same ship, destroyed with themselves those who were pure towards the gods; and that others, escaping death, have incurred the extremity of danger through such men. Many again, on standing beside the sacrifice, have been discovered to be impure and hinderers of the solemn rites. Now in all such cases an opposite fortune has been mine. First, all who have sailed with me have had excellent voyages: then, whenever I have assisted at a sacrifice it has in every instance been most favourable. These facts I claim as strong evidence touching the present charge and the falsity of the prosecutor's accusations."[2]

Coincidences of thought and tone such as these deserve notice just because they are general coin-

---

[1] Aesch. *Theb.* 593 ff. [2] *De caed. Herod.* §§ 82 ff.

cidences. There is no warrant for assuming a resemblance in any special features between the mind of Antiphon and the mind of Aeschylus: all the more that which the two minds have in common illustrates the broadest aspect of each. By pursuits and calling Antiphon belonged to a new Athenian democracy antagonistic to the old ideas and beliefs: by the bent of his intellect and of his sympathies he belonged, like Aeschylus, to the elder democracy. It is this which gives to his extant work a special interest over and above its strictly literary interest. All the other men whose writings remain to show the development of oratorical Attic prose have around them the atmosphere of eager debate or litigation; Antiphon, in language and in thought alike, stands apart from them as the representative of a graver public life. Theirs is the spirit of the ecclesia or the dicastery; his is the spirit of the Areiopagus.

CHAPTER III

ANTIPHON

WORKS

The φονικοί λόγοι alone extant.
SIXTY speeches ascribed to Antiphon were known in the reign of Augustus; but of these Caecilius pronounced twenty-five spurious.[1] Fifteen, including the twelve speeches of the Tetralogies, are now extant. All these relate to causes of homicide. The titles of lost speeches prove that Antiphon's activity was not confined to this province; but it was in this province that he excelled; and as the orations of Isaeus are now represented by one class only, the κληρικοί, so the orations of Antiphon are represented by one class only, the φονικοί.

The Tetralogies.
The Tetralogies have this special interest, that they represent rhetoric in its transition from the technical to the practical stage, from the schools to the law-courts and the ecclesia. Antiphon stood between the sophists who preceded and the orators who followed him as the first Athenian who was at once a theorist of rhetoric and a master of practical eloquence. The Tetralogies hold a corresponding place between merely ornamental exercises and real

[1] [Plut.] *Vitt. X. Oratt.*

orations. Each of them forms a set of four speeches, supposed to be spoken in a trial for homicide. The accuser states his charge, and the defendant replies; the accuser then speaks again, and the defendant follows with a second reply. The imaginary case is in each instance sketched as lightly as possible; details are dispensed with; only the essential framework for discussion is supplied. Hence, in these skeleton-speeches, the structure and anatomy of the argument stand forth in naked clearness, stripped of everything accidental, and showing in bold relief the organic lines of a rhetorical pleader's thought. It was the essence of the technical rhetoric that it taught a man to be equally ready to defend either side of a question. Here we have the same man—Antiphon himself—arguing both sides, with tolerably well-balanced force; and it must be allowed that much of the reasoning — especially in the Second Tetralogy—is, in the modern sense, sophistical. In reference, however, to this general characteristic one thing ought to be borne in mind. The Athenian law of homicide was precise, but it was not scientific. The distinctions which it drew between various degrees of guilt in various sets of circumstances depended rather on minute tradition than on clear principle. A captious or even frivolous style of argument was invited by a code which employed vague conceptions in the elaborate classification of accidental details. Thus far the Tetralogies bear the necessary mark of the age which produced them. But in all else they are distinguished as widely as possible from the essays of a merely artificial rhetoric;

not less from the "displays" of the elder sophists than from the "declamations" of the Augustan age.[1] They are not only thoroughly real and practical, but they show Antiphon, in one sense, at his best. He argues in them with more than the subtlety of the speeches which he composed for others, for here he has no less an antagonist than himself: he speaks with more than the elevation of his ordinary style,—for in the privacy of the school he owed less concession to an altered public taste.

First Tetralogy.

The First Tetralogy supposes the following case. A citizen, coming home at night from a dinner-party, has been murdered. His slave, found mortally wounded on the same spot, deposes that he recognised one of the assassins. This was an old enemy of his master, against whom the latter was about to bring a lawsuit which might be ruinous. The accused denies the charge: the case comes before the court of the Areiopagus. The speeches of accuser and defendant comprise a number of separate arguments, each of which is carefully, though very briefly, stated, but which are not systematised or woven into a whole. An enumeration of the points raised on either side in this case will give a fair general idea of the scope of the Tetralogies generally.

---

[1] "Antiphon is a sophist," says Reiske (*Orat. Att.* VII. p. 849)—"nay, in a manner the father of that *pedantic* (*umbratici*), hair-splitting, empty, affected kind of speaking with which the schools of the ancients were rife." The very phrase "scholae veterum" shows the vagueness of this assertion. Precisely that which distinguished Antiphon from the earlier sophists was his practical bent. No man could be less fairly called "umbraticus."

I. *First Speech of the Accuser*

1. §§ 1–3. (*Procm.*) The accused is so crafty that even an imperfect proof against him ought to be accepted: a proof complete in all its parts is hardly to be looked for. —It is not to be supposed that the accuser would have deliberately incurred the guilt of prosecuting an innocent person.

[Here a narrative of the facts would naturally follow: but as this is a mere practice-speech, it is left out, and the speaker comes at once to the proofs—first, those derived from argument on the circumstances themselves (the ἔντεχνοι πίστεις)—then, the testimony of the slave (which represents the ἄτεχνοι).]

2. § 4. The deceased cannot have been murdered by robbers; for he was not plundered.

3. Nor in a drunken brawl: for the time and place are against it.

4. Nor by mistake for some one else; for, in that case, the slave would not have been attacked too.

5. §§ 5–8. It was therefore a premeditated crime; and this must have been prompted by a motive of revenge or fear.

6. Now the accused had both motives. He had lost much property in actions brought by the deceased, and was threatened with the loss of more. The murder was the only means by which he could evade the lawsuit hanging over him. [Here follows a curious argument in a circle.] And he must have felt that he was going to lose the lawsuit, or he would not have braved a trial for murder.

7. § 9. The slave identifies him.

8. §§ 9–11. (*Epilogue.*) If such proofs do not suffice, no murderer can ever be brought to justice, and the State will be left to bear the wrath of the gods for an unexpiated pollution.

II. *First Speech of the Defendant*

1. §§ 1–4. (*Proem.*) The accused deserves the pity of the judge, for he is the most unlucky of men. In death, as in life, his enemy hurts him still. It is not enough if he can prove his own innocence; he is expected to point out the real culprit. The accuser credits him with craft. If he was so crafty, is it likely that he would have exposed himself to such obvious suspicion?

2. §§ 5–6. The deceased may have been murdered by robbers, who were scared off by people coming up before they had stripped him.

3. Or he may have been murdered because he had been witness of some crime.

4. Or by some other of his numerous enemies: who would have felt safe, knowing that the suspicion was sure to fall on the accused, his great enemy.

5. § 7. The testimony of the slave is untrustworthy, since, in the terror of the moment, he may have been mistaken; or he may have been ordered by his present masters to speak against the accused. Generally, the evidence of slaves is held untrustworthy; else they would not be racked.

6. § 8. Even if mere *probabilities* are to decide the case, it is more *probable* that the accused should have employed some one else to do the murder, than that the slave should, at such a time, have been accurate in his recognition.

7. § 9. The danger of losing money in the impending lawsuit could not have seemed more serious to the accused than the danger, which he runs in the present trial, of losing his life.

8. §§ 10–13. (*Epilogue.*) Though he be deemed the probable murderer, he ought not to be condemned unless he is proved to be the actual murderer.—It is his adver-

sary who, by accusing the innocent, is really answerable for the consequences of a crime remaining unexpiated.—The whole life and character of the accused are in his favour, as much as those of the accuser are against *him*.—The judges must succour the ill fortune of a slandered man.

III. *Second Speech of the Accuser*

1. § 1. (*Proem.*) The defendant has no right to speak of his "misfortune": it is his fault. The first speech for the prosecutor proved his guilt; this shall overthrow his defence.

2. § 2. Had the robbers been scared off by people coming up, these persons would have questioned the slave about the assassins, and given information which would have exculpated the accused.

3. Had the deceased been murdered because he had been witness of a crime, this crime itself would have been heard of.

4. § 3. His other enemies, being in less danger from him than the accused was, had so much less motive for the crime.

5. § 4. It is contended that the slave's testimony is untrustworthy because it was wrung from him by the rack. But, in such cases as these, the rack is not used at all. [Nothing is said about the hypothesis that the slave may have been suborned by his masters.]

6. § 5. The accused is not likely to have got the deed done by other hands, since *he* would have been suspected all the same, and could not have been so sure of the work being done thoroughly.

7. § 6. The lawsuit hanging over him—a certainty—would have seemed more formidable to him than the doubtful chance of a trial for murder.

8. §§ 7-8. (Notice of a few topics touched on by the defendant at the beginning and end of his speech.)—The

fear of discovery is not likely to have deterred such a man from crime : whereas the prospect of losing his wealth—the instrument of his boasted services to the State—is very likely to have driven him to it.—When the certain murderer cannot be found, the presumptive must be punished.

9. §§ 9–11. (*Epilogue.*) The judges must not acquit the accused — condemned alike by probabilities and by proofs — and thereby bring bloodguiltiness on themselves. By punishing him, they can take the stain of murder off the State.

IV. *Second Speech of the Defendant*

1. §§ 1–3. (*Proem.*) He is the victim of cruel malignity. Though bound only to clear himself, it is demanded of him that he shall account for the crime.

2. §§ 4–5. Suppose that robbers did the murder, but were scared, before they had taken their booty, by people coming up. Would these persons, as it is contended, have remained to make inquiries ? Coming on a bloody corpse and a dying man at dead of night, would they not rather have fled in terror from the spot ?

3. § 6. Suppose that the deceased was slain because he had been witness of a crime :—the fact of such crime not having been heard of, does not prove that it did not take place.

4. § 7. The slave, with death from his wounds close at hand, had nothing to fear if he bore false testimony.

5. § 8. But the accused can prove a distinct *alibi*. All his own slaves can testify that on the night in question—the night of the Diïpolia—he did not leave his own house.

[The assertion of the *alibi* has been reserved till this point, because now the prosecutor cannot reply.]

6. § 9. It is suggested that he may have committed the crime to protect his wealth. But desperate deeds, such

as this, are not done by prosperous men. They are more natural to men who have nothing to lose.

7. § 10. Even if he were the presumptive murderer, he would not have been proved the actual: but, as it is. the probabilities also are for him. On all grounds, therefore, he must be acquitted, or there is no more safety for any accused man.

8. §§ 11-12. (*Epilogue.*) The judges are entreated not to condemn him wrongfully, and so leave the murder unatoned for, while they bring a new stain of bloodguiltiness on the State.

A tolerably full analysis of this First Tetralogy has been given, because it is curious as showing the general line of argument which a clever Athenian reasoner, accustomed to writing for the courts, thought most likely to succeed on either side of such a case. It will be seen that, though other kinds of evidence come into discussion, the contest turns largely on general probabilities (εἰκότα) — a province for which Antiphon had the relish of a trained rhetorician, and on which he enlarges in the speech On the Murder of Herodes.[1] As regards style, in this as in the other Tetralogies the language is noble throughout, rising, in parts of the speeches of the accused, to an austere pathos;[2] it is always concise without baldness, but somewhat over-stiff and antique. There is also too little of oratorical life; at which, however, in short speeches written for practice, the author perhaps did not aim.

The subject of the Second Tetralogy is the death of a boy accidentally struck by a javelin while

Second Tetralogy

---

[1] See esp. *de caed. Herod.* §§ 57-63.   [2] Esp. B. §§ 1-4 : Δ. §§ 1-3.

watching a youth practising at the gymnasium. The boy's father accuses the youth — whose father defends him—of accidental homicide; and the case comes before the court of the Palladion. In order to understand the issues raised, it is necessary to keep in mind the Greek view of accidental homicide. This view was mainly a religious one. The death was a pollution. Some person or thing must be answerable for that pollution, and must be banished from the State, which would else remain defiled.[1] In a case like the supposed one, three hypotheses were possible :—that the cause of the impurity had been the thrower, the person struck, or the missile. Pericles and Protagoras spent a whole day in discussing a similar question. Epitimus, an athlete, had chanced to hit and kill a certain Pharsalian : did the guilt lie, they inquired, with Epitimus, with the man killed, or with the javelin?[2] There was a special court—that held at the Prutaneion—for the trial of inanimate things which had caused death. Here, however, the question is only of living agents. The judges have nothing whatever to do with the question as to how far either was morally to blame. The question is simply which of them is to be considered as, in fact, the author or cause of the death.

Analysis. The accused, in his first speech, assumes that the case admits of no doubt; states it briefly; and concludes with an

---

[1] This feeling about homicide comes out strongly in the custom of trying cases of φόνος in the open air: ἵνα τοῦτο μὲν οἱ δικασταὶ μὴ ἴωσιν εἰς τὸ αὐτὸ τοῖς μὴ καθαροῖς τὰς χεῖρας, τοῦτο δὲ ὁ διώκων τὴν δίκην τοῦ φόνου ἵνα μὴ ὁμωρόφιος γένηται τῷ αὐθέντῃ. Cf. supra, p. 40, *note* 2; and Dem. *Aristocr.* §§ 65-79.

[2] Plut. *Pericl.* 36.

appeal to the judges (A. §§ 1–2). The father of the accused, after bespeaking patience for an apparently strange defence (B. §§ 1–2), argues that the error, the ἁμαρτία, was all on the boy's side (§§ 3–5). The thrower was standing in his appointed place; the boy was not obliged to place himself where he did. The thrower knew what he was about; the boy did not—he chose the wrong moment for running across. He was struck; and so *punished himself for his own fault* (§§ 6–8).—The accuser answers in the tone of a plain man bewildered by the shamelessness of the defence (Γ. §§ 1–4). It is absurd, he says, to pretend that the boy killed himself with a weapon which he had not touched. On the showing of the defence itself, the blame is divided: if the boy ran, the youth threw: neither was passive (§§ 5–10).—The youth's father answers that his meaning has been perverted (Δ. §§ 1–2): he did not mean, of course, that the boy pierced himself, but that he became the *first cause* of his own death (§§ 3–5). The youth did no more than the other throwers, who did not hit the boy only because he did not cross their aim (§§ 6–8). Involuntary homicide is, doubtless, punishable by law; but, in this instance, the involuntary slayer—the deceased himself—has been punished already. To condemn the accused would be only to incur a new pollution (§§ 9–10).

The striking point of the whole Tetralogy is the ingenuity with which the defender inverts the natural view of the case. The guilt of blood is, he says, with the deceased alone, who has taken satisfaction for it from himself. "Destroyed by his own errors, he was punished by himself in the same instant that he sinned." (Δ. § 8.)

Another peculiarity of the Athenian law of homicide is illustrated by the third and last Tetralogy. An elderly man had been beaten by a younger

Third Tetralogy.

man so severely that in a few days he died. The young man is tried for murder before the Areiopagus.

Analysis. The accuser, in a short speech, appeals chiefly to the indignation of the judges, dwelling, in a striking passage, on the sin of robbing a fellow-mortal of the god's gift (A. §§ 1–4).—The defendant argues in reply that, if the homicide is to be regarded as *accidental*, then it rests with the surgeon, under whose unskilful treatment the man died; but, if it is to be regarded as *deliberate*, then the murderer is the deceased himself, since he struck the first blow, which set the train of events in motion (B. §§ 3–5).—The accuser answers that the elder man is not likely to have first struck the younger (Γ. § 2); and that to blame the surgeon is idle; it would not be more absurd to inculpate the persons who called in his aid (§ 5).—[Here the second speech of the accused could naturally follow. But the accused has, in the meantime, taken advantage of the Athenian law by withdrawing into voluntary exile. The judges have no longer any power to punish him. A friend, however, who was a bystander of the quarrel, comes forward to defend the innocence of the accused.] The guilt, he maintains, lies with the old man; he, as can be proved, gave the first blow (Δ. §§ 2–5): he is at once the murdered and the murderer (§ 8).

The line thus taken by the defence is remarkable. It relies chiefly on the provocation alleged to have been given by the deceased. But it does not insist upon this provocation as mitigating the guilt of the accused. It insists upon it as transferring the whole guilt from the accused to the dead man. Athenian law recognised only two kinds of homicide; that which was purely accidental, and that which resulted from some deliberate act. In the latter case, whether there had been an intent to kill or not, some one must be a murderer. Thus, here, it would not have been enough for the defence to show that the accused had, without intent to kill, and under provocation, done a fatal injury. It is necessary to go on to argue that the deceased was guilty of his own murder.

The literary form of the Third Tetralogy deserves notice in two respects: for the solemnity and majesty of the language in the accuser's first address; and for the vivacity lent by rhetorical question and answer to part of the first speech of the defendant[1]— a vivacity which distinguishes it, as regards style, from everything else in these studies.

Of extant speeches written by Antiphon for real causes, by far the most important is that On the Murder of Herodes. The facts of the case were as follows. Herodes, an Athenian citizen, had settled at Mytilene in 427 B.C. after the revolt and reduction of that town. He was one of the cleruchs among whom its territory was apportioned, but not otherwise wealthy.[2] Having occasion to make a voyage to Aenus on the coast of Thrace, to receive the ransom of some Thracian captives who were in his hands, he sailed from Mytilene with the accused,—a young man whose father, a citizen of Mytilene, lived chiefly at Aenus.[3] Herodes and his companion were driven by a storm to put in at Methymna on the north-west coast of Lesbos; and there, as the weather was wet, exchanged their open vessel for another which was decked. After they had been drinking on board

Speech On the Murder of Herodes.

---

[1] Tetral. III. B. §§ 2, 3.   [2] § 58.   [3] § 78.

together, Herodes went ashore at night, and was never seen again. The accused, after making every inquiry for him, went on to Aenus in the open vessel; while the decked vessel, into which they had moved at Methymna, returned to Mytilene.[1] On reaching the latter place again, the defendant was charged by the relatives of Herodes with having murdered him at the instigation of Lycînus, an Athenian[2] living at Mytilene, who had been on bad terms with the deceased. They rested their charge principally on three grounds. First, that the sole companion of the missing man must naturally be considered accountable for his disappearance. Secondly, that a slave had confessed under torture to having assisted the defendant in the murder. Thirdly, that on board the vessel which returned from Methymna had been found a letter in which the defendant announced to Lycînus the accomplishment of the murder.

Mode of legal procedure. It was necessary that the trial should take place at Athens, whither all subject-allies were compelled to bring their criminal causes. The ordinary course would have been to have laid an indictment for murder (γραφὴ φόνου) before the Areiopagus. Instead, however, of doing this the relatives of Herodes laid an information against the accused as a "malefactor."[3]

---

[1] Compare § 28 with § 23.

[2] See § 61; and also § 62, ἀπεστέρει μὲν ἐμὲ τῆς πατρίδος, ἀπεστέρει δὲ αὐτὸν ἱερῶν, which implies, as Blass points out, that Lesbos was not the πατρίς of Lycînus, as it was of the defendant.

[3] ἔνδειξις κακουργίας: cf. § 9, κακοῦργος ἐνδεδειγμένος. When the accused arrived in Athens, he was, on the strength of the ἔνδειξις, arrested by the Eleven: § 85, ἀπήχθην. Hence in § 9 he speaks of ταύτην τὴν ἀπαγωγήν. The terms ἔνδειξις κακουργίας and ἀπαγωγὴ κακουργίας do not denote two different processes, but two parts of the same process. Ἔνδειξις was the laying of information against a person not yet apprehended: ἀπαγωγή was the act of apprehending him.

He was accordingly to be tried by an ordinary dicastery under the presidency of the Eleven. "Malefactor," at Athens, ordinarily meant a thief, a housebreaker, a kidnapper, or criminal of the like class; but the term was, of course, applicable to murder, especially if accompanied by robbery. Instances of persons accused of murder being proceeded against, not by an indictment, but by an information, and being summarily arrested without previous inquiry, occur only a few years later than the probable date of this speech.[1] When, therefore, the accused contends that the form of the procedure was unprecedented and illegal, this is probably to be understood as an exaggeration of the fact that it was unusual. In two ways it must have been distasteful to the prisoner: first, as an indignity; secondly, as a positive disadvantage. Trial before the Areiopagus left to the prisoner the option of withdrawing from the country before sentences; and imposed upon the accuser a peculiarly solemn oath.[2] In this case,

---

[1] The two murderers of Phrynichus in 411 were "seized and put in prison" by his friends (ληφθέντων καὶ ἐς τὸ δεσμωτήριον ἀποτεθέντων), —that is, were proceeded against by ἀπαγωγή: Lycurgus *in Leocr.* §§12. The procedure in the case of Agoratus (391 B.C.), again, was by an ἔνδειξις, not by a γραφὴ φόνου, and there was an ἀπαγωγή of the accused (Lys. *in Agorat.* § 85). Strictly speaking the ἔνδειξις and ἀπαγωγή were applicable only to those cases in which the accused was taken ἐπ' αὐτοφώρῳ: that is, in which no further proof of his guilt was required. Thus Pollux defines ἔνδειξις as ὁμολογουμένου ἀδικήματος μήνυσις, οὐ κρίσεως ἀλλὰ τιμωρίας δεομένου. Agoratus appears to have raised this very point: Lys. *in Agor.* § 85. But, since the procedure of the Areiopagus was so highly favourable to the accused, a prosecutor would generally prefer the procedure by ἔνδειξις if there was any decent pretence for it. And the condition of *manifest* guilt does not seem to have been rigorously insisted upon by the authorities. There was, probably, a feeling that the forms of the Areiopagus would be in a manner profaned by application to criminals of the vilest class.

[2] *De caed. Herod.* § 12, δέον σε διομόσασθαι ὅρκον τὸν μέγιστον καὶ ἰσχυρότατον, ἐξώλειαν αὑτῷ καὶ γένει καὶ οἰκίᾳ τῇ σῇ ἐπαρώμενον.

moreover, the unusual (though not illegal) procedure was accompanied by unjust rigours. When the accused arrived in Athens, although he offered the three sureties required by law, his bail was refused; he was imprisoned. This treatment, of which he reasonably complains,[1] may have been due in part to the unpopularity of Mytileneans at Athens, and to the fact that Herodes had been an Athenian citizen.

Date of the speech. The date of the speech must lie between the capture of Mytilene in 427[2] B.C. and the revolt of Lesbos in 412 B.C. The accused says that in 427 B.C. he was too young[3] to understand the events which were passing, and that he knows them only by hearsay. On the other hand, he can hardly have been less than twenty at the time of the trial. Kirchner[4] and Blass are inclined to place the speech about 421 B.C.; it would perhaps be better to put it three or four years later, about 417 or 416 B.C. On the other hand, a slight indication — which seems to have escaped notice — appears to show that it was at least earlier than the spring of 415 B.C. The accused brings together several instances in which great crimes had never been explained.[5] If the mutilation of the Hermae had then taken place, he could scarcely have failed to notice so striking an example.

Analysis. The speech opens with a proem in which the defendant pleads his youth and inexperience (§§ 1–7); and which is followed by a preliminary argument (προκατασκευή) on the

---

[1] § 17.   [2] § 76.   [3] § 75.   *Antiphont.* pp. 2 ff., quoted by Blass,
[4] Kirchner, *De temporibus orationum*   *Attisch. Bereds.* p. 166.
[5] §§ 67–70.

informality of the procedure (§§ 8–18). The defendant then gives a narrative of the facts up to his arrival at Aenus (§§ 19–24); and shows that the probabilities, as depending upon the facts thus far stated, are against the story of the prosecutors (§§ 25–28). The second part of the narrative describes how the vessel into which Herodes and the defendant had moved at Methymna returned to Mytilene; how the slave was tortured, and under torture accused the defendant of murder (§§ 29–30).

The defendant now concentrates his force upon proving the testimony of the slave to be worthless (§§ 31–51). He next discusses the statement of the prosecutors that a letter, in which he announced the murder to Lycinus, had been found on board the returning vessel (§§ 52–56). He shows that he could have had no motive for the murder (§§ 57–63). He maintains that he cannot justly be required to suggest a solution of the mystery. It is enough if he establishes his own innocence. Many crimes have finally baffled investigation (§§ 64–73). He notices the reproaches brought against his father as having taken part in the revolt of Mytilene and having been generally disloyal to Athens (§§ 74–80).

Besides all the other proofs, the innocence of the prisoner is vindicated by the absence of signs of the divine anger. Voyages and sacrifices in which he has taken part have always been prosperous (§§ 81–84). In a concluding appeal the judges are reminded that, in any case, justice cannot be frustrated by his acquittal, since it will still be possible to bring him before the Areiopagus (§§ 85–95).

In reviewing the whole speech as an argument, the first thing which strikes us is the notable contrast between the line of defence taken here and that traced for a case essentially similar in the model-speeches of the First Tetralogy. There, the defendant

Remarks.

employs all his ingenuity in suggesting explanations of the mysterious crime which shall make the hypothesis of his own guilt unnecessary. Here, the defendant pointedly refuses to do anything of the kind. It is enough if he can show that he was not the murderer; it is not his business to show who was or might have been. On this broad, plain ground the defence takes a firm stand. The arguments are presented in a natural order, as they arise out of the facts narrated, and are drawn out at a length proportionate to their consequence,—by far the greatest stress being laid on the worthlessness of the slave's evidence; in discussing which, indeed, the speaker is not very consistent.[1] One apparent omission is curious. The prisoner incidentally says that he never left the vessel on the night when Herodes went on shore and disappeared;[2] but he does not dwell upon, or attempt to prove, this all-essential *alibi*. If the numerous commonplaces and general sentiments seem to us a source of weakness rather than strength, allowance must be made for the taste and fashion of the time; and every one must recognise the effectiveness of the appeal to divine signs in which the argument finds its rhetorical climax.

As a composition, the speech has great merits. The êthos, indeed, is not artistic; a style so dignified

---

[1] In § 39 it is contended that the slave cannot have represented himself as taking part in the murder, but only as helping to dispose of the corpse. In § 54, on the contrary, it is assumed that the slave represented himself as the actual murderer. Lastly, in § 68, the view taken in § 39 is not only reasserted, but is ascribed to the adversaries as their own.

[2] § 26, λέγουσι δὲ ὡς ἐν μὲν τῇ γῇ ἀπέθανεν ὁ ἀνήρ, κἀγὼ λίθον ἐπέβαλον αὐτῷ εἰς τὴν κεφαλήν, ὃς οὐκ ἐξέβην τὸ παράπαν ἐκ τοῦ πλοίου.

and so sententious is scarcely suitable to a speaker who is continually apologising for his youth and inexperience. Nor, except in the passage which touches on the ruin of Mytilene,[1] is there even an attempt at pathos. But there is variety and versatility; the opening passage is artistically elaborate, the concluding, impressive in a higher way; while the purely argumentative part of the speech is not encumbered with any stiff dignity, but is clear, simple, and sufficiently animated. Altogether the style has less sustained elevation, but shows more flexibility, greater maturity and mastery, than that of the Tetralogies.

The speech On the Choreutes relates to the death of Diodotus, a boy who was in training as member of a chorus to be produced at the Thargelia, and who was poisoned by a draught given to him to improve his voice.[2] The accused is the choregus, an Athenian citizen, who discharged that office for his own and another tribe, and at whose house the chorus received their lessons. The accuser, Philocrates, brother of the deceased Diodotus, laid an information for poisoning before the Archon Basileus; and after some delay, the case came before the Areiopagus.[3] It was not con-

Speech On the Choreutes.

---

[1] § 79: "For all Mytileneans, the memory of their past error has been made indelible; they exchanged great prosperity for great misery; they beheld their country made desolate."

[2] The object with which the draught was given is not stated in the speech itself: but the argument says εὐφωνίας χάριν ἔπιε φάρμακον καὶ πιὼν τέθνηκεν. Compare the passage in which Plutarch speaks of the pains taken to train the voices of the chorus (De glor. Athen. c. 6): οἱ δὲ χορηγοὶ τοῖς χορευταῖς ἐγχέλια καὶ θριδάκια καὶ σκελλίδας καὶ μυελὸν παρατιθέντες εὐώχουν ἐπὶ πολὺν χρόνον φωνασκουμένους καὶ τρυφῶντας.

[3] That the Areiopagus was the court which tried the case appears certain (1) because that court alone had jurisdiction in γραφαὶ φαρμάκων: (2) because the special compliment to the court as "the most conscientious and upright in Greece" (§ 51) points to the Areiopagus.

tended that the accused had intended to murder the boy, but only that he had ordered to be administered to him the draught which caused his death. According to Athenian law this was, however, a capital offence. The present speech is the second made by the defendant, and the last, therefore, of the trial. Its date may probably be placed soon after the Sicilian disaster.[1]

Analysis.

In a long proem, the accused dwells on the advantage of a good conscience—on the excellence of the court of the Areiopagus—and on the weight of a judicial decision in such a case (§§ 1–6). He goes on to complain of the manner in which the adversaries have mixed up irrelevant charges with the true issue; he will address himself to the latter, and then refute the former (§§ 7–10). A narrative of the

Some have supposed that this case came before court at the Palladion, because, in § 16, the accused is spoken of as βουλεύσας τὸν θάνατον, and, according to Harpocration, cases of βούλευσις were tried at the Palladion by the Ephetae. But the βούλευσις of Harpocration is a technical term, = ἐπιβούλευσις, and denotes the intent to kill in cases in which death had not ;actually followed. On the other hand, the accused here is said βουλεῦσαι τὸν θάνατον merely in the sense that it was *by his order* that the draught was given to the boy, though he did not hand the cup to him. No intent to murder was imputed to him: see § 19, οἱ κατήγοροι ὁμολογοῦσι μὴ ἐκ προνοίας μηδ' ἐκ παρασκευῆς γενέσθαι τὸν θάνατον.

[1] In §§ 12, 21, 55 the choregus speaks of having brought an action for embezzlement of public monies against Philinus and two other persons. Now Antiphon wrote a speech κατὰ Φιλίνου,—very probably, as

Sauppe conjectures, against this same Philinus when prosecuted by the choregus: and from the speech κατὰ Φιλίνου are quoted the words, τούς τε θῆτας ἅπαντας ὁπλίτας ποιῆσαι. Sauppe thinks this points to a time just after the Sicilian disaster: 'in illis enim rerum angustiis videntur Athenienses thetes ad arma vocasse." (*Or. Att.* vol. II. p. 144.) This is quite possible: but Sauppe's other argument that the fact of the choregus representing *two* tribes (§ 11) points to a contraction of public expenses in a time of distress, is not worth much, since we do not know that this may not have been the usual custom at the Thargelia. At any rate the decidedly modern character of the speech as compared with the *De caed*. *Herodis* warrants us in placing it some years after the latter, which (as has been said above) was probably spoken between 421 and 416 B.C.

facts is then begun; but he breaks it off with the remark that it would be easy to expose the falsehoods contained in the adversary's second speech, and that he will now bring proofs (§§ 11–15). The testimony of witnesses is adduced and commented upon (§§ 16–19). The defendant goes on to contrast his own conduct in the matter with that of the accuser; dwells on the refusal of his challenge to an examination of slaves; and urges the strength in all points of his case (§§ 20–32). The evidence closed, he digresses into a full review of the adversaries' conduct from the first, in order to illustrate their malice and dishonesty. "What judges," he asks in conclusion, "would they not deceive, if they have dared to trifle with the awful oath under which they came before this court?" (§§ 33–51).

It seems probable that the end of the speech has been lost. Standing last in the MSS. of Antiphon, it would thus be the more liable to mutilation; and in the concluding speech of a trial the orator would scarcely have broken the rule, which he observes in every other instance, of finishing with an appeal to the judges. The fact that a rhetorical promise made in the speech[1] is not literally fulfilled need not be insisted upon to strengthen this view.

In the speech On the Murder of Herodes, Antiphon had to rely mainly on his skill in argument; here, witnesses were available, the case against the accusers was strong, and little was needed but a judicious marshalling of proofs. This is ably managed; but,

Remarks.

---

[1] In § 8 the speaker says that he will first deal with the matter at issue, and then meet certain other charges which the adversaries have brought against him, but which he feels sure that he can turn to their own discomfiture. The promise, however, is conditional—ἐὰν ὑμῖν ἡδομένοις ᾖ: and is, in effect, if not literally, fulfilled by the digression (§§ 33–51) in which he brings out the malicious character of their whole conduct towards him.

as a display of power, the speech is necessarily of inferior interest. The Mytilenean defendant in the Herodes case and the choregus here speak in the same general tone—with a certain directness and earnestness; but the common êthos is more strongly marked here, as the personality of the speaker comes more decidedly forward. In other points of style there is a striking contrast between the earlier and the later oration. The proem here is, indeed, as measured and as elaborate as anything in the earlier work. But it stands alone; in the rest of the speech there is no stiffness. The language is that of ordinary life; the sentences are more flowing, if not always clear; the style is enlivened by question and exclamation, instead of being ornamented with antitheses and parallelisms; and already the beginning of a transition to the easier, more practical style of the later eloquence is well marked.

Speech Against a Step-mother.

The short speech entitled "Against a Step-mother, on a Charge of Poisoning," treats of a case which, like the preceding, belonged to the jurisdiction of the Areiopagus. The speaker, a young man, is the son of the deceased. He charges his step-mother with having poisoned his father several years before,[1] by the instrumentality of a woman who was her dupe. The deceased and a friend, Philoneôs, the woman's lover, had been dining together; and she was persuaded to administer a philtre to both, in hope of recovering her lover's affection. Both the men died; and the woman—a slave—was put to death forthwith. The accuser now asks that the real criminal,—the

[1] § 30.

true Clytaemnestra[1] of this tragedy,—shall suffer punishment.

After deprecating in a proem (§§ 1–4) the odium to which his position exposes him, and commenting on the refusal of the adversaries to give up their slaves for examination (§§ 5–13), the speaker states the facts of the case (§§ 14–20). He goes on to contrast his own part as his father's avenger with that of his brother, the champion of the murderess (§§ 21–25); appeals for sympathy and retribution (§§ 26–27); denies that his brother's oath to the innocence of the accused can have any good ground, whereas his own oath to the justice of his cause is supported by his father's dying declaration (§§ 28–30); and concludes by saying that he has discharged his solemn duty, and that it now remains for the judges to do theirs (§ 31). *Analysis.*

Two questions have been raised in connexion with this speech; whether it was written merely for practice; and whether it was the work of Antiphon. I. It has been urged that stories of this kind were often chosen as subjects by the rhetoricians of the schools; that the designation of the accused as Clytaemnestra is melodramatic; that the name Philoneôs (Φιλόνεως) seems fictitious; that the address to the Areiopagites as ὦ δικάζοντες in § 7 is strange; and that the speech stands in the mss. before the Tetralogies.[2] The last objection alone requires notice. *Remarks.*

---

[1] § 7.
[2] Spengel rejects the speech, but without assigning reasons (*συν. τεχνῶν*, p. 118). The special objections mentioned above were advanced by Maetzner, an editor of Antiphon, and are examined by Dr. P. G. Ottsen in a tract *De rerum inventione ac dispositione quae est in Lysiae atque Antiphontis orationibus* (Flensburg, 1847). If the speech was written as a mere exercise, then it certainly is not the work of Antiphon, who would have treated the subject as he treats the subjects of the Tetralogies —in outline merely, without needless details of name or place.

The place of the speech in the mss. is, as Blass observes, due to the fact that it is the only accusatory speech; the Tetralogies comprise both accusation and defence; then come the defensive orations.[1] On the other hand, the prominence of narrative and the entire absence of argument in this speech—in direct contrast to the Tetralogies, which are all argument and no narrative—and the unfitness of the subject for practising the ingenuity of an advocate, seem conclusive against the view that this was a mere exercise. II. The question of authenticity is more difficult. As regards matter, nothing can be weaker than the speech. There is no argument. An unsupported assertion that the accused had attempted the same crime before; the belief of the deceased that his wife was guilty; the refusal of the adversaries to give up their slaves; these are the only proofs. As regards style, there is much clumsy

But there is no good ground for assuming that the speech was not spoken in a real cause. The story has some melodramatic features, but contains nothing which might not have occurred in ordinary Greek life. With the designation of the accused as Clytaemnestra, compare Andoc. *de Myst.* § 129, τίς ἂν εἴη οὗτος; Οἰδίπους ἢ Αἴγισθος; ἢ τί χρὴ αὐτὸν ὀνομόσαι; Isaeus mentions Διοκλέα τὸν Φλυέα, τὸν Ὀρέστην ἐπικαλούμενον; *de Cir. hered.* (Or. VIII.) § 3. Maetzner derived the name Φιλόνεως from φίλος and ναῦς, and thought it suspicious that such a name should be given to a resident in the Peiraeus. Ottsen accepts the etymology, but does not share the suspicion. Even if Φιλόνεως could be equivalent to Φιλόναυς (cf. Λιπόναυς, μυριόναυς, etc.), the fact of a person so called living at a seaport would be about as strange as the fact of a person called Philip living at Ἄργος ἱππόβοτον. Lastly, as to the ὦ δικάζοντες in § 7, the great variety of forms used by Greek orators in addressing the judges would forbid us to pronounce this one inadmissible because it is unusual. But the genuineness of the words is not above suspicion. Blass, in his edition of Antiphon, brackets as spurious the words in § 7, πῶς οὖν περὶ τούτων, ὦ δικάζοντες—οὐκ εἴληφε. One good ms. omits them; and they seem like a scholium on what immediately precedes.

[1] *Attisch. Bereds.* p. 180.

verbiage.[1] On the other hand, the narrative (§§ 14—20) shows real tragic power, especially in the contrast drawn between the unconsciousness of the miserable dupe and the craft of the instigator; throughout there is a pathos of the same kind as that of the Tetralogies, but higher; and lastly there is a strong resemblance to a particular passage in the speech On the Choreutes.[2] The conclusion to which Blass comes appears sensible.[3] Our knowledge of Antiphon's style is not so complete as to justify this rejection of the speech; but it must in any case be assigned to a period when both his argumentative skill and his power as a composer were still in a rude stage of their development.

Besides the extant compositions, twenty-four others, bearing the name of Antiphon, are known by their titles. Among these three deserve especial notice, because their titles have occasioned different inferences as to their contents, and because it is now tolerably certain that they belong, not to Antiphon the orator, but to Antiphon the sophist.[4] These are the "speeches" (or rather essays) On Truth, On Concord, On Statesmanship.[5] As regards the first of these, indeed, the testimony of Hermogenes[6] that it

Lost works.

Authorship of the treatises On Truth, On Concord, On Statesmanship.

---

[1] e.g. § 21, τῷ τεθνεῶτι ὑμᾶς κελεύω καὶ τῷ ἠδικημένῳ.. τιμωροὺς γενέσθαι...ἄξιος καὶ ἐλέου καὶ βοηθείας καὶ τιμωρίας παρ' ὑμῶν τυχεῖν ...§ 22, ἀθέμιτα καὶ ἀτέλεστα καὶ ἀνήκουστα ... § 23, δικασταὶ ἐγένεσθε καὶ ἐκλήθητε.

[2] Compare § 1 with *de Choreuta* § 27.

[3] *Att. Bereds.* p. 184.

[4] See p. 2, note 3.

[5] ἀληθείας λόγοι B :—περὶ ὁμο-νοίας :—πολιτικός. The fragments are given in Sauppe's *Fragm. Oratt. Att.* pp. 145 ff. printed in Baiter and Sauppe's *Oratores Attici*, and in the edition of Antiphon by Blass, pp. 124-143 (Teubner, 1871).

[6] Hermog. περὶ ἰδεῶν. II. c. 11. p. 414. There were two Antiphons, he says, ὧν εἷς μέν ἐστιν ὁ ῥήτωρ, οὗπερ οἱ φονικοὶ φέρονται λόγοι καὶ δημηγορικοὶ καὶ ὅσοι τούτοις ὅμοιοι. ἕτερος δὲ ὁ καὶ τερατοσκόπος καὶ ὀνειροκρίτης

was the work of the Sophist has scarcely been
questioned. But the treatise On Concord has often
been given to the orator on the assumption that it
was a speech, enforcing the importance of harmony,
which he delivered in some political crisis, perhaps
at the moment when the Four Hundred were threatened with ruin by internal dissensions.[1] The treatise
on Statesmanship, again, might, as far as the title
witnesses, have been a practical exposition of oligarchical principles by the eloquent colleague of Peisander.
An examination of the fragments leads, however, to
the almost certain conclusion that all these three
works must be ascribed to the Sophist. The essay
On Truth was a physical treatise, in which cosmic
phenomena were explained mechanically in the fashion
of the Ionic School.[2] The essay On Concord was an

λεγόμενος γενέσθαι, οὕπερ οἵ τε περὶ
τῆς ἀληθείας λέγονται λόγοι καὶ ὁ
περὶ ὁμονοίας καὶ οἱ δημηγορικοὶ καὶ
ὁ πολιτικός. Spengel proposed to
detach the words καὶ ὁ περὶ ὁμονοίας
καὶ οἱ δημηγορικοὶ καὶ ὁ πολιτικός
from the last clause, and to insert
them in the first clause after φέρονται λόγοι (omitting, of course, the
καὶ δημηγ. which already stands
there, and the τε in οἵ τε περὶ τῆς
ἀληθείας). He would thus make
Hermogenes ascribe the περὶ ὁμονοίας and the πολιτικός to Antiphon
the orator, and the ἀληθείας λόγοι
only to Antiphon the sophist. But
this is an arbitrary and violent
treatment of the text. Sauppe is
no doubt right in thinking that
its only corruption is the recur-
rence of οἱ δημηγορικοὶ in the second
clause. The article had been accidentally left out where the word
first occurs, and a corrector wrote οἱ
δημηγορικοὶ at full length in the
margin, whence it crept into the
text a second time.

[1] In reference to the meeting of
the Four Hundred on the day after
the mutiny of the hoplites in the
Peiraeus (Thuc. VIII. 92, 93), Mr.
Grote says—"It may probably have
been in this meeting of the Four
Hundred that Antiphon delivered
his oration strongly recommending
concord." (*Hist. Gr.* c. 62, vol. VIII.
p. 94 *n.*) "In hoc autem libro"
(says Blass, *Antiphon*, p. 130) "sicut
fragmenta docent, de moribus so-
phista disserebat deque vitae brevi-
tate et aerumnis: rempublicam vero
civiumque concordiam nusquam at-
tigit."

[2] Protagoras called his Treatise
of Natural Philosophy ἀλήθεια, ἢ
περὶ τοῦ ὄντος. The most suggestive
fragment of the ἀληθείας λόγοι is
No. 13 in Sauppe's list (*fragm. Or.
Grace.* p. 149). Galen *ap.* Hippocr.
epidem. I. 3, vol. 17, 1. p. 681

ethical treatise, exhorting all men to live in harmony and friendship, instead of embittering their short lives by strife.¹ The essay on Statesmanship was no party-pamphlet, but a discussion of the training required to produce a capable citizen.² Besides the speeches known to the ancients, a work on the Art of Rhetoric,³ and a collection of Proems and Epilogues,⁴ were current under Antiphon's name. Sauppe and Spengel⁵ believe the Tetralogies to be examples taken from the Rhetoric; the latter, however, is expressly condemned as spurious by Pollux.⁶ The collection of Proems and Epilogues may, as Blass⁷ suggests, have furnished the opening and concluding passages of the Speech On the Murder of Herodes, and the opening passage of that On the Choreutes. In the latter case the difference of style between the proem and all that follows it is certainly striking.

The Rhetoric.

The collection of Proems and Epilogues.

(Kühn) says :—οὕτω δὲ καὶ παρ᾽ Ἀντιφῶντι κατὰ τὸ δεύτερον τῆς Ἀληθείας ἔστιν εὑρεῖν γεγραμμένην τὴν προσηγορίαν ἐν τῇδε τῇ ῥήσει· ὅταν οὖν γένωνται ἐν τῷ ἀέρι ὄμβροι τε καὶ πνεύματα ὑπενάντια ἀλλήλοις, τότε συστρέφεται τὸ ὕδωρ καὶ πυκνοῦται κατὰ πολλά, κ.τ.λ.

¹ See, for instance, fragments 1 and 4 of the περὶ ὁμονοίας in Sauppe :—ἀναθέσθαι δὲ ὥσπερ πεττὸν τὸν βίον οὐκ ἔστιν...πολλοὶ δ᾽ ἔχοντες φίλους οὐ γιγνώσκουσιν, ἀλλ᾽ ἑταίρους ποιοῦνται θῶπας, πλούτου καὶ τύχης κόλακας.

² For instance, in fragment 2 of the πολιτικός we have a precept on the value of a character for steady business habits—μήτε φιλοπότην κληθῆναι καὶ δοκεῖν τὰ πράγματα καταμελεῖν ὑπ᾽ οἴνου ἡσσώμενον.

³ ῥητορικαὶ τέχναι.

⁴ προοίμια καὶ ἐπίλογοι.

⁵ Sauppe, *Fragm. Oratt. Gr.* p. 145.

⁶ Pollux (VI. 143) quotes a word as used by Antiphon ἐν ταῖς ῥητορικαῖς τέχναις : but adds—δοκοῦσι δ᾽ οὐ γνήσιαι.

⁷ *Attisch. Bereds.* p. 103, where he quotes (note 7) Cic. *Brut.* 47 for the statement of Aristotle —*huic (Gorgiae) Antiphontem Rhamnusium similia quaedam habuisse conscripta :* —where *conscripta* seems to mean a collection of *communes loci* stored up to be used as they might be wanted.

CHAPTER IV

ANDOCIDES

LIFE

THE life of Andocides has, in one broad aspect, a striking analogy to the life of Antiphon. Each man stands forth for a moment a conspicuous actor in one great scene, while the rest of his history is but dimly known; and each, at that moment, appears as an oligarch exposed to the suspicion and dislike of the democracy. The Revolution of the Four Hundred is the decisive and final event in the life of Antiphon. The mutilation of the Hermae is the first, but hardly less decisive event, in the known life of Andocides; the event which, for thirteen years afterwards, absolutely determined his fortunes, and which throws its shadow over all that is known of their sequel.

Birth of Andocides.

Andocides was born probably about 440 B.C.[1] The deme Cydathene, of which he was a member, was included in the Pandionian tribe. His family was

---

[1] According to [Lys.] *in Andoc.* § 46, he was in 399 B.C. πλέον ἢ τετταράκοντα ἔτη γεγονώς. He speaks of his "youthfulness" in 415 B.C.: *de Red.* § 7. His father, Leogoras II., may have been born about 470: Andocides I. about 500: Leogoras I. about 540. The pseudo-Plutarch puts his birth in the archonship of Theagenides, Ol. 78. 1, 468 B.C.: probably on the assumption that the orator was the Andocides of Thuc. I. 51.

traced by Hellanicus the genealogist through Odysseus up to the god Hermes,[1] and had been known in Athenian history for at least three generations. Leogoras, his great-grandfather, had fought against the Peisistratidae.[2] Andocides, the elder, his grandfather, was one of ten envoys who negotiated the Thirty Years' Truce with Sparta in 445;[3] and had commanded with Pericles at Samos in 440,[4] and with Glaucon at Corcyra in 435.[5] Leogoras, father of the orator, was, to judge from Aristophanes, famous chiefly for his dinners and his pheasants.[6]

The only glimpse of the life of Andocides before 415 B.C. is afforded by himself. He belonged to a set or club, of which one Euphiletus was a leading member,[7] and with which his address "To His Associates" (πρὸς τοὺς ἑταίρους), mentioned by Plutarch, has sometimes been connected.[8] It was in May, 415, when he was about twenty-five, when the Peiraeus

Affair of the Hermae.

[1] [Plut.] *Vit. Andoc.* γένους Εὐπατριδῶν, ὡς δὲ Ἑλλάνικος, καὶ ἀπὸ Ἑρμοῦ· καθήκει γὰρ εἰς αὐτὸν τὸ Κηρύκων γένος. The pseudo-Plutarch seems to have inferred from the fact that the descent of Andocides was traced from Hermes, that he belonged to the priestly family of the Κήρυκες, who represented their ancestor Κῆρυξ as the son of Hermes (Paus. I. 38. 3). But Plutarch (*Alcib.* c. 21) tells us that Hellanicus traced Andocides up to Odysseus; the line from Hermes, then, was not through Ceryx, but through Autolycus, whose daughter Anticleia was mother of Odysseus.

[2] Andoc. *de Myst.* § 106. In *de Red.* § 26 Valckenär and Sauppe read ὁ τοῦ ἐμοῦ πατρὸς πάππος instead of ὁ τοῦ ἐμοῦ πατρὸς πρόπαππος.

[3] Andoc. *de Pace*, § 6.

[4] Schol. Aristid. III. 485, ap. Blass,

Att. Bereds. p. 270.

[5] Thuc. I. 51.

[6] Ar. *Vesp.* 1269: *Nub.* 109, τοὺς φασιανοὺς οὓς τρέφει Λεωγόρας. Athen. IX. p. 387 A, κωμῳδεῖται γὰρ ὁ Λεωγόρας ὡς γαστρίμαργος ὑπὸ Πλάτωνος ἐν Περιαλγεῖ. Besides his son Andocides, Leogoras had a daughter who married Callias a son of Telecles: *de Myst.* § 117: cf. §§ 42, 50.

[7] *De Myst.* §§ 61-63. Euphiletus is there described as proposing the sacrilege at a convivial meeting of the club (εἰσηγήσατο...πινόντων ἡμῶν, § 61). Its members were intimate associates (ἐπιτήδειοι, § 63: cf. οἷς ἐχρῶ καὶ οἷς συνῇσθα, § 49). There is nothing to show that this club of young men was anything so serious as a political ἑταιρεία.

[8] Plut. *Them.* c. 32. See ch. VI. *ad fin.*

was alive with preparations for the sailing of the fleet to Sicily, and all men were full of dreams of a new empire opening to the city, that Athens was astonished by a sacrilege, of which it is hard now to realise the precise effect upon the Athenian mind. When it appeared that the images of Hermes throughout the town—in the market-place, before the doors of houses, before the temples—had been mutilated in the night, the sense of a horrible impiety was joined to a sense of helplessness against revolution;[1] for to an Athenian it would occur instinctively that the motive of the mutilators had been not simply to insult, but to estrange, the tutelar gods of the city. This terror, while still fresh, was intensified by the rumoured travesties in private houses of the innermost sacrament of Greek religion, the Mysteries of Eleusis. In order to understand the position of Andocides, it is necessary to keep these two affairs distinct. There is nothing to show that he was in any way concerned, as accomplice or as informer, with the profanation of the Mysteries. As a matter of course, the author of the speech against him asserts it:[2] but his own denial is emphatic and clear,[3] and agrees with what is known from other sources. It was in the affair of the Hermae alone that he was implicated. The first important evidence in this matter was given by Teucrus, a resident-alien, who had fled to Megara, and who was brought back to give information under a promise of

[1] Thuc. VI. 27, καὶ τὸ πρᾶγμα μειζόνως ἐλάμβανον· τοῦ τε γὰρ ἔκπλου οἰωνὸς ἐδόκει εἶναι καὶ ἐπὶ ξυνωμοσίᾳ ἅμα νεωτέρων πραγμάτων καὶ δήμου καταλύσεως γεγενῆσθαι. Cf. Isocr. de Bigis, § 6.

[2] [Lys.] in Andoc. § 51, μιμούμενος τὰ ἱερὰ ἐπεδείκνυε τοῖς ἀμυήτοις, κ.τ.λ.

[3] Andoc. de Myst. § 29, περὶ μὲν τῶν μυστηρίων...ἀποδέδεικταί μοι ὡς οὔτε ἠσέβηκα οὔτε μεμήνυκα, κ.τ.λ.

impunity. This man denounced twelve persons as guilty in regard to the Mysteries, and eighteen as mutilators of the Hermae. Among the eighteen were Euphiletus and other members of the club to which Andocides belonged; of whom some were at once put to death, and others fled.[1]

But there was a very general belief that the bottom of the matter had not been reached, and that the conspiracy had been far more widely spread; a belief which the commissioners of enquiry, especially Peisander, seem to have encouraged. As usual in such cases, the demand for discoveries created the supply. Diocleides, the Titus Oates of this plot, came forward to state that the conspiracy included no less than three hundred persons. Forty-two of these were denounced, among whom were Andocides, his father, his brother-in-law and ten other of his relatives. They were imprisoned at once; Diocleides was feasted as a public benefactor at the Prytaneion; and the whole town spent the night under arms, panic-stricken by the extent of the conspiracy,—not knowing whence, when, or in what strength they might be attacked by the enemies of gods and men.[2] Andocides has described the first night in prison. Wives, sisters, children, who had been allowed to come to their friends, joined in their tears and cries of despair. Then it was that Charmides, one of his cousins, besought him to tell all that he knew, and to save his father, his relations and all the innocent citizens who were threatened with an infamous death. Andocides yielded. He was brought before the Council, and

[1] *De Myst.* § 35.   [2] *De Myst.* § 45.

stated that the story of Teucrus was true. The eighteen who had died or fled were indeed guilty. But there were four more whom Teucrus had left out, and whom Andocides now named. These four fled.[1]

The deposition of Andocides, confirming as it did the testimony of Teucrus, and at the same time supplementing that testimony, was accepted, at least at the time, as the true and complete account. The affair of the Hermae was dropped, and attention was fixed once more upon the affair of the Mysteries.[2] At some time not much later, Leogoras, the father of Andocides, gained an action which he brought against the senator Speusippus, who had illegally committed for trial Leogoras and the other persons accused by the slave Lydus of having profaned the Mysteries in the house of his master Pherecles.[3] Andocides himself was less fortunate. He had given his information under a promise of personal indemnity guaranteed by a decree of the ecclesia. After his disclosures, however, a new decree, proposed by Isotimides, cancelled the former. It provided that those who had committed impiety and confessed it should be excluded from the market-place and from the temples; a form of "disgrace" (atimia) virtually equivalent to banishment. Andocides was considered as falling under this decree, and was accordingly driven to leave Athens.

Decree of Isotimides.

This closes the first chapter of his life. Two

[1] *De Myst.* § 68.
[2] Thuc. VI. 61, ἐπειδὴ τὸ τῶν Ἑρμῶν ᾤοντο σαφὲς ἔχειν, πολὺ δὴ μᾶλλον καὶ τὰ μυστικὰ ὧν ἐπαίτιος ἦν μετὰ τοῦ αὐτοῦ λόγου καὶ τῆς ξυνωμοσίας ἐπὶ τῷ δήμῳ ἀπ' ἐκείνου (τοῦ Ἀλκιβιάδου) ἐδόκει πραχθῆναι.
[3] *De Myst.* § 17.

questions directly arising out of it suggest themselves for consideration here.

First, Does the speech On the Mysteries give the story which he really told before the Council at Athens in 415? In that speech, he represents himself as having stated that the mutilation of the Hermae had been proposed by Euphiletus at a convivial meeting of their club; that he had strenuously opposed it; and that, while he was confined to his house by illness, Euphiletus had seized the opportunity of executing the scheme, telling the others that Andocides had become favourable to it. Now it is a suspicious fact that in the speech On his Return, spoken in 410—that is, eleven years before the speech On the Mysteries—Andocides distinctly pleads guilty to certain offences committed in 415, and excuses them by his youth, his folly, his madness at the time.[1] It is suspicious, also, that not merely the author of the speech against him,[2] but also Thucydides in terms which can hardly be explained away,[3] and Plutarch still more explicitly,[4] represent him as having accused himself along with the rest. It can hardly be doubted that, in 415, he told the Council that the mutilation of the Hermae had been a mad freak committed by the club of young men to which he belonged,

The speech On the Mysteries.

---

[1] *De Red.* §§ 7, 25.
[2] [Lys.] *in Andoc.* §§ 36, 51.
[3] Thuc. VI. 60, καὶ ὁ μὲν αὑτός τε καθ' ἑαυτοῦ καὶ κατ' ἄλλων μηνύει τὸ τῶν Ἑρμῶν. Bishop Thirlwall thinks that this need not mean more than that Andocides confessed privity to the fact (*Hist. Gr.* vol. III. Appendix III. p. 500). But the words would naturally mean that he confessed participation in the fact. And so Mr. Grote understands them, vol. VII. p. 279.
[4] Plut. *Alc.* 21, οὗτος (Τίμαιος) ἀναπείθει τὸν Ἀνδοκίδην ἑαυτοῦ κατήγορον καὶ τινῶν ἄλλων γενέσθαι μὴ πολλῶν ... ὁ Ἀνδοκίδης ἐπείσθη καὶ γενόμενος μηνυτὴς καθ' αὑτοῦ καὶ καθ' ἑτέρων ἔσχε τὴν ἐκ τοῦ ψηφίσματος ἄδειαν αὐτός· οὓς δ' ὠνόμασε, κ.τ.λ.

and by himself among the number. Probably he felt that it would be useless to make a reservation of his own innocence. No one would believe him; and at the same time it would seriously damage the plausibility of his alleged acquaintance with the plans of the conspirators. It is very likely, however, that he did make excuses for himself, such as that his active part in the affair had been small, or that he had been drawn into it against his will, or in a moment of excitement. At the distance of sixteen years such excuses might easily grow into a denial of his having been concerned at all.

It is a further question whether, supposing that the story which he told at the time inculpated himself, this story was true. Was he really guilty? It ought to be remembered that the eighth book of Thucydides was probably written before the speech On the Mysteries had been delivered, or the exiles of 415 had returned; and that, therefore, we have perhaps larger materials than Thucydides himself had for forming a judgment on an affair which (as he says) had never been cleared up.[1] Great weight ought surely to be allowed to the circumstance that the Hermes before the house of Andocides was one of the very few[2] which had not been mutilated. The explanation of this given by Andocides himself in 399 is at least plausible. Euphiletus, he says, had told the other conspirators that Andocides had him-

---

[1] Thuc. VI. 60.

[2] The *only* one—μόνος τῶν Ἑρμῶν τῶν Ἀθήνησιν, according to Andocides himself, *de Myst.* § 62. But Plut. *Alc.* 21 says ἐν ὀλίγοις πάνυ τῶν ἐπιφανῶν μόνος σχεδὸν ἀκέραιος ἔμεινε; and Thuc. VI. 27 says only οἱ πλεῖστοι περιεκόπησαν.

self undertaken the mutilation of this particular image; and so it escaped, Andocides being ill and ignorant of the whole matter. Now if Euphiletus had a spite against Andocides for having condemned his proposal, he could not, in fact, have taken a more effectual revenge. The sparing of this Hermes was just the circumstance, which, in the event, turned suspicion most strongly upon Andocides. Had he been out himself that night and engaged in the sacrilege, he could scarcely have failed to think of a danger so evident, and would have taken care that his own house should not be marked out by its immunity. If the number of mutilators was as small as he states, the neglect of such a precaution is altogether inconceivable. The conjecture to which we should incline is that the Hermae were mutilated by the small club of young men to which Andocides belonged, but that, for some reason or other, he had no hand in it; that, however, when he gave his evidence at the time, he accused himself of having been actively concerned, thinking that otherwise the rest of his story would be disbelieved. It would follow that the version of the matter given in his speech On the Mysteries is, on the whole, true in itself, but is untrue as a representation of what he stated in 415.

The second chapter in the life of Andocides covers the years from 415 to 402. It is the history of his exile.

Life of Andocides from 415 to 402.

On leaving Athens in 415 he appears to have adopted a merchant's life. Archelaus, king of Macedonia, a friend of his family, gave him the right of cutting timber and exporting it.[1] In Cyprus according to the author of the speech against him, he was imprisoned by the king of Citium on account of some treachery;[2] a story from which it would be unsafe to infer more than that Andocides had visited the island. When, after the Sicilian disaster, Samos became the headquarters of the Athenian fleet, he endeavoured to conciliate his countrymen there by supplies of corn and cargoes of oar-spars and of bronze, which his mercantile connexion enabled him to get for them at a cheap rate.[3] In the spring of 411 he made his first attempt to re-establish himself at Athens. He was unaware, at the moment of his return, that the revolution of the Four Hundred had taken place. The hatred of the oligarchical clubs, incurred by his denunciation of his own associates, and the enmity of Peisander, whose desire to keep up a panic had been thwarted by his reassuring disclosures, would have been enough to have prevented him from expecting any other reception than that which he actually experienced.[4] He was instantly denounced to the Council by Peisander for supplying oars to the hostile democracy at Samos, and was thrown into prison.[5] Released by the downfall of the oligarchy, he again visited Cyprus,—where,

His first return to Athens.

---

[1] Andoc. *de Red.* § 11. Cf. Theophr. *Char.* xxiii., where the ἀλαζών boasts of having received, as a special honour from Antipater, the ἐξαγωγὴ ξύλων ἀτελής.

[2] [Lys.] *in Andoc.* § 26.

[3] *De Red.* § 11.

[4] He says (*de Red.* § 13) κατέπλευσα ὡς ἐπαινεθησόμενος ὑπὸ τῶν ἐνθάδε: and he would hardly have expected the "praise" of the Four Hundred for having ministered to the army at Samos. Earlier in the narrative, indeed, (§ 11) he says that he brought the supplies to Samos "when the Four Hundred had already seized the government:" but this is a way of fixing the date. It does not follow that the tidings from Athens had then reached Samos.

[5] *De Red.* § 15.

according to his accuser, he was once more imprisoned
"for a misdeed"—this time by Evagoras king of
Salamis;[1] but we may hesitate whether to recognise
here the monotony of fate or of invention.

In Cyprus Andocides found a new opportunity
to serve the interests of Athens. The loss of her
power in the Propontis had cut off her corn-trade
with the Euxine; and Andocides procured the despatch of corn-ships from Cyprus to the Peiraeus.
It must have been in the spring or summer of 410, *His second return to Athens.*
before the results of the victory at Cyzicus had
removed all fear of famine,[2] that Andocides was again
at Athens, and in a speech in the ecclesia pleaded
for the removal of the disabilities under which the
decree of Isotimides was held to have placed him.
He expresses penitence for his errors in 415; and
lays stress upon certain information which he had
given to the Senate, as well as upon his services in
procuring a supply of corn.[3] His application was
rejected; and for the third time he went into exile.
During the next eight years he is said to have visited
Sicily, Italy, the Peloponnesus, Thessaly, the Hellespont, Ionia and Cyprus.[4] In Cyprus he had received,
perhaps from Evagoras, a grant of land;[5] and the
fortune which afterwards enabled him to discharge
costly offices at Athens, although his patrimony had
been wrecked,[6] appears to show that he had been
active and successful as a merchant.

---

[1] [Lys.] *in Andoc.* § 28.

[2] For a discussion of the date of the speech On his Return, see Chap. VI.

[3] *De Red.* §§ 19 ff.

[4] [Lys.] *in Andoc.* § 6.

[5] In *De Myst.* § 4 he supposes his enemies saying of him—ἔστι πλεύσαντι εἰς Κύπρον, ὅθενπερ ἥκει, γῆ πολλὴ καὶ ἀγαθὴ διδομένη καὶ δωρεὰ ὑπάρχουσα.

[6] *ib.* § 144.

The general amnesty of 403 at last gave him the opportunity which he had so long sought in vain. He returned to Athens from Cyprus,[1] probably about the beginning of 402;[2] and for three years was not only unmolested, but was readmitted to the employments and honours of an active citizen. He was a choregus, and dedicated in the Street of Tripods the prize which he had won with a cyclic chorus;[3] he was gymnasiarch at the Hephaestia—head of sacred missions to the Isthmian and Olympian games—and steward of the sacred treasure;[4] he is heard of as speaking in the Senate and preferring accusations in the law-courts.[5] At length, in 399,[6] the zeal of his enemies—stimulated, perhaps, by his prosperity—appears to have revived. After one attempt which seems to have been abortive,[7] he was brought to trial, in the autumn of 399, on a charge of impiety. He had attended the Greater Mysteries at Eleusis; and

---

[1] *De Myst.* § 4.

[2] The contest between the exiles at the Peiraeus and the town party was not finally concluded till Boedromion (Sept.-Oct.) 403 B.C. See Clinton, *F. H.* At the time when the amnesty was sworn, Andocides was absent from Athens: [Lys.] *in Andoc.* § 39. It seems safe, then, to conclude that he did not return to Athens before the early part of 402.

[3] [Plut.] *Vit. Andoc.*

[4] *De Myst.* § 132.

[5] [Lys.] *in Andoc.* § 33, παρασκευάζεται τὰ πολιτικὰ πράττειν καὶ ἤδη δημηγορεῖ. Cf. *ib.* § 11, where mention is made of a γραφὴ ἀσεβείας brought by Andocides against one Archippus.

[6] Three years after his return to Athens: *de Myst.* § 132. The date 399 is confirmed by another consideration. In *de Myst.* § 132 the offices which he had held are enumerated in apparently chronological order:—πρῶτον μὲν γυμνασίαρχον Ἡφαιστίοις, ἔπειτα ἀρχιθεωρὸν εἰς Ἰσθμὸν καὶ Ὀλυμπίαζε, εἶτα δὲ ταμίαν ἐν πόλει τῶν ἱερῶν χρημάτων. Now the Olympic festival at which he was ἀρχιθεωρός must have been that of Ol. 95. 1, 400 B.C. After this architheoria he had been tamias; but clearly was so no longer at the time when the speech On the Mysteries was spoken.

[7] [Lys.] *in Andoc.* § 30, ἀφικόμενος εἰς τὴν πόλιν δὶς ἐν τῷ αὐτῷ [ἐνιαυτῷ?] ἐνδέδεικται. Neither Andocides nor his accuser says anything about the result of the earlier ἔνδειξις: probably, then, it never came to a trial.

his enemies contended that he had thereby violated the decree of Isotimides, by which he was excluded from all temples. Before the Eleusinian festival was over,[1] an information to this effect was laid before the Archon Basileus. The accusers were Cephisius, Epichares and Meletus, supported by Callias and Agyrrhius. The fact that Andocides was supported in court by Anytus and Cephalus,[2] two popular public men, as well as by advocates chosen by his tribe, shows that his assiduous services to the State, and perhaps the persevering malice of his adversaries, had at last produced their effect upon the general feeling towards him. He speaks like a man tolerably confident of a verdict; and he was acquitted.

Little is known of the life of Andocides after 399. From the speech On the Mysteries it appears that he was at that time unmarried and childless.[3] His uncle Epilycus had died leaving two daughters, whom Andocides and Leagrus, as the nearest kinsmen, had claimed in marriage before the Archon. The girl claimed by Andocides had died before the claim was heard; the other was now claimed by Callias, who had induced Leagrus to retire in his favour, and Andocides, to defeat this intrigue, had entered a counter-claim; but in 399 the case was still undecided.[4] If Andocides died without legitimate issue, his family became extinct.[5]

The first reappearance of Andocides in public life

---

[1] The great Eleusinia fell in the last half of Boedromion (end of Sept. and beginning of Oct.) The ἔνδειξις was laid ταῖς εἰκάσι, τοῖς μυστηρίοις τούτοις, de Myst. § 121.

[2] De Myst. § 150. [3] ib. § 148.

[4] ib. §§ 117-123. [5] ib. § 146.

is marked by the speech On the Peace with Lacedaemon, which belongs to 390, the fourth year of the Corinthian War.[1] Athens, Boeotia, Corinth and Argos were at this time allied against Sparta. The success of Agesilaus in 391 had led the Athenians, probably in the winter of 391–90, to send plenipotentiaries, among whom was Andocides, to treat for peace at Sparta. According to the terms proposed by the Lacedaemonians, Athens was to retain her Long Walls—rebuilt three years before by Conon —and her fleet; she was also to recover Lemnos, Imbros and Scyros: and Boeotia was to be gratified by the withdrawal of the Spartan garrison from Orchomenus. The plenipotentiaries did not use their powers, but requested that the Athenian ecclesia might have forty days in which to consider these proposals; and returned, accompanied by Spartan envoys, to Athens.[2] It was in the ensuing debate— early in the year 390—that the speech of Andocides was made.

This, his only recorded utterance on a public

---

[1] From the speech itself it appears that (1) the Boeotians had been now four years at war, § 20 : (2) Lechaeum had been taken by the Lacedaemonians, § 18: (3) The Lacedaemonians are spoken of as having been already thrice victorious—at Corinth, Coronea, and Lechaeum ; and nothing is said of any check which they had received : § 18. The destruction of the mora by Iphicrates —so tremendous a blow to the Spartan arms—can hardly, then, have taken place. Grote puts the victory of Iphicrates in 390: see his note, vol. ix. p. 455, which discusses Clinton's view that it occurred in 393.

Krüger places the speech of Andocides in 393: Grote and Kirchner in 391 ; but the data above mentioned seem in favour of 390 : which is the year for which Blass decides (*Att. Bereds.* pp. 282 f.).

[2] Xenophon and Diodorus say nothing about such an embassy from Sparta to Athens. But, according to the author of the Argument to the Speech, Φιλόχορος μὲν οὖν λέγει καὶ ἐλθεῖν τοὺς πρέσβεις ἐκ Λακεδαιμονίας καὶ ἀπράκτους ἀνελθεῖν μὴ πείσαντος τοῦ Ἀνδοκίδου. Philochorus, writing circ. 300–260 B.C., is a trustworthy witness for the fact of the embassy.

question, is temperate and sensible. He points out
that it is idle to wait either for the prospect of
crushing Sparta in war, or for the prospect of recovering by diplomacy all the possessions abroad which
Athens had lost in 405; her ships and walls are now,
as they always were, her true strength, and she ought
to accept thankfully the secured possession of these.
The soundness of this view was proved in the sequel.
By the Peace of Antalcidas three years later Athens
got only what she was offered in 390; and she got it,
not by treaty on equal terms with a Hellenic power,
but as part of the price paid by the Persian king for
the disgraceful surrender of Asiatic Hellas. The
advice of Andocides probably lost something of its
effect through the suspicion of "laconism" attaching
to all statesmen of oligarchical antecedents; and,
though he had long cast in his lot with the democracy, a certain odour of oligarchy must have clung
to him still. At any rate his advice was not
taken. The story that he was not only disobeyed,
but banished,[1] probably represents merely the
desire to add one disaster more to a history so full
of repulses.

A fair estimate of Andocides is made difficult by Character of Andocides.
the fact that he was first brought into notice by a
scandal, and that the memory of this scandal runs
through nearly all that is known of his after-life. At
the age of twenty-five he is banished for the Hermae
affair; he is defeated, on the same ground, in two
attempts to return; at the end of sixteen years he is

---

[1] [Plut.] *Vit. Andoc.* πεμφθεὶς δὲ περὶ τῆς εἰρήνης εἰς Λακεδαίμονα καὶ δόξας ἀδικεῖν ἔφυγε.

brought to trial for impiety; and his acquittal is the last thing recorded about him. At that time he was only forty-one; already, since his return in 402, he had discharged public services; and now, formally acquitted of the charges which had so long hung over him, he might hope for a new career. His speech On the Peace shows that in 390 he was sufficiently trusted by his fellow-citizens to have been sent as a plenipotentiary to Sparta; and proves also, by its statesmanlike good sense, his fitness for such a trust. But, except in this speech, nothing is recorded of his later and probably brighter years. History knows him only under a cloud. It was, moreover, his misfortune that while the informations which he laid in 415 made him hateful to the oligarchs, his hereditary connexion with oligarchy exposed him to the continual suspicion of the democrats. One year he is imprisoned by the Four Hundred; the next he is repulsed by the ecclesia. It would be an easy inference that there must have been something palpably bad and false in the man to whom both parties were harsh, did not a closer view show that one party may have been influenced by spite and the other by prejudice. Many of those who believed that Andocides was concerned in the mutilation of the Hermae must have regarded him with sincere horror. But on the other hand it should be remembered that such horror is never so loudly expressed, and is never so useful to personal enmity, as at a time when a popular religion, still generally professed, is beginning to be widely disbelieved. Diagoras and Socrates were accused of impiety with the more effect because the views ascribed to them resembled the real views of many who seemed orthodox. Besides those who hated Andocides as an informer, as an oligarch, or as an iconoclast, there were probably many who regarded him with that special kind of dislike which attaches to a person who drives the world into professing angry conviction on matters to which it is secretly indifferent. Viewed apart from the feelings which worked on his contemporaries, the facts of his life seem to warrant severe blame as little as they warrant high praise. His youthful associates were dissolute; through them he was involved, rightly or wrongly, in the suspicion of a great impiety; and this suspicion clung to him for years. But it was never proved; and when he was at last brought to trial, he was acquitted. As an exile he conferred on Athens services which, if not disinterested, were at all events valuable; after his return he discharged costly public services, and represented the State on an important mission.

To judge from his extant works he had not genius, but he was energetic and able. Hard and various experiences had sharpened his shrewdness; he had a quick insight into character, and especially the triumphant skill of a consciously unpopular man in exposing malignant motives. There was no nobleness in his nature, except such as is bred by self-reliance under long adversity; but he had practical good sense, which his merchant's life in exile must have trained and strengthened. If the counsel which he gives to Athens in his speech On the Peace with Lacedaemon may be taken as a sample of his statesmanship, he was an adviser of the kind rarest in the ecclesia; not only clearsighted in the interests of the city, but bold enough to recommend to Athenians a safe rather than a brilliant course.

CHAPTER V

ANDOCIDES

STYLE

ANDOCIDES differs in one important respect from all the other Attic orators of the canon. He is not an artist. Each of the rest represents some theory, more or less definite, of eloquence as an art; and is distinguished, not merely by a faculty, but by certain technical merits, the result of labour directed to certain points in accordance with that theory. Among these experts Andocides is an amateur. In the course of an eventful life he spoke with ability and success on some occasions of great moment and great difficulty. But he brought to these efforts the minimum of rhetorical training. He relied almost wholly on his native wit and on a rough, but shrewd, knowledge of men.

This accounts for the comparatively slight attention paid to Andocides by the ancient rhetoricians and critics. Dionysius mentions him only twice; once, where he remarks that Thucydides used a peculiar dialect, which is not employed by "Andocides, Antiphon, or Lysias;"[1] again, where he says

[1] Dionys. *de Thuc.* c. 51.

that Lysias is the standard for contemporary Attic,
"as may be judged from the speeches of Andocides,
Critias and many others."[1] Both these notices recognise Andocides as an authority for the idiom of
his own day; and it is evident that he had a
philological interest for the critic. On the other
hand it is clear that Dionysius discovered in him no
striking power; for Andocides does not occur in his
long list of men foremost in the various departments of oratory.[2] Quintilian names him only in
one slighting allusion. Who, he asks, is to be our
model of Attic eloquence? "Let it be Lysias; for his
is the style in which the lovers of 'Atticism' delight.
At this rate we shall not be sent back all the way
to Andocides and Coccus."[3] It has been thought
that Quintilian refers to the Coccus mentioned by
Suidas as a pupil of Isocrates; but, however this
may be, the context is enough to show that he
means to mark, not the antiquity, but the inferiority
(in his view) of the two men. When Herodes Atticus
was told by his Greek admirers that he deserved
to be numbered with the Attic Ten, he turned off
the compliment, with an adroitness which his biographer commends, by saying—"At all events I am
better than Andocides."[4] More definite censure is
expressed in the compact criticism of Hermogenes :—

---

[1] de Lys. c. 2.

[2] de Isaeo, cc. 19 ff.

[3] Quint. XII. 10. § 21. *Nam quis erit hic Atticus? Sit Lysias; hunc enim amplectuntur amatores istius nominis modum. Non igitur iam usque ad Coccum et Andocidem remittemur.*

[4] Philostratus, *Vit. Her. Att.* II. 1. § 14, p. 564 ed. Kayser. βοώσης δὲ ἐπ' αὐτὸν τῆς Ἑλλάδος καὶ καλούσης αὐτὸν ἕνα τῶν δέκα, οὐχ ἡττήθη τοῦ ἐπαίνου, μεγάλου δοκοῦντος, ἀλλ' ἀστειότατα πρὸς τοὺς ἐπαινέσαντας, Ἀνδοκίδου μὲν, ἔφη, βελτίων εἰμί.

"Andocides aims at being a political orator, but does not quite achieve it. His figures want clear articulation; his arrangement is not lucid; he constantly tacks on clause to clause, or amplifies in an irregular fashion, using parentheses to the loss of a distinct order. On these accounts he has seemed to some a frivolous and generally obscure speaker. Of finish and ornament his share is small; he is equally deficient in fiery earnestness. Again, he has little, or rather very little, of that oratorical power which is shown in method; general oratorical power he has almost none."[1]

The phrase "political oratory" as used by Hermogenes has two senses, a larger and a narrower. In the larger sense it denotes all public speaking as opposed to scholastic declamation, and comprises the deliberative, the forensic, the panegyric styles. In the narrower sense it denotes practical oratory, deliberative or forensic, as opposed not only to scholastic declamation but also to that species of panegyric speaking in which no definite political question is discussed.[2] Here, the narrower sense is

---

[1] Hermog. περὶ ἰδεῶν, B. c. XI. (vol. II. p. 416 Spengel *Rhet. Gr.*):—ὁ δὲ 'Ανδοκίδης πολιτικὸς μὲν εἶναι προαιρεῖται, οὐ μὴν πάνυ γε ἐπιτυγχάνει τούτου· ἀδιάρθρωτος γάρ ἐστιν ἐν τοῖς σχήμασι καὶ ἀδιευκρίνητος καὶ τὰ πολλὰ ἐπισυνάπτει τε καὶ περιβάλλει ἀτάκτως διὰ τὸ ταῖς ἐπεμβολαῖς χωρὶς εὐκρινείας χρῆσθαι, ὅθεν ἔδοξέ τισι φλύαρος καὶ ἄλλως ἀσαφὴς εἶναι· ἐπιμελείας δὲ αὐτῷ καὶ κόσμου πάνυ βραχὺ μέτεστι, γοργότητός τε ὡσαύτως. καὶ μέντοι καὶ τῆς κατὰ μέθοδον δεινότητος ὀλίγον ἀλλὰ καὶ σφόδρα ὀλίγον ἔχει, τῆς δ' ἄλλης σχεδὸν οὐδ' ὅλως.

[2] For the larger sense, see περὶ ἰδεῶν, B. c. X. περὶ τοῦ πολιτικοῦ λόγου: in which chapter he says, τούτου δὲ τοῦ λόγου τοῦ πολιτικοῦ ὁ μέν ἐστι συμβουλευτικὸς ὁ δὲ δικανικὸς ὁ δὲ πανηγυρικός. For the narrower sense, see c. XI. περὶ τοῦ ἁπλῶς πολιτικοῦ λόγου: and c. XII. περὶ τοῦ ἁπλῶς πανηγυρικοῦ. It is in the narrower sense—that is, as including deliberative and forensic speaking only, and excluding all epideictic speaking, on whatever subject—that πολιτικὸς λόγος is gener-

intended. When Hermogenes says that Andocides does not succeed in being a "political" speaker, he means that Andocides does not exhibit—for instance, in the speech On his Return and in the speech On the Peace—the characteristic excellences of deliberative speaking; nor—for instance in the speech On the Mysteries—the characteristic excellences of forensic speaking. What Hermogenes took these excellences to be, he explains at length in another place; the chief of them are these three :—clearness; the stamp of truth; fiery earnestness.[1]

The first and general remark of Hermogenes upon Andocides implies, then, that he is wanting in these qualities. The special remarks which follow develop it. They refer partly to his arrangement of subject-matter, partly to his style of diction. He is said to have little "power" (or "cleverness") "of method"; that is, little tact in seeing where, and how, each topic should be brought in ;[2] he "amplifies"[3] un-

ally used : see *c.g.* the Ῥητορικὴ πρὸς Ἀλέξανδρον, c. 1. (Spengel), δύο γένη τῶν πολιτικῶν εἰσὶ λόγων, τὸ μὲν δημηγορικὸν τὸ δὲ δικανικόν. Cf. Isocr. κατὰ σοφ. § 19.

[1] See περὶ ἰδ. B. c. X. passim : esp. *ad init.* φημὶ τοίνυν δεῖν ἐν τῷ τοιούτῳ λόγῳ πλεονάζειν μὲν ἀεὶ τόν τε τὴν σαφήνειαν ποιοῦντα τύπον καὶ τὸν ἠθικόν τε καὶ ἀληθῆ καὶ μετὰ τούτους τὸν γοργόν.

[2] The distinction drawn by Hermogenes in his criticism upon Andocides between ἡ κατὰ μέθοδον δεινότης and what he calls ἡ ἄλλη δεινότης is explained by his own writings. His treatise Περὶ μεθόδου δεινότητος discusses the proper occasion (καιρὸς ἴδιος, c. 1.) for using the various figures and arts of rhetoric. It is a treatise upon Rhetorical Tact. By ἡ ἄλλη δεινότης he means simply what he speaks of in περὶ ἰδ. B. c. XI., περὶ δεινότητος :—oratorical power in the largest and most general sense, including all particular excellences whatsoever.

[3] περιβάλλει. Hermogenes uses the terms περιβολή, περιβάλλειν in a special technical sense, for which it is difficult to find any precise English equivalent. "Amplification" perhaps comes nearest. There are two sorts of περιβολή: (1) κατ' ἔννοιαν—when some special statement is prefaced by a general statement : *e.g.* πονηρὸν ὁ συκοφάντης ἀεί· τοῦτο δὲ καὶ φύσει κίναδος τἀνθρώπιόν ἐστι: (2) κατὰ λέξιν, when a fact is related with all

necessarily, by detailing circumstances unnecessary for his point; he obscures the order of his ideas by frequent parentheses, or by adding, as an afterthought, something which ought to have come earlier. As regards diction, in the first place his "figures" are said to be "wanting in clear articulation" (ἀδιάρθρωτα). Hermogenes elsewhere[1] enumerates thirteen "figures" of rhetoric, which are either certain fixed modes of framing sentences, such as the antithesis and the period; or (in the phrase of Caecilius) "figures of thought," such as irony and dilemma.[2] Hermogenes means that Andocides does not use "figures" of either sort with precision; he does not work them out to an incisive distinctness; he leaves them "inarticulate"—still in the rough, and with their outlines dull. Again Andocides has little "finish" (ἐπιμέλεια)—a term by which his critic means refinement and smoothness in composition.[3] Lastly, Andocides is said to be wanting in "fiery earnestness." The word γοργότης, which we have attempted thus to paraphrase, plays a very important part in the rhetorical terminology of Hermogenes: it describes one of the three cardinal excellences of "political" oratory.[4] Perhaps no simple English equivalent can

its attendant circumstances: *e.g.* ὑπεσχόμην χορηγήσειν· πότε; τρίτον ἔτος τουτί· ποῦ; ἐν τῇ ἐκκλησίᾳ. διὰ τί; οὐ καθεστηκότος χορηγοῦ, κ.τ.λ. See Herm. περὶ ἰδ. A. c. XI.

[1] Hermog. περὶ εὑρέσεων Δ.—Ch. I. is περὶ λόγου σχημάτων in general: cc. II.-XIV. discuss the several σχήματα.

[2] See supra, p. 28.

[3] See the chapter περὶ ἐπιμελείας καὶ κάλλους, Hermog. περὶ ἰδ. A. c. XII.

where he opposes κάλλος τι καὶ εὐρυθμία to τὸ ἀμελὲς καὶ ἄρρυθμον: and observes, πλεῖον δέ τι τῆς ἐπιμελείας καὶ τοῦ κάλλους ἔχουσιν αἱ μικραὶ τῶν λέξεων καὶ δι' ὀλίγων συγκείμεναι συλλαβῶν· οἷον, περὶ τοῦ πῶς ἀκούειν ὑμᾶς ἐμοῦ δεῖ (from Dem. *de Coron.* § 2). So the use of short, simple words may be a mark of ἐπιμέλεια—showing how the notion of *refinement* comes into it.

[4] περὶ ἰδ. B. c. X. ad init.

be found for it. But Hermogenes has explained clearly what he means by it. He means earnest feeling, especially indignation, uttered in terse, intense, sometimes abrupt language. It is to a strong and noble emotion what "keenness" (ὀξύτης) and "tartness" (δριμύτης) are to a lower kind of eagerness. The lofty invectives of Demosthenes against Philip supply Hermogenes with his best examples of it.[1]

We have now seen the worst that can be said of Andocides from the point of view of the technical Rhetoric; and it must be allowed that, from that point of view, the condemnation is tolerably complete. Now the canon of the Ten Attic Orators was probably drawn up at the time when scholastic rhetoric was most flourishing, and when, therefore, the standard of criticism used by Hermogenes and Herodes was the common one. It may seem surprising, then, that Andocides was numbered in the decad at all. Critias, his contemporary, whom so many ancient writers praise highly, might be supposed to have had stronger claims; and the fact that the memory of Critias as a statesman was hateful, is not enough in itself to explain his exclusion from a literary group.[2] Probably one reason, at least,

---

[1] See the chapter περὶ γοργότητος (περὶ ἰδ. B. c. 1.). He there says that γοργότης is the opposite of slackness and languor (τὸ ἀνειμένον καὶ ὕπτιον):—that it usually expresses itself in the trenchant style (διὰ τοῦ τμητικοῦ γίνεται τύπου). He cites as examples of γοργότης the opening of the Third Philippic: also de Coron. § 10. ἔστι τοίνυν οὗτος ὁ πρῶτος: κ.τ.λ., and several other passages from the same speech: de falsa Legat. § 24. τί γὰρ καὶ βουλόμενοι κ.τ.λ.

[2] K. O. Müller says (Hist. Gr. Lit. c. XXXIII. Vol. II. p. 115 n., ed. Donaldson). "It is surprising that Critias was not rather enrolled among the Ten: but perhaps his having been one of the Thirty stood in his way."

for the preference given to Andocides was the great interest of the subjects upon which he spoke. The speech On the Mysteries, supplying, as it does, the picturesque details of a memorable event, had an intrinsic value quite apart from its merits as a composition. The speech On the Peace with Lacedaemon, again, gives a clear picture of a crisis in the Corinthian War; and is an illustration, almost unique in its way, of Athenian history, at the time just after the rebuilding of the walls by Conon, when, for the first time since Aegospotami, Athenian visions of empire were beginning to revive. As Lycurgus seems to have owed his place among the Ten chiefly to his prominence as a patriot, so Andocides may have been recommended partly by his worth as an indirect historian. Again, Dionysius, as we have seen, recognised at least the philological value of Andocides. It is further possible that even rhetoricians of the schools may have found him interesting as an example of merely natural eloquence coming between two opposite styles of art; between the formal grandeur of Antiphon and the studied ease of Lysias.

It is a result of the precision with which the art of rhetoric was systematized in the Greek and Roman schools that much of the ancient criticism upon oratory is tainted by a radical vice. The ancient critics too often confound literary merit with oratorical merit. They judge too much from the standpoint of the reader, and too little from the standpoint of the hearer. They analyse special features of language and of method; they determine with nicety

General tendency of ancient criticism upon oratory. Unjust to Andocides.

the rank of each man as a composer; but they too often forget that, for the just estimation of his rank as a speaker, the first thing necessary is an effort of imaginative sympathy. We must not merely analyse his style; we must try to realise the effect which some one of his speeches, as a whole, would have made on a given audience in given circumstances. As nearly all the great orators of antiquity had been trained in the rudiments of the technical rhetoric, the judgment upon their relative merits is not, as a rule, much disturbed by this tendency in their critics. It may often, indeed, be felt that the judgment, however fair in itself, is based too much upon literary grounds. But, in most cases, so far as we can judge, no great injustice is done. Criticism of this kind may, however, happen to be unjust; and it has certainly been unjust in the case of Andocides. Others far excel him in finish of style, in clearness of arrangement, in force and in fire; but no one can read the speech On the Mysteries (for instance) without feeling that Andocides was a real orator. The striking thing in that speech is a certain undefinable tone which assures even the modern reader that Andocides was saying the right things to the judges, and knew himself to be saying the right things. He is, in places, obscure or diffuse; he sometimes wanders from the issue, once or twice into trivial gossip; but throughout there is this glow of a conscious sympathy with his hearers. He may not absolutely satisfy the critics; but he was persuading, and he felt with triumph that he was persuading, the judges.

It is somewhat difficult to analyse the style of a speaker whose real strength lay in a natural vigour directed by a rough tact; and who, in comparison with other Greek orators, cared little for literary form. An attempt at such an analysis may, however, start from the four epithets given to Andocides in the Plutarchic Life.¹ He is there said to be "simple" (ἁπλοῦς); "inartificial in arrangement" (ἀκατάσκευος); "plain" (ἀφελής); and "sparing of figures" (ἀσχημάτιστος). The first two epithets apparently refer to the order in which his thoughts are marshalled; the last two, to the manner in which they are expressed. We will first speak of the latter, and then come back to the former.

Four epithets given to the style of Andocides by the author of the Plutarchic Life.

The sense in which the diction of Andocides is "plain" will be best understood by a comparison with Antiphon and Lysias. Antiphon consciously strives to rise above the language of daily life; he seeks to impress by a display of art. Lysias carefully confines himself to the language of daily life; he seeks to persuade by the use of hidden art. Andocides usually employs the language of daily life; he is free, or almost free, from the archaisms of Antiphon, and writes in the new-Attic dialect, the dialect of Lysias and his successors.² On the other hand, he does not confine himself to a rigid simplicity. In his warmer or more vigorous passages, especially of invective or of intreaty, he often employs phrases or

The diction of Andocides is "plain" (ἀφελής),

---

¹ [Plut.] *Vit. Andoc.* § 15, ἔστι δὲ ἁπλοῦς καὶ ἀκατάσκευος ἐν τοῖς λόγοις, ἀφελής τε καὶ ἀσχημάτιστος.

² As exceptions may be noted the frequent use of the formula τοῦτο μέν..τοῦτο δέ (*e.g. de Myst.* § 103: *de Red.* § 16: *de Pace*, § 40): and of the dative οἷ—avoided, as a rule, by the other orators: *e.g. de Myst.* §§ 15, 38, 40, 41, 42, etc.

expressions borrowed from the idiom of Tragedy.[1] These, being of too decidedly poetical a colour, have a tawdry effect; yet it is evident that they have come straight from the memory to the lips; they are quite unlike prepared fine things; and they remind us, in fact, how really natural a speaker was Andocides,—neither aiming, as a rule, at ornament, nor avoiding it on principle when it came to him. The "plainness" of Lysias is an even, subtle, concise plainness, so scrupulous to imitate nature that nature is never suffered to break out; the "plainness" of Andocides is that of a man who, with little rhetorical or literary culture, followed chiefly his own instinct in speaking. Lysias had at his command all the resources of technical rhetoric, but so used them towards producing a sober, uniform effect, that his art is scarcely felt at any particular point; it is felt only in the impression made by the whole. Andocides had few of such resources. As his biographer says, he is "sparing of figures." Here the distinction

and sparing of figures (ἀσχημάτιστος).

[1] *E.g. De Myst.* § 29, οἱ λόγοι τῶν κατηγόρων ταῦτα τὰ δεινὰ καὶ φρικώδη ἀνωρθίαζον: (cf. Aesch. *Choeph.* 271, ἐξορθιάζων πολλά). *Ib.* § 67, πίστιν τῶν ἐν ἀνθρώποις ἀπιστοτάτην. *Ib.* § 68, ὁρῶσι τοῦ ἡλίου τὸ φῶς—a phrase which, however, occurs also in the fragment of the speech of Lycurgus against Lysicles. *Ib.* § 99, ὦ συκοφάντα καὶ ἐπίτριπτον κίναδος: (cf. Soph. *Ai.* 104, τοὐπίτριπτον κίναδος). *Ib.* § 146 (γένος) οἴχεται πᾶν πρόρριζον: (cf. Soph. *Electra* 765 πρόρριζον... ἔφθαρται γένος). *De Pace,* § 34, εἰρήνης πέρι: cf. Arist. *Poet.* c. 22, where the collocation Ἀχίλλεως πέρι instead of περὶ Ἀχίλλεως is specially instanced as a violation of the idiom (διάλεκτος) of ordinary life. Add to these examples the use of the poetical φρενῶν in *De Red.* § 7, τοιαύτην συμφορὰν τῶν φρενῶν: which, however, occurs also in the peroration of Demosth. *de Corona,* § 324, τούτοις βελτίω τινὰ νοῦν καὶ φρένας ἐνθείητε. Both instances, perhaps, come under the principle of Aristotle (*Rhet.* III. 7. § 11) that unusual or poetical words μάλιστα ἁρμόττει λέγοντι παθητικῶς. The writer of the speech κατ' Ἀλκιβιάδου has imitated the tragic vein which appears in the genuine speeches of Andocides: § 22, παρανομώτερος Αἰγίσθου γέγονεν. Cf. § 23.

already noticed between "figures of language" and "figures of thought" must be kept in mind. Andocides uses scarcely at all the "figures of language": that is, he seldom employs antitheses — aims at parallelism between the forms of two sentences—or studies the niceties of assonance.[1] His neglect of such refinements—which, in his day, constituted the essence of oratorical art, and which must have been more or less cultivated by nearly all public speakers —has one noticeable effect on his composition. There is no necessary connexion between an antithetical and a periodic style. But, in the time of Andocides, almost the only period in use was that which is formed by the antithesis or parallelism of clauses. Hence, since he rarely uses antitheses or parallelisms, Andocides composes far less in a periodic style than Thucydides or Antiphon or even Lysias. His sentences, in the absence of that framework, are constantly sprawling to a clumsy length; they are confused by parentheses, or deformed by supplementary clauses, till the main thread of the sense is often almost lost.[2] But while he thus dispenses with the

[1] In technical language, he seldom attempts, (1) ἀντίθεσις, the opposition of words, or of ideas, or of both, in the two corresponding clauses of a sentence: (2) παρίσωσις, a general correspondence between the *forms* of two sentences or clauses: (3) παρομοίωσις, correspondence of sound between words in the same sentence. See on these, Mr. Sandys's ed. of Isocr. *Ad Demonicum*, and *Panegyricus*, p. xiv. One special form of παρομοίωσις, viz. ὁμοιοτέλευτον, occurs *e.g.* in Andoc. *De Pace*, § 2, διά τε τὴν ἀπειρίαν τοῦ ἔργου διά τε τὴν ἐκείνων ἀπιστίαν: another special form, viz. παρήχησις, *e.g.* in *De Red.* § 24, εἰ γὰρ ὅσα οἱ ἄνθρωποι τῇ γνώμῃ ἁμαρτάνουσι, τὸ σῶμα αὐτῶν μὴ αἴτιόν ἐστι, κ.τ.λ.: where there is a general resemblance of sound between γνώμῃ and σῶμα. But such artifices, so common in the other orators, are rare and exceptional in Andocides.

[2] See *e.g. De Myst.* § 57 : εἰ μὲν γὰρ ἦν δυοῖν τὸ ἕτερον ἑλέσθαι, ἢ καλῶς ἀπολέσθαι ἢ αἰσχρῶς σωθῆναι, ἔχοι ἄν τις εἰπεῖν κακίαν εἶναι τὰ γενόμενα· | καίτοι πολλοὶ ἂν καὶ τοῦτο

ornamental "figures of language," Andocides uses largely those so-called "figures of thought" which give life to a speech :—irony, indignant question, and the like.[1] This animation is indeed one of the points which most distinguish his style from the ordinary style of Antiphon, and which best mark his relative modernism.

The method of Andocides is simple (ἁπλοῦς) and inartificial (ἀκατάσκευος).

As Andocides is "plain" in diction and avoids ornamental figures, so he is also "simple" in treatment of subject-matter, and avoids an artificial ar-

εἵλοντο, τὸ ζῆν περὶ πλείονος ποιησάμενοι τοῦ καλῶς ἀποθανεῖν· | ὅπου δὲ τούτων τὸ ἐναντιώτατον ἦν, | σιωπήσαντι μὲν αὐτῷ τε αἴσχιστα ἀπολέσθαι μηδὲν ἀσεβήσαντι, ἔτι δὲ τὸν πατέρα περιιδεῖν ἀπολόμενον καὶ τὸν κηδεστὴν καὶ τοὺς συγγενεῖς καὶ ἀνεψιοὺς τοσούτους, οὓς οὐδεὶς ἀπώλλυεν ἢ ἐγὼ μὴ εἰπὼν ὡς ἕτεροι ἥμαρτον· | Διοκλείδης μὲν γὰρ ψευσάμενος ἔδησεν αὐτούς, σωτηρία δὲ αὐτῶν ἄλλη οὐδεμία ἦν ἢ πυθέσθαι Ἀθηναίους πάντα τὰ πραχθέντα· | φονεὺς οὖν αὐτῶν ἐγιγνόμην ἐγὼ μὴ εἰπὼν ὑμῖν ἃ ἤκουσα.

Here the parenthesis, καίτοι πολλοί ...τοῦ καλῶς ἀποθανεῖν, first of all disturbs the original plan of the antithesis; this plan is resumed by the words ὅπου δὲ τὸ ἐναντιώτατον ἦν: but then the speaker goes off into a new antithesis, σιωπήσαντι μέν, κ.τ.λ., which is never completed; for the clause οὓς οὐδεὶς ἀπώλλυεν ἢ ἐγώ, κ.τ.λ., leads to a new parenthesis in explanation, Διοκλείδης μὲν γὰρ ... τὰ πραχθέντα: and the final clause, φονεὺς οὖν αὐτῶν ἐγιγνόμην, κ.τ.λ., is a conclusion drawn from this parenthesis, not the proper completion of that second member of the original antithesis which the words ὅπου δὲ τὸ ἐναντιώτατον ἦν commenced.

This is a strong example; but it is typical of the perplexity in which many passages of Andocides are involved through the same cause—imperfect or careless structure of antithesis.

[1] Among the minor σχήματα διανοίας used by Andocides, asyndeton is one of the most frequent. It often adds life and vigour to his style: see e.g. De Myst. § 16 :—τρίτη μήνυσις ἐγένετο. ἡ γυνὴ Ἀλκμαιωνίδου, γενομένη δὲ καὶ Δάμωνος— Ἀγαρίστη ὄνομα αὐτῇ—αὕτη ἐμήνυσεν, κ.τ.λ.: cf. §§ 33, 115, 127. He also uses the figure called ἀναφορά— i.e. the emphatic repetition of a word at the beginning of successive clauses: and ὑποφορά—the "suggestion" of some argument or objection which is then refuted. In De Myst. § 148, ἀναφορά and ὑποφορά occur together:—τίνα γὰρ καὶ ἀναβιβάσομαι δεησόμενον ὑπὲρ ἐμαυτοῦ; τὸν πατέρα; ἀλλὰ τέθνηκεν. ἀλλὰ τοὺς ἀδελφούς; ἀλλ' οὐκ εἰσίν. ἀλλὰ τοὺς παῖδας; ἀλλ' οὔπω γεγένηνται. ὑμεῖς τοίνυν καὶ ἀντὶ πατρὸς ἐμοὶ καὶ ἀντὶ ἀδελφῶν καὶ ἀντὶ παίδων γένεσθε· εἰς ὑμᾶς καταφεύγω καὶ ἀντιβολῶ καὶ ἱκετεύω· ὑμεῖς με παρ' ὑμῶν αὐτῶν αἰτησάμενοι σώσατε.

rangement.[1] His two speeches before the ecclesia—
that On his Return and that On the Peace—show,
indeed, no distinct or systematic partition. In his
speech On the Mysteries he follows, with one difference, the arrangement usually observed by Antiphon and more strictly by Lysias. There is a
proem, followed by a short prothesis or general statement of the case; then narrative and argument;
lastly epilogue.[2] But the narrative as a whole is not
kept distinct from the argument as a whole. Each
section of the narrative is followed by the corresponding section of the argument. Dionysius notices
such interfusion as a special mark of art in Isaeus.[3]
In Andocides it is rather a mark of artlessness. He
had a long story to tell, and was unable, or did not

[1] As he is ἀφελής and ἀσχημάτιστος, so he is also ἁπλοῦς and
ἀκατάσκευος. The word ἀκατάσκευος
is, indeed, often closely synonymous with ἀφελής and ἁπλοῦς: e.g.
Dionys. *Isae.* c. 7, ἀκατάσκευον φαίνεται εἶναι καὶ ὡς ἂν ἰδιώτης τις
εἰπεῖν δύναιτο τὸ εἰρημένον: cf. Ernesti,
Lex. Tech. Gr. Rhet. s.v., who
quotes from Menander, διαιρ. ἐπιδ.
p. 624, εἶδος ἀπαγγελίας ἁπλοῦν
ἀφελές καὶ ἀκατάσκευον. But in one
or two places the usage of Dionysius
seems to confirm the view that the
author of the Plutarchic Life of
Andocides meant ἁπλοῦς and ἀκατάσκευος to refer mainly to arrangement of subject-matter, as the
other two epithets refer mainly to
diction. Contrasting the method
of Lysias with the method of Isaeus,
Dionysius says (*Isae.* c. 3): παρὰ
Λυσίᾳ μὲν οὐ πολλὴν τὴν ἐπιτέχνησιν
οὔτ' ἐν μερισμοῖς τῶν πραγμάτων
οὔτ' ἐν τῇ τάξει τῶν ἐνθυμημάτων
οὔτ' ἐν ταῖς ἐξεργασίαις αὐτῶν (τις)
ὄψεται· ἁπλοῦς γὰρ ὁ ἀνήρ. Again,
he says (*ib.*) that Isaeus "in proportion as he falls short of the
other's grace, excels him in cleverness of artificial arrangement"—ὅσον
ἀπολείπεται τῆς χάριτος ἐκείνης, τοσοῦτον ὑπερέχῃ τῇ δεινότητι τῆς
κατασκευῆς. In the essay of
Dionysius on Thucydides, again
(c. 27), τὸ φορτικὸν τῆς λέξεως καὶ
σκολιὸν καὶ δυσπαρακολούθητον
are opposed to τὸ ἀγενὲς καὶ χαμαι-
πετὲς καὶ ἀκατάσκευον.

[2] Proem, §§ 1–7: prothesis, §§ 8–
10: narrative and argument, §§ 11–
139: epilogue, §§ 140–150.

[3] Dionys. *Isae.* § 14: τότε δὲ με-
ρίσας αὐτὰς (τὰς διηγήσεις) εἰς τὰ
κεφάλαια, καὶ παρ' ἕκαστον αὐτῶν τὰς
πίστεις παρατιθείς, ἐκμηκύνει τε μᾶλλον
καὶ ἐκβαίνει τὸ τῆς διηγήσεως σχῆμα,
τῷ συμφέροντι χρώμενος: "sometimes
he divides his statement under
heads; and, presenting the proofs
under the several heads, adds somewhat to the length of the narrative,
while he departs, as may be expedient, from its strict form."

try, to tell it concisely. The very length of his narrative compelled him to break it up into pieces and to comment upon each piece separately. He has not effected this without some loss of clearness, and one division of the speech is thoroughly confused.[1] But it should be remembered that a defective ordering of topics, though a grave fault, was less serious for Andocides than it would have been for a speaker in a different style. The main object of Andocides was to be in sympathy with his audience—amusing them with stories, however irrelevant—putting all his arguments in the most vivid shape—and using abundant illustration. Lucid arrangement, though always important, was not of firstrate importance for him. His speeches were meant to carry hearers along with them rather than to be read and analysed at leisure.

Andocides has little skill in the commonplaces of rhetorical argument.

But it is not merely in special features of diction or of arrangement that Andocides is seen to be no technical rhetorician. A disciple of the sophistical rhetoric learned to deal copiously and skilfully with those commonplaces of argument which would be available in almost any case. His education taught him to prefer general argument to argument from particular circumstances, unless these were especially easy to manipulate. We see this in Antiphon's First Tetralogy: it is a model exercise in making the utmost of abstract probabilities as inferred from facts which are very slightly sketched. In the speech On the Murder of Herodes the statement of the facts is hurried over, and there is no attempt at a close and searching analysis of them. But for a speaker un-

[1] §§ 92-150.

skilled in rhetorical commonplace the particulars of any given subject would be everything. Picturesque narration, shrewd inference from small circumstances, lively illustration of character, would naturally be his chief resources. And so it is with Andocides. His strength is in narrative, as the strength of Antiphon is in argument. Andocides relies on his case, Antiphon on his science; it is only Lysias who hits the masterly mean, who makes his science the close interpreter of his case, who can both recount and analyse. But, although the narrative element in Andocides exceeds the just proportion always observed by Lysias, it is, from a literary point of view, a great charm. The speech On the Mysteries is full of good bits of description, lively without set effort to be graphic. For instance, the scene in the prison, when Andocides was persuaded to denounce the real mutilators of the Hermae:—

Strength of Andocides in narrative.

" When we had all been imprisoned in the same place; when night had come, and the gaol had been closed; there came, to one his mother, his sister to another, to another his wife and children; and there arose a piteous sound of weeping and lamentation for the troubles of the hour. Then Charmides (he was my cousin, of my own age, and had been brought up with me in our house from childhood) said to me: —' Andocides, you see how serious our present dangers are; and though hitherto I have always shrunk from saying anything to annoy you, I am forced by our present misfortune to speak now. All your intimates and companions except us your relations have either been put to death on the charges which threaten us with destruction, or have taken to flight and pronounced themselves guilty. If you have heard anything about this affair which has occurred, speak it out, and save our lives—save yourself in the first place, then your father, whom you ought to love very dearly, then your brother-in-law, the husband of your only sister,—your other kinsmen, too, and near friends, so many of them; and me also, who have never given you any annoyance in all my life, but am most zealous for you and for your interests, whenever anything is to be done.' When Charmides said this, judges, and when the others besought and entreated me severally, I thought to myself,—'most miserable and unfortunate of men, am I to see my own kinsfolk perish undeservedly—to see their lives sacrificed and their property confiscated, and in addition to this their names written up on tablets as sinners against the gods,—men who are wholly innocent of the matter,—am I to see moreover three hundred Athenians doomed to undeserved destruction and the State involved in the most serious calamities, and men nourishing suspicion against each other,—or shall I tell the Athenians just what I heard from Euphiletus himself, the real culprit?'"[1]

Another passage in the same speech illustrates the skill of Andocides in dramatising his narrative. He delighted to bring in persons speaking. Epichares, one of his accusers in this case, had been an agent of the Thirty Tyrants. He turns upon him.

[1] *De Myst.* §§ 48–51. Compare, as another graphic passage, the account in §§ 38–40 of the story told by Diocleides—how he had seen by moonlight the conspirators meeting in the orchestra of the theatre of Dionysus.

"Speak, slanderer, accursed knave—is this law valid or not valid? Invalid, I imagine, only for this reason,—that the operation of the laws must be dated from the archonship of Eucleides. So you live, and walk about this city, as you little deserve to do; you who, under the democracy, lived by pettifogging, and under the oligarchy—lest you should be forced to give back all the profits of that trade—became the instrument of the Thirty.

"The truth is, judges, that as I sat here, while he accused me, and as I looked at him, I fancied myself nothing else than a prisoner at the bar of the Thirty. Had this trial been in their time, who would have been accusing me? Was not this man ready to accuse, if I had not given him money? He has done it now. And who but Charicles would have been cross-examining me? 'Tell me, Andocides, did you go to Deceleia, and enforce the hostile garrison on your country's soil?'—'Not I.'—'How then? You ravaged the territory, and plundered your fellow-citizens by land or sea?'—'Certainly not.'—'And you did not serve in the enemy's fleet, or help to level the Long Walls, or to abolish the democracy?'—'None of these things have I done.'—'None? Do you think, then, that you will enjoy impunity, or escape the death suffered by many others?'

"Can you suppose, judges, that my fate, as your champion, would have been other than this, if I had been caught by the Tyrants? I should have been destroyed by them, as they destroyed many others, for having done no wrong to Athens."[1]

References of Andocides to the early history of Attica.

[1] *De Myst.* §§ 99-102.

The love of Andocides for narrative, wherever it can be introduced, is strikingly seen in his mode of handling his legal argument in the speech On the Mysteries. Instead of simply citing and interpreting the enactments upon which he relies, he reviews in order the events which led to the enactments being made.[1] The same tendency appears in his habit of drawing illustrations from the early history of Attica. These references are in many points loose and confused.[2] Andocides, however, is hardly a worse offender in this respect than (for instance) Aeschines;[3] and has more excuse. In the time of Andocides written history was a comparatively new invention, and most men knew the events even of their grandfathers' days only from hearsay. Nor does the apparent inaccuracy of Andocides in regard to earlier history affect his authority as a witness for events with which he was contemporary. The value of his testimony for the years 415–390 is unquestioned.

Love of Andocides for gossip.

Andocides sometimes shows his taste for narrative in a special form which deserves notice. He is a master of shrewd and telling gossip. He diverges from the main thread of his argument into anecdotes which will amuse his hearers, and either directly damage the adversary, or at least strike some chord favourable to himself. A part of the speech On the Mysteries is, in fact, made up of such stories (§§ 110–

---

[1] *De Myst.* §§ 70–91.
[2] Remarks on the historical references in *De Myst.* §§ 106–108, and in *De Pace*, §§ 3–7, will be found in ch. VI., in connexion with these speeches respectively.
[3] See *e.g.* Aeschin. *De Falsa Legat.*

§ 172, where Miltiades is spoken of as alive after Salamis: and *ib.* § 174, where the 1000 talents set apart in 431 B.C. against special need (Thuc. II. 24) are represented as the total sum then in the Athenian treasury.

136). Speaking, for instance, of the son of his accuser Callias, he reminds the judges that there was once a certain Hipponicus at Athens whose house was haunted by an avenging spirit—so said the children and the women: and the saying came true, for the man's son proved a very demon to him. Well, the house of Callias is haunted by a fiend of the same kind (§§ 130–131). In this trait Andocides resembles one, and one only, of the other Greek orators: it is precisely the impudent, unscrupulous cleverness of Aeschines. There is the same shrewd perception of what will raise a laugh or a sneer; the same adroitness, unchecked by self-respect, in making a point of this kind whenever the opportunity offers; the same command of coarse but telling abuse; the same ability and resolution to follow the workings, and profit by the prejudices, of low minds. Akin to this taste for gossip is a certain proneness to sink into low comedy. There is a fragment of Andocides, describing the influx of country-people into Athens in 431 B.C., which will illustrate this. It has exactly the tone of the *Acharnians*:— Proneness of Andocides to low comedy.

"Never again may we see the colliers coming in from the hills to the town—the sheep and oxen and the waggons—the poor women and old men—the labourers arming themselves! Never more may we eat wild greens and chervil!"[1]

In passing judgment upon Andocides, it must be Summary.

---

[1] μὴ γὰρ ἴδοιμέν ποτε πάλιν ἐκ τῶν ὀρέων τοὺς ἀνθρακευτὰς ἥκοντας καὶ πρόβατα καὶ βοῦς καὶ τὰς ἁμάξας εἰς τὸ ἄστυ, καὶ γύναια καὶ πρεσβυτέρους ἄνδρας καὶ ἐργάτας ἐξοπλιζομένους· μηδὲ ἄγρια λάχανα καὶ σκάνδικας ἔτι φάγοιμεν. Quoted by Suidas, p. 3327 B, from a scholium on Ar. *Acharn.* 477: Sauppe, *Fragm. Oratt. Gr.* p. 166: Blass, *Andoc.* (Teubner) p. 97.

allowed that he possesses neither literary merit nor properly oratorical merit which can entitle him to rank with the greatest masters of Greek rhetorical prose. His language has neither splendour nor a refined simplicity; he is not remarkably acute in argument; and, compared with his contemporaries, he is singularly without precision in the arrangement of his ideas. His extant works present no passage conceived in the highest strain of eloquence; he never rises to an impassioned earnestness. On the other hand, his naturalness, though not charming, is genuine; he has no mannerisms or affectations; and his speeches have a certain impetus, a certain confident vigour, which assure readers that they must have been still more effective for hearers. The chief value of Andocides is historical. But he has also real literary value of a certain kind: he excels in graphic description. A few of those pictures into which he has put all the force of a quick mind—the picture of Athens panic-stricken by the sacrilege [1]—the scene of miserable perplexity in the prison [2]—the patriotic citizen arraigned before the Thirty Tyrants [3]—have a vividness which no artist could easily surpass, combined with a freshness which a better artist might possibly have lost.[4]

[1] *De Myst.* §§ 43–45.
[2] *Ib.* §§ 48–51.
[3] *Ib.* §§ 70–91.
[4] Sluiter's judgment (*Lectiones Andocideae*, p. 3) does not show much discrimination :—"At equidem, quanquam Andocidi orationem non tribuam ratione et arte excultam et politam ; subtilitatem tamen, impetum atque *gravitatem* illius sum admiratus. Arte Lysiae cedit, nervos plures habet et lacertos : vehemens imprimis in reprehendendo, in defendendo se gravis, ad misericordiam erga se movendam odiumque in adversarios excitandum plane compositus, *in proponendis diiudicandisque argumentis subtilis et acutus, dictione purus et elegans, plenus Attici saporis:* ut iure a Grammaticis in numerum sit relatus et inter decem collocatus principes."

CHAPTER VI

ANDOCIDES

WORKS

FOUR speeches ascribed to Andocides are extant, bearing the titles "On the Mysteries": "On his Return": "On the Peace with the Lacedaemonians": "Against Alcibiades." The speech On the Mysteries, as the chief extant work of its author, stands first in the manuscripts and the editions. But the second oration relates to an earlier passage in the life of Andocides, and may conveniently be considered first.

The speech of Andocides "On his Return" affords no further internal evidence of its own date than that it was spoken later than 411 and earlier than 405 B.C.[1] Blass places it in 409.[2] But a circumstance which he has not noticed seems to us to make it almost certain that the speech cannot have been delivered later than the summer of 410. Andocides lays stress upon the service which he has rendered to Athens by securing a supply of corn from Cyprus.

Speech "On his Return."

---

[1] Later than 411—as being a considerable time after the fall of the Four Hundred in June 411, §§ 13–16, etc.: and obviously earlier than Aegospotami—since (*e.g.*) the Peiraeus is open to corn-ships, § 21.—The notice in [Lys.] *in Andoc.* § 29 gives no help towards fixing the date.

[2] *Attisch. Bereds.* p. 278.

There had been a disappointment about this supply;
but he states that he has overcome the difficulty,—
that fourteen corn-ships will be in the Peiraeus almost
immediately, and that others are to follow.[1] Now
the event which had made this supply a matter of
anxiety to Athens was the stoppage of the usual
importations from the south coast of the Euxine.
In 411 she had lost the command of the Bosphorus
by the revolt of Chalcedon, and the command of the
Hellespont by the revolt of Abydus.[2] But, in 410,
the battle of Cyzicus was followed by the re-establishment of Athenian power in the Propontis and in its
adjacent straits. The corn-trade of the Euxine once
more flowed towards Athens; and, in the autumn of
410, Agis, from his station at Deceleia, saw with
despair the multitude of corn-ships which were running into the Peiraeus.[3] The benefit, therefore, for
which Andocides claims so much credit, would have
been no great benefit, had it been conferred later
than the middle of the year 410. The Four Hundred
were deposed about the middle of June 411; and it
would have been natural that Andocides should have
endeavoured to return at least in the course of the
following year.

As a speech on a private matter before the public
assembly, this oration belongs to the same class as
that which Demosthenes is said to have written for
Diphilus in support of his claim to be rewarded by

[1] §§ 20-21.

[2] See Grote, VIII. pp. 171 ff.

[3] Xen. *Hellen.* I. i. 35, Ἄγις δὲ ἐκ τῆς Δεκελείας ἰδὼν πλοῖα πολλὰ σίτου εἰς Πειραιᾶ καταθέοντα οὐδὲν ὄφελος ἔφη εἶναι τοὺς μετ' αὐτοῦ πολὺν ἤδη χρόνον Ἀθηναίους εἴργειν τῆς γῆς, εἰ μή τις σχήσοι καὶ ὅθεν ὁ κατὰ θάλατταν σῖτος φοιτᾷ.

the State.¹ Andocides is charged, in the speech of the pseudo-Lysias, with having gained admittance to the ecclesia by bribing its presidents.² It is unnecessary to believe this story. But the emphasis which he himself lays on the valuable information which he had previously given to the Senate³ suggests that, without some such recommendation, he would have found it difficult to obtain a hearing from the people.

The object of the speech is to procure the removal of certain disabilities under which he was alleged to lie. His disclosures in 415 were made under a guarantee of immunity from all consequences. But the decree of Isotimides, passed soon afterwards, excluded from the market-place and from temples all "who had committed impiety and who had confessed it;" and his enemies maintained that this decree applied to him.

In the proem he points out the malice or stupidity of the men who persist in rejecting the good offices which he is anxious to render to Athens; and refers to the importance of the communications which he has made in confidence to the Senate (§§ 1–4). His so-called crimes—committed in

Analysis.

---

¹ That is to say, it is a δημηγορία, but not properly a *deliberative* speech: not a true συμβουλευτικὸς λόγος. Dionysius mentions (*De Deinarcho*, c. 11) a δημηγορικὸς λόγος written for Diphilus, in which the latter urged before the ecclesia his own claim to certain public honours (δωρεαί). Dionysius thinks that this must have been written by Demosthenes, not by Deinarchus. Cf. Sauppe, *Fragm. Oratt. Gr.* p. 251.

² [Lys.] *in Andoc.* § 29, καταπλεύσας δὲ ἐκεῖθεν δεῦρο εἰς δημοκρατίαν εἰς τὴν ἑαυτοῦ πόλιν τοῖς μὲν πρυτάνεσιν ἔδωκε χρήματα ἵνα αὐτὸν προσαγάγοιεν ἐνθάδε, ὑμεῖς δ' αὐτὸν ἐξηλάσατε ἐκ τῆς πόλεως.

³ Andoc. *De Red.* § 19, ἐμοὶ τοίνυν τὰ μὲν ἤδη πεπραγμένα σχεδόν τι ἅπαντες ἂν εἰδείητε, τὰ δὲ μέλλοντά τε καὶ ἤδη πραττόμενα ἄνδρες ὑμῶν πεντακόσιοι ἐν ἀπορρήτῳ ἴσασιν, ἡ βουλή. The words ἄνδρες πεντακόσιοι deserve notice as a clever rhetorical touch: they imply a congratulation on the recent abolition of the Senate of *Four* Hundred.

"youth" and "folly"—are, he contends, his misfortunes. For the disclosures which he was driven to make five years before he deserves pity—nay, gratitude—rather than hatred (§§ 5–9).

He then speaks of his life in exile: of his services to the army at Samos in 411; of his return to Athens in the time of the Four Hundred; and of his imprisonment at the instance of Peisander, who denounced him as the friend of the democracy (§§ 10–16). Statesmen and generals serve the State at the State's expense; he has served it at his own charge. Nor has the end of these services been yet seen. The people will be soon in possession of the secrets which he has imparted to the Senate; and will soon see supplies of corn, procured by his intercession, enter the Peiraeus (§§ 17–21). In return for so much, he asks but one small boon—the observance of the promise of impunity under which he originally laid his information, but which was afterwards withdrawn through the influence of his enemies (§§ 22–23).

The peroration opens with a singular argument. When a man makes a mistake, it is not his body's fault: the blame rests with his mind. But he, since he made his mistake, has got a new mind. All that remains, therefore, of the old Andocides is his unoffending body (§ 24). As he was condemned on account of his former deeds, he ought now to be welcomed for his recent deeds. His family has ever been patriotic; his great-grandfather fought against the Peisistratidae; he, too, is a friend of the people. The people, he well knows, are not to blame for the breach of faith with him; they were persuaded to it by the same advisers who persuaded them to tolerate an oligarchy. They have repented of the oligarchy; let them repent also of the unjust sentence (§§ 25–28).

Remarks. There is a striking contrast between this defence

before the ecclesia and that which Andocides made on the same charges, some eleven years later, before a law-court. There he flatly denies that he is in any degree guilty; he turns upon his adversaries with invective and ridicule; he carries the whole matter with a high hand, speaking in a thoroughly confident tone, and giving free play to his lively powers of narration. Here it is quite otherwise. He speaks with humility and remorse of the "folly"—the "madness" of his youth; he complains feelingly of the persecution which he has suffered; he implores, in return for constant devotion to the interests of Athens, just one favour—a little favour, which will give his countrymen no trouble, but which will be to him a great joy. In 399 he is defiant; in 410 he is almost abject. In 410 the traces of guilt to which his enemies pointed were still fresh. Before his next speech was spoken, they had been dimmed, not by lapse of time only, but by that great wave of trouble which swept over Athens in 405, and which left all older memories faint in comparison with the memory of the Thirty Tyrants. Andocides the wealthy choregus, the president of the sacred mission, the steward of the sacred treasure, supported on his trial by popular politicians and by advocates chosen from his tribe, was a different person from the anxious suitor who, in the speech On his Return, implored, but could not obtain tolerance.

In the style of the speech there is little to remark except that its difference from that of the speech On the Mysteries exactly corresponds with the difference of tone. There the orator is diffuse, careless, lively;

here he is more compact—for he dared not treat a hostile assembly to long stories—more artificial—and decidedly more dull. Once only does the dramatic force of his natural style flash out—where he describes his appearance before the Council of the Four Hundred. "Some of the Four Hundred learned that I had arrived; sought me at once; seized me; and brought me before the Council. In an instant Peisander was at my side:—'Senators, I impeach this man for bringing corn and oar-spars to the enemy'" (§ 14).

Speech On the Mysteries.

The events with which the speech On the Mysteries is connected have been related in the life of Andocides. After his return to Athens (probably early in 402 B.C.), under favour of the general amnesty which followed the overthrow of the Thirty Tyrants, he had spent three years in the discharge of various public offices. At length, in 399 B.C., his enemies renewed their attack. During the festival of the Great Mysteries, which Andocides attended, in the autumn of that year, Cephisius laid an information against him before the Archon Basileus.

Mode of legal procedure.

Some obscurity hangs over the form of the accusation; we will give the account of it which appears most probable. When, in 415 B.C., Andocides made his disclosures, he did so on the guarantee of impunity (ἄδεια) which a special decree of the ecclesia had given to all who should inform. Subsequently, however, Isotimides proposed and carried a decree that all *who had committed impiety and had confessed it* should be excluded from the market-place and from the temples. The enemies of Andocides maintained that he came under this decree. This was the immediate cause of his quitting Athens in 415. In 410 he was unsuccessful in applying to have the sentence of disfranchisement cancelled. On his return in 402, however, nothing had been said at first about his disabilities.

His accusers now contended that he had broken the decree of Isotimides by attending the Mysteries and entering the Eleusinian Temple. To attend the festival or enter the temple unlawfully would, of course, be an impiety. The information which they laid against him charged him, therefore, on this ground, with impiety. It was an ἔνδειξις ἀσεβείας. But, in order to prove it, it was necessary to show that he came under the decree of Isotimides. It was necessary to show that he had committed impiety, as well as given information, in 415 B.C.

His defence is therefore directed to showing, in the first place, that he had not committed impiety at that time either by profaning the Mysteries or by mutilating the Hermae. The speech takes its ordinary title from the fact that the Mysteries form one of its prominent topics. But a more general title would have better described the range of its contents. It might have been more fitly called a Defence on a Charge of Impiety.

This view of the matter explains some difficulties. Andocides says (*de Myst.* § 71), "Cephisius has informed against me according to the existing law, but bases his accusation on the decree of Isotimides." That is, Cephisius laid against Andocides an ordinary ἔνδειξις ἀσεβείας. But the charge of ἀσέβεια rested on the assumption that he had broken the decree of Isotimides. He was not *directly* charged either with profaning the Mysteries or with mutilating the Hermae; his guilt in one or both of these matters was assumed. He proceeds to prove that this assumption is groundless; and that, therefore, the decree does not apply to him.[1]

The charge, like all connected with religion, was brought into court by the Archon Basileus. Since details connected with the Mysteries might be put in evidence, the judges were chosen exclusively from the initiated of the higher grade.[2] Cephisius, the chief accuser,[3] was assisted by Meletus, who had been implicated in the murder of Leon under the Thirty,[4] and by Epichares, who had been a member of their government.[5] On the same side were Callias[6] and Agyrrhius,[7] each of whom had a private quarrel with the accused. Andocides was supported by Anytus and Cephalus, both politicians of mark, and both popular for the part which they had taken in the restoration of the democracy.[8] Advocates

---

[1] Blass says: "Kephisios, der als Hauptkläger auch die Hauptrede hielt, hatte nach Andokides seine Anklage gegründet auf das Psephisma des Isotimides." (*Att. Bereds.* p. 300.) This statement, though substantially true, is not calculated to convey a clear idea of the *form* in which the accusation was preferred. Andocides was not simply accused of usurping certain rights which the decree of Isotimides had taken from him. That would have been an ἔνδειξις ἀτιμίας. He was accused specifically of *impiety*—the result of usurping such rights: it was an ἔνδειξις ἀσεβείας. Thus alone can we understand why the cause was brought into court by the Archon Basileus; and why death was the penalty. (Cf. *de Myst.* § 146 : [Lys.] *in Andoc.* § 55.)

[2] § 29 οἱ μεμυημένοι : § 31 μεμύησθε καὶ ἑωράκατε τοῖν θεοῖν τὰ ἱερά.

[3] § 71.   [4] § 94.   [5] § 95.

[6] §§ 110-131.   [7] §§ 132-136.

[8] § 150. For Anytus, see Xen. *Hellen.* ii. 3 §§ 42, 44 : for Cephalus, Demosth. *de Cor.* § 219.

chosen for him by his tribesmen were also in court. It is remarkable if, as there is reason to believe, two men engaged on different sides in this trial were, in the same year, united in preferring a more famous charge of impiety. Anytus undoubtedly, Meletus[1] probably, was the accuser of Socrates.

The speech On the Mysteries falls into three main divisions. In the first, Andocides shows his innocence in regard to the events of 415 B.C. In the second he shows that, in any case, the decree of Isotimides is now obsolete. In the third he deals with a number of minor topics.

I. §§ 1–69

1. (*Proem.*) §§ 1–7. Andocides dwells on the rancour of his enemies; insists on the fact of his having remained to stand his trial—instead of withdrawing to his property in Cyprus—as a proof of a good conscience; and appeals to the judges.[2]

2. §§ 8–10. He is perplexed as to what topic of his defence he shall first approach. After a fresh appeal to

Analysis.

---

[1] Meletus is mentioned in §§ 12 f., 35, 63, 94. He was a partisan of the Thirty (§ 94), and is clearly identical with the Meletus who went to Sparta as one of the envoys of the Town Party in 403 to discuss the terms of peace between the Town and the Peiraeus (Xen. *Hellen.* II. 4 § 36). All this agrees with what is known about the age of the Meletus who accused Socrates. See the article by Mr. Philip Smith in the Dict. of Greek and Roman Biography.

[2] Parts of this proem, viz. § 1 to the words πολλοὺς λόγους ποιεῖσθαι, and §§ 6, 7 αἰτοῦμαι οὖν—ἀκούσητε ἀπολογουμένου occur, slightly varied, in Lysias *de bonis Aristophanis*, §§ 2–5. Spengel and Blass believe that both Andocides and Lysias used a proem written by some third person; Andocides interpolating in it some matter of his own. It is true that the transition from § 5 to § 6 in the speech of Andocides is harsh, as if a patch had been made; but the transition from § 3 to § 4 is hardly less harsh, as Blass himself observes: indeed he suggests that a *second* borrowed proem may have been used there; but this is improbable. I should prefer to suppose that the whole proem is the work of Andocides himself, and that Lysias (whose speech belongs to 387 B.C.) abridged it.

the judges he resolves to begin with the facts relating to the Mysteries.

3. §§ 11–33. *The Mysteries Case.* He neither profaned them himself, nor informed against others as having profaned them. Four persons, on four distinct occasions, did, in fact, so inform: viz.—(i) Pythonicus, who produced the slave Andromachus, § 11: (ii) Teucrus, § 15: (iii) Agariste, § 16: (iv) Lydus, § 17. Lydus implicated Leogoras the father of Andocides. Leogoras, however, not only cleared himself, but got a verdict in an action which he brought against the senator Speusippus, §§ 17, 18. (This occasions a parenthesis, in which Andocides defends himself against the imputation of having denounced his father and relations: §§ 19–24.) The largest reward for information ($μήνυτρα$) was adjudged to Andromachus; the second, to Teucrus: §§ 27, 28. Andocides calls upon the judges to recognise his innocence as regards the Mysteries: §§ 29–33.

4. §§ 34–69. *The Hermae Case.* In this matter the chief informants were (i) Teucrus: §§ 34–35: (ii) Diocleides, whose allegations caused a general panic: §§ 36–46: (iii) Andocides himself. The circumstances, motives and results of his disclosure are stated at length: §§ 47–69.

II. §§ 70–91

It is argued that the decree of Isotimides is now void, because it has been cancelled by subsequent decrees, laws and oaths, §§ 70–72. These are next enumerated, as follows.

1. §§ 73–79. During the siege of Athens by the Lacedaemonians in 405 B.C. the decree of Patrocleides was passed, reinstating all the disfranchised.

2. § 80. After the truce with Sparta in 404, when the Thirty Tyrants were established, all exiles received free permission to return.

3. § 81. After the expulsion of the Thirty in 403 a general amnesty was proclaimed.

4. §§ 82–89. At the same time, in accordance with the decree of Tisamenus, a revision of the laws was ordered. This revision having been completed, four new general laws (νόμοι) were passed:—viz. (i) That no "unwritten" law should have force: (ii) That no decree (ψήφισμα) of ecclesia or senate should overrule a law (νόμος): (iii) That no law should be made against an individual (ἐπ' ἀνδρί, § 87): (iv) That decisions of judges or arbiters, pronounced under the former democracy, should remain valid: but that, in future, all decisions should be based on the code as revised in the archonship of Eucleides in 403 B.C. [This is expressed by the phrase χρῆσθαι νόμοις ἀπ' Εὐκλείδου ἄρχοντος, § 87.]

5. §§ 90, 91. Returning to the subject of § 81, Andocides recalls the terms of the oath of amnesty taken in 403 B.C. He then quotes the official oath of Senators and the official oath of Judges.

III. §§ 92–150 (end).

1. §§ 92–105. He shows that, if the amnesty is to be violated in his case, it may be violated to the cost of others also. The accusers, Cephisius, Meletus, and Epichares, as well as others, would, in various ways, be liable to punishment.

2. §§ 106–109. He illustrates the good effect of general amnesties by two examples from the history of Athens:— (i) the moderation shown after the expulsion of the Peisistratidae: (ii) an amnesty in the time of the Persian Wars.

3. §§ 110–136. He answers a charge made against him by Callias. Callias asserted that Andocides, terrified by the accusation hanging over him, had laid a suppliant's bough (ἱκετηρία) on the altar in the temple at Eleusis during the festival of the Great Mysteries. To take sanctuary, or to place a symbol of supplication, in that temple at that season,

was a capital offence (as implying the approach of guilt to the temple at a holy season). Andocides explains the motive of this false charge. Callias was seeking for his son an heiress whose hand was claimed by Andocides (§§ 110–123). This leads to a digression about a scandal connected with the birth of this son (§§ 124–131). He then attacks the abettors of Callias in this slander—especially Agyrrhius, a fraudulent tax-farmer who had a grudge against Andocides (§§ 132–136).

4. §§ 137–139. He ridicules the assertion made by the accuser, that the gods must have preserved so great a traveller from the dangers of the sea because they reserved him for the hemlock.

5. §§ 140–150. Peroration, on three topics chiefly:—(i) the credit which Athens has gained by her policy of amnesties—credit which the judges are bound to sustain: (ii) the public services of the ancestors of Andocides: (iii) his own opportunities for usefulness to the State hereafter, if he is acquitted.

Andocides was acquitted. Before speaking of the method and style of his speech, it is due to its great historical interest to notice some of the disputed statements of fact which it contains.

Historical matter in the Speech. 1. Does the speech represent that account of his own conduct which Andocides gave in 415 when he made his disclosures before the Council of Four Hundred? Next—had he, as a matter of fact, taken part in the mutilation of the Hermae? These two questions have been shortly discussed in Chapter IV.[1] Some reasons are there suggested for believing (1) that, in 415, Andocides had criminated himself as well as others: (2) that he was, in fact, innocent.

[1] p. 75.

2. In § 11 Pythonicus, who brought forward the evidence of the slave Andromachus, is named as the first denouncer of Alcibiades. "Some resident-aliens and slaves in attendance on their masters" (ἀκολούθων) are said by Thucydides (VI. 28) to have been the first accusers; and Plutarch adds that these were brought forward by Androcles. Androcles is mentioned by Andocides only in § 27, as claiming the reward (μήνυτρα) from the Senate. In order to reconcile Andocides with Thucydides, it must be supposed either (1) that the "resident-aliens and slaves" of Thucydides (VI. 28) were the witnesses of Pythonicus, and not, as Plutarch states (*Alcib.* 19), of Androcles: or (2) that they were the witnesses, some of Pythonicus, some of Androcles; and that those brought forward by Androcles did not criminate Alcibiades, although Androcles *afterwards* found witnesses who did so. The former supposition, which makes Plutarch inaccurate, seems the most likely.

3. In § 13 it is stated that, on Pythonicus making his accusations, Polystratus was at once arrested and executed, and that the other accused persons fled. It is certain, as Grote[1] observes, that Alcibiades was accused, but neither fled nor was brought to trial; and it would seem more probable, therefore, that the charge was dropped, for the time, in reference to the others also. On this point, however, it does not seem necessary to assume inaccuracy in Andocides. The position of Alcibiades, as a commander of the expedition on which the hopes of the people were set and which was about to sail, was wholly exceptional.

[1] *Hist. Gr.* III. p. 243.

The evidence against him may also have been of a different nature.

4. In § 13 there is an oversight. Among those denounced by Pythonicus was Panaetius. And it is said that all persons so denounced—except Polystratus, who was put to death—fled. But in § 68 Panaetius appears as leaving Athens in consequence of the later denunciation of Andocides. As the list in § 13 contains ten names in all, the speaker might easily have made a mistake about one of the number. Or the evidence against Panaetius—who is named last of the ten—may have been so weak that he was acquitted upon this first charge.

5. In § 34 it is said that some of the persons accused by Teucrus were put to death. To this Mr. Grote[1] opposes the fact that Thucydides (VI. 60) names as having suffered death only some of those who were denounced by Andocides. It seems unsafe, however, to conclude that the orator has made a wrong statement. The language of Thuc. VI. 53, ξυλλαμβάνοντες κατέδουν, hardly warrants the inference that imprisonment was the utmost rigour used in other cases. The statement of Andocides in § 34 is incidentally confirmed by the words which he ascribes to Charmides in § 49.

6. In § 38 Andocides quotes, without comment, the statement of Diocleides that he had seen the faces of some of the conspirators by the light of a full moon. Now Plutarch says that one of the informers (he does not give the name), being asked how he had recognised the faces of the mutilators, answered, " by the

[1] *Hist. Gr.* VII. 268.

light of the moon"; and was thus convicted of falsehood, it having been new moon on the night in question.[1] Diodorus (XIII. 2) tells the same story, without mentioning any name; but his account does not apply to Diocleides. Mr. Grote is unquestionably right in treating the new-moon story as a later fiction.[2] Andocides would not have failed to notice so fatal a slip on the part of Diocleides; nor is it likely that the informer would have made it.

7. In § 17 the action brought by Leogoras against Speusippus is mentioned directly after the evidence of Lydus. But it should be observed that it is mentioned parenthetically; and that the indefinite κἄπειτα does not fix its date at all. Leogoras was in the prison with his son (§ 50); and the action was doubtless not brought until after the disclosures of Andocides.

8. In § 45 the panic, during which the citizens kept watch under arms through the night, is placed in immediate connection with the informations of Diocleides, who caused this panic by representing the plot as widely spread. It is said, also, that the Boeotians took advantage of the alarm at Athens to march to the frontier. Now Thucydides (vi. 60) states that, during one night an armed body of citizens garrisoned the Theseion; but he puts this after the disclosures of Andocides, and connects it with the appearance of a Spartan force at the isthmus. Bishop Thirlwall justly remarks that, unless there were

---

[1] Plut. *Alc.* c. 20, εἰς δ' αὐτῶν ἐρωτώμενος ὅπως τὰ πρόσωπα τῶν ἑρμοκοπιδῶν γνωρίσειε, καὶ ἀποκρινάμενος ὅτι πρὸς τὴν σελήνην, ἐσφάλη τοῦ παντός, ἕνης καὶ νέας οὔσης ὅτε ταῦτ' ἐδρᾶτο.

[2] *Hist. Gr.* VII. p. 271.

two or more occasions on which the citizens kept armed watch, Andocides, who goes into minute detail, is more likely than Thucydides to be right about the time of it.[1]

9. In § 106 the expulsion from Athens of the tyrants—that is Hippias and his adherents—is described as following upon a battle fought ἐπὶ Παλ-ληνίῳ, which seems to mean "at the Pallenion," the temple of Athena Pallenis at Pallene, about 10 miles E.N.E. of Athens.[2] Now it was near this temple that Peisistratus, on his third return, won the victory which led to the final establishment of his tyranny, probably in 545 B.C.[3] But no battle at the same spot, or anywhere near it, is mentioned by any other authority in connexion with the expulsion of the Peisistratidae. According to Herodotus, the Lacedaemonians sent, in 510, an expedition under Cleomenes. Cleomenes, on entering Attica from the isthmus, met and routed the Thessalian cavalry of Hippias; advanced to Athens; and besieged the Peisistratidae, who presently capitulated.[4] Herodotus and Andocides can be reconciled only by supposing that the account of Herodotus is incomplete.[5] It

---

[1] *Hist. Gr.* III. p. 499 (appendix III. to ch. XXV.).

[2] Professor Rawlinson, in the *Journal of Philology*, Vol. I. No. 2, p. 25, questions whether the Παλ-λήνιον of Andocides means the temple of Athena at Pallene. The proper name of that temple was, he thinks, "the Pallenis." It appears to me, as I have endeavoured to show (*Journ. Philol.* Vol. II. No. 3, p. 48), that Παλληνίς is always the epithet of the goddess, not the name of the temple. I believe Παλλήνιον to be identical with what Herodotus (I. 62)

calls Παλληνίδος Ἀθηναίης ἱρόν.

[3] This is the date fixed on by Curtius (*Hist. Gr.* Vol. I. p. 359 tr. Ward). Clinton (*F. H.* II. p. 202) thinks 537 more probable.

[4] Her. v. 64.

[5] Professor Rawlinson thinks that there was a second battle (after that won by Cleomenes on entering Attica), in which the Alcmaeonidae and the other exiles fought on the Spartan side: and this battle, he suggests, may have been fought near Pallene (*Journ. Phil.* I. 2. pp. 25 ff.).

seems more probable, however, that Andocides has confused the scene of a battle won by Peisistratus with the scene of a battle lost by the Peisistratidae.¹

10. In § 107 it is said that when, later, the Persian king made an expedition against Greece, the Athenians recalled those who had been banished, and reinstated those who had been disfranchised, when the tyrants were expelled. No such amnesty is recorded in connexion with the first Persian invasion in 490; but Plutarch mentions such a measure as having been passed shortly before the battle of Salamis in 480.² Now the Persian invasion in 490 was undertaken for the purpose of restoring Hippias; and the invasion in 480 was undertaken partly at the instance of his family. Men (or their descendants) who had been banished or disfranchised in 510 would certainly not have been restored to Athenian citizenship in 490 or 480. Andocides seems, then, to have remembered vaguely that an act of amnesty was passed at Athens on some occasion during the Persian wars; to have placed this act in 490 instead of 480; and to have represented it as passed in favour of the very persons who would probably have been excluded from it.

11. In § 107 it is said of the Athenians:—
"They resolved to meet the barbarians at Marathon. ... They fought and conquered; they freed Greece and saved their country. And having done so great a deed, they thought it not meet to bear malice

---

¹ The view that the battle described by Andocides as fought ἐπὶ Παλληνίῳ is identical with that mentioned in Herod. v. 64 is held by Sluiter, Lect. Andoc. p. 6: Wordsworth, Athens and Attica, p. 198 note: Thirlwall, Hist. Gr. II. p. 80 note: Grote, Hist. Gr. IV. p. 165 note.

² Plut. Them. c. 11.

against any one for the past. Therefore, although through these things *they entered upon their city desolate, their temples in ashes, their walls and houses in ruins*, yet by concord they achieved the empire of Greece," etc. From this passage Valckenär,[1] Sluiter and Grote infer that Andocides has transferred the burning of Athens by Xerxes in 480 to the first invasion in 490. This is hardly a necessary inference. Andocides is speaking of the struggle with Persia— extending from 490 to 479—as a whole. He names Marathon: he does not name Salamis or Plataea. He merely says that, after the Athenians had "freed Greece," they came back to find their city in ruins.[2]

<small>Arrangement and Style of the Speech.</small>

It is impossible to read the speech On the Mysteries without feeling that, as a whole, it is powerful in spite of some evident defects. The arrangement is best in what we have called the first division (§§ 1–69), which deals with two distinct groups of facts, those relating to the Mysteries case and those relating to the Hermae case. These facts are stated in an order which is, on the whole, clear and natural, though not free from the parentheses of which Andocides was so fond, and of which sections 19–24 form an example. Less praise is due to the second part of the speech (§§ 70–91), devoted to the various enactments which had made the decree of

---

[1] See Valckenär's note, quoted and endorsed by Sluiter, *Lect. Andoc.* p. 48, and by Grote, IV. p. 165 n.:— "Confundere videtur Andocides diversissima: Persica sub Miltiade et Dario et victoriam Marathoniam, quaeque evenere sub Themistocle, Xerxis gesta. Hic urbem incendio delevit, non ille. Nihil magis est manifestum quam diversa ab oratore confundi.

[2] See the *Journal of Philology*, Vol. I. No. 1, p. 165, for a discussion of this passage.

Isotimides obsolete. It is at once full and obscure, giving needless, and withholding necessary, details. The third part (§§ 92–end) is a mere string of topics, unconnected with each other, and but slightly connected with the case. This confused appendix to the real defence is, however, significant. It shows the anxiety of Andocides to make the judges understand the rancorous personal feeling of his enemies; an anxiety natural in a man who for sixteen years had been pursued by unproved accusations. The passages about Callias and Agyrrhius probably had a stronger effect upon the court than any conventional appeal to compassion would have produced.

As regards style, the language of the speech is thoroughly unaffected and easy, plain without studied avoidance of ornament, and rising at the right places —as when he speaks of the old victories of freedom (§§ 106–109), and in the peroration (§§ 140–150). But the great merit of the composition is its picturesqueness, its variety and life. The scene in the prison (§§ 48–53) and the description of the panic at Athens (§§ 43–45) are perhaps the best passages in this respect. If Andocides had not many rhetorical accomplishments, he certainly had perception of character, and the knack of describing it. Diocleides bargaining with Euphemus (§ 40)—Charmides exhorting Andocides to save the prisoners (§§ 49, 50) —Peisander urging that Mantitheus and Aphepsion should be put on the rack (§ 43)—are well given in a few vivid touches.

The speech On the Peace with the Lacedaemonians belongs, as has been noticed in a former

Speech On the Peace with the Lacedaemonians.

chapter,[1] to the year 390. Athens, Thebes, Corinth and Argos had then been four years at war with Sparta. Andocides had just returned from an embassy to Sparta with a view to peace. The terms proposed by the Lacedaemonians were, as regarded Athens, permission to retain her walls and ships, and the restoration of Lemnos, Imbros and Scyros. The orator, speaking in debate in the ecclesia, urges that these terms should be accepted.

Analysis. The opponents of peace contend that peace with Lacedaemon is fraught with danger to the democracy (§§ 1–2). He meets this objection by instancing a number of cases in which peace with Sparta, so far from injuring the Athenian democracy, was productive of the greatest advantage to it. He cites (1) a peace with Sparta negotiated by Miltiades during a war in Euboea: §§ 3–5. (2) The Thirty Years' Truce, 445 B.C.: §§ 6–7. (3) The Peace of Nicias, 421 B.C.: §§ 8, 9.—The compulsory truce with Sparta in 404, followed by the establishment of the Thirty Tyrants, was not, properly speaking, a peace at all; and is therefore no exception to the rule that peace with Sparta has always been found salutary (§§ 10–12).

There is no good reason for continuing the war. The claims of Athens have now been recognised; the Boeotians desire peace; the hope of finally crushing Sparta is idle (§§ 13–16). Athens is the power which gains most by the peace now proposed (§§ 17–23). If Boeotia makes peace, Athens will be left with one weak ally, Corinth, and another who is a positive encumbrance—selfish Argos (§§ 24–27). Athens must not, here, prefer weak friends, as formerly she preferred Amorges to Xerxes II.; Egesta to Syracuse; Argos to Sparta (§§ 28–32). The speaker goes on to notice a variety of objections to the peace. Some say that walls

[1] Ch. IV. p. 82.

and ships are not money, and wish to recover their property abroad [τὰ σφέτερ' αὐτῶν τῆς ὑπερορίας, § 36] which was lost when the Athenian empire fell. But such men ought to remember that walls and ships were just the means by which the empire was won in the first instance (§§ 33–39).

In a peroration the assembly is reminded that the decision rests wholly with it; Argive and Corinthian envoys have come urging war; Spartan envoys, offering peace. The true plenipotentiaries are not the ambassadors, but those who vote in the ecclesia (§§ 40, 41).

According to the author of the Argument, the speech On the Peace was judged spurious by Dionysius[2] and Harpocration also doubted its authenticity.[3] Among modern critics, Taylor[4] and Markland[5] are the chief who have taken the same view; but they have a majority of opinions against them.[6] Probably the suspicions of Dionysius, like those of Taylor, arose mainly from the difficulties of the historical passage (§§ 3-6); and from the fact that this passage is found, slightly modified, in the speech of Aeschines On the Embassy. *Question of authenticity.*

It is said in §§ 3-5 that, when the Athenians "had the war in Euboea"—being then masters of Megara, Troezen and Pegae—Miltiades, son of Cimon, who had been ostracised, was recalled, and was sent to treat for peace at Sparta. A peace was *Historical difficulties.*

---

[1] πρεσβευτὰς οὖν πάντας ὑμᾶς ἡμεῖς οἱ πρέσβεις ποιοῦμεν.

[2] Auct. Argum. *ad fin.* ὁ δὲ Διονύσιος νόθον εἶναι λέγει τὸν λόγον.

[3] He quotes it thrice, but always with the addition εἰ γνήσιος.

[4] *Lectiones Lysiacae,* c. vi. (Vol. ii. p. 260, ed. Reiske).

[5] *Ad* Aeschin. *De Falsa Legat.* p. 302.

[6] Sluiter, *Lect. Andoc.* c. x. p. 205, and Valckenär quoted there: Ruhnken, *Hist. Crit. Or. Graec.* (Opusc. Vol. i. p. 325); Wesseler *ad* Diod. Sic. xii. c. 8; and Blass, *Att. Bereds.* p. 322, are among the defenders of the speech as authentic.

concluded between Athens and Sparta for fifty years;[1] and was observed on both sides for thirteen years. During this peace the Peiraeus was fortified (478 B.C.), and the Northern Long Wall was built (457 B.C.). Now (1) the only recorded war of Athens in which Euboea was concerned, during the life of Miltiades, was *circ*. 509 B.C., when the Chalcidians were defeated and their territory given to the first cleruchs. (2) Megara, Troezen and Pegae were not included in the Athenian alliance until long after 478 B.C. (3) Miltiades was never ostracised; having been sent to the Chersonese before the invention of ostracism by Cleisthenes. (4) No such peace as that spoken of is known; though in 491, an Athenian embassy went to Sparta with a different object—to denounce the medism of the Aeginetans.[2] Most critics have assumed that Andocides refers to the Five Years' Truce between Athens and Sparta, concluded in 450 B.C., mainly through the influence of Cimon, son of Miltiades; and that he names the father instead of the son.[3] But all agree that the passage as it stands is full of inaccuracies, and can be reconciled with history only by conjectural emendation.[4]

Again, in § 6 it is said that Athens having been plunged into war by the Aeginetans, and having done and suffered much evil, at last concluded the

[1] Taylor, correcting Andocides from Aeschin. *De Fals. Legat.* § 172, reads πεντήκοντα for πέντε : and so Blass.

[2] Her. VI. 49.

[3] This view, briefly stated by Sluiter, *Lectiones Andocideae*, c. x. p. 135, is discussed and approved by Clinton, *Fasti Hellen.* Vol. II. Append.

c. 8, p. 257; and adopted by Grote, v. p. 453, *note* 3. For the Five Years' Truce Clinton gives the date 450, which I take: Grote, 452: Curtius (*Hist. Gr.* II. p. 402 tr. Ward) 451-450.

[4] Cf. Curtius, *Hist. Gr.* Vol. II. p. 412 (tr. Ward): Grote, v. pp. 455-464.

Thirty Years' Peace with Sparta (445 B.C.) The impression conveyed by this statement is wrong. The war between Athens and Aegina began about 458, and ended in 455 with the reduction of Aegina. In 450 Athens and Sparta made a truce for five years. A new train of events began with the revolution in Boeotia in 447, followed by the revolt of Megara and Euboea; and it was this which led up to the peace of 445 B.C.

These inaccuracies are in regard only to the earlier history of Athens: and the undoubtedly genuine speech On the Mysteries contains allusions which are no less inaccurate. In regard to contemporary events the speaker makes no statement which can be shown to be incorrect: and on one point—the position of Argos at the time—he is incidentally confirmed in a striking manner by Xenophon.[1] A forger would have studied the early history with more care, and would not have known

---

[1] The speech On the Peace speaks of the Argives as having "made a peace on their own account" which protected their territory: § 27 αὐτοὶ δ' ἰδίᾳ εἰρήνην ποιήσαντες τὴν χώραν οὐ παρέχουσιν ἐμπολεμεῖν. Now Xenophon tells us that in 392 the Corinthian government had formed a close alliance with Argos. The boundary-stones between the territories were taken up; an Argive garrison held the citadel of Corinth; and the very name of Corinth was changed to Argos (*Hellen.* IV. 4-6). In 391 Agesilaus had ravaged the Argive territory before taking Lechaeum (*Hell.* IV. 4-19). The next year, 399, Ol. 97. 3, was the year of the Isthmia. The Argives assumed the presidency of the festival, and offered the sacrifice to Poseidon, on the ground that "Argos was Corinth" —ὡς "Αργους τῆς Κορίνθου ὄντος (*Hell.* IV. 5. 1). Consequently they claimed the privilege of the Sacred Month (ἱερομηνία) for Argolis. And so, precisely in the year 390, to which we saw that the speech On the Peace belongs, it was true that the Argive territory enjoyed a special immunity. This had not been the case in 391; nor was it any longer the case in 388 (the next Isthmian year), when Agesipolis asked Zeus at Olympia and Apollo at Delphi whether he was bound to respect this fictitious extension of the ἱερομηνία—was absolved by the gods from respecting it—and ravaged Argolis (*H.* IV. 7. 2).

Passage common to Andocides and Aeschines.

the details of the particular situation so well. But how does it happen that the whole historical passage (§§ 3–12) reappears, with modifications, in the speech of Aeschines On the Embassy?[1] Either Aeschines copied this speech, or a later writer copied the speech of Aeschines. There can be little doubt that the former was the case. Andocides, grandfather of the orator, is mentioned in the speech On the Peace[2] as a member of the embassy to Sparta in 445 B.C. In the speech of Aeschines[3] he is named as chief of that embassy. This Andocides—an obscure member, if he was a member, of the embassy which, according to Diodorus,[4] was led by Callias and Chares—would not have been named at all except by his own grandson. Again, there are traces in Aeschines of condensation—not always intelligent—from the speech On the Peace. Thus the latter[5] says (referring to the years before the Peloponnesian war)—"we laid up 1000 talents in the acropolis, *and set them apart by law for the use of the people at special need*": Aeschines, leaving out the qualifying clause, makes it appear that the sum of 1000 talents was the total sum laid up in the Athenian treasury[6] during the years of peace.

---

[1] Aeschin. *De Fals. Legat.* § 172, συνταραχθέντες δέ... to § 176, ἠναγκασμένοι. The topics are the same as those of Andoc. *De Pace*, §§ 3–12 : the language is coincident in several points, yet, on the whole, much altered.

[2] § 6, ἡρέθησαν δέκα ἄνδρες ἐξ Ἀθηναίων ἁπάντων πρέσβεις ἐς Λακεδαίμονα αὐτοκράτορες, ὧν ἦν καὶ Ἀνδοκίδης ὁ πάππος ὁ ἡμέτερος.

[3] Aesch. *De Fals. Legat.* § 174,

Ἀνδοκίδην ἐκπέμψαντες καὶ τοὺς συμπρέσβεις.

[4] XII. 7.

[5] Andoc. *De Pace*, § 7, πρῶτον μέν... ἀνηνέγκαμεν χίλια τάλαντα εἰς τὴν ἀκρόπολιν καὶ νόμῳ κατεκλείσαμεν ἐξαίρετα εἶναι τῷ δήμῳ· τοῦτο δὲ τριήρεις ἄλλας ἑκατόν, κ.τ.λ.

[6] Aeschin. *De Fals. Legat.* § 174, χίλια μὲν γὰρ τάλαντα ἀνηνέγκαμεν νομίσματος εἰς τὴν ἀκρόπολιν, ἑκατὸν δὲ τριήρεις ἑτέρας, κ.τ.λ.

The treatment of the subject certainly affords no argument against the authenticity of the speech. Andocides gave little care to arrangement, and here there is no apparent attempt to treat the question methodically. On the other hand, the remarks about Corinth and Argos,[1] and the answer to those who demanded the restoration of lands abroad,[2] are both acute and sensible. In this, as in his other speech before the ecclesia, the descriptive talent of Andocides had little scope; but, as in the speech On the Mysteries, the style is spirited and vigorous.

Remarks on the Speech.

   The speech against Alcibiades is certainly spurious. It discusses the question whether the speaker, or Nicias or Alcibiades, is to be ostracised. The situation resembles one which is mentioned by Plutarch. Alcibiades, Nicias and Phaeax were rivals for power, and it had become plain that one of the three would incur ostracism.[3] They therefore made common cause against Hyperbolus, who was ostracised, probably in 417 B.C.[4]

Speech against Alcibiades.

   The supposed date of this speech is fixed by a reference in § 22 to the capture of Melos. Melos was taken in the winter of 416–415 B.C. Nicias left Athens, never to return, in the spring of 415.

---

[1] §§ 24–27.
[2] §§ 36–39.
[3] Plut. *Alc.* c. 13. In *Aristid.* c. 7 and in *Nic.* c. 11 Plutarch names only Alcibiades and Nicias as the rivals; adding, in *Nic.* c. 11, that Theophrastus substitutes Phaeax for Nicias.
[4] The Schol. on Ar. *Vesp.* 1007 quotes Theopompus for the statement

ἐξωστράκισαν τὸν Ὑπέρβολον ἐξ ἔτη. ὁ δὲ καταπλεύσας εἰς Σάμον...ἀπέθανε. The death of Hyperbolus is fixed by Thuc. VIII. 73 to 411 B.C. Blass, with Cobet and others, thinks that the "six years" of Theopompus represent simply the number of years which intervened between the banishment of Hyperbolus and his death. This brings the ostracism to 417 B.C.

Therefore the speech could have been spoken only in the early part of 415 B.C.

Analysis. The orator, after stating the point at issue, and censuring the institution of ostracism (§§ 1–6), enters upon an elaborate invective against Alcibiades (§§ 10–40). The latter is attacked for having doubled the tribute of the allies (§§ 10–12); for having ill-used his wife (§§ 13–15); for contempt of the law (§§ 16–19); for beating a choregus (§§ 20, 21); for insolence after his Olympian victory (§§ 24–33). He is then contrasted with the speaker (§§ 34–40), who concludes with a notice of his own public services (§§ 41, 42).

The Speech not by Andocides. The speech is twice cited without suspicion by Harpocration: it is also named as genuine by Photius.[1] The biographer of Andocides does not mention it; but, in its place, mentions a Defence in reply to Phaeax.[2] There are traces of its ascription in antiquity both to Lysias[3] and to Aeschines.[4] But an examination of the speech will show that it cannot have been spoken by Andocides, or written by him for the use of another; that it was probably not written by any one who lived at the time of which it treats; and that there is good reason for believing it to be the work of a late sophist.

That Andocides spoke this speech is inconceivable. The speaker says (§ 8) that he has been four times tried; and (§ 41) that he has been ambassador to

---

[1] Phot. *Cod.* 261.

[2] [Plut.] *Vit. Andoc.* ἀπολογία πρὸς Φαίακα.

[3] Athenaeus (IX. p. 408 c) quotes some words from § 29 of the speech, as from Λυσίας κατ᾽ Ἀλκιβιάδου.

[4] This may be surmised from Diogenes Laertius, II. 63, who says, speaking of Aeschines *the Socratic*, ἦι δὲ καὶ ἐν τοῖς ῥητορικοῖς ἱκανῶς γεγυμνασμένος, ὡς δῆλον ἔκ τε τῆς ἀπολογίας [τοῦ πατρός—Blass ὑπὲρ] Φαίακος τοῦ στρατηγοῦ καὶ Δίωνος.

Molossia, Thesprotia, Italy and Sicily. But elsewhere, excusing himself for acts committed in the very year in which this speech is supposed to have been delivered—in 415—Andocides pleads that he was young and foolish at the time.[1] Moreover, no writer mentions Andocides as having been in danger of ostracism at the same time as Nicias and Alcibiades.

Nor is it credible that Andocides wrote the speech for another person—Phaeax, for instance, as Valckenär[2] suggests. The style is strongly against this. It is far more artificial than anything by Andocides which we possess; it approaches, indeed, more nearly to the style of Isocrates. The formal antitheses in the proem (§§ 1–2) are a striking example of this character.[3]

Taylor[4] and others have ascribed the speech to Phaeax himself. Plutarch names Phaeax, Alcibiades and Nicias as the three men over whom ostracism was hanging at the same time; and quotes from a speech against Alcibiades, with which the name of Phaeax is connected, a story which appears (in a different form) in our speech.[5] Then it is known

Was Phaeax the author?

---

[1] *De Reditu*, § 7.

[2] See Valckenär's dissertation, given at the end of Chap. I. of Sluiter's *Lect. Andoc.*

[3] Compare also § 21, ἀλλ' ὑμεῖς ἐν μὲν ταῖς τραγῳδίαις τοιαῦτα θεωροῦντες δεινὰ νομίζετε, γιγνόμενα δὲ ἐν τῇ πόλει ὁρῶντες οὐδὲν φροντίζετε, with Isocr. *Panegyr.* § 168, ἐπὶ μὲν ταῖς συμφοραῖς ταῖς ὑπὸ τῶν ποιητῶν συγκειμέναις δακρύειν ἀξιοῦσιν, ἀληθινὰ δὲ πάθη πολλὰ καὶ δεινὰ γιγνόμενα διὰ τὸν πόλεμον ἐφορῶντες τοσούτου δέουσιν ἐλεεῖν, κ.τ.λ.

[4] *Lect. Lysiac.* c. VI.

[5] Plut. *Alc.* c. 13, φέρεται δὲ καὶ λόγος τις κατ' Ἀλκιβιάδου καὶ Φαίακος γεγραμμένος ἐν ᾧ μετὰ τῶν ἄλλων γέγραπται καὶ ὅτι τῆς πόλεως πολλὰ πομπεῖα χρυσᾶ καὶ ἀργυρᾶ κεκτημένης Ἀλκιβιάδης ἐχρῆτο πᾶσιν αὐτοῖς ὥσπερ ἰδίοις πρὸς τὴν καθ' ἡμέραν δίαιταν. For καὶ Φαίακος Taylor (l.c.) and Vater (Rerum Andocidearum, cap. IV.) propose ὑπὸ Φαίακος: Blass (*All. Bereds.* 330) ὑπὲρ Φαίακος. Blass thinks that, whoever the author of the speech was, the person meant to

from Thucydides that Phaeax went on an embassy at least to Sicily and Italy.[1] Valckenär's and Ruhnken's[2] arguments against Taylor are inconclusive. If the speech was really written at the time of which it treats, it cannot be disproved, any more than it can be proved, that Phaeax was the author.

The Speech probably by a late sophist.

But an overwhelming amount of evidence tends to show that the speech is the work of a later sophist. First stand two general reasons: the supposed occasion of the speech, and the style of its composition.

Ostracism misconceived.

As far as the nature of ostracism is known to us, the whole speech involves a thorough misconception of it: it assumes a situation which could never have existed. Once every year the ecclesia was formally asked by its presidents whether, in that year, an ostracism should be held. If it voted affirmatively, a day was fixed. The market-place was railed in for voting, every citizen might write any name he pleased on the shell which he dropped into the urn; and if against any one name there were six thousand votes, the person so indicated was banished for ten — in later times, for five — years. The characteristic feature of the whole proceeding was the absence of everything like an open contest between definite

---

be defended was Phaeax; and that the ἀπολογία πρὸς Φαίακα in [Plut.] *Vit. Andoc.* may have come from an original ἀπολογία Φαίακι, i.e. ὑπὲρ Φαίακος.

The story of the sacred vessels can hardly have been taken by Plutarch *only* from § 29 of the speech, where it runs:—τὰ πομπεῖα παρὰ τῶν ἀρχιθεωρῶν αἰτησάμενος ὡς εἰς τἀπι-

νίκια τῇ προτεραίᾳ τῆς θυσίας χρησόμενος ἐξηπάτησε καὶ ἀποδοῦναι οὐκ ἤθελε.

[1] Thuc. v. 4.

[2] Ruhnken. *Historia Crit. Orat. Graec.* (Opusc. I. p. 326). Ruhnken, as Sluiter points out, borrows largely from Valckenär's dissertation (see above), which had appeared 12 years before.

rivals. The very object of ostracism was to get rid of a dangerous man in the quietest and least invidious way. No names were mentioned; far less was discussion dreamed of. The idea of a man rising in the ecclesia or other public gathering, and stating that he was one of three persons who were in danger of ostracism; then inveighing at great length and with extraordinary bitterness against one of the other two; and concluding with a vindication of his own consequence—would have probably seemed to Athenians of the days of ostracism incredibly indecent and absurd. In the first place, they would have been offended by his open assumption—whether true or not—that *he* was one of the citizens who had rendered the resort to ostracism necessary; secondly, they would have resented his attempt to prejudice the ballot; and if, in the end, he had escaped, his escape would probably have been due to their conviction that, as the poet Plato said of Hyperbolus, "it was not for such fellows that shells were invented."[1] But the speaker against Alcibiades does not only himself speak thus; he asserts that Alcibiades is about to address the house next, and to endeavour to move it by his tears.[2]

If the nature of the situation supposed were not enough, the style of the composition would in itself be almost decisive. The speaker begins with a formal

Style.

---

[1] *Ap.* Plut. *Alc.* c. 13, οὐ γὰρ τοιούτων εἵνεκ' ὄστραχ' εὑρέθη.
[2] § 39. Grote (IV. p. 202, *note*) remarks on the erroneous conception of ostracism involved in the speaker complaining that he is going to be ostracised *without* any secret voting —as if by a show of hands. But in § 2 the οὔτε before διαψηφισαμένων κρύβδην is now omitted by Schleiermacher and Blass.

statement of the matter in hand, evidently meant for a reader; and then goes on to string together all the tritest stories about Alcibiades. This — the body of the speech — has the unmistakable air of a compilation.

<small>Particular errors.</small>

The arguments from the supposed occasion and from the style are confirmed by the evidence of particular misstatements. In §§ 22, 23 Alcibiades is said to have had a child by a Melian woman who came into his power after the capture of Melos; but the speech, as has been shown, can refer only to the spring of 415: and Melos was taken only in the winter of 416–415. In § 33 Cimon is said to have been banished because he had married his own sister. In § 13 the commander at Delium—a battle fought but nine years before the supposed date of the speech—is called Hipponicus instead of Hippocrates. The two last blunders would have been impossible for an Athenian of that age. On the whole there can be little doubt that in this speech we must recognise the work of a late rhetorician who saw, in the juxtaposition of Alcibiades, Nicias and Andocides, a dramatic subject; who had only an indistinct notion of how ostracism was managed in olden times; and who believed himself sufficiently prepared for his task when he had read in Plutarch all the scandalous stories relating to Alcibiades.

<small>Lost Works.</small>

Beside the extant speeches of Andocides, the titles of four others have been preserved. (1) Plu-

<small>Address to the Associates.</small>

tarch quotes an address "To the Associates," or members of the oligarchical clubs, as authority for a statement that the remains of Themistocles had been dishonoured at Athens; but adds that the statement was made by Andocides merely for the purpose of exasperating the oligarchs against the people.[1] Ruhnken,[2] with whom Sauppe[3] agrees, thought that this Address was a letter written by Andocides, then in exile, to the fellow-conspirators of Peisander in 411. But the breach of Andocides with the oligarchical party, after his informations in 415, was decisive and final; when he returned to Athens in 411 he was at once denounced by Peisander and imprisoned. It seems better, then, with Kirchhoff[4] and Blass,[5] to refer this Address to an earlier time than 415: perhaps to the years 420–418, a period of keen struggle between the oligarchical and popular parties at Athens.[6]

Deliberative Speech.

(2) The "Deliberative Speech" quoted by the lexicographers[7] is identified by Kirchhoff with the last mentioned. Its title seems, however, to show plainly that it was of a different kind, and was either spoken, or supposed to be spoken, in debate in the ecclesia.

Speech On the Information.

(3) Harpocration once quotes a "Speech On the Information" ($\pi\epsilon\rho\grave{\iota}$ $\tau\hat{\eta}s$ $\grave{\epsilon}\nu\delta\epsilon\acute{\iota}\xi\epsilon\omega s$) for the word $\zeta\eta\tau\eta\tau\acute{\eta}s$, which occurs twice in the speech On the Mysteries.[8] Hence the two speeches have sometimes been identified. But the pseudo-Plutarch expressly distinguishes them.[9] And the author of the speech against Andocides states

---

[1] Plut. *Themist.* c. 32.
[2] *Hist. Crit. Or. Gr.* (Opusc. I. p. 326).
[3] *Or. Att.* II. p. 165.
[4] *Andocidea*, Hermes I. pp. 1–20.
[5] *Att. Bereds.* p. 286; and *Andoc.* (Teubner) p. 96.
[6] Cf. Plut. *Alc.* c. 13.
[7] Antiatticista, Bekker, *Anecd.* vol. I. p. 94, v. 25. Photius, p. 288, 23.
[8] §§ 36, 40.
[9] [Plut.] *Vit. Andoc.* mentions first the speeches On the Mysteries and On his Return; and then adds, σώζεται δὲ αὐτοῦ καὶ ὁ περὶ τῆς ἐνδείξεως λόγος καὶ ἀπολογία πρὸς Φαίακα καὶ ὁ περὶ τῆς εἰρήνης.

that two informations had been laid against him in the same year.¹ It is true that there is no proof of the earlier information having resulted in a trial; and that the title of the lost speech, if really distinct from the *De Mysteriis*, was ill-chosen. But it is difficult to suppose that the biographer could have made such a blunder as to quote the same speech by two different titles in the same sentence. On the whole, Sauppe's² view, that the speech On the Mysteries and the speech On the Information were distinct, appears most probable. If the lost speech referred, like the *De Mysteriis*, to the Hermae case, it must have contained the word which Harpocration quotes; and it would have been natural for him to quote it from the earlier of the two compositions in which it occurred. (4) The "Reply to Phaeax" is known only from the pseudo-Plutarch, who does not name the speech "Against Alcibiades."³ It has been shown that the latter is probably the work of a late sophist; and it is likely that Phaeax, rather than Andocides, was intended to be the speaker. If, then, it could be assumed that "Reply to Phaeax" is an inaccurate quotation of the title, which ought to have been cited as "Reply *for* Phaeax," there is no difficulty in supposing the identity of this work with the extant speech Against Alcibiades.

Reply to Phaeax.

Doubtful fragments.

Besides the names of these four speeches, two fragments of unknown context have been preserved.⁴ One of them expresses the hope that Athens may

---

¹ [Lys.] *in Andoc.* § 30.
² *O. A.* II. p. 165.
³ [Plut.] *Vit. Andoc.* l. c.
⁴ Sauppe, *O. A.* II. p. 166 : Blass, *Andoc.* (Teubner) p. 97.

not "again" see the country people thronging in to seek shelter within the walls. This seems to refer to the invasion by Archidamus in 431. If this be so, the speech to which the fragment belonged was probably older than 413, when Agis occupied Deceleia, and when the scenes of 431 must have been to some extent repeated. Such a passage might have found place either in the address To the Associates or in the Deliberative Speech.[1] The other fragment speaks of Hyperbolus as then at Athens; and is therefore older, at least, than 417.[2]

---

[1] Sauppe refers the fragment to the πρὸς τοὺς ἑταίρους. So, also, does Kirchhoff, identifying the πρὸς τοὺς ἑταίρους with the συμβουλευτικός. If these, however, were distinct, the fragment may belong just as well to the συμβουλευτικός.

[2] On the date of the ostracism of Hyperbolus, see above, p. 131, note 4.

CHAPTER VII

LYSIAS

LIFE

LYSIAS, though he passed most of his years at Athens, did not possess the citizenship, and, except in the impeachment of Eratosthenes, appears to have had no personal contact with the affairs of the city. Yet, as in literary style he is the representative of Atticism, so in his fortunes he is closely associated with the Athenian democracy. He suffered with it in its two greatest calamities—the overthrow in Sicily and the tyranny of the Thirty; he took part in its restoration; and afterwards, in his speeches for the law-courts, he became perhaps the best, because the soberest, exponent of its spirit—the most graceful and most versatile interpreter of ordinary Athenian life.

Cephalus, the father of Lysias, was a Syracusan, who settled at Athens as a resident alien on the invitation of Pericles.[1] Such an invitation would scarcely have carried much weight before Pericles had begun to be a leading citizen,—*i.e.* before about 460 B.C.; and the story which represented Cephalus as having been driven from Syracuse when the democracy

---

[1] Lys. *in Eratosth.* § 4.

was overthrown by Gelon (485 B.C.) is therefore not very probable.[1]

Lysias was born at Athens after his father had come to live there. The year of his birth cannot be determined. Dionysius assumes the same year as the pseudo-Plutarch—Ol. 80. 2., 459 B.C. ; but admits, what the latter does not, that it is a mere assumption.[2] And the ground upon which the assumption rested is evident. Lysias was known to have gone to Thurii when he was fifteen. Thurii was founded Ol. 84. 2., 443 B.C. : it was inferred, then, that Lysias was born in 459 B.C. But there is nothing to prove that Lysias went to Thurii in the year of its foundation. The date 459 B.C. must be regarded, therefore, as a mere guess. It is the guess, however, which had the approval of the ancients ; and it is confirmed by this circumstance—that Lysias was reported to have died at about eighty,[3] and that, in fact, his genuine works, so far as they are extant, cease at about 380 B.C.[4] In the absence of certainty, then, it seems probable that the date 459 is not far wrong.

This is not, however, the prevalent modern view.

---

[1] [Plut.] *Vit. Lys.* ὡς δέ τινες, ἐκπεσόντα τῶν Συρακουσῶν ἡνίκα ὑπὸ Γέλωνος ἐτυραννοῦντο.

[2] Dionys. *Lys.* c. 1 says that in the archonship of Callias (412 B.C.) Lysias was forty-seven, *as one might conjecture*—ὡς ἄν τις εἰκάσειεν. Again in c. 12 he *supposes* that Lysias may have died in 379 at the age of 80. The pseudo-Plutarch *Vit. Lys.* says boldly :—γενόμενος Ἀθήνησιν ἐπὶ Φιλοκλέους ἄρχοντος τοῦ μετὰ Φρασικλῆ, κατὰ τὸ δεύτερον ἔτος τῆς ὀγδοηκοστῆς Ὀλυμπιάδος.

[3] Dionys. *Lys.* c. 12 : [Plut.] *Vit. Lys.*

[4] The speech *Against Evandrus* (382 B.C.), and that *For Pherenicus*, of which a fragment remains (381 or 380 B.C.)—are his latest known works. The two lost speeches *For Iphicrates* (Sauppe. *Frag.* XVIII. and LXV, *Att. Or.* II. pp. 178, 190) belonged respectively to the years 371 and 354 ; but the judgment of Dionysius in rejecting them (*Lys.* c. 12) has been generally confirmed by modern writers.

Lysias was said to have gone to Italy after his father's death;[1] and this fact is the criterion for the date of his birth on which C. F. Hermann[2] and Baur[3] rely, as the ancient writers relied on the foundation-year of Thurii. Cephalus is introduced in Plato's *Republic*, of which the scene is laid (C. F. Hermann thinks) in 430 B.C. Lysias, then, it is agreed, cannot have gone to Thurii before 429, or have been born before 444. Blass justly objects to a dialogue of Plato being used as an authority for a date of this kind; but he himself arrives at the same conclusion on another ground —viz. because Cephalus cannot have come to Athens earlier than 460, and had lived there (as his son says[4]) thirty years. Again, Lysias was certainly older than Isocrates,[5] who was born in 436. The birth of Lysias must therefore be put (Blass thinks) between 444 and 436.

This view depends altogether on the statement that Lysias remained at Athens till his father's death —a statement vouched for only by the Plutarchic biographer, who is surely untrustworthy on such a point. Further, it assumes both the date and the literal biographical accuracy of the *Republic;* or else

---

[1] τοῦ πατρὸς ἤδη τετελευτηκότος: pseudo-Plut. *Vit. Lys.*

[2] *Gesammelte Abhandlungen,* p. 15.

[3] *Uebersetzung d. Reden d. Lys.* pp. 5 ff. — Blass, *Attisch. Bereds.* p. 333.

[4] Lys. *in Eratosth.* § 4.

[5] A dialogue of Plato can seldom be safely cited to prove that one of the persons of the imaginary conversation was, or was not, alive at a given time long before. But when, in such a dialogue, one of two persons contemporary with Plato is represented as very decidedly older than the other, it must be assumed that this was the case. To infer from the *Republic* that Cephalus was alive in 430 B.C. would be rash. But it is perfectly safe to infer from the *Phaedrus* (p. 278 E, etc.) that Lysias was an orator of matured powers when Isocrates was a boy.

—what is at least doubtful—that Cephalus could not have come to Athens before 460. Lastly, it makes it difficult to accept the well-accredited account of Lysias having reached, or passed, the age of eighty; since all traces of his industry, hitherto constant, cease when, at this rate, he would have been no more than sixty-six.[1] The question must be left uncertain. But the modern hypothesis that Lysias was born between 444 and 436 B.C. does not seem, at least, more probable than the ancient hypothesis that he was born about 459.[2]

Besides Lysias, Cephalus had two other sons, Polemarchus and Euthydêmus[3]—Polemarchus being the eldest of the three; and a daughter, afterwards married to Brachyllus. The hospitable disposition of Cephalus is marked in the opening of the *Republic*, of which the scene is laid at the house of his eldest son. He complains that Socrates does not come often now to see them at the Peiraeus, and begs that in future he will come to them without ceremony, as to intimate friends.[4] It is easy to believe that, in

---

[1] Blass distinctly admits this:—"Starb also Lysias bald nach diesem Jahre, so sind freilich jene Angaben über das Alter, welches er erreichte, völlig aufzugeben." *Att. Bereds.* p. 336.

[2] Stallbaum, in his *Lysiaca ad illustrandas Phaedri Platonici origines* (Leipzig, 1851) pp. 6 f., takes the following dates: Birth of Lysias, 459: Foundation of Thurii, 446: Cephalus comes to Athens, 444: Lysias goes to Thurii, 443: Death of Lysias, 378.

[3] Plato (*Rep.* p. 328 B) mentions Lysias and Euthydêmus as the brothers of Polemarchus. Dionysius (*Lys.* 1) speaks of *two* brothers of Lysias. But the pseudo-Plutarch gives him three — Polemarchus, Eudidus (Euthydêmus), and Brachyllus. Blass seems right in concluding from Demosth. *Neaer.* § 22 that Brachyllus was not brother, but brother-in-law, of Lysias. It is there said that Lysias married the daughter of Brachyllus, his own niece (ἀδελφιδῆ). Hence, probably, the mistake of the so-called Plutarch.

[4] Plat. *Rep.* p. 328 D.

the lifetime of Pericles, the house of the wealthy Sicilian whom his friendship had brought to Athens was an intellectual centre, the scene of many such gatherings as Plato imagined at the house of Polemarchus; and that Lysias really grew up, as Dionysius says, in the society of the most distinguished Athenians.[1]

Lysias at Thurii.

At the age of fifteen[2]—his father, according to one account, being dead[3]—Lysias went to Thurii, accompanied certainly by his eldest brother Polemarchus; perhaps also by Euthydêmus.[4] At Thurii, where he passed his youth and early manhood, he is said to have studied rhetoric under Tisias[5] of Syracuse, himself the pupil of Corax, reputed founder of the art. If, as is likely, Tisias was born about 485 B.C. and did not go to Athens till about 418, there is nothing impossible in this account. At any rate it is probable that Lysias had lessons from some teacher of the Sicilian school, a school the trammels of which his maturer genius so thoroughly shook off. The overthrow of the Athenian arms in Sicily brought into power an anti-Athenian faction at Thurii. Lysias and his brother, with three hundred persons accused of "Atticising,"[6] were driven out, and fled to Athens in 412 B.C.[7] A tradition, idle, indeed, but picturesque,

---

[1] Dionys. *Lys.* 1: συνεπαιδεύθη τοῖς ἐπιφανεστάτοις Ἀθηναίων. The pseudo-Plut. repeats the words: τὸ μὲν πρῶτον συνεπαιδεύετο τοῖς ἐπιφ. Ἀθην.

[2] Dionys. *Lys.* 1.

[3] [Plut.] *Vit. Lys.*

[4] Dionysius (l. c.) says σὺν ἀδελφοῖς δυσί: the pseudo-Plut. mentions Polemarchus only.

[5] The pseudo-Plut. says παιδευόμενος παρὰ Τισίᾳ καὶ Νικίᾳ τοῖς Συρακουσίοις. Blass thinks that the name of the unknown Nicias arose out of Τισίᾳ by a dittography.

[6] Ἀττικισμὸν ἐγκληθεῖσι. Dionys. *Lys.* 1.

[7] Dionysius and the pseudo-Plut. both mark the date by the archonship of Callias.

connected the Athenian disaster in Sicily with the last days of Lysias in southern Italy. To him was ascribed a speech, possessed by the ancients, in which the captive general Nicias implored the mercy of his Sicilian conquerors.[1]

The next seven years at Athens—from 412 to 405—seem to have been years of peace and prosperity for the brothers. They were the owners of three houses, one in the town, in which Polemarchus lived;[2] another in the Peiraeus, occupied by Lysias; and, adjoining the latter, a shield-manufactory, employing a hundred and twenty slaves. Informers —who were especially dangerous to rich foreigners— did not vex them;[3] they had many friends; and, in the liberal discharge of public services, were patterns to all resident-aliens.[4] The possession of house-property[5] shows that they belonged—as their father Cephalus had doubtless belonged—to that privileged class of resident-aliens who paid no special tax as such, and who, as being on a par in respect of taxes with citizens, were called isoteleis. If Lysias continued his rhetorical studies during this quiet time, he probably had not yet begun to write speeches for

His life at Athens from 412 to 405 B.C.

---

[1] See the short fragment of this speech ὑπὲρ Νικίου in Sauppe O. A. II. p. 199. Dionysius unhesitatingly rejected it, and the few remaining words suffice in themselves to betray a vulgar rhetorician:—κλαίω τὸν ἀμάχητον καὶ ἀναυμάχητον ὄλεθρον, κ.τ.λ. But it must have been at least as old as the latter part of the fourth century B.C., since Theophrastus quoted it (Dionys. *Lys.* 14).

[2] This follows from Lys. *In Eratosth.* § 16.

[3] *In Eratosth.* § 4.

[4] Cf. *In Eratosth.* § 20, where Lysias speaks of himself and his brother as πάσας τὰς χορηγίας χορηγήσαντας—and, in contrast with the Thirty, οὐχ ὁμοίως μετοικοῦντας ὥσπερ αὐτοὶ ἐπολιτεύοντο.

[5] Boeckh, *Publ. Econ.* Bk. I. c. 24. A resident-alien could under no circumstances be an owner of land; and only an isoteles could be owner of a house.

the law-courts. A rich man, as he then was, had no motive for taking to a despised drudgery; and the only extant speech ascribed to him which refers to a date earlier than 403—that for Polystratus—is probably spurious. Cicero,[1] quoting Aristotle, says that Lysias once kept a rhetorical school, but gave it up because Theodôrus surpassed him in technical subtlety. If this story is worth anything, there is perhaps one reason for referring it to the years 412–405; it certainly imputes to Lysias the impatience of a wealthy amateur. At any rate the ornamental pieces enumerated in the lists of his works—the encomia, the letters, the show-speeches—may have belonged in part to this period of his life. After 403 he wrote for the law-courts as a profession, and wrote with an industry which can have left little time for the rhetoric of display.

The Anarchy.

Soon after the Thirty had taken power in the spring of 404, two of them, Theognis and Peison, proposed that measures should be adopted against the resident-aliens; nominally, because that class was disaffected—really, because it was rich. Ten resident-aliens were chosen out for attack, two poor men being included for the sake of appearances. Lysias and Polemarchus were on the list. When Theognis and Peison, with their attendants, came to the house of Lysias in the Peiraeus, they found him entertaining a party of friends. The guests were driven off, and their host was left in the charge of Peison, while Theognis and his companions went to the shield-

---

[1] Cic. *Brut.* c. 48: *nam Lysiam primo profiteri solitum artem dicendi, deinde, quod Theodorus esset in arte subtilior, in orationibus ieiunior, orationes cum scribere aliis coepisse, artem removisse.*

manufactory close by to take an inventory of the slaves. Lysias, left alone with Peison, asked if he would take a sum of money to save him. "Yes," said Peison, "if it is a large sum." They agreed on a talent; and Lysias went to bring it from the room where he kept his money-box. Peison, catching sight of the box, called up two servants, and told them to take its whole contents. Thus robbed of more than thrice the amount bargained for, Lysias begged to be left at least enough to take him out of the country. Peison replied that he might consider himself lucky if he got off with his life. They were then going to leave the house, when they met at the door two other emissaries of the Thirty. Finding that Peison was now going to the house of Polemarchus in the town, these men relieved him of Lysias, whom they took to the house of one Damnippus. Theognis was there already with some other prisoners. As Lysias knew Damnippus, he took him aside, and asked him to assist his escape. Damnippus thought that it would be best to speak directly to Theognis, who, he was sure, would do anything for money. While Theognis and Damnippus were talking in the front hall, Lysias slipped through the door, which chanced to be open, leading from the first court of the house to the second.[1] He had still two doors to pass through—luckily they were both unlocked. He escaped to the house of Archeneôs, the master of a merchant-ship, close by, and sent him up to Athens to learn what had become of Polemarchus. Archeneôs came back with the news

---

[1] *In Eratosth.* § 16, τριῶν δὲ θυρῶν οὐσῶν ἃς ἔδει με διελθεῖν ἅπασαι ἀνεῳγμέναι ἔτυχον. The first of these must have been the μέταυλος θύρα, leading from the outer to the inner αὐλή.

that Polemarchus had been met in the street by Eratosthenes, one of the Thirty, and taken straight to prison. The same night Lysias took boat to Megara.

Polemarchus received the usual message of the Thirty[1]—to drink the hemlock. Although the property of which the brothers had been despoiled was so valuable—including almost the whole stock of the shield-manufactory, gold and silver plate, furniture, and a large sum of money—the decencies of burial were refused to Polemarchus. He was laid out in the prison on a common stretcher,—one friend gave a cloth to throw over the body, another a cushion for the head, and so forth. A pair of gold earrings were taken from the ears of his widow.[2]

Lysias aids the Exiles.

During the ten or twelve months of the exile—from the spring of 404 to the spring of 403—Lysias seems to have been active in the democratic cause. According to his biographer[3]—whose facts were probably taken from Lysias himself—he presented the army of the patriots with two hundred shields, and with a sum of two thousand drachmas; gained for it, with the help of one Hermon,[4] upwards of three hundred recruits; and induced his friend Thrasydaeus of Elis[5] to contribute no less than two talents. Immediately upon the return from the Peiraeus to the

---

[1] τὸ ὑπ' ἐκείνων εἰθισμένον παράγελμα, πίνειν κώνειον: *In Eratosth.* § 17.

[2] *In Eratosth.* § 19. For the whole account of the arrest, see that speech, §§ 6-20.

[3] [Plut.] *Vit. Lys.* The facts mentioned there may have been taken from the speech of Lysias on the motion of Archinus (*ib.* § 11),

and also from that περὶ τῶν ἰδίων εὐεργεσιῶν (quoted by Harpocration, s. vv. Κεῖοι, Φηγαιεῦσι, μεταπύργιον), if indeed this was distinct from the former.

[4] Ἑρμᾶνι in the *Vit. Lys.* § 7 ought probably to be Ἕρμωνι, as Blass assumes, *Att. Bereds.* p. 340.

[5] [Plut.] *Vit. Lys.* Cf. Xen. *Hellen.* III. 2. 27.

city in the spring of 403, Thrasybulus proposed that the citizenship should be conferred upon Lysias; and the proposal was carried in the ecclesia. In one respect, however, it was informal. No measure could, in strictness, come before the popular assembly which was not introduced by a preliminary resolution (probouleuma) of the Senate. But at the moment when this decree was passed, the Senate had not yet been reconstituted after the anarchy;[1] and the probouleuma had therefore been wanting. On this ground Archînus, a colleague of Thrasybulus, arraigned the decree (under the Graphê Paranomôn) as unconstitutional, and it was annulled.[2] The whole story has been doubted;[3] but it is difficult to reject it when the Plutarchic biographer expressly refers to the speech made by Lysias in connexion with the protest of Archînus.[4] Whether this speech was or was not identical with that of Lysias On his own Services[5] cannot be decided; but the latter must at least have been made upon this occasion.

Stripped of a great part of his fortune by the Thirty Tyrants, and further straitened, probably, by

The professional life of Lysias.

---

[1] This appears from the statement of the pseudo-Plut. *Vit. Lys.* § 8, that the proposal was made μετὰ τὴν κάθοδον ἐπ' ἀναρχίας τῆς πρὸ Εὐκλείδου, that is, immediately after the return in the spring of the year 403. Later in the same year Eucleides became archon; and with the revival of the constitutional forms which commenced in his archonship the ἀναρχία was held to have ended.

[2] [Plut.] *Vit. Lys.* ὁ μὲν δῆμος ἐκύρωσε τὴν δωρεάν, ἀπενεγκαμένου δὲ Ἀρχίνου γραφὴν παρανόμων διὰ τὸ ἀπροβούλευτον εἰσαχθῆναι ἑάλω τὸ ψήφισμα.

[3] As by Scheibe (Blass, p. 340), who thinks that the biographer assumed it from the vague allusion in Aeschin. *in Ctes.* § 195: Ἀρχῖνος γὰρ ὁ ἐκ Κοίλης ἐγράψατο παρανόμων Θρασύβουλον τὸν Στειριέα γράψαντά τι παρὰ τοὺς νόμους, ἕνα τῶν συγκατελθόντων αὐτῷ ἀπὸ Φυλῆς, καὶ εἷλε. This says only, τι.

[4] ἔστι δ' αὐτοῦ καὶ ὁ ὑπὲρ τοῦ ψηφίσματος (λόγος) ὃ ἐγράψατο Ἀρχῖνος, τὴν πολιτείαν αὐτοῦ περιελών: *Vit. Lys.* § 11.

[5] See p. 148, *note* 3.

his generosity to the exiles, Lysias seems now to have settled down to hard work at Athens. His activity as a writer of speeches for the law-courts falls—as far as we know—between the years 403 and 380 B.C. That it must have been great and constant is shown by the fact that Dionysius speaks of him as having written "not fewer than two hundred forensic speeches."[1] No other of the Attic orators was credited with so many as a hundred compositions of all kinds.[2]

The impeachment of Eratosthenes. First in time and first, too, in importance among the extant orations of Lysias is that Against Eratosthenes, in whom he saw not only one of the Thirty Tyrants, but the murderer of his brother Polemarchus. It was probably in 403 that Eratosthenes was impeached. The speech of Lysias, memorable as a display of eloquence, valuable, too, as a sufferer's picture of a dreadful time, has this further interest, that it is the only forensic speech known to have been spoken by Lysias himself, and that it marks his only personal contact with the politics of Athens.

Lysias and Socrates. Lysias had probably been a professional speech-writer for about four years when Socrates was brought to trial in 399. According to the popular account, Lysias wrote a defence for Socrates to speak in court, but Socrates declined to use it.[3] In the story itself there is nothing improbable; Cephalus and his son Lysias had been the intimate friends of Socrates. But it may be suspected that the story arose from a confusion. At some time later than 392 B.C. the

---

[1] *De Lys.* c. 17.
[2] Even including doubtful speeches, as Blass observes, *Att. Bereds.* p. 344.
[3] Diog. Laert. II. 40 : [Plut.] *Vit. Lys.*: Cic. *de Orat.* I. 54 § 231 : Quint. II. 15 § 30, XI. 1 § 9 : Valer. Max. VI. 4. 2 : Stob. *Flor.* VII. 56.

sophist Polycrates published an epideictic [*deictic*] Accusation of Socrates,[1] and, in reply to it, Lysias wrote a speech In Defence of Socrates.[2] This was extant in antiquity; and some one who had heard of it, but who knew nothing of the circumstances under which it was written, probably invented the story that it had been offered to, and declined by, the philosopher. The self-denial of Socrates would be complete when, after rejecting the aid of money, he had rejected the aid of the best contemporary rhetoric.[3]

Lysias is named in the ordinary text of his own speech On the Property of Aristophanes as taking part in an embassy to Dionysius the elder of Syracuse, an embassy of which the date cannot be put below 389 B.C. But there can be little doubt as to

Lysias at Olympia.

---

[1] The κατηγορία Σωκράτους of Polycrates is mentioned by Suidas, s. v. Πολυκράτης : Isocr. *Bus.* §§ 3, 5, and auctor Argum.: Aelian, *V. H.* xi. 10 : Quint. ii. 17, cf. iii. 1 : Diog. Laert. ii. 38. Diogenes notices, from Favorinus, that Polycrates had referred to the rebuilding of the walls by Conon : therefore, as Bentley first pointed out (*de Epist. Socr.* § 6, p. 51), the speech cannot have been written before 392 B.C.

[2] Schol. ad Aristid. p. 113. 16 (vol. iii. p. 480 Dind.), οἶδε τὸν Σωκράτην πρὸς τοὺς νέους ἀεὶ τὸν Ὀδυσσέα θαυμάζοντα…ὡς Πολυκράτης ἐν τῷ κατ' αὐτοῦ λόγῳ φησὶ καὶ Λυσίας ἐν τῷ πρὸς Πολυκράτην ὑπὲρ αὐτοῦ. The title of the speech probably was Ὑπὲρ Σωκράτους πρὸς Πολυκράτην.

[3] Dr. L. Hölscher (*Quaestiunculae Lysiacae*, Herford, 1857, pp. 4 ff.) defends the ordinary account, believing that Lysias really composed a defence which Socrates declined to use. He thinks that the ἀπολογία Σωκράτους mentioned among the works of Lysias by Phot. *Cod.* 262, Antiatt. in Bekker *Anecd.* p. 115. 8, Schol. ad Plat. *Gorg.* p. 331 B, and [Plut.] *Vit. Lys.*, was distinct from the speech ὑπὲρ Σωκράτους written in reply to Polycrates, and cited by the scholiast on Aristides. He remarks that in the Plutarchic life the Apologia is described as ἐστοχασμένη τῶν δικαστῶν—which is meant, he thinks, to mark that it was more practical, more forensic, than Plato's Apologia Socratis. He observes also that the scholiast on the *Gorgias* (l. c.) notices the speech of Lysias as having contained matter about Anytus and Melêtus. But neither of these references affords any good ground for assuming that there was an Ἀπολογία Σωκράτους by Lysias distinct from his reply to Polycrates. The latter had been read by the scholiast on Aristeides. Sauppe shows that the supposed Apologia was at all events not extant in antiquity (*O. A.* ii. p. 203).

the correctness of the emendation which removes his name from that passage.¹ There is better reason for believing another story in which the name of Lysias is associated with that of the elder Dionysius. We have good authority² for the statement that the *Olympiacus*, of which a large fragment remains, was spoken by Lysias in person at the Olympic festival of 388 B.C., to which Dionysius had sent a splendid embassy. In that speech Lysias pointed out that two great enemies—the despot of Syracuse in the west, the king of Persia in the east—threatened Greece; and urged union among Greeks with all the eagerness and with more than the sagacity of Isocrates.

<small>Chronological limit of his known work.</small>

As has already been noticed, the indisputably genuine works of Lysias, so far as they are known, cease about 380 B.C. The latest, the speech for Pherenicus of which a fragment remains, belongs to 381 or 380. Of the two speeches for Iphicrates, also represented by fragments only, one belonged to 371, the other to 354;³ but Dionysius pronounced both spurious, partly on the external ground that Lysias could not then have been living; partly—which, for us, is the important point—on the internal evidence of style.⁴ It seems probable that

---

¹ Lys. *de bonis Aristoph.* § 19, βουλομένου Κόνωνος πέμπειν τινὰ εἰς Σικελίαν ['Αριστοφάνης] ᾤχετο ὑποστὰς μετὰ Εὐνόμου καὶ Λυσίου, φίλου ὄντος καὶ ξένου, τὸ πλῆθος τὸ ὑμέτερον πλεῖστα ἀγαθὰ πεποιηκότος, κ.τ.λ. Sauppe substitutes Διονυσίου for the words καὶ Λυσίου. Obviously the words φίλου ὄντος καὶ ξένου require to be defined by the mention of the person whose friend he was. Kayser proposed to insert Διονυσίῳ between Λυσίου and φίλου. Sauppe's remedy is, as Blass says, simpler and better.

² Dionys. *Lys.* c. 29: Diod. XIV. 109.

³ See Sauppe, *O. A.* II. p. 178, 190.

⁴ Dionys. *Lys.* c. 12.

Lysias died in, or soon after, 380 B.C., at the age of about eighty.[1]

The character, as well as the capacity, of Lysias must be judged from the indirect evidence of his own writings. Circumstances kept him out of political life, in which his versatility and shrewdness would probably have held and improved the position which great powers of speech must soon have won. The part which he took during the troubles under the Thirty proved him a generous friend to Athens, as the *Olympiacus* shows him to have been a wise citizen[2] of Greece; but his destiny was not that of a man of action. It is not likely that he regretted this much, though he must have felt his exclusion from the Athenian franchise as the refusal of a reward to which he had claims. His real strength—as far as can be judged now—lay in his singular literary tact. A fine perception of character in all sorts of men, and a faculty for dramatising it, aided by a sense of humour always under control; a certain pervading gracefulness and flexibility of mind; rhetorical skill, masterly in a sense hardly dreamed of at that day, since it could conceal itself—these were his most distinctive qualities and powers. His liberal discharge of public services, and his generosity to the exiles in 404, accord with the disposition which is suggested by the fragments

Character of Lysias.

---

[1] [Plut.] *Vit. Lys.* ἐτελεύτησεν ὀγδοήκοντα ἔτη βιούς, ἢ ὥς τινες ἐξ καὶ ἑβδομήκοντα, ἢ ὥς τινες ὑπὲρ ὀγδοήκοντα, ἰδὼν Δημοσθένην μειράκιον ὄντα [Schäfer places the birth of Demosthenes in 384]. Dionys. *Lys.* c. 12, εἰ γὰρ ὀγδοήκοντα ἔτη γενόμενον θήσει τις τελευτῆσαι Λυσίαν, κ.τ.λ.

[2] The expression is his own: he claims to give counsel as a good citizen (*Olymp.* § 3)—with the thought in his mind, perhaps, that if he was still but a μέτοικος of Athens he was at least a πολίτης of Hellas.

of his letters. He was a man of warm nature, impulsive, hospitable, attached to his friends; fond of pleasure, and freely indulging in it; but, like Sophocles at the Chian supper-party described by Ion,[1] carrying into social life the same intellectual quality which marks his best work—the grace and the temperate brightness of a thoroughly Athenian mind.

[1] Athenaeus XIII. pp. 603 E-604 D.

CHAPTER VIII

LYSIAS

STYLE

AN appreciation of Lysias is, in one sense, easy for modern criticism. He was a literary artist, and his work bears the stamp of consummate literary skill. The reader may fail to realise the circumstances under which a particular speech was delivered, the force with which it appeals to emotion or to reason, the degree in which it was likely to prove persuasive or convincing. But he cannot fail to be aware that he is reading admirable prose. The merit of Lysias as a writer is secure of recognition. It is his oratorical power which runs some danger of being too lightly valued, unless attention is paid to the conditions under which it was exerted. The speech Against Eratosthenes, indeed, in which he expresses the passionate feeling of his own mind, would alone suffice to prove him in the modern sense eloquent. But a large majority of his other speeches are so comparatively tame, so poor in the qualities of the higher eloquence, that his oratorical reputation, to be understood, needs to be closely interpreted by the scope of his oratory.

Although on a few occasions he himself came forward as a speaker, the business of his life was to write for others. All sorts of men were among his clients; all kinds of causes in turn occupied him. Now he lent his services to the impeachment of an official charged with defrauding the Athenian treasury, or to the prosecution of some adherent of the Thirty, accused of having slandered away the lives of Athenian citizens; now he supplied the words in which a pauper begged that his obol a day from the State might not be stopped, or helped one of the parties to a drunken brawl to demand satisfaction for a black eye. The elderly citizen who appeals against the calumny of an informer to his past services as trierarch or choregus; the young man checked on the threshold of public life by some enemy's protest at his dokimasia for his first office,—in turn borrow their eloquence from Lysias. If he had been content to adopt the standard which he found existing in his profession, he would have written in nearly the same style for all these various ages and conditions. He would have treated all these different cases upon a uniform technical system, merely seeking, in every case alike, to obtain the most powerful effect and the highest degree of ornament by applying certain fixed rules. Lysias was a discoverer when he perceived that a purveyor of words for others, if he would serve his customers in the best way, must give the words the air of being their own. He saw that the monotonous intensity of the fashionable rhetoric—often ludicrously unsuited to the mouth into which it was put—was fatal to real impressiveness; and, instead of lending to all speakers the same false brilliancy, he determined to give to each the vigour of nature. It was the desire of treating appropriately every case entrusted to him, and of making each client speak as an intelligent person, without professional aid, might be expected to speak in certain circumstances, which chiefly determined the style of Lysias.

This style, imitated by many, but marked in Lysias by an original excellence, made him for antiquity the representative of a class of orators. It was in the latter part of the fourth century B.C. that Greek critics began regularly to distinguish three styles of rhetorical composition, the grand, the plain and the middle. The grand style aims constantly at rising above the common idiom; it seeks ornament of every kind, and rejects nothing as too artificial if it is striking. The plain style may, like the first, employ the utmost efforts of art, but the art is concealed; and, instead of avoiding it, imitates the language of ordinary life. The "middle" style explains itself by its name. Theophrastus appears to have been the first writer on Rhetoric who attempted such a classification; there is, at least, no hint of it in Aristotle or in the Rhetorica ad Alexandrum.[1] Vague as the classification necessarily is, it was frequently modified according to the taste of individual teachers. The two extremes—the grand and the plain styles—were

Lysias the representative of the Plain Style.

---

[1] Dionysius, speaking of the third or middle style, declares himself unable to decide whether it was first used by Thrasymachus of Chalcêdon, "*as Theophrastus thinks*," or by some one else: *De Demosth.* c. 3. From this, Francken infers with great probability that the distinction between the three styles was first made by Theophrastus in his lost work περὶ λέξεως (*Commentationes Lysiacae*, p. 9).

recognised by all; but some discerned two,[1] some three[2] shades between them; while others thought it needless to distinguish anything intermediate.[3] On the whole, however, the tripartite division kept its ground down to Roman times. It was adopted, with variations of detail, by Cicero,[4] Dionysius[5] and Quintilian.[6] The characteristics of the "plain" style —with which we are most concerned at present—are only sketched by Dionysius;[7] but they are more precisely given by Cicero. There is a difference, indeed, between the points of view of the two critics. Dionysius treats the three styles historically; Cicero treats them theoretically. The "middle" style of Cicero differs, therefore, from the "middle" style of Dionysius in being an ideal. But Cicero's description of the "plain" style, at least, would probably have

<small>General characteristics of the Plain Style.</small>

---

[1] Thus Demetrius (περὶ ἑρμην. c. 36, Walz, *Rh. Graec.* vol. IX. p. 21) distinguishes four types or χαρακτῆρες —the plain (ἰσχνός), the grand (μεγαλοπρεπής), the polished (γλαφυρός), and the forcible (δεινός)— meaning by the last a terse, vigorous style, suited to controversy in court or council.

[2] Syrianus, in his commentary on the περὶ ἰδεῶν of Hermogenes (Walz, *Rh. Graec.* vol. VII. p. 93), says that Hipparchus (a rhetorician who wrote a treatise περὶ τρόπων, *ib.* VI. p. 337) recognised five styles — the plain (ἰσχνός), the copious (ἁδρός—another name for the μεγαλοπρεπής), the middle (μέσος), the graphic (γραφικός), and the florid (ἀνθηρός).

[3] Demetrius says that his γλαφυρὸς χαρακτήρ was considered by some as a branch of the ἰσχνός, and his δεινὸς χαρακτήρ as a branch of the μεγαλοπρεπής: περὶ ἑρμ. c. 36, Walz, IX. 21.

[4] Cic. *Orator*, c. 6, § 20, *grandiloqui —tenues, acuti—medius et quasi temperatus.*

[5] Dionysius describes the grand style as ἐξηλλαγμένη, περιττή, ἐγκατάσκευος (*De Demosth.* 1), or ὑψηλὴ λέξις (*ib.* 34): the plain, as λιτή, ἀφελής (*ib.* 2), or ἰσχνή, ἀπέριττος (*ib.* 34): the middle as μέση (*ib.* 34) or μικτή (*ib.* 3).

[6] Quint. XII. c. 10, § 58. *Unum subtile (genus), quod ἰσχνόν vocant, alterum grande atque robustum, quod ἁδρόν dicunt, constituunt; tertium alii medium ex duobus, alii floridum (namque id ἀνθηρόν appellant) addiderunt.*

[7] Dionys. *De Demosth.* c. 2, ἡ ἑτέρα λέξις, ἡ λιτὴ καὶ ἀφελής, καὶ δοκοῦσα κατασκευήν τε καὶ ἰσχὺν τὴν πρὸς ἰδιώτην ἔχειν λόγον καὶ ὁμοιότητα — a vague description, which tells us only that this style is based upon ἰδιώτης λόγος—the language of ordinary life.

been accepted in the main by Dionysius; and it is clear that for Cicero, as for Dionysius, Lysias was the canon of that style. According to Cicero, the chief marks of the "genus tenue" are these:—1. In regard to composition—a free structure of clauses and sentences, not straining after a rhythmical period.[1] 2. In regard to diction—(*a*) purity,[2] (*b*) clearness,[3] (*c*) propriety.[4] 3. Abstemious use of rhetorical figures.[5]

With certain exceptions, which will be noticed in their place, Lysias has these characteristics, and is the best representative of the plain style, whether viewed historically or in the abstract. That style gradually came to be used by almost all writers for the ecclesia or the law-courts; but it was Lysias, says Dionysius, who "perfected" it, and "brought it to the summit of the excellence proper to it."[6] In order that the originality of Lysias may not be underrated, attention must be given to the precise meaning of this statement. It appears to speak of him merely as having succeeded better than others in a style used by nearly all writers of speeches for the law-courts. But what was, in fact, common to him and them was this only—the avoidance of decidedly poetical ornament and the employment of sober prose. This is all that the "plain" style, as opposed to the

Originality of Lysias.

---

[1] Cic. *Orator*, § 77, *Primum igitur cum tanquam e vinculis numerorum eximamus......Solutum quiddam sit, nec vagum tamen.*

[2] *ib.* § 79, *sermo erit purus et Latinus.*

[3] *ib. dilucide planeque dicetur.*

[4] *ib. quid deceat circumspiciatur.*

[5] *ib.* § 80, *verecundus erit usus oratoriae quasi supellectilis. supellex est enim quodammodo nostra quae est in ornamentis, alia rerum, alia verborum.*

[6] Dionys. *De Demosth.* c. 2, ἐτελείωσε δ' αὐτὴν καὶ εἰς ἀκρὸν ἤγαγε τῆς ἰδίας ἀρετῆς Λυσίας ὁ Κεφάλου.

"elaborate," necessarily means. That which he had, and which no other had in the same degree, was the art of so writing this prose that it should be in character with the person who spoke it. Their style was monotonously plain; his was plain too, but it was more, it was variously natural. Dionysius shows elsewhere that he appreciated to the full the originality of Lysias; but he has hardly brought it out with sufficient clearness in the passage which has just been noticed. Lysias may, in a general sense, be regarded as the perfecter of a style already practised by many others; but it is closer to the truth to call him the founder of a new one, and of one in which he was never rivalled.[1]

It does not, perhaps, strike the modern mind as very remarkable that a man whose business was to write speeches for other people should have conceived the idea of making the speech appropriate to the person. In order to understand why this conception was, at the time, a proof of genius, it is necessary to remember how rhetoric was then viewed. Prose composition in its infancy was a craft, a close profession, just as much as poetry. Beside the sacred band of "wise" poets stood the small group of experts skilled to fashion artistic prose. When a man wished for help in a lawsuit he applied, as a matter of course,

---

[1] The question, "How far is Lysias the true representative of the genus tenue?" has been exhaustively discussed by Dr. F. Berbig, in an essay "Ueber das genus dicendi tenue des Redners Lysias" (Gymnasium-program, Cüstrin, 1871; reviewed in the Philologischer Anzeiger, III. 5. p. 252). The essay will be referred to below. Its general conclusion is that "In all his writings Lysias must be pronounced, by any judgment not absolutely rigorous, an excellent model of the plain style;" though both his composition and his language depart from it in certain points.

if he could afford it, to one of these; and it was equally a matter of course that the speech supplied to him should bear the same stamp as others turned out by the same machine. There was no pretence of its being the work of the speaker, and no expectation, therefore, that it should reflect his nature; a certain rhetorical colour, certain recognised forms of argument and appeal, were alone looked for. The idea of writing for a client so that he should have in court the whole advantage of professional aid, and, in addition to this, the advantage of appearing to have dispensed with it, was not only novel but daring. This is what Lysias first undertook to do, and did admirably.

His dramatic purpose—if it may be so called—decided the special characteristics of his style. But, even without this purpose, an instinctive dislike of exaggeration would of itself have given his style some general characteristics, sufficient to distinguish it from that of any of his contemporaries. On this account we must dissent from a view advanced by K. O. Müller in his History of Greek Literature.[1] Lysias had, he thinks, two distinct styles at two different periods of his life; the earlier, "forced and artificial"; the later, plain. Müller recognises the former in the speech in the Phaedrus, and in the Epitaphius. The turning-point was, he conceives, the impeachment of Eratosthenes, when "a real feeling of pain and anger" in the mind of Lysias gave "a more lively and natural flow both to his spirits and to his speech." "This occasion"—Müller adds—

Had his style been florid before it became plain?

[1] Vol. II. p. 143 (transl. Donaldson).

"convinced Lysias what style of oratory was both the most suited to his own character and also least likely to fail in producing an effect upon the judges." Ingenious as the theory is, we have no belief in the fact of any such abrupt transition as it supposes. That temperate mastery with which Lysias cultivated the "plain" style is doubly a marvel if it was only a sudden practical experience which weaned him from his first love for a forced and artificial rhetoric. Converts are not proverbial for discretion; and the exquisite judgment shown by Lysias after his supposed reformation ought to have prevented its necessity. Like all his contemporaries, he must, unquestionably, have had his earliest training in the florid Sicilian school; but there is nothing to show that its precepts ever took a strong hold upon him; and there is overwhelming reason to believe that a genius of the bent of his must very early have thrown off such pedantic trammels. It is true that the speech in the Phaedrus—assuming its genuineness—is more stiffly composed than any of his presumably later writings: but, on the other hand, it is, as Müller allows, entirely free from the ornaments of Gorgias. As for the Epitaphius, its spuriousness is now a generally recognised fact.[1]

Special characteristics of his style.

Plainness and an easy versatility are, then, the general characteristics of Lysias. We propose now to consider in detail his special characteristics; speaking first of his style in the narrower sense, his composition and diction; next of his method of handling subject-matter.

[1] See below.

Cicero, as we have seen, counts among the marks His Composition. of the "plain" style a free structure of sentences and clauses, not straining after a rhythmical period.[1] Dionysius, speaking of êthopoiïa in Lysias, says that he composes "quite simply and plainly, aware that ethos is best expressed, not in rhythmical periods, but in the lax (or easy) style" (ἐν τῇ διαλελυμένῃ λέξει).[2] In another place, however, he praises Lysias for a vigour, essential in contests, "which packs thoughts closely and brings them out roundly" (στρογγύλως)[3] —that is, in terse periods. Both remarks are just. Nothing more strikingly distinguishes Lysias from his predecessors and from nearly all his successors than the degree in which the structure of his sentences varies according to his subject. His speeches may in this respect be classified under three heads. First, those which are of a distinctly public character; in which the composition is thoroughly rhythmical, and which abound with artistic periods, single or combined.[4] Secondly, those speeches which, from the nature of their subjects, blend the private with the public character; which show not only fewer combinations or groups of periods, but a less careful formation of single periods.[5] Thirdly, the essentially private speeches; which differ from the second class, not in the mould of such periods as occur, but in the larger

[1] Cic. *Orator*, § 77, quoted above.

[2] Dionys. *De Lys.* c. 8.

[3] *ib.* c. 6.

[4] In this class, Berbig (in the essay mentioned above "Ueber das genus dicendi tenue des Redners Lysias," p. 8) places these speeches: 1. Or. XXVII. (κατὰ Ἐπικράτους): 2. Or. XXVIII. (κατὰ Ἐργοκλέους): 3. Or. XXIX. (κατὰ Φιλοκράτους): 4. Or. XXXIII. (Ὀλυμπιακός): 5. Or. XXXIV. (περὶ τοῦ μὴ καταλῦσαι τὴν πολιτείαν).

[5] *e.g.* 1. Or. XII. (κατὰ Ἐρατοσθένους): 2. Or. XIII. (κατὰ Ἀγοράτου): 3. Or. XVI. (κατὰ Φίλωνος): 4. Or. XIX. (περὶ τῶν Ἀριστοφάνους χρημάτων).

mixture with these of sentences or clauses not periodic.[1] Further, in each of these three classes, a greater freedom of composition distinguishes the narrative from the argument. The narrative parts of the properly public speeches are usually thrown into what may be called the historical as opposed to the oratorical period; that is, the sentences are more loosely knit and are drawn out to a greater length. According as the speech has more of a private character, these freer periods are more and more relaxed into a simple series (λέξις εἰρομένη) of longer or shorter clauses. Yet, while there are so many shades in the composition of Lysias, the colour of the whole is individual. Isocrates develops period out of period in long, luxuriant sequence; Demosthenes intersperses the most finished and most vigorous periods with less formally built sentences which relieve them; Lysias binds his periods, by twos or threes at the most, into groups always moderate in size but often monotonous in form; excelling Isocrates in compactness, but yielding to Demosthenes in life.[2]

His Diction—its purity.

The diction of Lysias is distinguished in the first place by its purity. This is a quality upon which no modern could have pronounced authoritatively, but

---

[1] In this third class two grades may be distinguished, according to the importance of the subject and the use, greater or less accordingly, of a periodic style. I. 1. Or. I. (περὶ τοῦ Ἐρατοσθένους φόνου): 2. Or. III. (κατὰ Σίμωνος): 3. Or. IV. (περὶ τραύματος ἐκ προνοίας): 4. Or. VII. (περὶ τοῦ σηκοῦ). II. 1. Or. XVII. (περὶ δημοσίων χρημάτων): 2. Or. XXIII. (κατὰ Παγκλέωνος): 3. Or. XXXII. (κατὰ Διογείτονος).

[2] Cf. Dionys. De Lys. c. 6 (speaking of the terse periodic style)—ἡ συστρέφουσα τὰ νοήματα καὶ στρογγύλως ἐκφέρουσα λέξις, Dionysius says, ταύτην ὀλίγοι μὲν ἐμιμήσαντο, Δημοσθένης δὲ καὶ ὑπερεβάλετο· πλὴν οὐχ οὕτως εὐτελῶς οὐδὲ ἀφελῶς ὥσπερ Λυσίας, χρησάμενος αὐτῇ, ἀλλὰ περιέργως καὶ πικρῶς.

for which the ancient Greek critic vouches. In the
Augustan age the reaction from florid Asianism to
Atticism had set in strongly, and especial attention
was paid by Greek grammarians to the marks of a
pure Attic style. Dionysius may be taken as a competent judge. He pronounces Lysias to be "perfectly
pure in expression, the best canon of Attic speech,—
not of the old used by Plato and Thucydides," but of
that which was in vogue in his own time.[1] This
may be seen, he adds, by a comparison with the
writings of Andocides, Critias and many others. Two
ideas are included under the "purity" praised here:
abstinence from words either obsolete (γλῶσσαι) or
novel, or too decidedly poetical; and abstinence from
constructions foreign to the idiom of the day—an
excellence defined elsewhere as "accuracy of dialect."[2]
Lysias is not rigidly pure in these respects. The only
instance of an old-fashioned syntax, indeed, which
has been noticed in him, is the occasional use of τε as
a copula;[3] nor does he use such pedantic words as
were meant by "glossae"; but rare or poetical words
and phrases occur in many places.[4] The praise of
purity must be taken in a general and relative sense.
Of those who came after Lysias, Isocrates most nearly

---

[1] Dionys. De Lys. c. 2.

[2] ib. c. 13, where the "purity" spoken of in c. 2 is defined as consisting of two elements—τὸ καθαρὸν τῶν ὀνομάτων and ἡ ἀκρίβεια τῆς διαλέκτου.

[3] This use occurs seven times in all: Or. 1. § 17: XIII. §§ 1, 82: XXXI. §§ 1. 5: XXXII. §§ 1, 22. Berbig, p. 13.

[4] e.g. Or. XXXIII. § 3, μικρολογησόμενος: § 7, οἰκοῦντες ἀπόρθητοι καὶ ἀτείχιστοι καὶ ἀστασίαστοι καὶ ἀήττητοι: Or. IV. § 8, παρωξυμμένος ὀξύχειρ λίαν καὶ πάροινός ἐστιν: § 9, ἐς τοῦτο βαρυδαιμονίας ἥκει: § 20, ἀνήκεστος συμφορά: Or. XVIII. § 49, ἀρχαιόπλουτος: Or. XIII. § 45, ἀκλεής—γηροτροφεῖν: Or. XXVI. § 4, ἀείμνηστος: Or. XXX. § 35, μισοπονηρεῖν: Or. XXIV. § 3, δυστυχήματα ἰᾶσθαι: Or. XXXIII. § 7, ἀθάνατος ἐλευθερία.

approached him in this quality;[1] but Isaeus is also commended for it.[2]

Simplicity. Next, in contrast with the Sicilian school of rhetoric, Lysias is characterised by a general avoidance of ornamental figures. Such figures as occur are mostly of the kind which men use in daily life without rhetorical consciousness,—hyperbole, metaphor, prosopopoiïa and the like.[3] As a rule, he expresses his meaning by ordinary words employed in their normal sense.[4] His panegyrical speeches and his letters are said to have presented a few exceptions to this rule; but all his business-works, as Dionysius calls them—his speeches for the ecclesia and for the law-courts—are stamped with this simplicity. He seems, as his critic says, to speak like the ordinary man, while he is in fact the most consummate of artists,[5]—a prose poet who knows how to give an unobtrusive distinction to common language, and to bring out of it a quiet and peculiar music.[6] Isocrates had the same command of familiar words, but he was not content to seek effect by artistic harmonies of these. His ambition was to be ornate; and hence one of the differences remarked

---

[1] Dionys. *De Lys.* c. 2, Ἰσοκράτης —καθαριώτατος δὴ τῶν ἄλλων μετά γε Λυσίαν.

[2] Dionys. *De Isaeo*, c. 3.

[3] As an instance of a common prosopopoiïa see *e.g.* Or. XXI. § 8, οὕτω παρεσκευασμένην τριήρη πόσα οἴεσθε ...τοὺς πολεμίους εἰργάσθαι κακά; Other common figures which occur in Lysias are synecdoche, *e.g.* Or. XXXIII. § 9, τὰς ἐλπίδας τῆς σωτηρίας: antonomasia, Or. § 15, ὁ σεμνὸς Στειριεύς: metonymia, Or. XII. § 60, τὰς πόλεις ἐπάγοντες: epanaphora, Or. XXX. § 3, πολλὰ μέν...

πολλὰ δέ: synathroismus, Or. XXXIII. § 3, καί...καί...καί...καί: periphrasis, Or. XVIII. § 3, τρόπαιον ἱστάναι, etc.

[4] Dionys. *De Lys.* c. 3 (ἀρετή) ἡ διὰ τῶν κυρίων τε καὶ κοινῶν καὶ ἐν μέσῳ κειμένων ὀνομάτων ἐκφέρουσα τὰ νοούμενα.

[5] *ib.* ὁμοίως δὲ τοῖς ἰδιώταις διαλέγεσθαι δοκῶν πλεῖστον ὅσον ἰδιώτου διαφέρει.

[6] *ib.* κράτιστος ποιητὴς λόγων λελυμένης ἐκ μέτρου λέξεως, ἰδίαν τινὰ λόγων εὑρηκὼς ἁρμονίαν, ᾗ τὰ ὀνόματα κοσμεῖ τε καὶ ἡδύνει, μηδὲν ἔχοντα ὀγκῶδες,μηδὲ φορτικόν.

by Dionysius : Isocrates is sometimes vulgar ;[1] Lysias never is. There is one kind of ornament, however, which Lysias uses largely, and in respect to which he deserts the character of the plain style. He delights in the artistic parallelism (or opposition) of clauses. This may be effected : (1) by simple correspondence of clauses in length (isokôlon) ; (2) by correspondence of word with word in meaning (antitheton proper) ; (3) by correspondence of word with word in sound (paromoion).[2] Examples are very numerous both in the public and in the private speeches. This love of antithesis—shown on a larger scale in the terse periodic composition—is the one thing which sometimes blemishes the êthos in Lysias.

Closely connected with this simplicity is his clearness. Lysias is clear in a twofold sense : in thought, and in expression. Figurative language is often a source of confusion of thought ; and the habitual avoidance of figures by Lysias is one reason why he not only speaks but thinks clearly. In regard to this clearness of expression Dionysius has an excellent remark. This quality might, he observes, result merely from "deficiency of power," i.e. poverty of language and of fancy which constrained the speaker to be simple. In the case of Lysias it does, in fact, result from *wealth of the right words.*[3] He uses only

Clearness.

---

[1] Dionys. *De Isocr.* c. 3, σχηματίζει φορτικῶς.

[2] Isokôla and homoioteleuta constantly occur together : see esp. Or. XII. (§§ 1, 4, 6, 19, 26, 32, 39, etc.) and Or. XXXIII. passim. A special form of the paromoion, viz. paronomasia, is frequent in Lysias : *e.g.* Or. XXXI. § 11, γνώμη—συγγνώμης : § 24 τιμωρηθήσεται—τετιμήσεται : Or. XXX. § 29, τὰ πάτρια—κατὰ πατέρα.

[3] *De Lys.* c. 4, καὶ εἰ μὲν δι' ἀσθένειαν δυνάμεως ἐγίγνετο τὸ σαφὲς οὐκ ἄξιον ἦν αὐτὸ ἀγαπᾶν· νῦν δὲ ὁ πλοῦτος τῶν κυρίων ὀνομάτων ἐκ πολλῆς αὐτῷ περιουσίας ἀποδείκνυται ταύτην τὴν ἀρετήν.

Conciseness.

plain words; but he has enough of these to express with propriety the most complex idea. The combination of clearness with conciseness is achieved by Lysias because he has his language thoroughly under command; his words are the disciplined servants of his thoughts.[1] Isocrates is clear; but he is not also concise. In the union of these two excellences, Isaeus [2] perhaps stands next to Lysias. There are, indeed, exceptions to the conciseness of Lysias, as there are exceptions to the purity and the plainness of his diction. Instances occur in which terms nearly synonymous are accumulated, either for the sake of emphasis or merely for the sake of symmetry;[3] but such instances are not frequent.

Vividness.

Vividness, ἐνάργεια—"the power of bringing under

---

[1] *ib.* c. 4, οὐ τοῖς ὀνόμασι δουλεύει τὰ πράγματα παρ' αὐτῷ, τοῖς δὲ πράγμασιν ἀκολουθεῖ τὰ ὀνόματα.

[2] It is remarkable that Dionysius expressly denies to Demosthenes the *invariable* clearness of Lysias, De Lys. c. 4, τῆς μὲν Θουκυδίδου λέξεως καὶ Δημοσθένους, οἳ δεινότατοι τὰ πράγματα ἐξειπεῖν ἐγένοντο, πολλὰ δυσείκαστά ἐστιν ἡμῖν καὶ ἀσαφῆ.

[3] For *emphasis* (e.g.) in Or. XIII. § 63, οἱ δ' αὐτῶν περιγενόμενοι καὶ σωθέντες, οὓς οὗτος μὲν ἀπέκτεινεν ὠμῶς καὶ θάνατος αὐτῶν κατεγνώσθη, ἡ δὲ τύχη καὶ ὁ δαίμων περιεποίησε . . . τιμῶνται ὑφ' ὑμῶν. For *symmetry* (e.g.) in Or. XXVIII. § 3, καὶ γὰρ δὴ δεινὸν ἂν εἴη εἰ νῦν μὲν οὕτως αὐτοὶ πιεζόμενοι ταῖς εἰσφοραῖς συγγνώμην τοῖς κλέπτουσι καὶ τοῖς δωροδοκοῦσιν ἔχοιτε, ἐν δὲ τῷ τέως χρόνῳ καὶ τῶν οἴκων τῶν ὑμετέρων μεγάλων ὄντων καὶ τῶν δημοσίων προσόδων μεγάλων οὐσῶν, θανάτῳ ἐκολάζετε τοὺς τῶν ὑμετέρων ἐπιθυμοῦντας: where, as Blass observes, the words μεγάλων οὐσῶν are superfluous, and the phrase τοὺς τῶν ὑμετέρων ἐπιθυμοῦντας, where τοὺς τοιούτους would have sufficed, is meant to balance τοῖς κλέπτουσι καὶ τοῖς δωροδοκοῦσιν.

Another strong instance of redundancy of the former kind—the emphatic—is Or. XXI. § 24, οὐδεπώποτ' ἠλέησα οὐδ' ἐδάκρυσα οὐδ' ἐμνήσθην γυναικὸς οὐδὲ παίδων τῶν ἐμαυτοῦ, οὐδ' ἡγούμην δεινὸν εἶναι εἰ τελευτήσας ὑπὲρ τῆς πατρίδος ὀρφανοὺς καὶ τοῦ πατρὸς ἀπεστερημένους αὐτοὺς καταλείψω. Favorinus, according to Gellius (II. v.), used to say:—"If you remove a single word from a passage of Plato, or alter it, however suitably to the sense, you will still have taken away something from the elegance; if you do so in Lysias, you will have taken away something from the sense." This praise, as we have seen, needs modification.

the senses what is narrated"[1]—is an attribute of the style of Lysias. The dullest hearer cannot fail to have before his eyes the scene described, and to fancy himself actually in presence of the persons introduced as speaking. Lysias derives this graphic force from two things :—judicious use of detail, and perception of character. A good example of it is his description, in the speech Against Eratosthenes, of his own arrest by Theognis and Peison.[2] Dionysius ascribes vividness as well as clearness, to Isocrates also;[3] but there is perhaps only one passage in the extant work of Isocrates which strictly justifies this praise.[4] A description may be brilliant without being in the least degree graphic. The former quality depends chiefly on the glow of the describer's imagination; the latter depends on his truthfulness and skill in grouping around the main incident its lesser circumstances. A lifelike picture demands the union of fine colouring and correct drawing. Isocrates was a brilliant colourist; but he was seldom, like Lysias, an accurate draughtsman.

From this trait we pass naturally to another which has just been mentioned as one of its sources—the faculty of seizing and portraying character. Of all the gifts of Lysias this is the most distinctive, and is the one which had greatest influence upon his style. It is a talent which does not admit of definition or analysis; it can be understood only by studying its results. It is shown, as Dionysius says, in three

Ethopoiia.

---

[1] Dionys. *De Lys.* c. 7, δύναμίς τις ὑπὸ τὰς αἰσθήσεις ἄγουσα τὰ λεγόμενα.
[2] *In Eratosth.* §§ 8–17.
[3] *De Isocr.* c. 2.
[4] The passage in the Aegineticus in which the speaker describes his care of Thrasylochus: §§ 24–27.

things—thought, diction, and composition;[1] that is, the ideas, the words, and the style in which the words are put together, always suit the person to whom they are ascribed.[2] There is hardly one of the extant speeches of Lysias upon which this peculiar power has not left its mark. Many of them, otherwise poor in interest, have a permanent artistic value as describing, with a few quiet touches, this or that type of man. For instance, the Defence which is the subject of the Twenty-first Oration is interesting solely because it embodies to the life that proud consciousness of merit with which a citizen who had deserved well of the State might confront a calumny. In the speech on the Sacred Olive, if the nameless accused is not a person for us, he is at least a character —the man who shrinks from public prominence of

---

[1] *De Lys.* c. 8, τριῶν τε ὄντων ἐν οἷς καὶ περὶ ἃ τὴν ἀρετὴν ταύτην συμβέβηκεν εἶναι, διανοίας τε καὶ λέξεως καὶ τρίτης τῆς συνθέσεως, ἐν ἅπασι τούτοις αὐτὸν ἀποφαίνομαι κατορθοῦν.

[2] Francken (*Commentationes Lysiacae*, pp. 5-7) thinks it doubtful whether by the ἠθοποιΐα of Lysias Dionysius meant the appropriate delineation of each several character, or the attribution to all characters alike of a certain attractive simplicity. Francken inclines to the latter view. He refers to cases in which, as he thinks, Lysias has failed, or has not tried, to mark individual character, or in which the general stamp of simplicity is exaggerated. The appreciation of ἔθος depends much upon taste; it scarcely admits of argument. But it is clear to me what Dionysius, at least, meant by the ἠθοποιΐα of Lysias. He meant the appropriate delineation of each several character. Surely he says so very plainly : *De Lys.* c. 8, οὐ γὰρ διανοουμένοις μόνον ὑποτίθεται χρηστὰ καὶ ἐπιεικῆ καὶ μέτρια τοὺς λέγοντας, ὥστε εἰκόνας εἶναι δοκεῖν τῶν ἠθῶν τοὺς λόγους ἀλλὰ καὶ τὴν λέξιν ἀποδίδωσι τοῖς ἤθεσιν οἰκείαν. Cf. K. O. Müller. *Hist. Gr. Lit.* II. p. 143 (tr. Donaldson) :—" Lysias distinguished, with the accuracy of a dramatist, between the different characters into whose mouths he put his speeches, and made every one, the young and the old, the rich and the poor, the educated and the uneducated, speak according to his quality and condition: this is what the ancient critics praise under the name of his *Ēthopoiïa*. The prevalent tone, however, was that of the average man."

any kind, but who at the same time has a shy pride in discharging splendidly all his public duties.[1] The injured husband, again, who has taken upon Eratosthenes the extreme vengeance sanctioned by the law, is the subject of an indirect portrait, in which homeliness is combined with the moral dignity of a citizen standing upon his rights.[2] The steady Athenian householder of the old type, and the adventurous patriot of the new, are sketched in the speech On the Property of Aristophanes.[3] The accuser of Diogeiton, unwilling to prosecute a relative, but resolved to have a shameful wrong redressed;—Diogeiton's mother, pleading with him for her sons;—are pictures all the more effective because they have been produced without apparent effort.[4] But of all such delineations—and, as Dionysius says, *no* character in Lysias is inartistically drawn or lifeless [5]—perhaps the cleverest and certainly the most attractive is that of Mantitheus, the brilliant young Athenian who is vindicating his past life before the Senate. Nowhere is the ethical art of Lysias more ably shown than in the ingenuous words of apology with which, as by an afterthought, Mantitheus concludes his frank and high-spirited defence :—

"I have understood, Senators, that some people are annoyed with me for this too—that I presumed, though rather young, to speak in the Assembly. It was about my own affairs that I was first compelled

---

[1] *De sacra Olea*, §§ 1-3, 30.
[2] *De caed. Eratosth.* (Or. I.) §§ 5 ff., 47-50.
[3] *De Aristoph. bonis*, §§ 18-23, 55-64.
[4] *In Diogeit.* §§ 1-3, 12-17.
[5] *De Lys.* c. 8, ἁπλῶς γὰρ οὐδὲ εὑρεῖν δύναμαι παρὰ τῷ ῥήτορι τούτῳ πρόσωπον οὔτε ἀνηθοποίητον οὔτε ἄψυχον.

to speak in public; after that, however, I *do* suspect myself of having been more ambitiously inclined than I need have been,—partly through thinking of my family, who have never ceased to be statesmen,— partly because I saw that you (to tell the truth) respect none but such men; so that, seeing this to be your opinion, who would not be invited to act and speak in behalf of the State? And besides—why should you be vexed with such men? The judgment upon them rests with none but yourselves."[1]

The "propriety" of Lysias.

The "propriety" which has always been praised in Lysias depends mainly on this discernment of what suits the character of each speaker; but it includes more—it has respect also to the hearers and to the subject, and generally to all the circumstances of the case. The judge, the ecclesiast, the listener in the crowd at a festival are not addressed in the same vein; different excellences of style characterise the opening, the narrative, the argument, the final appeal.[2]

His "charm."

It remains to say a few words on the peculiar and crowning excellence of Lysias in the province of expression,—his famous but inexplicable "charm." It is noticeable that while his Roman critics merely praise his elegance and polish, regarding it as a simple result of his art,[3] the finer sense of his Greek critic

---

[1] *Pro Mantith.* §§ 20, 21.

[2] The distinction between *Ēthopoiïa* and the *Propriety* praised in Lysias will appear from a careful reading of Dionys. *De Lys.* cc. 8, 9. Ethopoiïa is the adaptation of the speech to the intrinsic character of the speaker. Propriety is the adaptation of the speech to the circumstances:—on the one hand, to the age, quality, occupation, etc., of the speaker; on the other hand, to the cause and to the audience.

[3] Cic. *Brut.* § 35, *egregie subtilis scriptor atque elegans:* ib. § 285. *ieiunitas polita, urbana, elegans.* Quint. x. 1. 78, *subtilis atque ele-*

apprehends a certain nameless grace or charm, which
cannot be directly traced to art,—which cannot be
analysed or accounted for : it is something peculiar to
him, of which all that can be said is that it is there.
What, asks Dionysius, is the freshness of a beautiful
face ? What is fine harmony in the movements and
windings of music ? What is rhythm in the measure-
ment of times ? As these things baffle definition, so
does the charm of Lysias. It cannot be taken to
pieces by reasoning ; it must be seized by a cultivated
instinct.[1] It is the final criterion of his genuine work.
"When I am puzzled about one of the speeches
ascribed to him, and when it is hard for me to find
the truth by other marks, I have recourse to this
excellence, as to the last piece on the board. Then,
if the Graces of Speech seem to me to make the writing fair, I count it to be of the soul of Lysias ; and I
care not to look further into it. But if the stamp of
the language has no winningness, no loveliness, I am
chagrined, and suspect that after all the speech is not
by Lysias ; and I do no more violence to my instinct,
even though in all else the speech seems to me clever
and well finished ; believing that to write well, in
special styles other than this, is given to many men ;

---

gens: ix. 4. 17, *gratia quae in eo maxima est simplicis atque inaffectati coloris.* It must be allowed to Cicero that he felt the plainness of Lysias to have a charm of its own. But he did not, like Dionysius, feel this charm to be something independent of the plainness, which could be used as a distinct test of genuine work. See *Orator,* § 78, *nam ut mulieres esse dicuntur nonnullae inornatae, quas id ipsum deceat, sic haec subtilis oratio atque incompta delectat. fit enim quiddam in utroque, quo sit venustius, sed non ut appareat.*

[1] Dionys. *De Lys.* c. 11. Note the words—τίς ἡ παρ' αὐτῷ χάρις ἐστι, βουλομένοις μαθεῖν ὑποθείμην ἂν ἐπιτηδεύειν χρόνῳ μακρῷ καὶ μακρᾷ τριβῇ, καὶ ἀλόγῳ πάθει τὴν ἄλογον συνασκεῖν αἴσθησιν—"and to train their critical sense by a feeling as instinctive as itself."

but that to write winningly, gracefully, with loveliness, is the gift of Lysias."[1]

A modern reader would be sanguine if he hoped to analyse the distinctive charm of Lysias more closely than Dionysius found himself able to do. He may be content if study by degrees gives him a dim apprehension of something which he believes that he could use, as Dionysius used the qualities detected by his "instinct," in deciding between the genuine and the false. Evidently the same cause which in great measure disqualifies a modern for estimating the "purity" of the language of Lysias also disqualifies him for estimating its charm. This charm may be supposed to have consisted partly in a certain felicity of expression,—Lysias having a knack of using the word which, for some undefinable reason, was felt to be curiously right; partly in a certain essential urbanity, the reflection of a nature at once genial and refined. The first quality is evidently beyond the sure appreciation of a modern ear: the second less so, yet scarcely to be estimated with nicety, since here too shades of expression are concerned. At best a student of Lysias may hope to attain a tolerably true perception of what he could *not* have written: but hardly the faculty of rejoicing that he wrote just as he did.

His treatment of subject-matter.

Having now noticed the leading characteristics of Lysias in regard to form of language, we will consider some of his characteristics in the other great department of his art—the treatment of the subject-matter. In this the ancient critics distinguished two chief elements, Invention and Arrangement.[2]

[1] Dionys. *De Lys.* c. 11. [2] εὕρεσις—τάξις: Dionys. *De Lys.* c. 15.

By "invention" was meant the faculty of dis- *Invention.* covering the arguments available in any given circumstances; the art, in short, of making the most of a case. Socrates, criticising the speech in the *Phaedrus*, is made to express contempt for the inventive power of Lysias.[1] Arguments, however, which would not pass with a dialectician, might do very well for a jury. If Plato found Lysias barren of logical resource, Dionysius emphatically praises his fertile cleverness in discovering every weapon of controversy which the facts of a case could yield to the most penetrating search.[2] The latter part of the speech against Agoratus may be taken as a good example of this exhaustive ingenuity.[3] It is a fault, indeed, that there the speaker attempts to make too many small points in succession; and one, at least, of these is a curious instance of overdone subtlety.[4]

In regard to arrangement, Lysias is distinguished *Arrangement.* from all other Greek orators by a uniform simplicity. His speeches consist usually of four parts, which follow each other in a regular order: proem, narrative, proof, epilogue.[5] In some cases the nature of the subject renders a narrative, in the proper sense, unnecessary; in others, the narrative is at the same time the proof; in a few, the proem is almost or entirely dispensed with. But in no case is there

---

[1] Plat. *Phaedr.* pp. 234 E–236 A.
[2] Dionys. *Lys.* c. 13.
[3] *In Agorat.* §§ 49–90.
[4] *ib.* §§ 70–90, in which it is argued that the amnesty of 403 does not hold good as between two members of the same political party.
[5] ἔστι δὲ τὰ τῆς ὑποθέσεως στοιχεῖα τέσσαρα, προοίμιον, διήγησις, πίστεις, ἐπίλογος: Dionys. *Art. Rhet.* x. c. 12. Aristotle's enumeration is προοίμιον, πρόθεσις, πίστις, ἐπίλογος: *Rhet.* III. 13.

anything more elaborate than this fourfold partition, —and in no case is the sequence of the parts altered. This simple arrangement, contrasting with the manifold subdivisions which Plato notices as used by the rhetoricians of his day,[1] is usually said to have been first made by Isocrates.[2] This may be true in the sense that it was he who first stated it theoretically. In practice, however, it had already been employed by Lysias; and more strictly than by Isocrates himself.[3] The difference between their systems, according to Dionysius, is precisely this:—Lysias uses always the same simple framework, never interpolating, subdividing or defining;[4] Isocrates knows how to break the uniformity by transpositions of his own devising, or by novel episodes.[5] The same difference, in a stronger form, separates Lysias here from his imitator in much else, Isaeus. Every kind of artifice is used by Isaeus in shifting, subdividing, recombining the four rudimentary elements of the speech according to the special conditions of the case.[6] It was this versatile tact in disposing his forces—this generalship,[7] as Dionysius in one place calls it — which chiefly procured for Isaeus the reputation of unequalled adroitness in fighting a bad cause.[8] Lysias had consummate literary skill and much acuteness; but his

---

[1] *Phaedr.* pp. 266 E, 267 E. Cf. Arist. *Rhet.* IV. 13.

[2] Dionys. *Lys.* 16 : Sauppe, *O. A.* II. 224 : Cope, *Introd. to Arist. Rhetoric*, p. 332.

[3] Westermann (*Griech. Bereds.* p. 75) seems to recognise Lysias as the inventor of the fourfold partition.

[4] Dionys. *De Lys.* c. 15.

[5] Id. *De Isocr.* c. 4, τὸ διαλαμβάνεσθαι τὴν ὁμοειδίαν ἰδίαις μεταβολαῖς καὶ ξένοις ἐπεισοδίοις.

[6] Id. *De Isae.* c. 14.

[7] τοὺς δὲ δικαστὰς καταστρατηγεῖ, *De Isae.* 3.

[8] His reputation in this respect was of a somewhat sinister kind :— ἦν δὲ περὶ αὐτοῦ δόξα παρὰ τοῖς τότε γοητείας καὶ ἀπάτης, ὡς δεινὸς ἀνὴρ τεχνιτεῦσαι λόγους ἐπὶ τὰ πονηρότερα. Dionys. *De Isae.* 4.

weapons were better than his plan of campaign; he was not a subtle tactician. "In arranging what he has invented he is commonplace, frank, guileless;"[1] while Isaeus "plays all manner of ruses upon his adversary,"[2] Lysias "uses no sort of knavery."[3] Invention and selection are admirable in him: arrangement is best studied in his successors.[4]

If we turn from his general plan to his execution of its several parts, Lysias will be found to show very different degrees of merit in proem, narrative, proof and epilogue.

His proem, or opening, is always excellent, always *Proem.* gracefully and accurately appropriate to the matter in hand. This inexhaustible fertility of resource calls forth the special commendation of Dionysius. "The power shown in his proems will appear especially marvellous if it is considered that, though he wrote not fewer than 200 forensic speeches, there is not one in which he is found to have used a preface which is not plausible, or which is not closely connected with the case. Indeed, he has not twice hit upon the same syllogisms, or twice drifted into the same thoughts. Yet even those who have written little are found to have had this mischance,—that, I mean, of repeating commonplaces; to say nothing of the fact that nearly all of them borrow the prefatory remarks of others, and think no shame of doing so."[5] The opening of the speech against Diogeiton may be

---

[1] ἔστιν ἀπέριττός τις καὶ ἐλεύθερος καὶ ἀπόνηρος οἰκονομῆσαι τὰ εὑρεθέντα: Dionys. *De Lys.* c. 15.
[2] πρὸς τὸν ἀντίδικον διαπονηρεύεται, *De Isae.* c. 3.
[3] οὔτε γὰρ προκατασκευαῖς [κ.τ.λ.], ...οὔτε ταῖς ἄλλαις τοιαύταις πανουργίαις εὑρίσκεται χρώμενος: *De Lys.* c. 15.
[4] *Ib.*
[5] *Ib.* c. 17.

cited as an example of a difficult case introduced with singular delicacy and tact.

Narrative. The same kind of cleverness which never fails to make a good beginning finds a more important scope in the next stage of the speech. In narrative Lysias is masterly. His statements of facts are distinguished by conciseness, clearness and charm, and by a power of producing conviction without apparent effort to convince.[1] If these qualities mark almost equally some of the narratives in the private orations of Demosthenes,[2] it is yet Lysias and not Demosthenes to whom Dionysius points as the canon of excellence in this kind.[3] He goes so far as to say that he believes the rules for narrative given in the current rhetorical treatises to have been derived from study of models supplied by Lysias.

Proof. In the third province—that of proof—this supremacy is not maintained. Rhetorical proofs are of three kinds: (1) direct logical proofs which appeal to the reason; and indirect moral proofs which appeal (2) to the moral sense, and (3) to the feelings.

In the first sort Lysias is strong both by acuteness in discovering, and by judgment in selecting, arguments. In the second he is effective also; and succeeds, even when he has few facts to go upon, in making characters seem attractive or the reverse by

---

[1] His narratives τὴν πίστιν ἅμα λεληθότως συνεπιφέρουσιν, Dionys. *De Lys.* c. 18.

[2] After comparing an extract from the lost speech of Lysias Against Tisis with an extract from the speech of Demosthenes Against Conon, Dionysius asks—ταῦτα οὐ καθαρὰ καὶ ἀκριβῆ καὶ σαφῆ καὶ διὰ τῶν κυρίων καὶ κοινῶν ὀνομάτων κατεσκευασμένα ὥσπερ τὰ Λυσίου; and goes on to notice other excellences which both have alike. *De Demosth.* c. 13.

[3] ὅρον τε καὶ κανόνα τῆς ἰδέας ταύτης αὐτὸν ἀποφαίνομαι: *De Lys.* c. 18.

incidental touches. In the third he is comparatively weak; he cannot heighten the force of a plea, represent a wrong, or invoke compassion,[1] with sufficient spirit and intensity. Hence in the fourth and last department, the epilogue, he shows, indeed, the neatness which suits recapitulation, but not the power which ought to elevate an appeal. The nature of his progress through a speech is well described by an image which his Greek critic employs.[2] Like a soft southern breeze, his facile inspiration wafts him smoothly through the first and second stages of his voyage; at the third it droops; in the last it dies.

Epilogue.

The manner in which Lysias handles his subject-matter has now been spoken of so far as concerns its technical aspect. But, besides these characteristics of the artist which may be discovered in particular parts, there are certain general qualities, resulting from the character of the man, which colour the whole; and a word must now be said of these.

Foremost among such qualities is tact. One of its special manifestations is quick sympathy with the character of the speaker; another is perception of the style in which a certain subject should be treated or a certain class of hearers addressed. Both these have already been noticed. But, above and beyond these, there is a certain sureness in the whole conduct of a case, a certain remoteness from liability to

The tact of Lysias.

---

[1] In the technical language of Dionysius, Lysias understands οὔτε αὐξήσεις οὔτε δεινώσεις οὔτε οἴκτους: *De Lys.* c. 19.

[2] αὕτη μέντοι (ἡ χάρις), καθάπερ νότιός τις αὔρα, μέχρι προοιμίου καὶ διηγήσεως αὐτὸν ἄγει· ὅταν δὲ εἰς τοὺς ἀποδεικτικοὺς ἔλθῃ λόγους, ἀμυδρά τις γίγνεται καὶ ἀσθενής· ἐν δὲ δὴ τοῖς παθητικοῖς εἰς τέλος ἀποσβέννυται: Dionys. *De Demosth.* c. 13.

blunder, which is the most general indication of the tact of Lysias. Among his genuine extant speeches there is only one which perhaps in some degree offers an exception to the rule :—the speech Against Evandrus.[1] In the case of the speech Against Andocides, the conspicuous absence of a fine discretion is one of the most conclusive proofs that Lysias was not the author.[2] In relation to treatment, this tact is precisely what the "charm" praised by Dionysius is in relation to language; it is that quality, the presence or absence of which is the best general criterion of what Lysias did or did not write.

His humour. A quality which the last almost implies is humour; and this Lysias certainly had. The description of an incorrigible borrower, in the fragment of the lost speech against the Socratic Aeschines, shows this humour tending to broad farce,[3] and illustrates what Demetrius means by the "somewhat comic graces"[4]

---

[1] See the remarks below upon this speech.

[2] The internal evidence against the authenticity of the speech Against Andocides is discussed below.

[3] Fragment 1 in Sauppe, *O. A.* II. p. 172. The passage especially meant here begins at ἀλλὰ γάρ, ὦ ἄνδρες δικασταί, οὐκ εἰς ἐμὲ μόνον τοιοῦτός ἐστιν, and goes down to ἢ τούτῳ συμβάλλειν :—

"But indeed, judges, I am not the only person to whom he behaves in this way; he is the same to every one else who has had to do with him. Have not the neighbouring shopkeepers, from whom he gets on credit goods for which he never pays, shut up their shops and gone to law with him? Are not his neighbours so cruelly used by him that they have left their houses and are trying to take others at a distance? Whenever he has collected club-subscriptions, he fails to hand over the payments of the other members, and they are wrecked on this little tradesman like chariots at the turning-post of the course. Such a crowd goes at daybreak to his house to demand the sums due to them, that passers-by fancy the people have come to attend a funeral. As for the inhabitants of the Peiraeus, they are in such a mind that they think it much safer to sail to the Adriatic than to encounter this man."

[4] Demetr. περὶ ἑρμηνείας, § 128 (Walz, *Rhet. Gr.* IX. 58): τῶν δὲ χαρίτων αἱ μέν εἰσι μείζονες καὶ σεμνότεραι, αἱ δὲ εὐτελεῖς μᾶλλον καὶ κωμικώτεραι, οἷον αἱ Ἀριστοτέλους χάριτες καὶ Σώφρονος καὶ Λυσίου.

of Lysias. But, as a rule, it is seen only in sudden touches, which amuse chiefly because they surprise; as in the speech for Mantitheus, and most of all in that for the Invalid.[1] Really powerful sarcasm must *Sarcasm.* come from earnest feeling; and Lysias, though intellectual acuteness gave him command of irony, was weak in sarcasm for the same reason that he was not great in pathos. There is, properly speaking, only one extant speech — that against Nicomachus — in which sarcasm is a principal weapon.[2] Here he is moderately successful, but not in the best way; for, just as in his attack upon Aeschines, vehemence, tending to coarseness, takes the place of moral indignation.

The language, the method, the genius of Lysias *Defects of Lysias as an orator.* have now been considered in reference to their chief positive characteristics. But no attempt to estimate what Lysias was would be true or complete if it failed to point out what he was not. However high the rank which he may claim as a literary artist, he cannot, as an orator, take the highest. The defects which exclude him from it are chiefly two; and these are to a certain extent the defects of his qualities. As he excelled in analysis of character and in elegance, so he was, as a rule, deficient in pathos and in fire.

It would be untrue to say that Lysias never *The limits of pathos in Lysias.* appeals to the feelings with effect, and unfair to assume that he lacked the power of appealing to them with force. But the bent of his mind was

---

[1] *e.g. In Mantith.* (Or. XVI.) § 15: *Pro Inval.* (Or. XXIV.) § 9. Cf. *De sacra Olea* (Or. VII.) §§ 1, 14.   [2] See esp. *In Nicom.* (Or. XXX.) §§ 11, 27.

critical; his artistic instinct shrank from exaggeration of every sort; and, instead of giving fervent expression to his own sense of what was pitiable or terrible in any set of circumstances, it was his manner merely to draw a suggestive picture of the circumstances themselves. This self-restraint will be best understood by comparing a passage of Lysias with a similar passage of Andocides. The speech On the Mysteries describes the scene in the prison when mothers, sisters, wives came to visit the victims of the informer Diocleides.[1] A like scene is described in the speech Against Agoratus, when the persons whom he had denounced took farewell in prison of their kinswomen.[2] But the two orators take different means of producing a tragic effect. "There were cries and lamentations," says Andocides, "weeping and wailing for the miseries of the hour."[3] Lysias simply remarks that the wife who came to see her husband had already put on mourning.[4] For hearers of a certain class the pathos of facts is more eloquent than an express appeal; but the speaker who is content to rely upon it renounces the hope of being found pathetic by the multitude. It was only now and then that, without going beyond the limits which his own taste imposed, Lysias could expect to stir general sympathy. In the defence which he wrote for the nephews of Nicias, the last survivors of a house made desolate by violent deaths and now threatened with spoliation, he found such an opportunity. He used it well, because, though declamation would have been

---

[1] Andoc. *De Myst.* §§ 48–51.
[2] Lys. *In Agorat.* §§ 39–42.
[3] *De Myst.* § 48.
[4] *In Agorat.* § 40.

easy, he abstained from everything rhetorical and hollow. The few words in which the defendant speaks of his claim to the protection of the court are plain and dignified:—

"Judges, I have no one to put up to plead for us; for of our kinsmen some have died in war, after showing themselves brave men, in the effort to make Athens great; some, in the cause of the democracy and of your freedom, have died by the hemlock of the Thirty; and so the merits of our kinsmen, and the misfortunes of the State, have become the causes of our friendlessness. It befits you to think of these things and to help us with good will, considering that under a democracy those deserve to be well treated at your hands who, under an oligarchy, had their share of the troubles."[1]

After inquiring how far Lysias fails in pathos, it remains to speak of the other principal defect noticed above. How far, and in what sense, does he want fire? By "fire" is meant here the passion of a speaker stirred with great ideas. Dionysius says (in effect) that, besides pathos, Lysias wants two other things, grandeur and spirit.[2] He has not—we are told—the intensity or the force[3] of Demosthenes; he touches, but does not pierce, the heart;[4] he charms, but fails to astonish or to appal.[5] This is true; but it should be remembered that in a great majority of the causes with which he had to deal the attempt

The eloquence of Lysias rarely passionate.

---

[1] *De bonis Niciae fratris* (Or. XVIII.) §§ 24, 25.
[2] Dionysius says that the style of Lysias is not ὑψηλή and μεγαλοπρεπής: nor θυμοῦ καὶ πνεύματος μεστή: *De Lys.* c. 13.
[3] τόνος—ἰσχύς: Dionys. *Demosth.* 13.
[4] He wants τὸ πικρόν: id. *Lys.* 13.
[5] His style being neither θαυμαστή nor καταπληκτική: *ib.*

at sublimity would have been ridiculous. It may be granted that, had Lysias been called upon to plead for Olynthus or to denounce Philip, he would not have approached even distantly the lofty vehemence of Demosthenes. The absence of passion cannot properly be regarded as a defect in his extant speeches; but they at least suggest that under no circumstances could he have excelled in passionate eloquence. They indicate a power which sufficed to elaborate them, rather than a power which gave them their special qualities out of an affluence of resource. Two speeches, however, must be named, one of which shows (in what remains of it) the inspiration of a great idea, the other, the inspiration of an ardent feeling. These are the *Olympiacus* and the speech Against Eratosthenes. If in each of these Lysias has shown himself worthy of his subject, the inference in his favour should be strengthened by the fact that, so far as we know, these are the noblest subjects which he treated.

In the *Olympiacus* he is enforcing the necessity of union among Greeks and calling upon Sparta to take the lead :—

"It befits us, then, to desist from war among ourselves and to cleave, with a single purpose, to the public weal, ashamed for the past and apprehensive for the future; it befits us to imitate our forefathers, who, when the barbarians coveted the land of others, inflicted upon them the loss of their own; and who, after driving out the tyrants, established liberty for all men alike. But I wonder most of all at the Lacedaemonians, and at the policy which can induce them to view passively the conflagration of Greece. They are the leaders of the Greeks, as they deserve to be, both for their inborn gallantry and for their warlike science; they alone dwell exempt from ravage, though unsheltered by walls; unvexed by faction; strangers to defeat; with usages which never vary; thus warranting the hope that the freedom which they have achieved is immortal, and that, having proved themselves in past perils the deliverers of Greece, they are now thoughtful for her future."[1]

In the speech Against Eratosthenes, he concludes the impeachment with an appeal to the two parties who had alike suffered from the Thirty Tyrants:—the Townsmen, or those who had remained at Athens under the oligarchy; and the democratic exiles who had held the Peiraeus:—

"I wish, before I go down, to recall a few things to the recollection of both parties, the party of the Town and the party of the Peiraeus; in order that, in passing sentence, you may have before you as warnings the calamities which have come upon you through these men.

"And you, first, of the Town—reflect that under their iron rule you were forced to wage with brothers, with sons, with citizens a war of such a sort that, having been vanquished, you are the equals of the conquerors, whereas, had you conquered, you would have been the slaves of the Tyrants. They would have gained wealth for their own houses from the administration; you have impoverished yours in the

[1] *Olympiacus* (Or. XXXIII.) §§ 6, 7.

war with one another; for they did not deign that you should thrive along with them, though they forced you to become odious in their company; such being their consummate arrogance that, instead of seeking to win your loyalty by giving you partnership in their prizes, they fancied themselves friendly if they allowed you a share of their dishonours. Now, therefore, that you are in security, take vengeance to the utmost of your power both for yourselves and for the men of the Peiraeus; reflecting that these men, villains that they are, were your masters, but that now good men are your fellow-citizens,—your fellow-soldiers against the enemy, your fellow-counsellors in the interest of the State; remembering, too, those allies whom these men posted on the acropolis as sentinels over their despotism and your servitude. To you—though much more might be said—I say thus much only.

"But you of the Peiraeus—think, in the first place, of your arms—think how, after fighting many a battle on foreign soil, you were stripped of those arms, not by the enemy, but by these men in time of peace; think, next, how you were warned by public criers from the city bequeathed to you by your fathers, and how your surrender was demanded of the cities in which you were exiles. Resent these things as you resented them in banishment; and recollect, at the same time, the other evils that you have suffered at their hands;—how some were snatched out of the market-place or from temples and put to a violent death; how others were torn from children, parents, or wife, and forced to become their own murderers, nor allowed the common decencies of burial, by men who believed their own empire to be surer than the vengeance from on high.

"And you, the remnant who escaped death, after perils in many places, after wanderings to many cities and expulsion from all, beggared of the necessaries of life, parted from children, left in a fatherland which was hostile or in the land of strangers, came through many obstacles to the Peiraeus. Dangers many and great confronted you; but you proved yourselves brave men; you freed some, you restored others to their country.

"Had you been unfortunate and missed those aims, you yourselves would now be exiles, in fear of suffering what you suffered before. Owing to the character of these men, neither temples nor altars, which even in the sight of evil-doers have a protecting virtue, would have availed you against wrong;— while those of your children who are here would have been enduring the outrages of these men, and those who are in a foreign land, in the absence of all succour, would, for the smallest debt, have been enslaved.

"I do not wish, however, to speak of what might have been, seeing that what these men have done is beyond my power to tell; and indeed it is a task not for one accuser, or for two, but for a host.

"Yet is my indignation perfect for the temples which these men bartered away or defiled by entering them; for the city which they humbled; for the arsenals which they dismantled; for the dead, whom you, since you could not rescue them alive, must vindicate in their death. And I think that they are listening to us, and will be aware of you when you give your verdict, deeming that such as absolve these men have passed sentence upon *them*, and that such as exact retribution from these have taken vengeance in *their* names.

"I will cease accusing. You have heard—seen—suffered: you have them: judge."[1]

Place of Lysias in the history of Rhetoric.

On reviewing the general position of Lysias among the Attic orators, it will be seen to result mainly from his discovery, made at a time when Rhetoric had not yet outlived the crudest taste for finery, that the most complete art is that which hides itself. Aided not only by a delicate mastery of language but by a peculiar gift for reading and expressing character, he created a style of which the chief mark was various naturalness. It was long before the art of speaking reached, in general practice, that sober maturity which his precocious tact had given to it in a limited field; it was long before his successors freed themselves to any great extent—few wholly freed themselves—from the well-worn allurements which he had decisively rejected when they were freshest. But at least no one of those who came after dared to neglect the lesson taught by Lysias; the attempt to be natural, however artificially or rarely, was henceforward a new element in the task which professors of eloquence conceived to be set before them. Lysias remains, for all after-times, the master of the plain style.

[1] *In Eratosth.* §§ 92–100.

This supremacy in a definite province is allowed to him by the general voice of antiquity through the centuries in which its culture was finest; the praise becoming, however, less discriminating as the instinct which directed it became less sure.

The ancient critics upon Lysias.

Plato's satire [1] upon Lysias—for not having seen that the writing of love-letters is a branch of Dialectic—is joined to a notice of the clearness, compactness, finished polish of his language;[2] and it would perhaps be unfair to Plato to assume that in the one place where he seems at all just to Lysias he meant to be altogether ironical. Isaeus was a careful student of Lysias.[3] If Aristotle[4] seldom quoted him, if Theo-

---

[1] Plat. *Phaedr.* p. 264 B: οὐ χύδην δοκεῖ βεβλῆσθαι τὰ τοῦ λόγου; ἢ φαίνεται τὸ δεύτερον εἰρημένον ἔκ τινος ἀνάγκης δεῖν δεύτερον τεθῆναι; It is on this ground—the *unphilosophic* character of Lysias—that Plato gives such a decided preference to Isocrates. Compare the remark of Dionysius that Isaeus differs from Lysias in this among other things—τῷ μὴ κατ' ἐνθύμημά τι λέγειν ἀλλὰ καὶ κατ' ἐπιχείρημα (*De Is.* 16). That is, Isaeus frequently makes an attempt (ἐπιχείρημα) at strict logical proof; whereas Lysias rarely goes beyond the rhetorical syllogism (ἐνθύμημα).

[2] *Phaedr.* p. 234 E: τί δέ; καὶ ταύτῃ δεῖ τὸν λόγον ἐπαινεθῆναι, ὡς τὰ δέοντα εἰρηκότος τοῦ ποιητοῦ, ἀλλ' οὐκ ἐκείνῃ μόνον, ὅτι σαφῆ καὶ στρογγύλα, καὶ ἀκριβῶς ἕκαστα τῶν ὀνομάτων ἀποτετόρνευται;

[3] Dionys. *De Is.* 2: [Plut.] *Vit. Isae.*

[4] In the extant works of Aristotle there occur but two quotations from authentic speeches of Lysias: (1) In *Rhet.* III. ad fin. εἴρηκα, ἀκηκόατε, ἔχετε, κρίνατε: cited as an example of effective asyndeton. This is probably an inaccurate citation of the ἀκηκόατε, ἑωράκατε, πεπόνθατε, ἔχετε, δικάζετε with which the speech Against Eratosthenes closes. (2) In *Rhet.* II. c. 23, § 18, there is a quotation from § 11 of the speech of Lysias περὶ τῆς πολιτείας (Or. XXXIV.): εἰ φεύγοντες μὲν ἐμαχόμεθα ὅπως κατέλθωμεν, κατελθόντες δὲ φευξόμεθα ὅπως μὴ μαχώμεθα.

The citation in *Rhet.* III. c. 10, § 7 (διότι ἄξιον ἦν ἐπὶ τῷ τάφῳ—συγκαταθαπτομένης τῇ ἀρετῇ αὐτῶν τῆς ἐλευθερίας) from § 60 of the ἐπιτάφιος ascribed to Lysias (Or. II.) cannot be reckoned, since that speech is unquestionably spurious. Blass remarks that the words quoted by Demetrius (περὶ ἑρμ. § 28) from a lost work of Aristotle περὶ δικαιοσύνης resemble what we read in § 39 of the speech Against Eratosthenes. (*Att. Bereds.* p. 377, note 3.)

phrastus[1] appears to have missed, and Demetrius[2] to have underrated his peculiar merits, one of the first orators of their generation, Deinarchus,[3] often took him for a model. When the taste for Attic simplicity, lost during two centuries in the schools of Asia, revived at Rome, Lysias was recognised as its truest representative. Though most of his Roman imitators appear to have become feeble in seeking to be plain, one of them, Licinius Calvus, is allowed at least the praise of elegance.[4] Cicero's criticism of Lysias is not close; it does not analyse with any exactness the special qualities of his style; but the general appreciation which it shows is just. For Cicero, Lysias is the model, not of a plain style merely, but of Attic refinement;[5] he has also the highest degree of

---

[1] Dionysius expresses indignant astonishment at the assertion of Theophrastus (ἐν τοῖς περὶ λέξεως) that Lysias had a taste for vulgar redundancy of ornament (φορτικῶν καὶ περιέργων αὐτὸν οἴεται ζηλωτὴν γενέσθαι λόγων). Moderns may share this surprise, when they find that Theophrastus referred in support of his opinion to a speech said to have been composed by Lysias for the captive general Nicias. The few words quoted by Theophrastus suffice to indicate the work of a third-rate rhetorician: see above, p. 145. Cf. Sauppe's remarks on the fragment, O. A. II. p. 199.

[2] In a passage of the περὶ ἑρμηνείας (§ 128) already noticed, the epithets which Demetrius gives to the "graces" of Lysias are εὐτελεῖς —κωμικώτεραι. It is significant that Demetrius should have mistaken ἀφέλεια for εὐτέλεια, plainness for paltriness. He lived at the time when Greek eloquence, in the first stage of its decline, was beginning to affect the tawdry ornament of the Rhodian school. (See Westerm. Griech. Bereds. p. 165.)

[3] Dionysius names certain speeches of Deinarchus as bearing especially the Λυσιακὸς χαρακτήρ. Hypereides and (of course) Demosthenes were the two other masters by whom Deinarchus was chiefly influenced. (Dionys. De Dein. c. 5.)

Among the less eminent imitators of Lysias who belonged nearly to the age of Deinarchus, Cicero names Charisius and Hegesias of Magnesia (Brut. § 286: Orator, § 226).

[4] Cic. Brutus, § 283, Accuratius quoddam dicendi et exquisitius afferebat genus. He treated this style scienter eleganterque, though with a certain self-conscious and overwrought care which deprived it of freshness and force.

[5] De Oratore, III. 7, § 28, Suavitatem Isocrates, subtilitatem Lysias, acumen Hyperides, sonitum Aeschines, vim Demosthenes habuit. Compare Orator,

vigour;[1] and though grandeur was seldom possible in the treatment of such subjects as he chose, some passages of his speeches have elevation.[2] Yet, while Demosthenes could use the simplicity of Lysias, it is doubtful (Cicero thinks) whether Lysias could ever have risen to the height of Demosthenes;[3] Lysias is "almost" a second Demosthenes,[4] or, what is the same thing, "almost" a perfect orator;[5] but his mastery is limited to a province. The Augustan age produced by far the best and fullest of known ancient criticisms upon Lysias, that of Dionysius.[6] The verdict of Caecilius has perished with his work on the Ten Orators; but the remark preserved from it, that Lysias was abler in the invention than in the arrangement of arguments,[7] shows discernment. This quality marks in a less degree the judgments of subsequent writers. Quintilian[8] only commends Lysias in general terms for plain elegance of language and mastery of

§ 29, *intelligamus hoc esse Atticum in Lysia, non quod tenuis sit atque inornatus, sed quod nihil habeat insolens aut ineptum.*

[1] *Brutus*, § 64, *Quanquam in Lysia saepe sunt etiam lacerti, ita sic ut fieri nihil possit valentius.*

[2] *De opt. gen. Oratorum*, § 9, *Est enim (Lysias) multis locis grandior; sed quia et privatas ille plerasque et cas ipsas aliis et parvarum rerum caussulas scripsit, videtur esse ieiunior, quom se ipse consulto ad minutarum genera caussarum limaverit.*

[3] *ib.* § 10, *Ita fit ut Demosthenes certe possit summisse dicere, elate Lysias fortasse non possit.*

[4] *Orator*, § 226, *Lysiam—alterum paene Demosthenem.*

[5] *Brutus*, § 35, *Quem iam prope audeas oratorem perfectum dicere; nam plane quidem perfectum, et cui nihil admodum desit, Demosthenem facile dixeris.*

[6] Besides the special essay on Lysias, and the short notice in the κρίσις ἀρχαίων, v. 1, there is much criticism upon him in the essays upon Isocrates, Isaeus, Demosthenes and Deinarchus. It is necessary to study these in connexion with the essay on Lysias; they explain, or limit, many statements found there.

[7] The criticism is cited, and contested, by Photius, p. 489 B, quoted below.

[8] Quint. IX. 4. 16: X. 1. 78 (Lysias) *...quo nihil, si oratori satis est docere, quaeras perfectius.*

clear exposition; Hermogenes[1] especially praises, not his winningness, but his hidden force, classing him with Isaeus and Hypereides, next to Demosthenes in political eloquence. Photius[2] goes wide of the mark; he praises Lysias for those things in which he was relatively weak, pathos and sublime intensity; and disputes the just observation of Caecilius that Lysias excelled in invention rather than in arrangement.

Lysias and his Successors. A few words will be enough to mark the broad differences between Lysias and those three of his successors who may best be compared with him,— Isaeus, Isocrates and Demosthenes. Isocrates, like Lysias, has purity of diction and accuracy of idiom; command of plain language (though he is seldom content with it); power of describing, though not of dramatising, character; propriety and persuasiveness. But while Lysias hides his art in order to be more winning, Isocrates aims openly at the highest artificial ornament, and escapes being frivolous or frigid only by the greatness of most of his subjects and the earnestness with which he treats them. Isaeus, a direct student of Lysias, resembles him most in his diction, which is not only, like that of Isocrates, clear and pure, but concise also; further, he strives, like

---

[1] In the περὶ ἰδεῶν, II. c. 41, Hermogenes ranks Lysias, with Isaeus and Hypereides, next to Demosthenes in mastery of the πολιτικὸς λόγος. In his chapter περὶ δεινότητος (περὶ ἰδ. II. 9) he says that there are three kinds of δεινότης—that which is and seems, that which seems and is not, and that which is but does not seem. The last, or hidden, δεινότης is, he thinks, most perfectly exemplified in Lysias.

[2] Photius, *cod.* 262 : ἔστι δὲ ὁ Λυσίας δεινὸς μὲν παθήνασθαι, ἐπιτήδειος δὲ τοὺς πρὸς αὔξησιν διαθεῖναι λόγους.—Id. p. 489 b. 13 : Καικίλιος δὲ ἁμαρτάνει εὑρετικὸν μὲν τὸν ἄνδρα εἴπερ ἄλλον τινὰ συνομολογῶν, οἰκονομῆσαι δὲ τὰ εὑρεθέντα οὐχ οὕτως ἱκανόν· καὶ γὰρ κἂν τούτῳ τῷ μέρει τῆς ἀρετῆς τοῦ λόγου οὐδενὸς ὁρᾶται καταδεέστερος—injudicious praise indeed.

his master, to conceal his art, but never quite succeeds in this. The excellence of Demosthenes comprises that of Lysias, since, while the latter is natural by art, the former is so by the necessary sincerity of genius; but Demosthenes is not, like Lysias, plain; nor has he the same delicate charm; grandeur and irresistible power take its place.

Lastly—it should be remembered that it is not only as an orator but also, and even more, as a writer that Lysias is important; that, great as were his services to the theory and practice of eloquence, he did greater service still to the Greek language. He brought the everyday idiom into a closer relation than it had ever before had with the literary idiom, and set the first example of perfect elegance joined to plainness; deserving the praise that, as in fineness of ethical portraiture he is the Sophocles, in delicate control of thoroughly idiomatic speech he is the Euripides of Attic prose.

Services of Lysias to the prose idiom.

CHAPTER IX

LYSIAS

WORKS

The Extant Collection.—Epideictic and Deliberative Speeches

THE Plutarchic biographer of Lysias says:—"425 compositions pass under his name; of which 233 are pronounced genuine by Dionysius and Caecilius."[1] The precise number 233 was probably given by Dionysius *or* Caecilius, not by both; but it may be taken as representing roughly the proportion of genuine to spurious allowed by the Augustan Atticists. It is not difficult to understand how the list of works attributed to Lysias had become so large and so inaccurate. His fertility was known to have been great; his style was distinguished less by any salient features than by marks needing for their recognition a finer sense, especially an instinct for the

---

[1] [Plut.] *Vit. Lys.* φέρονται δ' αὐτοῦ λόγοι τετρακόσιοι εἴκοσι πέντε· τούτων γνησίους φασὶν οἱ περὶ Διονύσιον καὶ Καικίλιον εἶναι διακοσίους τριάκοντα. Photius, in his transcript of the passage (*cod.* 262), has διακοσίους τριάκοντα τρεῖς: and probably τρεῖς is to be replaced in [Plut.]. The general term λόγοι is to be understood as including Letters: Cf. Dionys. *de Lys.* 1, γράψας λόγους εἰς δικαστήρια ... πρὸς δὲ τούτοις ... ἐπιστολικούς.— Suidas (s. v. Λυσίας) says λόγοι δ' αὐτοῦ λέγονται εἶναι γνήσιοι ὑπὲρ τοὺς τ' (300) perhaps a mere slip for σ'— (200).

niceties of Attic idiom; and it was not until the Attic revival under Augustus that such an instinct, dead during two centuries, was brought back to an artificial life. Meanwhile the grammarians of Pergamus and Alexandria, presuming on the reputation of Lysias for industry, had probably been lavish in ascribing to him such anonymous forensic speeches as bore the general stamp of the "plain" style.

Thirty-four speeches, entire, or represented by large fragments, are extant under the name of Lysias. A hundred and twenty-seven lost speeches are known from smaller fragments or by their titles. Three letters, cited by grammarians, are identified by the names of the persons to whom they were addressed. If to this list is added the disputed Eróticus in Plato's Phaedrus, 165 of the 425 compositions mentioned in the Plutarchic Life have been accounted for; 260 remain unknown.[1]

Proportion of Extant to Lost Works.

Of the 34 speeches now usually reckoned as extant, three are mere fragments, though large fragments, preserved by Dionysius alone, and printed with the rest only in the more recent editions of Lysias. These are Nos. XXXII. (Against Diogeiton); XXXIII. (Olympiacus); XXXIV. (Defence of the Constitution). Of the other 31 speeches eight are more or less mutilated. In the first place an entire quaternion (eight pages), and three pages of another, are wanting in the Palatine MS. The lost quaternion contained the end of Or. XXV. (Defence on a Charge of abolishing the Commonwealth), the speech Against

Condition of the Extant Speeches.

---

[1] For the titles and fragments of the 127 lost speeches, and of the letters, see Sauppe, *Or. Att.* II. pp. 170–210. Blass reckons 170 (instead of 165) compositions known by name: *Att. Bereds.* pp. 348–365.

Nicides, and the beginning of Or. XXVI. (Against Evandrus). The imperfect quaternion contained on its first two pages the end of Or. V. (For Callias), and the beginning of Or. VI. (Against Andocides); on its last page, a passage in Or. VI. corresponding to the lacuna in § 49 after ἀνταποδούς. In the next place the archetype of the Palatine MS. itself was defective. The gaps are at the beginning of Or. IV. (On Wounding with Intent); at the end of Or. XVII. (On the Property of Eraton); at the beginning of Or. XVIII. (On the Property of Eucrates); and at the beginning of Or. XXI. (On a Charge of taking Bribes). Thus of the 34 speeches only 23 are entire.[1]

Arrangement in the MSS.

Leaving aside the three speeches known only from Dionysius, the other 31, as arranged in the MSS., form three divisions. The first division consists of the solitary epideictic speech, No. II. (the Epitaphius) —interpolated, as it were, by accident, and (considering its almost certain spuriousness) possibly at a late time. The second division consists of Orations I. and III. to XI. inclusive,—all forensic, except VIII., and arranged with an attempt at classification of subjects. Oration I. refers to a case of murder; III. and IV. to cases of wounding with murderous intent; V. VI. VII. deal with cases of impiety; VIII.–XI. (inclusive) concern, directly or indirectly, cases of libel (κακηγορία); —No. VIII., though not forensic, being numbered with these for convenience. In the third division, consisting of Orations XII.–XXXI. inclusive, no such system of arrangement can be discovered; but the

---

[1] These facts are taken partly from Baiter and Sauppe's edition of the text of Lysias, and the critical notes thereto; partly from the references of Blass to Sauppe's *Epistola Critica* (*Att. Bereds.* pp. 368–371).

twenty speeches have this in common, that all relate to causes either formally or virtually public. Oration XVII. (On Eraton's Property — in the MSS. περὶ δημοσίων ἀδικημάτων), though not formally public, is so virtually, as concerning a confiscation to the treasury; the case dealt with by Or. XXIII. (Against Pancleon), though private in form, is so far akin to a public cause that it turns upon a disputed claim to Athenian citizenship.

It seems probable that each of these two divisions —Or. I. with III. to XI., and Or. XII. to XXXI.—is a fragment of a manuscript edition which originally comprised all the speeches of Lysias; but whether both fragments belong to the same edition can hardly be decided.[1]

The extant speeches of Lysias may be considered under the heads of Epideictic, Deliberative and Forensic. After these, it will remain to speak of the Miscellaneous Writings ascribed to him, represented by the Address to his Companions (Or. VIII.) and the Platonic Eróticus. Lastly, the Fragments of speeches and letters will claim notice.

Epideictic Speeches

Of the Epideictic speeches of Lysias at least one genuine specimen remains—the fragment of an

---

[1] If both fragments belong to the same edition, then this edition would seem to have contained (1) the public speeches, classed together as such, but not arranged according to subjects, with the great speeches Against Eratosthenes and Against Agoratus (XII. XIII.) at their head: (2) the private speeches—whether technically private, or only virtually so, as concerning the individual more than the State—arranged according to subjects. But then it is difficult to explain why Orat. VI., Against Andocides—essentially a δημόσιος λόγος—should appear among the latter.

<small>Oratory at the Panhellenic festivals.</small>

oration delivered at the Olympic festival. The fashion of addressing a set harangue to the Panhellenic concourse at the great national meetings had been set by the earliest sophists. Hippias "used to charm Greece at Olympia with ornate and elaborate speeches."[1] The Olympic oration of Gorgias was renowned; and at Delphi his golden statue stood in the temple where, during the panegyris, he had "thundered his Pythian speech from the altar."[2] If only as displays of rhetorical art, such harangues were in harmony with the character of the great Panhellenic meetings, the central idea of which was open competition in every sort of excellence, physical and mental. But the speaker at such a time would have certain practical themes suggested to him by the occasion itself, and would enjoy a rare opportunity of treating them with practical effect. He could interpret and apply to passing events the thought, necessarily present to every mind in such an assemblage, of a common Hellenic brotherhood. Gorgias had not failed to strike this chord. "His speech at Olympia dealt with the largest of political questions. Seeing Greece torn by faction, he became a counsellor of concord, seeking to turn the Greeks against the barbarians, and advising them to take for the prizes of their arms not each others' cities but the land of the barbarians."[3] Hellenic nationality as a tie no less real than local citizenship, the Hellenic cause as paramount to all individual interests, must, in one form or another, have always been

---

[1] ἔθελγε τὴν Ἑλλάδα ἐν Ὀλυμπίᾳ λόγοις ποικίλοις καὶ πεφροντισμένοις εὖ, Philostr. *Vit. Sophist.* I. 11.

[2] τὸν λόγον τὸν Πυθικὸν ἀπὸ τοῦ βωμοῦ ἤχησεν, *ib.* I. 9.

[3] Philostr. *l. c.*

the foremost topic of speakers at the Panhellenic festivals.

This topic had a special significance at the moment when the Olympiacus of Lysias was spoken.[1] It was spoken, according to Diodôrus, in the first year of the 98th Olympiad, 388 B.C.—the year before the Peace of Antalcidas, by which the Corinthian War was brought to a close. Athens, Thebes, Argos and Corinth had in 388 been seven years at war with Sparta. During this time two powers, both dangerous to the freedom of Greece, had been rapidly growing. In the east the naval strength of Persia had become greater than it had been for a century. In the west Dionysius, tyrant, since 405, of Syracuse, had reduced Naxos, Catana, and Leontini; had twice defeated Carthage; and was threatening the Greek towns of Italy.

The Olympiacus.

A magnificent embassy from the court of Dionysius, with his brother Thearides at its head, appeared at the Olympic festival of 388. Tents embroidered with gold were pitched in the sacred enclosure; a number of splendid chariots were entered in the name of Dionysius for the four-horse chariot-race; while rhapsodists, whose skill in recitation attracted crowds, repeated poems composed by their royal master.[2] While eye and ear were thus allured by the glories of the Syracusan tyrant, Lysias lifted up his voice to remind the assembled Greeks

The Embassy from Dionysius.

---

[1] xiv. 107, 109. Grote (x. 103, note) rejects the statement of Diodôrus, and assumes 384 B.C.—the next festival—as the date; but on grounds which do not appear conclusive. The oration distinctly speaks of a war as going on at the time: ὥστε ἄξιον τὸν μὲν πρὸς ἀλλήλους πόλεμον καταθέσθαι, § 6: and in 384 the Corinthian war had been over for three years.

[2] Diod. xiv. 109.

that in Dionysius they must recognise one of the two great enemies of Greece. Let them not admit to their sacred festival the representatives of an impious despotism. Let them remember that their duty is to overthrow that tyranny and to set Sicily free; and let the war be begun forthwith by an attack upon those glittering tents.[1]

Only the first part of the speech has been preserved; but, to judge from the scale on which the topics are treated and from the point in the argument which the extract reaches, the whole cannot have been much longer.

Analysis. After praising Heracles for having founded the Olympic festival in order to promote goodwill among all Hellenes (§§ 1, 2), the speaker says that he is not going to trifle with words like a mere sophist, but to offer serious counsel upon the dangers of Greece. Part of the Greek world is already subject to barbarians, part to tyrants. Artaxerxes is rich in ships and money; so is Dionysius. Greeks must lay aside civil strife, and unite like their fathers against their common foes (§§ 3–6). The Lacedaemonians are the acknowledged leaders of Greece, unconquered abroad, untroubled by faction at home. Why do they not bestir themselves? (§ 7). Instant action is needful. Greece must not wait until the enemy in the east and the enemy in the west close in upon her together (§§ 8, 9).

Remarks. Here the extract ends—probably at the point where Lysias addressed himself more particularly to the state of Sicily, before concluding with an invective against the envoys of Dionysius. It is natural to compare with this fragment the great

[1] Dionys. *Lys.* c. 29.

speech in which eight years later the same subject was treated,—the Panegyricus of Isocrates. In each case a Panhellenic audience is reminded of the political unity of Hellas and is urged to common action against the barbarian; in each case there is an appeal to the most powerful of the Greeks to become organisers and leaders of the rest; in each case the speaker claims to be a more practical adviser than his predecessors. This last claim would not be easy to decide. It would be hard to say which was the more hopeful scheme : in 388, that Sparta should persuade the other Greek cities to lay aside all jealousies and unite for the common defence under her leadership; or in 380, that Sparta and Athens should jointly achieve that task, and act as harmonious colleagues in such a leadership. As regards form, the vigorous plainness which stamps the fragment of the Olympiacus is perhaps in better keeping with counsel given at a grave national crisis than is the artistic finish of the Panegyricus. Dionysius says that in the epideictic style Lysias is " somewhat languid," and wants that power of " rousing the hearer " which Isocrates, like Demosthenes, possessed.[1] It is not certainly in this fragment that we find the justification of the criticism.

The Olympiacus compared with the Panegyricus.

The Funeral Oration ascribed to Lysias purports to have been spoken, in the course of the Corinthian War, over Athenians who had been sent to the support of Corinth. The precise date cannot be determined. In § 59 there is an allusion to the

The Epitaphius.

---

[1] Dionys. *de Lys.* c. 28, ἐν μὲν δὴ τοῖς ἐπιδεικτικοῖς λόγοις μαλακώτερος .. οὐ διεγείρει δὲ τὸν ἀκροατὴν ὥσπερ Ἰσοκράτης ἢ Δημοσθένης.

battle of Cnidos in 394, and to the visit of the Persian fleet to Greece in 393 ; and in § 63 there is an allusion to the rebuilding of the walls of Athens in the latter year. If it were supposed that the speech was retouched after delivery, it might have been spoken over those who fell in the battle of Corinth in 394. Otherwise the fight in the Long Walls of Corinth in 392, or that in 391 when Agesilaus took Lechaeum, might be assumed as the occasion. To any one of these three hypotheses there is, indeed, the objection that the speaker seems to refer to the battle in question as one in which the deceased were on the winning side (§ 70).

Analysis. The oration opens by contrasting the greatness of the theme with the shortness of the time allowed to the speaker for preparation (§§ 1–3). It goes on, in the usual fashion of such discourses, to commemorate the exploits of Athens from the earliest times. It relates the war in which Theseus repelled the Amazons; the part taken by Athenians in obtaining burial for the Argives who fell before Thebes in the war of the Seven ; the brave refusal of Athens to give up the children of Heracles to Eurystheus (§§ 4–16). Then a brief digression on the character of the Athenians as autochthones, and on the early growth of democracy (§§ 17–19). The Persian wars—the siege of Aegina in 458—and the expulsion of the Thirty Tyrants are successively noticed, with remarks on the contrast between the Athenian and the Spartan empire (§§ 20–66). Then comes a curiously short tribute to the departed (§§ 67–70), and a most gloomy address to their surviving relatives (§§ 71–76); followed by the usual commonplace about the immortal honours of the dead (§§ 77–81).

Two questions have to be considered in regard to

the Epitaphius: whether it was written for a real *Character and authorship of the Epitaphius.* occasion or merely as an exercise; and whether it is or is not the work of Lysias.[1]

If it was written for a real occasion, then it can hardly be his work; for Lysias, not being an Athenian citizen, could not have spoken it himself; and it is unlikely that he should have composed it for another, since the citizen chosen by the Senate to pronounce a funeral harangue was usually an orator of repute.[2] But two things are in favour of the view that the Epitaphius was a mere rhetorical exercise: first, the character of the references to supposed contemporary events,—references particular enough to have been inserted by a composer anxious for the appearance of reality, yet not exactly corresponding with any known situation; secondly, the neglect of topics which a mere exercise could afford to ignore, but which in a real oration would, according to all fitness and all usage, be prominent—the topics of practical advice and of consolation. This Epitaphius says little enough about the dead; it scarcely attempts to exhort or to comfort the living. If, then, we may assume what the general character

---

[1] The case for, and the case against, the authenticity of the Epitaphius are well argued in two essays—(1) *Lysias Epitaphios als echt erwiesen*, by Dr. Le Beau, Stuttgart, 1863: (2) *De Epitaphio Lysiae Oratori falso tributo*, by H. Eckert, Berlin [1865 ?]. Le Beau's able essay is clear and admirably thorough, but defends a hopeless cause: Eckert's is a full re-statement, in reply to Le Beau, of the arguments against the genuineness.

[2] Cf. Thuc. ii. 34, ἀνὴρ ᾑρημένος ὑπὸ τῆς πόλεως ὅς ἂν γνώμῃ τε δοκῇ μὴ ἀξύνετος εἶναι καὶ ἀξιώσει προήκῃ. A third hypothesis has been advanced by Le Beau (pp. 37 ff.)—that the oration was written by Lysias to be spoken by the Archon Polemarch at one of the annual commemorations of citizens who had died during the past year; but Eckert maintains that such annual commemorations were not instituted before the time of Alexander (pp. 6 ff.).

of the speech indicates—that it was composed merely as a rhetorical essay—the next question is—Was Lysias the author? The external evidence is inconclusive. Harpocration and Theon[1] ascribe it without suspicion to Lysias. Aristotle quotes from "*the* Epitaphius" a passage which is found in our speech, but does not name Lysias, though in the same chapter he cites Pericles, Isocrates and others by name. Nothing, however, can fairly be inferred from this except that in Aristotle's time the speech was celebrated.[2] Dionysius nowhere mentions an Epitaphius by Lysias; and his silence is suspicious. Turning from the external to the internal evidence, we find that this is overwhelmingly against the authorship of Lysias. All his leading characteristics—simplicity, grace, clearness, the sense of symmetry—are conspicuous by their absence. The structure of the whole is clumsy; the special topics are ill arranged, and receive a treatment sometimes meagre, sometimes extravagantly diffuse; the language is affected, turgid and in many places obscure to a degree which makes it inconceivable that this oration and the fragment of the Olympiacus can be the work of the same man.[3]

[1] Theon, προγυμνάσματα, p. 164 (Spengel, *Rhet. Gr.* II. p. 68) ἔχομεν δὲ καὶ Ἰσοκράτους μὲν τὰ ἐγκώμια, Πλάτωνος δὲ καὶ Θουκυδίδου καὶ Ὑπερείδου καὶ Λυσίου τοὺς ἐπιταφίους.

[2] Arist. *Rhet.* III. 10, καὶ οἷον ἐν τῷ ἐπιταφίῳ, διότι ἄξιον ἦν ἐπὶ τῷ τάφῳ τῷ τῶν ἐν Σαλαμῖνι τελευτησάντων κείρασθαι τὴν Ἑλλάδα, κ.τ.λ. The passage occurs in nearly the same words in § 60 of our Epitaphius.

[3] Eckert, in the essay referred to above, examines at length (pp. 19–48) the arrangement (τάξις), "invention" (εὕρεσις), and diction (λέξις) of the speech, and shows how thoroughly each is foreign to the manner of Lysias. It has not been judged necessary here to follow his analysis into details. The broad impression left upon the mind by the speech as a whole will be enough for most readers. As Dobree said—"Lysias in genere epideictico quantumvis plenus et diffluens; nugax, salebrosus, indigestus nunquam esse potuit." (*Advers.* I. p. 15.)

There are several resemblances of expression between this Epitaphius and the Panegyricus of Isocrates, and these have often been explained by supposing Isocrates to have borrowed from Lysias. But let any careful reader note how thoroughly the more rhetorical parts of the Epitaphius bear the stamp of a cento, and he will prefer to suppose that some very inferior writer has borrowed from Isocrates.[1] No weight can be allowed to the argument that Plato in the Menexenus (386 B.C. ?) had this particular Epitaphius in view. The Menexenus goes, indeed, over very nearly the same range of subjects; but these subjects were the commonplaces of commemorative oratory, and the coincidence is no warrant for assuming a direct imitation. If it may be taken for granted that Aristotle's citation in the Rhetoric is from our Epitaphius, the composition of the speech, whoever was the author, may be placed between 380 and 340 B.C.[2] In any case, considering the general character of the Greek,[3] it can scarcely be put much below the first half of the second century B.C.

Deliberative Speech

The speeches of Lysias for the ecclesia have had the same fate as his epideictic speeches. These, too, are represented by one fragment alone—that which

---

[1] Cf. Panegyr. § 72 with Epitaph. § 9 : Pan. § 88 with E. § 29 : Pan. § 115 with E. § 59 ; etc. "Illic" (i.e. in the Panegyricus), says Dobree, "summum oratorem videas, hic nugacem compilatorem."

[2] Aristotle's *Rhetoric* having been written probably during his second residence at Athens, 335-323 B.C. : see Grote's *Aristotle*, I. 34.

[3] "Sermone utitur sat bene Graeco atque Attico, et in universum spectanti non videtur in sermonis puritatem et verborum delectum admodum peccasse" (Dobree, *Adv.* p. 14). Cf. Eckert, p. 52.

Or. XXXIV., a Plea for the Constitution.

now stands last in the collection as Oration xxxiv. Like the fragment of the Olympiacus, it is given by Dionysius as a specimen of a class. The title which it usually bears describes it as a Plea against abolishing the ancient Constitution of Athens. When, after the fall of the Thirty, the democracy was restored in 403, it was the aim of Sparta to restrict it. One Phormisius proposed in the ecclesia that only landowners should have the franchise, a measure which, according to Dionysius, would have excluded about five thousand citizens. The speech from which he gives an extract was made against this motion during a debate in the ecclesia. It appears to have been written by Lysias for some wealthy citizen who was not personally affected by the proposal, and may probably be regarded as the earliest of the orator's works now known.

Analysis.

A censure on the proposers and supporters of the motion is followed by a statement of the speaker's political faith. Nothing but a full democracy, he says, can save the country. When Athens was imperial, did she limit the franchise? On the contrary, she gave one of the special privileges of citizenship to the Euboeans. Then, to take the landowners' point of view, it is not they who have ever profited by oligarchies. In fact, it is just on their property that the advocates of this, as of former oligarchies, have designs (§§ 1–5).

If it is said that Athens can be safe only by obeying Sparta, it should be remembered how desperate are the terms which Sparta would like to impose. Surely it is better to die fighting for one's rights than to pass sentence of death upon oneself. But there is a danger for Sparta also, which will to a certain extent restrain her. She leaves

Argos and Mantineia at peace, because she knows that
nothing can be gained, and that much would be risked, by
driving them to extremities: she will feel the same in
regard to Athens. This was the policy of Athens herself
when she was greatest (§§ 6–9). It would be strange if
the democrats who fought bravely in exile should lose heart
now that they are restored; if the sons of men who saved
Hellas should shrink from delivering Athens (§§ 10, 11).

Dionysius remarks on this speech that there is
nothing to prove that it was actually delivered on the
occasion supposed, but that "at all events it is in a
style suitable for debate."[1] For that very reason, the
smooth finish of the extract from the Olympiacus is
not to be looked for here; a rougher vigour takes its
place. Regarded historically, it has one point of
interest—the analogy suggested between Sparta's contemptuous forbearance towards Argos and Mantineia
and her probable attitude towards Athens. Nothing
could show more strikingly the prostrate condition
in which Athens was left by the Thirty Tyrants than
that a speaker in the ecclesia should have ventured
to use such an illustration.

[1] *De Lys.* c. 32, εἰ μὲν οὖν ἐρρήθη τότε, ἄδηλον· σύγκειται γοῦν ὡς πρὸς
ἀγῶνα ἐπιτηδείως.

CHAPTER X

LYSIAS

WORKS

Forensic Speeches in Public Causes

<small>Principle of distinction between "public" and "private" law-speeches.</small> IN classifying forensic speeches, the first thing to be done is to fix the principle of distinction between the public and the private. One method is to consider solely the form of procedure, and to distinguish "public" and "private" as they were technically distinguished by Greek law. Another method is to consider rather the substance than the form of each cause, and to arrange the causes according as their practical interest was more directly for the State or for the individual. Blass adopts the latter plan.[1]

---

[1] Blass's classification is as follows:—

I. *Public Causes:* Against Epicrates [Or. XXVII]: Against Ergocles [XXVIII]: Against Philocrates [XXIX]: Against Nicomachus [XXX]: Against the Corndealers [XXII]: Against Evandrus [XXVI]: Against Philon [XXXI]: Against Alcibiades [XIV, XV]: Defence on Charge of Taking Bribes [XXI]: For Polystratus [XX]: Defence on a Charge of seeking to abolish the Democracy [XXV]: For Mantitheus [XVI]: On the Property of the Brother of Nicias [XVIII]: On the Property of Aristophanes [XIX].

II. *Private Causes in which the person of the accused, or the consequences of the offence in question, had a specially high importance for the Commonweal (Att. Bereds.* p. 539*)*. Against Eratosthenes [XII]: Against Agoratus [XIII]: Against Andocides [VI].

III. *Properly Private Causes.* On the Murder of Eratosthenes [I]: Against Simon [III]: On Wounding with Intent [IV]: For Callias [V]:

The speech On the Murder of Eratosthenes [Or. I.], for instance, is referred by Blass to the private class, since the cause, though formally public (as being a γραφὴ φόνου), was of no properly political interest. The obvious objection to such a mode of classification is its uncertainty. The definite technical distinction once abandoned, it becomes hard to say what is or is not a "public" cause. Thus the speeches Against Eratosthenes [Or. XII.] and Against Agoratus [Or. XIII.] are placed by Blass in a rank by themselves, intermediate between the properly public and the properly private, because in each case, though an individual is mainly concerned, the issue is of high moment to the State. Such differences have a real *literary* importance, and have already been recognised (p. 163) as corresponding to different shades of style. But they appear too indefinite to form a good basis for scientific classification. The necessity of drawing a doubtful or arbitrary line is avoided by taking the classification supplied by Greek law itself. Classified as public and private (δημόσιοι and ἰδιωτικοί) in the Greek sense, the speeches of Lysias will stand thus :—

A.—Speeches in Public Causes

I. *Causes relating to Offences directly against the State* (γραφαὶ δημοσίων ἀδικημάτων); *such as treason, malversation in office, embezzlement of public moneys.*

On the Sacred Olive [VII]: For the Soldier [IX]: Against Theomnestus [X, XI]: Against Diogeiton [XXXII]: On the Property of Eraton [XVII]: Against Pancleon [XXIII].

IV. *Bagatelle Speeches.* For the Invalid [XXIV]: To his Companions [VIII].—*Ill. Bords.* pp. 445-660.

1. For Polystratus [Or. xx.]
2. Defence on a Charge of Taking Bribes [Or. xxi.]
3. Against Ergocles [Or. xxviii.]
4. Against Epicrates [Or. xxvii.]
5. Against Nicomachus [Or. xxx.]
6. Against the Corndealers [Or. xxii.]

II. *Cause relating to Unconstitutional Procedure* (γραφὴ παρανόμων).

On the Property of the Brother of Nicias [Or. xviii.]

III. *Causes relating to Claims for Money withheld from the State* (ἀπογραφαί).
1. For the Soldier [Or. ix.]
2. On the Property of Aristophanes [Or. xix.]
3. Against Philocrates [Or. xxix.]

IV. *Causes relating to a Scrutiny* (δοκιμασία), *especially the Scrutiny by the Senate of Officials-designate.*
1. Against Evandrus [Or. xxvi.]
2. For Mantitheus [Or. xvi.]
3. Against Philon [Or. xxxi.]
4. Defence on a Charge of seeking to abolish the Democracy [Or. xxv.]
5. For the Invalid [Or. xxiv.]

V. *Causes relating to Military Offences* (γραφαὶ λειποταξίου, ἀστρατείας, κ.τ.λ.)
1. Against Alcibiades, I. [Or. xiv.]
2. Against Alcibiades, II. [Or. xv.]

VI. *Causes relating to Murder or Intent to murder* (γραφαὶ φόνου, τραύματος ἐκ προνοίας).

1. Against Eratosthenes [Or. XII.]
2. Against Agoratus [Or. XIII.]
3. On the Murder of Eratosthenes [Or. I.]
4. Against Simon [Or. III.]
5. On Wounding with Intent [Or. IV.]

VII. *Causes relating to Impiety* (γραφαὶ ἀσεβείας).

1. Against Andocides [Or. VI.]
2. For Callias [Or. V.]
3. On the Sacred Olive [Or. VII.]

B.—SPEECHES IN PRIVATE CAUSES

I. *Action for libel* (δίκη κακηγορίας).
Against Theomnêstus[1] [Or. X.]

II. *Action by a Ward against a Guardian* (δίκη ἐπιτροπῆς).
Against Diogeiton [Or. XXXII.]

III. *Trial of a Claim to Property* (διαδικασία).
On the Property of Eraton[2] [Or. XVII.]

IV. *Answer to a Special Plea* (πρὸς παραγραφήν).
Against Pancleon [Or. XXIII.]

SPEECHES IN PUBLIC CAUSES

I. CAUSES RELATING TO OFFENCES DIRECTLY AGAINST THE STATE (γραφαὶ δημοσίων ἀδικημάτων).

1. *For Polystratus.* [Or. XX.] — Harpocration describes this as a "Defence for Polystratus on a

---

[1] The MSS. give κατὰ Θεομνήστου A. as Or. X. and κατὰ Θεομνήστου B. as Or. XI. But the so-called Second Speech is a mere epitome of the first: see below.

[2] Entitled in the MSS. περὶ δημοσίων ἀδικημάτων.

charge of seeking to abolish the Democracy."[1] But from the speech itself the precise nature of the charge cannot be gathered. All that can be safely inferred is that the offence alleged was of a political nature, and was connected with the oligarchical revolution of 411 B.C. Polystratus had held several offices under the oligarchy (§ 5), and had been elected to a vacancy in the Council of the Four Hundred just eight days before the defeat of the Athenian fleet by the Spartans at Eretria, immediately after which the government fell (§ 14). His most important employment had been that of enrolling the 5000 persons to whom the Council conceded the franchise; and he takes credit for having placed, in his capacity of registrar, 9000 instead of 5000 on the roll. It was only in their last peril that the Oligarchy took steps for giving a real existence to the nominal body of 5000; and this agrees with the account of Polystratus, who dates his registrarship from his entry into the Council only eight days before its overthrow (§ 14). When the democracy was re-established, Polystratus was prosecuted and heavily fined: probably on the ground of malversation in some office which he had held under the Oligarchy.

Probable nature of the charge. In the present case malversation in his registrarship may have been the special charge against him. The penalty threatened was pecuniary; but he says that, as he has no money with which to meet it, the result for him, if condemned, will be disfranchisement as a state-debtor.

Date. The date must lie between 411 and 405. The

---

[1] s.v. Πολύστρατος—ὑπὲρ Π. δήμου καταλύσεως ἀπολογία.

war in the Hellespont is noticed (§ 29); but there is no reference to Arginusae or subsequent events; and the early part of 407 is therefore the latest date which appears probable.

Polystratus, who was a man past sixty (§ 10), is represented by the eldest of his three sons (§ 24).

The first part of the speech sets forth that Polystratus *Analysis.* was one of the least prominent and least culpable of the oligarchs; that he had already suffered severely, and is now accused maliciously; and that the general tenor of his past life proves his patriotism (§§ 1–23). The speaker then relates his own services in Sicily after the disaster of 413, and reads a patriotic letter written to him by his father at that time. He recounts also the services of his brothers, the second and third sons of Polystratus; of whom the former had been active at the Hellespont, and the latter at home (§§ 24–29). In return for all that the father and his three sons have done for the city, they ask only to be spared a verdict which would rob them of citizenship (§§ 30–36).

The only ancient notice of this speech is by Harpocration, who once refers to it; then, indeed, without suspicion.[1] But the general opinion of recent critics[2] pronounces it spurious. In one respect alone it has at first sight a resemblance to the style of Lysias. It is thoroughly natural. Yet the naturalness is not that of Lysias. It is the absence, not the concealment, of art; the simplicity, not of a master, *The speech probably spurious.*

---

[1] s. v. Πολύστρατος.
[2] As of Baiter, Sauppe and Blass. It is curious to find—in an essay published at Munich in 1830, *Dissertatio de locis quibusdam Lysiae arte critica persanandis*, by J. Franz —numerous minute emendations proposed in the text of this speech (pp. 7–10), all depending on close observation of the language of Lysias; while the general character of the whole composition—so unlike that of its reputed author's work—entirely escapes criticism.

but of a composer wholly untrained. A want of logical method renders the statements in the first part (§§ 1–23) confused, and the language throughout clumsy, sometimes obscure. Instead of the compact sentences of Lysias, there are long strings of clauses loosely joined; — see especially § 14. Were the speech genuine, it would be the only known forensic speech of Lysias earlier than the fall of the Thirty Tyrants. But it seems hardly doubtful that it must be rejected.

I. 2. Defence on a Charge of Taking Bribes.

2. *Defence on a Charge of Taking Bribes.* [Or. XXI.]—The first part of this speech, in which the accused met the specific charges against him, has been lost; the part which remains contains only his appeal to his previous character generally. The precise nature of the charge is therefore doubtful. In § 21 the speaker asks that he may not be adjudged guilty of taking bribes; hence the title given to the fragment. The accused had probably held some office, and was charged, when he gave account of it, with corrupt practices.

Date.

A clue to the date is given by the fact that the speaker became of full age (*i.e.* eighteen) in the archonship of Theopompus (§ 1), 411 B.C.; and had performed leiturgies yearly to the archonship of Eucleides (§ 4), 403 B.C. No reason appears why his public services should have ceased abruptly in that year. On the other hand, if he had performed leiturgies later than 403 B.C., he would probably have mentioned them. The year of the speech may therefore be conjectured to be 402, and the age of the speaker 26.[1]

[1] Blass, *Att. Ber.* p. 496.

Having already answered the accusers in detail, he goes *Analysis.* on, in the extant fragment, to enumerate his public services. As choregus and trierarch he has spent upwards of ten talents in eight years—more than four times the amount which would have satisfied legal requirements (§§ 1–5). His trireme, when he was trierarch, was so good that Alcibiades, as admiral, had done him the unwelcome honour of sailing in it (§ 7); and it was one of the twelve which made good their escape from Aegospotami (§ 10).

He might fairly claim some substantial recognition of these costly services; but he asks only not to be deprived of his own property (§§ 11–19). In conclusion he reminds the judges that one who had risked his life and whole fortune for the State was not likely to have taken bribes to defraud it (§§ 21, 22). Beggary had often enough hung over his wife and children when he was fighting for Athens; it would be hard if it should at last actually befall them by the sentence of an Athenian court (§§ 24–52).

Lysias shows here strikingly his power of adapting *The ethos.* language to character; the êthos is the merit of the speech. It expresses the strong, honest feeling of a man who has made sacrifices for his country, who is conscious of his desert, and who claims, rather than begs, acquittal. "I think, judges, that it would be much fairer for you to be indicted by the revenue-officers for keeping my property, than for me to be now in peril on a charge of keeping the property of the Treasury ... I am not proud of what is left to me, but of what I have spent upon you. My fortune came to me from others—the credit for its use is my own" (§§ 16, 17).

3. *Against Ergocles.* [Or. XXVIII.]—In 390 B.C. *I. 3.* a fleet of forty triremes was sent to the coast of Asia *Against Ergocles.*

Minor under the command of Thrasybulus. After many successes in the Hellespont and a victory over the Lacedaemonians at Lesbos, Thrasybulus was slain at Aspendus in Pamphylia by a party of natives who surprised his camp by night.[1] Meanwhile anger had been excited at Athens by reports that the commanders of the expedition had embezzled moneys levied on the towns in Asia, and had been treacherous to the cause of the city. A decree was passed demanding an account of all funds so raised, and recalling the commanders. Thrasybulus died before he could obey the summons; his colleagues, of whom Ergocles was one, were brought to trial in 389 B.C. The procedure was apparently by impeachment. Ergocles was condemned to death and his property was confiscated.[2]

Date.

The short speech of Lysias was spoken by one of the Public Prosecutors; who, as others had already gone fully into the charges, does little more than recapitulate them.

Analysis.

Ergocles is charged with having betrayed Greek towns in Asia, with having injured citizens and friends of Athens, and with having enriched himself at the public cost. All this time the fleet was allowed to go to ruin, with the connivance of Thrasybulus—who would never have been given the command, had it been foreseen that only his "flatterers" (§ 4) were to benefit by it (§§ 1–7). Thrasybulus had done well to die; the partners of his guilt are now seeking to buy their lives by wholesale bribery; but this must not be suf-

---

[1] Xen. *Hellen.* IV. viii. 25–30.
[2] See § 2 of the speech Against Philocrates, who was accused of having in his hands part of the confiscated property of Ergocles.

fered (§§ 8–11). Ergocles pleads his patriotism at the restoration of the democracy; but he has since shown himself worse than the Tyrants (§§ 12–14). His condemnation and that of his associates is necessary as an example to Greece, and is due to the cities, such as Halicarnassus,[1] which they betrayed (§§ 15–17).

Decision and vigorous brevity are the chief characteristics of this speech, as of that Against Epicrates (XXVII.) and that Against Philocrates (XXIX.); both of which, like this, were spoken by Public Prosecutors. An address by an official afforded less scope for artistic individual colouring than a speech which had to be fitted to the character and circumstances of a private speaker.

4. *Against Epicrates.* [Or. XXVII.]—The title, "Against Epicrates and his Fellow-Envoys," which one Theodôrus[2] affixed to this speech, is clearly wrong. In the first place, each of the "Fellow-Envoys" would have been the subject of a separate accusation; in the next place, there is absolutely no reference to an embassy except in the opening words,[3] which have probably been interpolated to match the title. The grammarian, it can hardly be doubted, was thinking of the Epicrates mentioned by Demosthenes as having been condemned, with his colleagues in an embassy,

I. 4.
Against Epicrates.

---

[1] Xenophon does not name Halicarnassus: but he describes Thrasybulus, after his victory at Lesbos, as levying money for his troops from some towns on the Greek coast:—ἐκ δὲ τούτου τὰς μὲν προσηγάγετο τῶν πόλεων, ἐκ δὲ τῶν οὐ προσχωρουσῶν λεηλατῶν χρήματα τοῖς στρατιώταις ἔσπευσεν εἰς τὴν Ῥόδον ἀφικέσθαι. ὅπως δ' ἂν καὶ ἐκεῖ ὡς ἐρρωμενέστατον τὸ στράτευμα ποιήσαιτο, ἐξ ἄλλων τε πόλεων ἠργυρολόγει, κ.τ.λ. (*H.* IV. viii. 30).

[2] The MSS. having ΚΑΤΑ ΕΠΙΚΡΑΤΟΥΣ ΚΑΙ ΤΩΝ ΣΥΜΠΡΕΣΒΕΥΤΩΝ ΕΠΙΛΟΓΟΣ ΩΣ ΘΕΟΔΩΡΟΣ.

[3] κατηγόρηται μέν, ὦ ἄνδρες Ἀθηναῖοι, Ἐπικράτους ἱκανὰ καὶ τῶν συμπρεσβευτῶν· ἐνθυμεῖσθαι δὲ χρή. κ.τ.λ. The words καὶ τῶν συμπρεσβευτῶν are probably spurious.

by a decree of the people.[1] Whether this Epicrates is the same person or not, cannot be decided. But, in the present case, the charge against him is of having embezzled public moneys while he held the office of comptroller of the treasury (§ 3). The charge must have been made either at his audit ($εὔθυναι$) or by a special impeachment ($εἰσαγγελία$). The only clue to the date is the fact that a war had now lasted some time (§ 10). The latter part of the Corinthian War—about the year 389—is probably indicated.

<small>Date.</small>

Like the speech against Ergocles, this was preceded by others for the prosecution, and gives therefore only a general view of the case.

<small>Analysis.</small>

Corrupt officers of the treasury, like Ergocles, often tell the judges, in asking for a verdict against some one whom they have wrongfully accused, that if it is not given, the city will soon lack funds to pay its public servants. And now this lack of funds is caused by the corrupt officials themselves. The State must punish heavily those guardians of the revenue who so often procure the confiscation of private property while they enrich themselves out of the property of the public (§§ 1–7). If such men were condemned without the forms of a trial, it would be no breach of justice; their guilt is notorious. This is war-time; yet these men can not only pay heavy taxes, but at the same time live in the best houses—men who, in quieter times, had not bread to eat (§§ 8–10). No appeal to mercy should be admitted from such a quarter. The courts have lately been too lenient. Epicrates and his like must be made to suffer loss, since they are insensible to shame (§§ 11–16).

5. *Against Nicomachus.* [Or. xxx.]—Soon after

---

[1] *De Falsa Legat.* § 277: Blass, p. 445.

the fall of the First Oligarchy in 411 B.C., a decree of the ecclesia (probably in 410) appointed a board of special Commissioners (Nomothetae[1]) for the revision of the laws; especially for the recension of those old laws of Solon, written on the sides of the wooden prisms called Kurbeis or Axones, which now needed to be freed from corruptions and interpolations. Nicomachus[2] was a member of the Commission. Four months were assigned for the work;[3] but Nicomachus contrived to extend his share of it over six years—*i.e.* until the overthrow of the democracy in 404—without rendering an account.

I. 5.
Against Nicomachus.

After the fall of the Second Oligarchy in 403, a second Revising Commission was appointed by the Senate. These special Nomothetae were to report *within one month* to the Senate and the 500 ordinary Nomothetae selected by the demes.[4] Nicomachus

---

[1] Nicomachus is called in §§ 2 and 27 νομοθέτης. This was probably the ordinary official designation of the special Commissioners both in 411 and 403: the title ἀναγραφεὺς τῶν νόμων, "Recorder" of the laws, also applied to Nicomachus in § 2, being sometimes used, perhaps, to distinguish the special from the ordinary Nomothetae.—Rauchenstein notices in Demosth. *Olynth.* III. § 10 another trace of the occasional appointment of special Nomothetae: see his Introduction to this speech, *Ausgewählte Reden des Lysias*, p. 130, n.

[2] In § 11, as once in a quotation by Harpocration (s. v. ἐπιβολή), Nicomachus is called Nicomachides:— πείθουσι Νικομαχίδην νόμον ἀποδεῖξαι ὡς χρὴ καὶ τὴν βουλὴν συνδικάζειν. Rauchenstein (ad loc.) thinks that is merely an instance of the pat- ronymic used convertibly with the simple name, as Eubulides for Eubulus in Or. XIX. § 29; cf. Androcleides for Androcles in Isac. Or. VI. 46. Blass, with more likelihood, suspects a mere blunder. Is it possible that in § 11 we ought to insert τοῦτον after πείθουσι, and understand :—" they persuade the defendant to enunciate a law of which he was himself the parent" (Νικομαχίδην νόμον)—a law invented by Nicomachus for the occasion? This would be quite in keeping with the sarcastic tone of the speech.

[3] § 2, προσταχθὲν γὰρ αὐτῷ τεσσάρων μηνῶν ἀναγράψαι...ἐξέτη τὴν ἀρχὴν ἐποιήσατο.

[4] The psephisma of 403 for the revision of the laws is given in full by Andocides in the speech On the Mysteries, § 83.

was again employed; his special duty on this occasion being to revise the laws which concerned the public sacrifices.[1] Again he failed to discharge his task within the prescribed term. At the date of this speech he had held office for four years. The speech probably belongs, therefore, to 399 B.C. Nicomachus is accused before the Board of Auditors (the ten Logistae) of having failed to render an account of his office (ἀλογίου δίκη).[2]

The speaker is one of several accusers (§ 34), probably not the principal; the penalty demanded is death (§§ 23, 27).

Analysis.   The first part of the speech sets forth the antecedents of Nicomachus. His father was a public slave; he himself, after late enrolment in a phratria, became an under-scribe to a magistrate. His present offence was not the first of the kind which he had committed. After the First Oligarchy, as after the Second, commissioners for the revision of the laws were appointed. Nicomachus had been one of these also; and had retained the appointment for six years (§ 2) —(that is, till 404 B.C.)—(§§ 1–6).

He will perhaps try to cast upon his accuser the suspicion of oligarchical sympathies. It ought not to be for-

---

[1] See § 25, καὶ τῶν ὁσίων καὶ τῶν ἱερῶν ἀναγραφεὺς γενόμενος εἰς ἀμφότερα ταῦτα ἡμάρτηκεν. Here τῶν ὁσίων refers to the first Commission of 410 B.C., when the laws entrusted to the revision of Nicomachus were only secular; τῶν ἱερῶν to the second Commission of 403 B.C., when the laws which came under his revision were those relating to public worship.

[2] The description in the MS. heading of the speech—εὐθυνῶν κατηγορία—is inaccurate, as Rauchenstein points out (*Introd.* p. 131). This would mean that Nicomachus had rendered an account, and that, when he rendered it, an accusation was brought against him by some citizen: which would then have been heard by the εὔθυνοι. The charge against Nicomachus was that he had never rendered any account to the Logistae. The points of law connected with this speech are discussed in an essay entitled *Diatribe in Lysiae orationem in Nicomachum*, by F. V. Weijers, Leyden, 1839.

gotten that it was he himself who, by a forged law, enabled the oligarchs to destroy Cleophon[1] in 405. His sufferings under the Thirty were involuntary, and cannot be set against an action which was deliberate (§§ 7–16). The speaker will be taunted by Nicomachus with impiety because he complained in the ecclesia of the number of public sacrifices which this self-authorised legislator had ordered. But the truth is that, by ordering a number of new sacrifices, Nicomachus has caused those prescribed by the laws of Solon (τὰ ἐκ τῶν κύρβεων, § 17) to be neglected; and has in two years spent twelve talents more than was necessary (§ 21). Hence the city, from want of funds, has been driven to confiscations (§ 22). Nicomachus ought to suffer the extreme penalty, as a warning to the corrupt officials who, confident in their powers of speech, are reckless of public or private misery (§§ 17–25).

Neither service in war, nor liberality at home, nor the merit of ancestors, nor the hope of his own gratitude, can be pleaded as a reason for acquitting him. The people themselves might well be denounced for entrusting to such as he the powers once held by a Solon, a Themistocles, a Pericles (§ 28). Nicomachus has sought in vain to bribe his accusers; let his judges do their duty as firmly (§§ 26–35).

Unsparing and rather coarse sarcasm is the strength of this attack. Throughout, Nicomachus is treated, not as the recorder of laws, but as the son of the public slave, as the ex-under-scribe. "Are we to acquit him for his ancestors?" asks the accuser. "Nay, for his own sake he deserves death; and for theirs—the slave-market" (§ 27).

6. *Against the Corndealers.* [Or. XXII.]—The

---

[1] Cleophon, ὁ λυροποιός, the demagogue: Ar. *Ran.* 677: Arist. *Rhet.* 1. 15, etc. Cf. Lys. *de bonis Aristoph.* (Or. XIX.) § 48: Κλεοφῶντα πάντες ἴστε ὅτι πολλὰ ἔτη διεχείρισε τὰ τῆς πόλεως πάντα.

Guild of Corndealers (σιτοπῶλαι) was composed of aliens (§ 5) resident in the Peiraeus, who bought corn as it came into port and sold it in small quantities to the citizens. The trade was a good one, and was watched with jealousy both by citizens and by wholesale importers (ἔμποροι, § 27). Stringent laws, administered by a board of Corn-Inspectors (σιτοφύλακες, § 8), were framed to limit the gains of the retail-dealers. One of these laws forbade them to charge more than one obol a bushel over cost-price (§ 8); another, in order to check monopoly, provided that no one should buy more than 50 phormoi (about 50 bushels) of corn at one time (§ 6).

It is this second law which is here alleged to have been broken by the guild or by some of its members. The case is tried before an ordinary court under the presidency of the Thesmothetae: the penalty is death.

Date. The date of the speech cannot be fixed. All that can be said is that it was certainly later than the beginning of the Corinthian War in 394 B.C.; possibly later than the Peace of Antalcidas in 387 B.C.[1]

Analysis. The speaker begins by deprecating the notion that the charge preferred by him is vexatious or spiteful. On the contrary, he says, he was at the beginning of the business suspected of unduly favouring the Guild. An impeachment

---

[1] See § 14, which speaks of the rumours spread by the Corndealers in orders to raise the price of corn:—
ἢ τὰς ναῦς διεφθάρθαι τὰς ἐν τῷ Πόντῳ ἢ ὑπὸ Λακεδαιμονίων ἐκπλεούσας συνειλῆφθαι ἢ τὰ ἐμπόρια κεκλεῖσθαι ἢ τὰς σπονδὰς μέλλειν ἀπορρηθήσεσθαι.

"The ships in the Euxine" are the ships which brought corn to Athens from those regions: cf. Xen. H. 1. 35. The σπονδαί possibly refer to the Peace of Antalcidas or to negotiations which preceded it.

was first laid before the Senate, who were inclined to deliver the Corndealers then and there to the Eleven. It was he who then counselled moderation and the observance of the usual legal course. Accordingly the case was heard before the Senate (which was itself the preliminary court in cases of impeachment). No one came forward as accuser; and the speaker then made the accusation himself. The case was sent by the Senate for trial by an ordinary court (§§ 1–4).

One of the Corndealers is then questioned, and admits having bought more than fifty bushels at once, but says that he did so by the recommendation of the Corn-Inspectors. The speaker shows, first, that this is no defence; next, that the statement is false (§§ 5–10). The dealers plead that their object in buying large quantities was to be able to sell cheap; but their claim to public spirit can be refuted (§§ 11–16). They have acknowledged their combination against the wholesale importers. Their death is the satisfaction due to these and to the officials who have so often been punished for inability to check such frauds (§§ 17–22).

Compact and clear, without any attempt at ornament, this short speech is at least good of its kind,—a specimen of the strictly business-like style of Lysias.

II. Indictment for proposing an Unconstitutional Measure (γραφὴ παρανόμων).

On the Confiscation of the Property of the Brother of Nicias. [Or. XVIII.]—Eucrates, brother of the General Nicias, was put to death by the Thirty Tyrants in 404 B.C. Several years afterwards a certain Poliochus[1] proposed and carried in the ec-

II. 1. On the Confiscation of the Property of the Brother of Nicias.

---

[1] There is some doubt about the name. The MSS. have Πολίαχος: or Πόλισχος: Galen, in his citation (XVIII. 2. 657 Kühn), Πολιοῦχος. Taylor has been followed by Sauppe and other recent editors in reading Πολίοχος, a proper name recognised by Harpocration.

clesia a decree for confiscating the estate left by Eucrates. In this speech the elder of the two sons of Eucrates pleads against the execution of the decree.

Form of the cause.   The legal form of the cause is doubtful. Two views are possible. (1) The sons of Eucrates may have indicted Poliochus under the Graphê Paranomôn for proposing an unconstitutional measure. In this case the speech is an Accusation. (2) Poliochus may have indicted the sons of Eucrates for withholding property due to the State under the decree; the action being in form an apographê, or claim for moneys withheld from the Treasury. In this case the speech is a Defence.[1]

One point is in favour of the latter view. The speaker appeals in his peroration, first, to the judges generally, then to the Syndici (§ 26). Now these fiscal officers would have had the presidency of the court in a cause affecting the treasury. But it is not clear why they should have had jurisdiction in a trial under the Graphê Paranomôn.

On the other hand, a passage in § 14 supports the first view. "All men will know" [i.e. if Poliochus gains the cause] "that on the former occasion you fined[2] in 1000 drachmas the man who wished to confiscate our land, whereas on this occasion he has carried his proposal; and that, therefore, in these two cases Athenian judges gave two opposite verdicts, *the*

---

[1] Francken (*Commentationes Lysiacae*, pp. 124 ff.) thinks that Hamaker has proved beyond all doubt that the cause is an ἀπογραφή, not a γραφὴ παρανόμων. But the arguments brought are unavailing without a satisfactory emendation of the words in § 14—to be noticed presently.

[2] Scheibe's emendation of ἐζημι- ώσατε for ἐζημίωσε seems certain.

same man being on his trial for a breach of the Constitution.

The last words—παρανόμων φεύγοντος τοῦ αὐτοῦ ἀνδρός—may possibly be corrupt.[1] But if they are right, then they prove that this trial, like the former, was a Graphê Paranomôn against Poliochus. And this is confirmed by the fact that "Against Poliochus" is the title under which the speech is cited by Galen.[2] On the whole, the probabilities appear to lean to this side. But the evidence does not suffice to decide the question.

The date may be inferred from two circumstances. (1) The speaker and his brothers were children in 404 (§ 10), but are now adults, holding the office of trierarchs (§ 21). (2) On the other hand, Athens and Sparta are at peace (§ 15). The Corinthian War (394–387 B.C.), therefore, either has not begun or is over. And as the son of Nicêratus (§ 10), the first cousin of the speaker, is not mentioned as having yet taken any part in public affairs, the earlier date is more likely—396 or 395 B.C., approximately.

Date.

The following stemma shows the relationship of the persons with whom the speech is concerned :—

Stemma of the family of Nicias.

---

[1] Francken (*Comm. Lys.* p. 126) suggests that Lysias may have written something like παρανόμων φυγόντος τότε τοῦ ἀνδρός [not τοῦ αὐτοῦ ἀνδρός, as Blass quotes it, *Att. Bereds.* p. 524], νῦν δὲ νικήσαντος. But this is too violent a change : and besides, as Blass says, one would require τότε μὲν παρανόμων φυγόντος, νῦν δὲ νικήσαντος.

[2] Vol. XVIII. 2. 657 (Kühn), ap. Sauppe, *Or. Att.* p. 112 and Blass *Att. Bereds.* p. 522. It seems very probable that κατὰ Πολιόχου is the right title.

VOL. I   Q

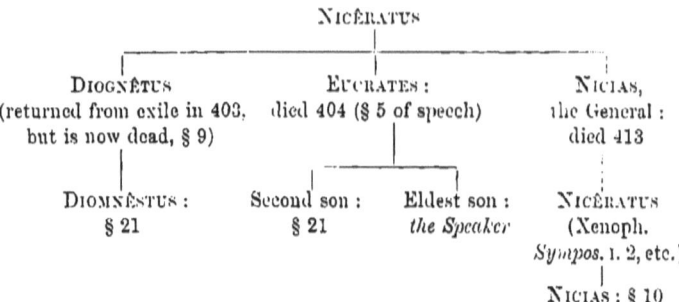

Analysis. The speaker begins by dwelling on the public services of his uncles Nicias and Diognêtus and his father Eucrates (§§ 1–12). He next argues that a confiscation is never in any true sense a gain to the State. First, it endangers the most precious of all the city's treasures—concord among citizens. In the next place, property thus confiscated is always sold below its true value, and part even of the sum which it fetches is made away with by the proposer of the measure. Left in the hands of patriotic owners—like the speaker, his brother, and his cousin, who, all three, are trierarchs—it is far more profitable to the State (§§ 13–23).

They can produce no relatives to weep and pray for them; they are the last of their house; they can only appeal to the judges to protect the kinsmen of those who suffered for the democracy. Let the judges remember the time when, in exile and poverty, they prayed to the gods for a day when they might be able to show their gratitude to the children of their champions. This gratitude is claimed now. The danger which threatens the accused is nothing less than utter ruin (§§ 24–27).

This fragment is interesting as giving a sequel, in the history of his family, to the personal fortunes of Nicias; it is interesting, too, as being distinguished by a quality somewhat rare in the works of Lysias. Few of his speeches have so much pathos. The address is emphatically an appeal to pity; and excites it less by direct appeals than by its simplicity and a tone of manly self-restraint. One passage is especially striking — the description of Diognêtus bringing the orphan children of his brothers to Pausanias, and imploring the Spartan king to remember all that their fathers had suffered (§ 10).

III. CLAIMS FOR MONEYS WITHHELD FROM THE STATE

1. *For the Soldier.* [Or. IX.] — The accused, Polyaenus, is prosecuted under a writ (ἀπογραφή, §§ 3, 21) for the recovery of a fine alleged to be due from him to the Treasury. He states that, two years before, he had returned to Athens from a campaign, but had not been two months at home before he was again placed upon the list for active service. Hereupon he appealed to the General of his tribe (τῷ στρατηγῷ, § 4); but obtained no redress. He spoke indignantly on the subject in conversation at one of the bankers' tables in the market-place; and, this having been reported to the authorities, he was fined under the law against reviling magistrates. The Generals did not, however, take any steps to levy the fine; but at the expiration of their year of office, left a note of it with the Stewards of the Treasury (τοῖς ταμίαις, § 6). These, after inquiry, were satisfied that the fine had been inflicted maliciously (§ 7), and cancelled it. The accusers,

ignoring this decision, now prosecute the soldier, at an interval of more than a year, as a state-debtor. In case of conviction the penalty would be the payment of twice the original fine; but not the loss of civic rights (§ 21). From § 4 the speech may be referred to the time of the Corinthian War, 394 387 B.C.

<small>Analysis.</small>   After complaining that his adversaries have wandered from the special issue into general attacks upon his character, the speaker sketches the facts of the case (§§ 1-7). He then argues, first, that the fine was originally illegal, since the offence contemplated by the law was that of speaking against a magistrate in court (ἐν συνεδρίῳ, § 6), which he had not done; secondly, that in any case the reversal of the sentence by the stewards had absolved him (§§ 8–12).

The malice of his enemies had been provoked, he says, by the favour which he had formerly enjoyed with Sôstratos, an influential citizen. They are resolved to ruin him. The matter at issue is nominally a fine, but really his citizenship; for, if the court also takes part against him, he will be driven to fly from a city in which justice is not to be had (§§ 13–22).

<small>Question of genuineness.</small>   Harpocration doubted the authenticity of this speech;[1] some recent critics have decisively rejected it.[2] There are several traces of mutilation in the extant version. Thus the direct question with which the speech opens is oddly abrupt; in § 5 a conversation is referred to (τὰ προειρημένα) as if it had been given in terms; and in § 9 the speaker alludes to

---

[1] s. v. δικαίωσις:—Λυσίας ἐν τῷ περὶ στρατιώτου, εἰ γνήσιος.

[2] Especially Francken, *Commen-* *tationes Lysiacae*, pp. 64 f.: Blass, *Att. Bereds.* pp. 606 f.

witnesses whom he has called, but of whom there is no other trace. It would be easier to vindicate the authorship of Lysias if the speech, as it stands, could be assumed to be a mere extract or epitome, like the so-called Second Speech Against Theomnêstus. But the epitomic character, distinct there, is absent here; there, proem and epilogue have been compressed; here their redundancies of expression are left untouched.

Francken thinks that the language is in some points doubtful Attic;[1] and that the law is questionable.[2] He argues further that, if the text is right in § 6, "Ctesicles the archon," there mentioned, must be the archon of Ol. CXI. 3, 334 B.C.; and notices that, in that year, an armament was prepared, but not despatched, by Athens[3]—which agrees with the fact that Polyaenus, when enrolled the second time, was not called upon to serve. These arguments seem to point to different conclusions. If the diction and the law are not classically Attic, then the speech is a late work, probably a rhetorical exercise. If Ctesicles is the Ctesicles of 334, then the speech was probably written for a real cause of about that date.[4]

---

[1] *e.g.* ἐντός for ἔνδον in § 10—already noticed by Dobree; δικαίωσις for δικαίωμα ("plea" or "argument") in § 8, noticed by Harpocr.; τὸ πέρας in the sense of "at last" in § 17.

[2] He infers from Dem. *Meid.* § 33 that the penalty for reviling a magistrate *in court*, as for striking τὸν ἄρχοντα ἐστεφανωμένον, would have been, not a fine, but atimia; and he thinks it strange that the ταμίαι, inferior magistrates, should summon their superiors, the strategi, before them (§ 7). We do not know enough to decide such points: and nothing can be safely argued from them.

[3] See Schäfer, *Demosthenes und seine Zeit*, vol. III. p. 162.

[4] Blass assumes (*Att. Bereds.* p. 607) that Ctesicles was one of the strategi, and this is certainly easier. But, in that case, the words τοῦ ἄρχοντος must be a gloss; added by a commentator who associated the name only with the archon of 334. A strategus could not have been called ἄρχων.

The general style proves the Speech spurious. Far stronger than these special objections is the general objection arising from the style. This, indeed, appears conclusive. The passage in §§ 15–18, where the speaker attacks his adversaries, could hardly have come from Lysias. It is overwrought in tone, overloaded with antitheses, and too epideictic for its place. The whole defence is meagre, yet not concise—a reversal of the manner of Lysias. It was probably written by a bad imitator of his style; but for a real cause rather than as an exercise.[1]

III. 2. On the Property of Aristophanes. 2. *On the Property of Aristophanes.* [Or. XIX.] —Nicophêmus, father of Aristophanes, was the friend of Conon, and his comrade in the naval campaigns of 394–390 B.C. When Conon visited the Persian Court in 394, he left Nicophêmus and Hierônymus in joint command of the Persian fleet;[2] and when he took Cythêra in 393 Nicophêmus was appointed harmost.[3] While Conon and Nicophêmus had their home at Cyprus (§ 36), their sons, Timotheus and Aristophanes, lived at Athens; the latter poor, until the battle of Cnidus in 394 and the campaigns of the following years brought some wealth to his father and himself (§ 28). On two important occasions Aristophanes was engaged in the service of the State. He went on an embassy to Sicily (in what year is doubtful) with proposals from Evagoras, king of Cyprus, to Dionysius; and succeeded in dissuading

---

[1] I cannot see that, as Blass thinks, a sophistic exercise is indicated by the accumulation of *unknown* proper names in § 5;—by the fact of the "influential" Sôstratus (§ 13) being lost to fame;—by the absence of clearness in the statement of the case;—or by the uncertainty of the date. The subject would surely have been a poor one for a declamation.

[2] Diod. XIV. 81: Νικόδημος, in that passage, being a mere clerical error for Νικόφημος.

[3] Xen. *Hellen.* IV. viii. 8.

the latter from affording his promised aid to Sparta (§§ 19, 20). Again in 389 B.C. he sailed with an Athenian expedition to the aid of Evagoras (§§ 21–23). From this expedition he never returned. He and his father Nicophêmus were suddenly put to death at Cyprus without trial (§ 7); doubtless on a suspicion of treachery or of embezzlement similar to that which raised a storm of indignation against Thrasybulus and his colleagues in 390 B.C.

After the death of Aristophanes, one Aeschines proposed the confiscation of his property. The proposal, like that of Poliochus in the case of the property of Eucrates, was resisted on the ground of illegality, and a speech was written by Lysias against it.[1] It was, however, carried into effect, and so stringently that not even the debts left by Aristophanes were discharged, nor was the dowry of his widow repaid to her family (§ 32). But the amount of property which was found disappointed the general belief in the wealth of Nicophêmus (§§ 11, 53). It was thought that something must have been withheld; and suspicion fell upon the father-in-law of Aristophanes. A writ was therefore issued against him for the recovery of moneys due to the treasury (§ 11). Before the trial came on, he died, at the age of more than seventy (§ 60); and his only son, a man of thirty (§ 55), was left to defend the action. The Fiscal Board of Syndici were the presidents of the court.

Origin of the Action.

---

[1] Harpocration s.v. Χύτροι:—Λυσίας ἐν τῷ κατ' Αἰσχίνου περὶ τῆς δημεύσεως τῶν Ἀριστοφάνους χρημάτων: Sauppe O. A. II. p. 173. In his *Onomasticum Fragmentorum* Sauppe seems to identify this Aeschines with the Socratic, against whom Lysias wrote on another occasion. That the proposal of Aeschines was met with a γραφὴ παρανόμων is indicated in § 8 of Or. XIX.

Date.

The date is indicated by § 50. It is there said that Diotimus had lately (ἔναγχος) been accused of having forty talents unaccounted for in his possession; but had, on returning to Athens, disproved the charge. Diotimus had held a command in the Hellespont in 388 and 387[1] B.C.; 387 is therefore probably the year of the speech.

Analysis.

The defence is approached with timidity, as if under the consciousness that a strong prejudice has to be met. The speaker represents the gravity of the task which has devolved upon him; his father's good fame, his own, and all his fortunes are at stake. He sets forth the restless malice of his accusers, and reminds the court that experience has proved how little such accusations are to be trusted.[2] The cruel fate of Nicophêmus and Aristophanes;—the destitution of his brother-in-law's children, and the persecutions to which his own family have been exposed in addition to the burden thus thrown upon them;—the current delusions, lastly, about the wealth of Nicophêmus, delusions so dangerous in the present impoverished state of the Treasury—all these are urged as claims to the sympathetic attention of the court (§§ 1–11).

The next division of the speech is devoted to showing that Aristophanes was not originally a rich man, and was at all times lavish. He was not chosen by the speaker's father as a son-in-law on account of his wealth: indeed, his last act before sailing for Cyprus was to come to their house and borrow seven minae; and it could be proved that shortly afterwards he was in want of a very small sum of ready

---

[1] Xen. *H.* v. 1. 25.
[2] On the almost verbal coincidence between §§ 2–5 of this proem and §§ 1, 6, 7 of Andoc. *De Mysteriis*, see above, p. 115.

money. Then follows a formal inventory of the property left by the deceased (§§ 12–27).

But why, it may be asked, was this property so small? Aristophanes had scarcely any fortune until four years before his death; and within these four years he was twice choregus, besides buying a house and lands. The defendant had taken precautions for the due transference to the Government of every article left in the house of Aristophanes: a watch had even been set to see that the doors were not torn off, as sometimes happened to confiscated houses. He is ready to take the most solemn oath before the Syndici that nothing remains in his hands; nay, that his sister's dowry and the debt of seven minae still remain unpaid. Supposing that the property of Timotheus, son of Conon, were confiscated and only four talents realised, would *his* relatives be thought to deserve ruin? Yet the father of Timotheus was at least ten times as rich as the father of Aristophanes (§§ 28–41). There are many instances in which the popular estimate of a man's fortune has been proved, at his death or on inquiry during his lifetime, to have been enormously exaggerated. The recent case of Diotimus (§ 50) and the case of the great Alcibiades (§ 52) are among those in point (§§ 42–54).

The good character borne by himself and by his father ought to be remembered. If their property were confiscated now, the State would not get two talents. At this moment he is a trierarch: his father spent his fortune on the State and for its honour; he kept good horses, had athletes in his pay, and won victories at the Isthmus and at Nemea (§ 63). On all these grounds the defendant claims the protection of the court against a malignant attack (§§ 55–64).

This very clever speech gives a formidable idea of the dangers to which an Athenian of the time was exposed if he or any member of his family was sup-

Light thrown by the speech on a danger of public service abroad.

posed to have made a fortune on foreign service. The city was poor;[1] it was full of informers, ready to prefer any accusation on the chance of sharing the spoil; and by a vague charge of treachery or embezzlement abroad it was easy to inflame the ecclesia.[2] There is nothing to show why Aristophanes or his father was put to death without trial. The point which is most strikingly brought out by this defence is the strength of the popular feeling which it had to combat. It is remarkable in how diffident a tone the speaker begins, how careful he is to put in the front of his case everything that can excite compassion, how he avoids directly praising or even defending Aristophanes. He gradually insinuates that Aristophanes was a worthy man—poor, but generous and patriotic. The speech is nearly half over before it comes directly to the real issue (§ 28), and argues that Aristophanes cannot, in fact, have left more property than appeared. Perhaps the modesty of the speaker is a little overwrought; but there is consummate art in the sketch of his father, the quiet citizen of the old school, and of Aristophanes, the adventurous patriot of the new. On the whole, this is one of the masterpieces of Lysias, in which all the resources of his tact were brought into play by a subject difficult enough to be worthy of them.

---

[1] See especially § 11, χαλεπὸν μὲν οὖν ἀπολογεῖσθαι πρὸς σπάνιν ἀργυρίου ἣ νῦν ἐστιν ἐν τῇ πόλει. Compare Or. XXX. (Against Nicomachus) § 22, and the case of Eraton (Or. XVII.): Francken, *Comment. Lysiacae*, p. 130.

[2] Rauchenstein, in his Introduction to this Speech (p. 146), aptly quotes Or. XXVII. (Against Epicrates) § 11: οὐκέτι ὧν οὗτοι (the corrupt demagogues) κλέπτουσι ὀργίζεσθε, ἀλλ' ὧν αὐτοὶ λαμβάνετε χάριν ἴστε, ὥσπερ ὑμεῖς τὰ τούτων μισθοφοροῦντες ἀλλ' οὐ τούτων τὰ ὑμέτερα κλεπτόντων.

3. *Against Philocrates* [Or. XXIX.]—This case may be regarded as a sequel to that of Ergocles [Or. XXVIII.].[1] Philocrates had sailed, as steward or purser (ταμίας, § 3), under command of Ergocles as trierarch. Ergocles had now been put to death and his property had been confiscated. But a sum of thirty talents, which he was said to have gained by corrupt practices, had not been found (§ 2). A writ was therefore issued against Philocrates on the supposition that, since he had been in the confidence of Ergocles, he must know what had become of the money.

The speaker is one of several Public Prosecutors (συνήγοροι) and, as in the case of Ergocles, merely follows others with a summary of the leading points. The case Against Philocrates has been stated, and the evidence cited, by former speakers; this is the concluding speech for the prosecution; hence the title of epilogue or peroration[2] given in the MSS. to this as well as to the speech Against Ergocles. The date is probably the year of the trial of Ergocles —389 B.C.

Many persons, says the speaker, who had promised to appear against Philocrates have failed; an additional proof that he has the money, and has been able to buy off numerous accusers. The thirty talents have not been discovered:

---

[1] See above, p. 215.

[2] Κατὰ Φιλοκράτους ἐπίλογος. The speaker says in § 1 that many persons who had promised to appear against Philocrates have not done so; but obviously this does not justify Francken's inference,—"Altera pars inscriptionis (ἐπίλογος) manifesto falsa est; statim enim ab initio totidem verbis neminem esse praeter se accusatorem orator testatur" (*Comment. Lys.* p. 226). The absence of witnesses and proofs in this speech is conclusive, as Blass says (*Att. Bereds.* p. 454), on the other side.

who can have them but the most intimate friend of Ergocles, his subaltern and his steward? It rests with Philocrates to show either that Ergocles was wrongly condemned, or that some one else now has the missing sum (§§ 1–5). Three talents, it is well known, had been promised to public speakers if they could save Ergocles. Philocrates has got this money back, and has possessed himself of the rest of his late chief's property; yet now he has the effrontery to pretend that he was his enemy. Is it likely that in that case he would have volunteered to sail with him as trierarch? (§§ 6, 7).

The Athenians ought to defend their own interests, and compel Philocrates to give up their property. It is hard if those who cannot pay taxes incur the public anger, while the embezzlers of State-property escape. Indeed, the accomplices of Ergocles deserve not only a pecuniary penalty, but the same punishment which he suffered—death. While his trial was pending, his friends went about boasting that they had bribed upwards of 2000 men (§ 12). Let it be proved to them that no amount of bribery can save evil-doers. If the citizens are wise, they will reclaim what is their own (§§ 8–14).

Like the speeches Against Ergocles and Against Epicrates, this is the address of an official prosecutor, and of one who had but a subordinate part to perform. It has the characteristic excellences of the other two, compactness and vigour; but it is necessarily inferior to the speech Against Ergocles, in which the greater importance of the cause calls forth more oratorical vigour.

IV. Causes relating to a Scrutiny (δοκιμασία) before the Senate; especially of Officials designate

1. *Against Evandrus.* [Or. xxvi.]—In the second year of the 99th Olympiad (38½ B.C.) Leôdamas[1] drew the lot to be First Archon for the following year; and Evandrus was at the same time designated First Archon in reserve.[2] Leôdamas, before entering upon the archonship, had to pass a scrutiny (δοκιμασία) before the Senate. On this occasion he was accused by Thrasybulus of Collytus; the Senate rejected him; and the office thus came to Evandrus. But Evandrus also had to pass a scrutiny; and the present speech is made to the Senate in order to prove that he is ineligible.

The case is heard on the last day but one of Ol. 99. 2, *i.e.* at about midsummer of our year 382 B.C.[3] The last day of the Attic year was a public holiday, on which no law-court could sit, and on which a sacrifice to Zeus Sôtêr was celebrated by the First Archon. If, therefore, the Senate rejected Evandrus,

---

[1] Not the orator of Acharnae, who was the advocate of Leptines in 355 B.C., but a man of whom nothing is known except from this speech and from a notice in Arist. *Rh.* II. 23. Thrasybulus had said in his accusation that the name of Leôdamas had been inscribed on a pillar [recording traitors, etc.] on the acropolis (ἢν στηλίτης γεγονὼς ἐν τῇ ἀκροπόλει), but was erased in the time of the Thirty. Leôdamas answered that he was not likely to have erased it then. The Thirty would have trusted him the more for his enmity to the people being registered (ἐγγεγραμμένης τῆς ἔχθρας πρὸς τὸν δῆμον).

[2] ἐπέλαχε: Harpocr. s. v. Cf. Aesch. *in Ctes.* § 62.

[3] The Olympic year, reckoned from July to July, is counted as that year B.C. in which its first half falls. The year 382 B.C. comprised the second half of Ol. 99. 2 and the first half of Ol. 99. 3. Hence the date of this speech, which belongs to the end of Ol. 99. 2, is, in strictness, 382 B.C.; and the following Greek year, Ol. 99. 3, in which Evandrus was Archon, is also *conventionally* 382 B.C.

no time remained for an appeal to an ordinary court; and the State would be left without its chief magistrate at one of its great solemnities (§ 6).

Evandrus actually Archon in 382 B.C.

The election of Evandrus was, in fact, ratified; for he appears in the lists as Archon for the following year, Ol. 99. 3. This date is confirmed by allusions in the speech.

Thrasybulus the Collytean is charged in § 23 with having estranged Boeotia from Athens and with having lost Athenian ships. The first accusation refers to the establishment of oligarchies in the Boeotian cities, through Spartan influence, after the Peace of Antalcidas; and is curiously illustrated by the reference of Aeschines to Thrasybulus of Collytus as a man of great influence at Thebes.[1] The second accusation refers to an incident of the war on the Hellespont five years before. In 387 B.C. eight triremes under the command of this Thrasybulus were captured by Antalcidas near Abydus.[2]

All the first part of the speech has been lost in those eight pages of the Palatine MS. which contained the conclusion of the Twenty-fifth Speech and the whole of that Against Nicides.[3] The special charges made by the accuser, and the depositions to which he alludes (§ 8), were in this part. What remains is chiefly his answer to certain pleas which he conceives that Evandrus may urge.

Analysis.

It is hard—the speaker says—that, not content with

---

[1] Aeschin. *in Ctes.* § 138.
[2] Xen. *Hellen.* v. 1. 27. Xenophon's account, it may be observed, gives no support to the accuser's statement (§ 23) that Thrasybulus *betrayed* his ships.
[3] See p. 195.

impunity for his offences against the people, Evandrus should ask for office. Evandrus relies on the recent sobriety (*ἡσυχιότης*, § 5) of his life—which has been compulsory: and on his father's liberality—who used the influence thus gained to overthrow the democracy (§§ 1–5). He has contrived to delay his scrutiny until the last day but one of the year, when there is no time to appoint another First Archon. But the sacrifices of the morrow will surely be more pleasing to the gods, though offered only by the King Archon and his colleagues, than if the celebrant were a man whose hands are stained with the blood shed in the days of the Thirty Tyrants (§§ 6–8). One of the principal objects of the law of Scrutinies (*ὁ περὶ τῶν δοκιμασιῶν νόμος*, § 9) is to exclude from office in a democracy those who have abused power under an oligarchy. The mere fact of having been an ordinary knight or senator under the Thirty disqualifies a man for a place in the Council of Five Hundred. Evandrus was more than this; he was guilty of special crimes against the people; and shall he be First Archon? He will thus become a member of the Areiopagus for life, and murderers will be tried by a murderer. And this through the influence of Thrasybulus, a traitor to Athens. It must not be supposed that the speaker opposes Evandrus for the sake of Leôdamas. Leôdamas would be well pleased that the Senate should prove itself oligarchical by confirming so unpopular an appointment (§§ 10–15).

Evandrus appeals to the Amnesty [of 403 B.C.]; but that Amnesty did not mean that the honours, as well as the toleration, of the State should be accorded to its recent enemies (§§ 16–20). Let the Senate compare the accuser with the advocate of Evandrus. The accuser is pure of all connexion with oligarchies; his ancestors fought against the Peisistratidae; his family have exhausted a large fortune upon the State. Thrasybulus has alienated the Boeotians from Athens; has lost her ships, and brought her to despair.

If the Court reflects which of these two men ought rather to prevail, it will decide rightly upon the claims of Evandrus (§§ 21–24).

Tone of the Speech.

Unwillingness to mar a great annual festival may have influenced the Senate when they confirmed the election; but there is no proof that the grounds upon which it was opposed were good. The accuser must have felt that his case was well-nigh hopeless. This, and the feeling of Lysias himself towards all who had been concerned in the violence of the Anarchy, will partly account for the extreme bitterness and unfairness of this speech. In two places the tone is especially marked. First, where the accuser admits that since the restoration of the democracy Evandrus has been a thoroughly good citizen, and then argues that he deserves no credit for it (§§ 3–5); again, where he maintains that the dokimasia was instituted for the express purpose of keeping oligarchs out of office (§ 9). The outburst against Thrasybulus at the end is of a piece with this (§ 23). A certain boldness of expression, hardly congenial to Lysias, corresponds with the excited tone of the speech,[1] which has the air of having been written in haste, to support a cause already desperate.

IV. 2. For Mantitheus.

2. *For Mantitheus.* [Or. XVI.]—The name occurs only in the title, which, contrary to the general rule, is perhaps of the same age as the speech—"A Defence for Mantitheus on his Scrutiny before the Senate." What the office was to which this scrutiny related, can only be guessed; perhaps it was that of an ordinary senator, since in § 8 the speaker cites in-

[1] See especially §§ 3, 4.

stances of persons who had really done what he is
charged with doing, and had yet been admitted to
the Senate. The complaint against him was that his
name appeared on the list (σανίς, cf. § 6) of those who
had served as Knights in the time of the Thirty. As
the speech Against Evandrus shows (§ 10), the fact
of such service under the Tyrants became, after the
restoration of the democracy, a disqualification for the
office of senator. Mantitheus must, then, have been
at least eighteen years of age in 405 B.C., and so must
have been born before 422. He refers to his share
in campaigns subsequent to that of 394 B.C. (§§ 15–18).
On the other hand, the tone of the joke in § 15 rather
suggests that Thrasybulus, its object, was still alive ;—
that is, that the speech is earlier than 389 B.C.[1] The *Date.*
date may have been about 392 B.C. The speaker, who
was taunted with youthful presumption (§ 20), cannot
have been much more than thirty.

The speaker first disproves the charge against him of *Analysis.*
having served as a Knight under the Thirty Tyrants. Before
the disaster on the Hellespont [405 B.C.], his father had
sent him and his brother to the Euxine, to Satyrus [king of
the Cimmerian Bosporus] ; and they did not return to Athens
till five days before the democratic exiles captured the
Peiraeus [404 B.C.] (§ 4). The appearance of his name upon
the list of Knights at that time proves nothing ; the list
has many false entries and many omissions. Here is a
better proof on the other side :—When the democracy was
restored, the phylarch (captain of cavalry) of each tribe was
directed to recover from each Knight who had served under

---

[1] Thrasybulus died in Ol. 97. 3 (Diod. XIV. 94, 99 : Xen. *Hellen.* IV. 8. 30), i.e. 390–389 B.C. : probably, as Clinton (*F. H.*) says, in the early part of 389.

the Tyrants *the sum paid to him by the State for his equipment*
when he was first enrolled (κατάστασις, § 6). Now Mantitheus was never called upon to refund, nor brought before
the Fiscal Board (σύνδικοι, § 7)—(§§ 1–8).

Having disproved the charge against him, he goes on to
urge his positive merits. His private life has been blame-
less. After his father's death, he portioned his two sisters
and helped his brother. Men who are fond of dice and
wine have a marked aversion to him (§ 11). Then his
public services have been constant. He volunteered on the
expedition for the relief of Haliartus [395 B.C.] (§ 13). In
the next year he fought in the disastrous battle of Corinth,
and retreated later than " the majestic Steirian [Thrasybulus],
who has taunted all the world with cowardice " (§ 15). In
the autumn of the same year [394 B.C.] he and his company
volunteered for service against Agesilaus in Boeotia. Since
then, he has constantly served in the field or in garrison
(§ 18)—(§§ 9–19).

Some have taunted him with forwardness because,
though so young, he has spoken in the ecclesia. His own
affairs, however, compelled him to do so at first. Perhaps,
indeed, he has been too ambitious. But he could not help
thinking of his forefathers, who had always been in public
life and served the State; and he saw that Athenians, to
tell the truth, respected none but those who could act and
speak for the city. " And why should you be annoyed with
such men ? You yourselves and none else are their judges "
(§§ 20, 21).

The character of Mantitheus.

Perhaps hardly anything in Greek literature has
a fresher or brighter charm than this short speech
—the natural, wonderfully vivid expression of an
attractive character. Mantitheus is the brilliant,
ambitious young Athenian, burning to fulfil the
Homeric ideal by distinguishing himself in council as

in war; an Alcibiades made harmless by the sentiment of chivalry. The general tone of simple self-reliance, and possibly the gibe at Thrasybulus, may have been found refreshing by elderly senators. Mantitheus had really done good service in the field; and his statement of this is followed by an ingenuous apology for over-eagerness to shine in the ecclesia. The last passage is masterly. The virtue of "minding one's own affairs" (ἀπραγμοσύνη) was often praised at Athens; but Mantitheus goes to the centre of Athenian instincts when he tells the judges that "to say the truth" they respect no men who do not take part in public life.[1]

3. *Against Philon.* [Or. XXXI.]—This speech may be considered as a companion-piece to the last; being an Accusation, as the other is probably a Defence, at a dokimasia for the Senate. Philon—a man otherwise unknown—had been chosen by lot a member of the Senate of Five Hundred; and had appeared before that body, with others designated to places in it, in order to pass the scrutiny. The speaker, himself a senator, comes forward to oppose the admission of Philon. The date cannot be fixed. Philon is accused of having gone about Attica, plundering "the oldest of the citizens," who had stayed quietly in their demes (§ 18); and some of these citizens were still alive: some time between 404 and 395 B.C. may therefore be assumed.

IV. 3. Against Philon.

Probable date.

---

[1] The speech is described by Dobree (*Adv.* I. 192) as "vividis et paene comicis coloribus exprimens στρατιωτικὴν αὐθάδειαν ea simul arte ut hoc ipso placeat"—a description which does no justice to the delicacy of the delineation. "Ex verbis Dobrei alterum quendam Pyrgopolinicen expectes," as Francken says (*Comment. Lys.* p. 118).

Analysis. The speaker begins by protesting that no private enmity, but only regard to his oath as senator, induces him to appear against Philon. What is the definition of a worthy senator? One who both is, and desires to be, a citizen (§ 5). Now when the troubles came on Athens [405 B.C.], Philon proved how little he valued his citizenship. He neither stayed with the oligarchs in the town, nor joined the exiles at Phylê, but went to Orôpus—paid the resident-alien's tax, and lived under the protection of a patron. This shall be proved by witnesses (§§ 1–14). If he says that he was unfit for fighting, it can be shown that his name does not appear among those of the citizens who, instead of personal service, paid money or armed their demesmen (§§ 15, 16). Nor was he merely passive: he did positive wrong to aged citizens of Athens whom he met with in the country (§§ 17–19). This corresponds with his treatment of his own mother, who transferred the keeping of her money from her son to a stranger (§§ 20–23). Why should such as he be a senator? The betrayer of a garrison, a fleet, or a camp is punished; but Philon has betrayed the State itself (§§ 24–26).

"He has broken no law," he says. No: for an offence so enormous was never expressly contemplated by any legislator (§§ 27, 28). If the aliens who helped Athens in her need were honoured, surely the citizens who abandoned her should be disgraced. The advocates who claim honour for Philon now would have done better had they advised him to deserve it then (§§ 29–33). Let each senator ask himself why *he* was admitted to that dignity, and he will see why Philon ought to be shut out from it (§ 34).

The attack strong, but temperate. The tone of this address is in contrast with that of the protest against the election of Evandrus: it is severe and decided, but not bitter or unfair. A character which seems to have been really contemptible is drawn without passion, each statement being supported by evidence; and the assertion of the speaker, that only a sense of duty prompted him to accuse, is at least not contradicted by his method. The style is rhetorical, and rather more openly artificial than is usual with Lysias (see esp. §§ 11, 32); but it has all his compactness and force—of which the short appeal at the end is a good example. One point of historical interest comes out. Philon is accused of having taken part, in 405 B.C., neither with oligarchs nor with democrats. He pleads:—"Had it been an offence not to be present at such a time, a law would have been made expressly on that subject." The answer is, that, owing to the inconceivable enormity of the offence, no law has been enacted on the subject (§ 27). So completely had Solon's enactment against neutrality—to which the speaker could have appealed with so much rhetorical effect—passed out of the remembrance of that generation.[1]

Allusion to the crime of Neutrality.

4. *Defence on a Charge of seeking to abolish the Democracy.* [Or. XXV.]—This title, given to the speech in the MSS., is clearly wrong. The speaker is, indeed, chiefly concerned to prove that he is guiltless of any share in the crimes of the Thirty Tyrants; but it is clear that he was not upon his trial for high treason. There is no reference to any penalties which

IV. 4. Defence on a Charge of seeking to abolish the Democracy.

---

[1] Rauchenstein, in his introduction to the speech (p. 116), brings together the chief passages in which Solon's law is mentioned:— Plut. *Sol.* c. 20 (ἄτιμον εἶναι τὸν ἐν στάσει μηδετέρας μερίδος γενόμενον): Cic. *ad Att.* X. 1: Gellius II. 12 (translating an extract from Aristotle—perhaps from his πολιτεῖαι) *si ob hanc discordiam dissensionemque seditio atque discessio populi in duas partes fieret et ob eam caussam irritatis animis utrinque arma caperentur pugnareturque, tum qui in eo tempore in eoque casu civilis discordiae non alterutri parti se adiunxerit sed solitarius separatusque a communi malo civitatis secesserit, is domo patria fortunisque omnibus careto, exul extorrisque esto.*

threatened him. The question is whether he shall,
or shall not, be admitted to certain privileges. Thus
in § 3 he insists on his claim to participation in the
advantages of citizenship; in § 4 he speaks of rights
which citizens who have done no evil ought to share
with positive benefactors of the State; in § 14 he
says to the judges:—"If, when I might have had
office, I declined it, I have a right to receive honour
from you *now*." Clearly this speech was delivered on
the occasion of a dokimasia for some office to which
the speaker had been designated, but his admission
to which was opposed. The cause is heard by an
ordinary court—probably under the presidency of the
Thesmothetae[1]—and on appeal from a decision for
the speaker already given by the Senate. The date
must be placed between 402 and 400 B.C.; probably
nearer to the lower limit.[2] The accusers were Epi-
genes, Diophanes and Cleisthenes (§ 25). The
defendant is not named.

<small>The Speech really connected with a Dokimasia.</small>

<small>Date.</small>

---

[1] Since the Thesmothetae had jurisdiction in causes connected with δοκιμασίαι: Pollux 8. 44.

[2] Rauchenstein (*Introduct.* p. 91) supposes 402 B.C.; Blass (*Att. Bereds.* p. 509) prefers 401 or 400.

The arguments for the *earlier* date are these:—(1) The general tone of the speech, referring to the troubles of the Anarchy as recent: (2) § 17, where the speaker says προθυμήσομαι χρηστὸς εἶναι—as if he had not yet had time to prove his reformed character: (3) §§ 23–24, where the exiled adherents of the Thirty are described as still hoping for a reaction at Athens: (4) § 28, from which (Rauchenstein thinks) it appears that the law of Archinus was not yet passed—a law enacted soon after the restoration of the democracy, providing that persons against whom, in despite of the Amnesty, accusations were brought in violation of the Amnesty, should be allowed at once to enter a παραγραφή, and to speak *first* at its hearing (Isocr. *Call.* § 2).

For the *later* date it is argued (1) that in one place at least—§ 21—the events under the Thirty are spoken of as if some considerable interval had elapsed: (2) that the restored democracy was old enough for abuses to have grown up,—§ 30 [this is, I think, a strong point]: (3) that § 28 does not prove the law of Archinus to be non-existent, since that law would have had no bearing on a δοκιμασία.

It would not be strange, he says, if the speeches made against him had excited the indignation of the judges against all, without distinction, who had remained at Athens under the Thirty. Much more might, indeed, have been said about the crimes of the Tyrants. But it is unmeaning to charge those crimes upon men who had no share in them. If he can prove that he is innocent, he may surely claim at least the ordinary privileges of citizenship in common with men of more distinguished services (§§ 1–6). No man is born an oligarch or a democrat. He becomes one or the other according to his private interest (τῶν ἰδίᾳ συμφερόντων, § 10). This is proved by history. Phrynichus and Peisander were demagogues before they become oligarchs. Men who helped to overthrow the Four Hundred were afterwards numbered with the Thirty: many of the Four Hundred themselves were with the democrats at the Peiraeus; some of those who had expelled the Four Hundred were afterwards among the Thirty; and some of the men who gave in their names for the march against Eleusis, after going forth with the people, were besieged along with the Tyrants.[1]

The explanation is simply that their interests varied at different times. Now, the interest of the speaker lay wholly with the democracy. He had been five times trierarch and had been in four sea-fights (§ 12). The establishment

---

[1] § 9 εἰσὶ δὲ οἵτινες τῶν Ἐλευσῖναδε ἀπογραψαμένων, ἐξελθόντες μεθ' ὑμῶν, ἐπολιορκοῦντο μετ' αὐτῶν. The Thirty Tyrants, when their government fell and was succeeded by that of the Ten, withdrew to Eleusis. After the restoration of the democracy, an expedition was made from Athens against Eleusis, and they were dislodged: Xen. *Hell.* II. iv. 39, 43.

The question is, whether οἱ Ἐλευσῖναδε ἀπογραψάμενοι are (1) men who enrolled themselves at Athens for this expedition, but afterwards deserted to the Tyrants—in which case ἐξελθόντες means "having marched out": or (2) men who, having been driven from Athens by the Thirty, remained in Attica, and, instead of joining the democrats, joined the tyrants at Eleusis—in which case ἐξελθόντες means "having left Athens" under stress of the Tyranny. I prefer the former view as giving (a) a clearer meaning to ἀπογραψαμένων, (b) a clearer contrast between ἐξελθόντες μεθ' ὑμῶν and ἐπολιορκοῦντο μετ' αὐτῶν.

of the Thirty destroyed his chance of reward for these services. Neither under the First Oligarchy nor under the Second did he hold office (§§ 7–14). If he did no wrong in the Anarchy, much more will he be a good citizen under the restored Democracy. The victims of the Tyrants must not be confounded with their agents. It was the error of the Thirty that they visited the sins of a few corrupt demagogues on all the citizens: let not the people so err now (§§ 15–20). Dissensions among the Thirty gave the exiles their first hopes of success; let not disunion in the democracy now give occasion to the enemies of Athens, but let the oaths of amnesty be kept towards all (§§ 21–24). After the fall of the Four Hundred, the rigours which bad advisers caused to be adopted against their political opponents brought the city to ruin. And now sycophants, counselling a revengeful policy, oppose themselves to the views of those who were really active in restoring the democracy. Such men show what they would have been had they shared the power of the Thirty. The friends of the city advise differently. Let the Amnesty hold good for all. When those who are really answerable for the past troubles are brought to account, severity is excusable; but innocent men must not be mixed up with them (§§ 25–35).

The Speech over-praised.

The speaker had evidently been closely connected with the party of the Tyrants; for though he states his services to the democracy before 405 B.C., of his political character since that time he has nothing better to say than that it has been harmless; indeed, he implies a contrast between himself and those who had been true to the democracy at its need (§ 4). It is hard to understand the high praise which has been given to this speech by some critics of Lysias;[1] it

---

[1] As by Reiske ("egregia, luculenta, Lysiae nomine dignissima," *Or. Att.* v. p. 759): and by Francken (*Comment. Lys.* p. 184).

is barely conceivable that one of the ablest of them should count it his best work.[1] The speaker's interpretation of the Amnesty is, indeed, larger and truer than the opposite view taken by the accuser of Evandrus;[2] and his elaborate exposition of the doctrine that political creed is purely an affair of self-interest may claim the praise of candour. The style has vigour, but neither brilliancy nor dignity; and the êthos of the speaker, as a moderately intelligent and thoroughly practical man, can scarcely be accounted persuasive.[3]

5. *For the Invalid.* [Or. XXIV.]—This speech may conveniently be classed with the four preceding, since it was written for a dokimasia, although the scrutiny in this case was of a different kind. At Athens a certain allowance was made by the State to the ἀδύνατοι:[4] that is, to persons who were unable, through bodily ailment, to earn a livelihood, and who had less than three minae of private property. Once a year, or perhaps oftener, the list of applicants for such relief was scrutinised by the Senate[5] and then passed by the ecclesia (§ 22). It is on the occasion of such a scrutiny that the present

IV. 5. For the Invalid.

Public Charity at Athens.

---

[1] "Lysiam relegenti videtur haec oratio esse omnium optima." Dobree, *Adv.* I. 247.

[2] Or. XXVI. §§ 16–20: see above, p. 244.

[3] It is difficult not to suspect that Lysias—himself a loyal friend of the democracy in two disasters—wrote this defence of easy tergiversation with deliberate, though disguised, irony; irony which perhaps ran no danger from the acuteness of his client.

[4] It is not clear whether the term ἀδύνατος, in this technical sense, referred *only* to bodily infirmity, or included (as Francken thinks, p. 171 n.) also the idea of poverty. The Invalid was said by his adversary (1) τῷ σώματι δύνασθαι καὶ οὐκ εἶναι τῶν ἀδυνάτων, § 4, and (2) δύνασθαι συνεῖναι δυναμένοις ἀνθρώποις ἀναλίσκειν, § 5, a phrase evidently as an antithesis — possibly humorous — to ἀδύνατος.

[5] Aeschin. *in Timarch.* § 104.

speech is made. The speaker had for years (§ 8) been in receipt of an obol daily (§ 26) from the State ; but lately it had been attempted to show that he was not entitled to public relief. This objection is termed in the title to the speech (not in the speech itself) an eisangelia; but had, of course, nothing in common with eisangeliae technically so called except that it was an accusation laid immediately before the Senate. *Date.* The date appears from § 25 to have been later than 403 B.C.

Analysis. Having premised that jealousy is the only conceivable motive for this attack upon him, the speaker comes to the two objections which have been made to his receiving the public alms :—that he is not really a cripple ; and that he has a trade (§§ 1–4). He answers the second objection first (§§ 5–9) ; and then refutes the other with a good deal of grim humour (§§ 10–14). Lastly, he defends his general character (§§ 15–20), and concludes with an entreaty not to be deprived of his obol a day (§§ 21–27).

No ground for doubting the genuineness. Harpocration seems[1] to have doubted the genuineness of this speech ; possibly on the ground taken by Boeckh[2]—that Lysias would not have written, nor the Senate endured, so elaborate an address on such a subject. This seems a most unsafe argument against

---

[1] *seems*, for his words are (s. v. ἀδύνατος), ἔστι δὲ καὶ λόγος τις ὡς Λυσίου περὶ τοῦ ἀδυνάτου: some MSS. having ὡς λέγεται Λυσίου (Blass, *Att. Bereds.* p. 648).

[2] *Stautsh.* 1. p. 260 ff. referred to by Blass *l. c.* Blass classes this speech with such "bagatelle" speeches as λόγος περὶ τῆς ἐγγυθήκης, λόγος περὶ τοῦ χρυσοῦ τρίποδος, etc., ascribed to Lysias: and remarks that all such trifles, without distinction, were held spurious by the old critics, whom Harpocration and Athenaeus follow. But it should be noticed that Athenaeus, while he adds εἰ γνήσιος to his mention of the περὶ τοῦ χρ. τρίποδος (VI. p. 231 B), only says of the περὶ τῆς ἐγγυθήκης that it is "ascribed" to Lysias—acquiescing, apparently, in the ascription (V. p. 209 F).

a composition excellent of its kind, and excellent in a way suggestive of Lysias. The humour, broad, but stopping short of burlesque, exactly suits the condition of the speaker; and there is true art in the ironical pathos of the invalid, when, using an Attic illustration, he remarks that his infirmity is disputed with him by his adversary as eagerly as if it were an heiress (§ 14).

V. Causes relating to Military Offences
(λιποταξίου—ἀστρατείας)

1. *Against Alcibiades, on a Charge of Desertion* [Or. XIV.].

2. *Against Alcibiades, on a Charge of Failure to Serve* [Or. XV.].

V. 1. Against Alcibiades,
I.
2. Against Alcibiades.
II.

These speeches do not refer to two distinct accusations, but are merely two different ways of stating the same accusation. Alcibiades, son of the famous Alcibiades, had taken part in the expedition sent from Athens to the relief of Haliartus when Boeotia was invaded by Lysander in 395 B.C. But, instead of serving with the heavy-armed infantry, he had chosen to serve with the cavalry, although he had not passed the scrutiny (dokimasia) required before enrolment among the Knights. His accusers might have indicted him under a special law which attached the penalty of disfranchisement to such a fraud (Or. XIV. § 8). They preferred, however, to bring against him a more invidious charge—desertion of military duty.

The two Speeches concern the same fact.

The principal military offences were dealt with at

Law about Military Offences.

Athens by one law. Under this law a citizen was liable to indictment and if convicted to disfranchisement for 1. Failure to join the army—ἀστρατείας: 2. Cowardice in battle—δειλίας: 3. Desertion of his post—λιποταξίου. This third term properly denoted an offence distinct from the other two. But it was sometimes so extended as to include either of the other two.[1] Now Alcibiades had served, indeed, but had not served with the hoplites. His offence, then, might be looked at from two points of view. He might be considered as a man who, on service, had been found out of his place, and who was liable to an indictment for Desertion of his Post—γραφὴ λιποταξίου. Or he might be considered as a man who had never been present in his place, and who was liable to an indictment for Failure to Serve—γραφὴ ἀστρατείας. The First Speech takes the former point of view; the Second takes the latter.

Date.

The date and occasion of the speeches are not directly indicated, but can be determined almost certainly. This was the first military trial since "the

---

[1] It does not appear quite certain whether there was a γραφὴ δειλίας distinct from a γραφὴ λιποταξίου. In § 6 of the First Speech Against Alcibiades they appear to be identified. But in the following passages (among others) they are distinguished :— Aeschin. *in Ctes.* § 175 Σόλων—ἐν τοῖς αὐτοῖς ἐπιτιμίοις ᾤετο δεῖν ἐνέχεσθαι τὸν ἀστράτευτον καὶ τὸν λελοιπότα τὴν τάξιν καὶ τὸν δειλὸν ὁμοίως : Andoc. *de Myst.* § 73 ὁπόσοι λίποιεν τὴν τάξιν ἢ ἀστρατείας ἢ δειλίας ἢ ἀναυμαχίου ὄφλοιεν ἢ τὴν ἀσπίδα ἀποβάλοιεν: and Plato's distinction (*Legg.* XII. 943 F) of ἀστρα- τείας—λιποταξίου—ῥιφθέντων (the last equivalent to δειλίας) may be supposed to correspond to a like distinction in the actual Attic law. Obviously a γραφὴ λιποταξίου might be needed for cases in which a γραφὴ δειλίας could not be preferred. On the other hand, the γραφὴ λιποταξίου might probably include the case of ἀστρατεία : just as the δίκη λιπομαρτυρίου (compared by Francken, *Comment. Lys.* p. 111) lay against a man who *refused* to give evidence ; not merely against one who, having undertaken to do so, failed to appear.

peace" (XIV. § 4);—a campaign had just taken place, but no battle had been fought (§ 5), though the generals had given satisfaction to the State (XV. § 1). All this corresponds with the campaign of the year 395. It was the first since the peace, or rather truce, with Sparta in the spring of 404. No battle had been fought, because, before the Athenian force arrived at Haliartus, the Lacedaemonians had already been defeated, and Lysander slain. The Athenian Generals had only to assist at the arrangement of the humiliating truce under which Pausanias led his army out of Boeotia.[1] In 395 B.C. the younger Alcibiades must have been about twenty years of age.[2]

The Court was composed of soldiers (στρατιώτας δικάζειν, Or. XIV. § 5), the Generals presiding (τῶν στρατηγῶν δέομαι, XV. 1). Archestratides, the chief accuser, had opened the cause and produced the evidence; these two speakers are his friends and supporters. (Or. XIV. 3; XV. 12.)

The accuser explains his appearance in that capacity. An explanation is, indeed, hardly necessary, considering the character of Alcibiades: but in his own case a feud inherited from his father supplies a special motive (§§ 1–3). He then addresses himself to a technical point. The law against Desertion is so worded (it has been argued) that it does not apply where there has been no battle. He answers that one of the two offences which that law contemplates—namely Failure to Serve—is manifestly proved

Analysis. —First Speech.

---

[1] Xen. *Hellen.* III. v. 16.
[2] Since from Isocr. *de Bigis* (*Or.* XVI.) § 45 it appears that the younger Alcibiades was born in, or just before, 415 B.C.

against Alcibiades, who did not take his place among the
hoplites. Of the other offence—Desertion of his Post
through cowardice—he is virtually guilty, since his reason
for preferring to serve with the cavalry was that there he
would run less risk. Others, who were really knights,
waived their privilege in this instance,[1] and served as
hoplites. Alcibiades seized a privilege to which he had no
claim (§ 10). Such audacity must be punished for public
example. Let the soldiers who sit in judgment remember
how much each of them sacrificed to his duty, and
then decide what punishment is merited by such contempt of duty (§§ 4–15). The advocates of Alcibiades will
plead his youth and his parentage. Neither his own nor
his father's character deserves sympathy. If relatives
plead for him, it is they who ought to have restrained
him; if officials, they must show that he is legally innocent
(§§ 16–22).

Then follows a bitter attack upon the defendant and his
father. Alcibiades the younger is described as vicious from
his youth, and as a traitor to his own father;[2] all the
treasons of the elder Alcibiades are recounted at length.
He prompted the Spartan occupation of Deceleia—he
incited Chios to revolt — he preferred a home even in
Thrace to Athens. He betrayed the Athenian fleet to
Lysander: both his great-grandfathers, Megacles and Alcibiades, were *ostracised* (§§ 23–40). An attack on the family
in their private relations, as stained with every impurity

---

[1] This statement is exactly illustrated by the Speech For Mantitheus
(Or. XVI) § 12, where Mantitheus,
speaking of this very expedition to
Haliartus, says:—ὅτε...εἰς Ἁλίαρτον
ἔδει βοηθεῖν, ὑπὸ Ὀρθοβούλου κατειλεγ-
μένος ἱππεύειν,...ἑτέρων ἀναβάντων
ἐπὶ τοὺς ἵππους ἀδοκιμάστων
παρὰ τὸν νόμον ἐγὼ προσελθὼν
ἔφην τῷ Ὀρθοβούλῳ ἐξαλεῖψαί με
ἐκ τοῦ καταλόγου.

[2] An allusion in § 26 is obscure.
It is said that the younger Alcibiades
μετὰ Θεοτίμου ἐπιβουλεύσας τῷ πατρὶ
Ὠρεοὺς προύδωκεν. Francken suggests Ὀρνεάς (the town in the Argeia);
and thinks that the young Alcibiades
may have had something to do with
a betrayal of that place to the Lacedaemonians in 416 B.C.: cf. Thuc.
VI. 7 (*Comment. Lys.* p. 106).

and impiety, leads to the conclusion. Much, the accuser says, has been omitted: the judges must imagine it. He then causes to be read the laws on which he relies; the judicial oath: and the indictment (§§ 41–47).

The Generals, the presidents of the Court, say that they allowed Alcibiades as a special favour to serve with the cavalry. Why, in that case, was he rejected by the phylarch of his own tribe, and not struck off the list of hoplites by the taxiarch? Why, when he took the field, was he treated with scorn by all the knights, and driven to place himself among the mounted bowmen? It is strange if the Generals can enrol a man among the knights at their pleasure, when they cannot so enrol him among the hoplites. If, however, the Generals have exceeded their real powers, then the Court cannot recognise their arbitrary act (§§ 1–8). The law is, indeed, severe: but the judges must administer it as unflinchingly as if they were marching against the enemy (§§ 9–12). *Second Speech.*

The first, especially, of these two speeches should be compared with the Defence written shortly before by Isocrates—probably in 397 or 396 B.C.—for the same man. Both bear striking witness to the hatred felt for the memory of the elder Alcibiades in the early years of the restored democracy. Here, denunciations of the father fill about one-half of the speech against the son; there, the son devotes more than three-fourths of his address to a defence of his father. The speech Against Alcibiades ascribed to Andocides, but probably the work of a late sophist, indirectly illustrates the same feeling; being, in fact, an epitome of the scandalous stories about Alcibiades current at the same period. *Feeling towards the elder Alcibiades.*

Doubt of the genuineness—not well founded.

Harpocration refers to Oration XIV. with a doubt of its authenticity;[1] Oration XV. is cited by no ancient author. The genuineness of each has been called in question by modern critics;[2] chiefly on grounds of internal evidence. It has been noticed that the composition varies in some points from the usual Lysian character; and that the special marks of his power are absent.[3] The two speeches must stand or fall together. If not the work of Lysias, they are certainly the work of a contemporary writer for the law-courts. But the evidence, external or internal, against their genuineness appears too slight to warrant even a strong suspicion.

VI. Causes relating to Murder or Intent to Murder (γραφαὶ φόνου—τραύματος ἐκ προνοίας)

VI. 1. Against Eratosthenes.

1. *Against Eratosthenes.* [Or. XII.]—Polemarchus, brother of Lysias, had been put to death by the Thirty Tyrants. Eratosthenes, one of their number, was the man who had arrested him and taken him to prison. In this speech Lysias, himself the speaker, charges Eratosthenes with the murder of Polemarchus, and, generally, with his share in the Tyranny.

---

[1] s. v. Ἀλκιβιάδης.

[2] See Francken (*Comment. Lys.* pp. 110-115), who refers to the doubts of Boeckh and others, but himself expresses positive suspicion only of Or. XV: Blass (*Att. Bereds.* pp. 491-4), who adds Scheibe to the sceptics, and himself inclines to doubt *both* speeches; though allowing, with Francken, that they certainly are not mere sophistic exercises. Taylor thought the *second* spurious (Reiske *Or. Att.* v. 553).

[3] Blass notices especially the heaping together of homoioteleuta in §§ 41 and 35. Markland observes on Or. XIV § 47, μεγάλη δ' εὐτυχία τὸ τοιούτων πολιτῶν ἀπαλλαγῆναι πόλει, "hi non sunt numeri Lysiani: ille potius scripsisset μεγάλη δ' εὐτυχία τῇ πόλει τοιούτων πολιτῶν ἀπαλλαγῆναι (ap. Reiske *O. A.* v. 553). The absence of ἦθος and χάρις is the more general accusation—a vague one.

A question has to be considered in regard to the form of the accusation. Was Eratosthenes prosecuted under an ordinary indictment for murder? Or was he accused on the occasion of his coming forward to render account of his office as one of the Thirty?

Form of procedure.

On the former supposition it is hard to say before what court the trial took place. Clearly it was not the Areiopagus. If it was the Delphinion, then Eratosthenes must have pleaded some justification of the homicide; but he admits its guilt, and lays the blame on his colleagues (§ 24). If it was an ordinary heliastic court under the presidency of the Eleven, then there must have been an arrest (ἀπαγωγή) by the Eleven; but this does not seem to have taken place.[1]

The other supposition offers less difficulty. A special clause in the Amnesty of 403 B.C. excluded the Thirty Tyrants, the Ten who had succeeded them, and the Eleven who had served them. But any one even of these might enjoy the Amnesty if he chose to stand a public inquiry, and was acquitted.[2] When the oligarchy was finally overthrown, Pheidon

---

[1] The arguments against the hypothesis of an ordinary γραφὴ φόνου are well given by Blass (*Att. Ber.* pp. 540–1.). Scheibe (*ib.*) thinks that the trial was "fortasse apud heliastas ad Delphinium"; Rauchenstein apparently (*Introd.* p. 16) before an ordinary heliastic court. Francken also (*Comment. Lys.* p. 79) seems to reject the idea of an accusation at the εὔθυναι.

[2] Xenophon (*Hellen.* II. iv. 38) mentions the exclusion from the Amnesty of the Thirty, the Eleven, and "the Ten who had ruled in the Peiraeus." Andocides (*De Myst.* § 90) gives the words of the Amnesty: καὶ οὐ μνησικακήσω τῶν πολιτῶν οὐδενί, πλὴν τῶν τριάκοντα καὶ τῶν ἕνδεκα [καὶ τῶν δέκα]· οὐδὲ τούτων ὃς ἂν ἐθέλῃ εὐθύνας διδόναι τῆς ἀρχῆς ἧς ἦρξεν. Francken cannot be right in referring τούτων here to τῶν ἕνδεκα *only* (*Comment. Lys.* p. 79). The words τῶν δέκα are added by Sauppe and Baiter with Schneider and others.

and Eratosthenes were the only members[1] of it who stayed at Athens. As they dared to do this, they must have availed themselves of the permission to give account of their office. And Lysias could have had no better opportunity for preferring his accusation than that which would be given by the public inquiry into the conduct of Eratosthenes. Two things in the speech itself tend to show that it was spoken on this occasion. First, its general scope. It has a wider range, and deals more generally with the history of the Anarchy, than would be natural if it was concerned exclusively with an ordinary indictment for murder. Only the first third of the speech relates to Polemarchus; thenceforth to the end his name is not mentioned, even in the peroration; the political offences of Eratosthenes are exclusively dwelt upon. It may be noticed, too, that at the commencement Lysias speaks in the plural of "the defendants" and their hostility to Athens, as if Eratosthenes was only in the same predicament with several other persons. Secondly, an expression in § 37 should be noticed. The speaker there says that he has done enough in having shown that the guilt of the accused reaches the point at which death is deserved. He would not have said this if death had been the necessary penalty in case of conviction. But he might well say it if his charge was preferred, among many others, when Eratosthenes was giving his account, and when

---

[1] Pheidon had been one of the Thirty and also one of the Ten. Eratosthenes had been one of the Thirty, but *not* one of the Ten. This is clear from §§ 54, 55.

the question was what degree of punishment, if any, he was to suffer.[1]

The date must be 403 B.C., the year of Eucleides. After their flight from Athens the Thirty maintained themselves for a short time at Eleusis. Soon after the restoration of the democracy, an expedition was made against Eleusis; the generals of the Thirty, who came out to ask for a parley, were seized and put to death; and the Tyrants, with their chief adherents, fled from Attica.[2] But it is clear from § 80 of the speech that this expedition had not yet taken place.

Again, in §§ 92 f. Lysias addresses successively two distinct parties — the "men of the city" who remained in Athens under the Thirty, and the "men of the Peiraeus." The line of demarcation could have been drawn so sharply only while the war of parties was quite recent; not two or three years later, when exiles and oligarchs had long been fused once more into one civic body. It was, no doubt, remembered for years who had been on one side and who on the other. But in a speech made (say) in 400 B.C., we should not find the "men of the city" and the "men

---

[1] The view that Lysias accused Eratosthenes at his εὔθυναι is taken by Blass (*Att. Ber.* p. 540) and by Grote (vol. VIII. p. 402). I have purposely abstained from bringing into the question the fact that Lysias was only an isoteles. On the one hand, as Rauchenstein says, a resident-alien was probably allowed to prosecute personally, instead of being represented by his προστάτης, when the duty of avenging blood came upon him as the nearest relative. On the other hand, it can hardly be doubtful that a resident-alien would, as Blass thinks, have been allowed to prefer an accusation at the euthunae of any official whose acts had touched him: it certainly is not doubtful that such a man as Lysias would have been allowed, under the democracy which he had just helped to restore, to impeach one of the Thirty Tyrants.

[2] Xen. *Hellen.* II. iv. 43.

of Peiraeus" addressed separately as if they still formed two distinct camps.

The speech falls into two divisions. The first and shorter (§§ 1–36) deals with the special charge against Eratosthenes; the second, with his political character and with the crimes of the Tyrants generally.

I. §§ 1–36

Analysis. The difficulty here is not how to begin, but where to stop. Ordinarily the accuser is expected to show that he has some motive for hostility to the accused. Here it would be more natural to ask the accused what motive he and his fellows have had for their hostility to Athens (§§ 1–3).

Lysias then enters on his narrative of the facts. His father had been invited by Pericles to settle at Athens as a resident-alien, and had lived there peaceably for thirty years. His family had never been involved in any troubles until the time of the Thirty Tyrants. Theognis and Peison, members of that body, suggested the policy of plundering the resident-aliens. These two men first paid a visit to the shield-manufactory of Lysias and his brother, and took an inventory of the slaves. They next came to the dwelling-house of Lysias, and got all his ready money, about three talents. He managed to slip away from them, and took refuge with a friend in the Peiraeus; then, hearing that his brother Polemarchus had been met in the street by Eratosthenes and taken to prison, he escaped by night to Megara. Polemarchus received the usual mandate of the Thirty—to drink the hemlock; and had a beggar's burial. Though he and Lysias had yielded such rich plunder, the very earrings were taken from the ears of his wife (§ 19). Now the murderer of Polemarchus was Eratosthenes (§§ 4–23). Here he is briefly cross-examined :—

"Did you arrest Polemarchus or not?" "Terrified by

the orders of the authorities, I proceeded to do so." "And were you in the council chamber when we were being talked about?" "I was." "Did you support, or oppose, those who advised our execution?" "Opposed them." "Opposed our being put to death?" "Yes." "Considering such treatment of us to be unjust—or just?" "Unjust."

Lysias comments indignantly on these answers. If Eratosthenes had really protested against the sentence, he would not have been selected to make the arrest. He was one of the Thirty themselves and had nothing to fear. All the circumstances disprove his pretence of good-will: instead of contenting himself with a visit to the house of Polemarchus, he seized him in the street; he gave him no friendly hint beforehand. If it is true that he opposed the sentence, he must at least prove that he did not make the arrest, or did not make it in a harsh manner. The judges are then reminded of the importance which their decision will have as an example for both citizens and foreigners. The fate of the generals who conquered at Arginusae is contrasted with the deserts of those who profited by the defeat at Aegospotami. If those suffered death, what is due to these? (§§ 24–36).

II. §§ 37–100

To say more is superfluous: the guilt of Eratosthenes has already been shown to be capital. But lest he should appeal to his past life, this must be exposed. In the first oligarchy [411 B.C.] he had to fly from the Hellespont after an unsuccessful attempt to corrupt the democratic crews of Athenian vessels there. After the defeat of Athens [405 B.C.] he and Critias were first among the Five Ephori and afterwards among the Thirty Tyrants. Perhaps he will say that he obeyed the Thirty through fear. No; in the cause of Theramenes he dared to oppose them. But this opposition was not patriotic: all the quarrels among the

Thirty were selfish. The so-called moderate party to which Theramenes belonged was represented by the later Board of Ten. And the Ten, instead of promoting peace, waged war with the exiles more bitterly than the Thirty (§§ 37–61).

Theramenes is the man whom Eratosthenes takes credit for having defended. It can be fancied how eagerly he would have claimed friendship with Themistocles, who built the walls of Athens, if he is proud of friendship with Theramenes—who pulled them down. Theramenes, when a member of the first oligarchy, betrayed his own closest friends, Antiphon and Archeptolemus; after Aegospotami, he undertook to make peace without loss of honour, and yet it was he who proposed at Sparta that Athens should lose her walls and her fleet; it was he who advocated the proposal of Dracontides for the establishment of the Thirty; and it is this man—twice the enslaver of Athens—whom Eratosthenes glories in having defended! (§§ 62–78).

This is no season for mercy. The man who condemned, untried, the fathers, sons, brothers of those who now judge him, does not deserve even a trial. His advocates can urge no merits either of his or of their own. His witnesses are mistaken if they think that they can shield from peril of death the men who made it dangerous to attend a burial. They will say that Eratosthenes was the least criminal of the Thirty. Is he to escape because there are twenty-nine greater villains in Greece? (§§ 79–91).

Lysias now addresses himself, first, to those who remained in Athens during the Anarchy, then to the exiles who returned from the Peiraeus—speaking as if he had before him two definite bodies of men. He reminds each party of their peculiar reasons for hating the Thirty. The "men of the city" should hate that despotism; for it shared with them nothing but its shame, and forced upon them an unholy strife. The "men of Peiraeus" should hate it: it proscribed them, persecuted them, severed them from country and kinsfolk. Had it triumphed, no sanctuary would have protected them, nothing could have saved their children from outrage at home or slavery abroad. But it is needless to speak of what might have been: what has been is too great for words. It can only be *felt*—felt, with boundless resentment for the shrines which these men desecrated, for the city which they humbled,—for the dead, who are listening now to mark if the judges will avenge them.

"I will cease to accuse. You have heard, seen, suffered:—you have them:—judge" (§§ 92–100).

Result of the Trial. The result is unknown. But as the accused had evidently strong support, and as Lysias complains of the difficulty which he had experienced in finding witnesses to some of the principal facts, it is probable that the penalty of death, at least, was not inflicted.[1]

Character of the Speech. The Speech Against Eratosthenes must take the first place among the extant orations of Lysias. In the two parts into which it naturally falls the speech presents, in perhaps unique combination, two distinct styles of eloquence,—first, the plain earnestness of a private demand for redress—then the lofty vehemence of a political impeachment. The compass of the power shown may best be measured by the two passages which mark its limits—on the one hand, the account of the arrest of Polemarchus, which has almost the flow of Herodotean narrative;—on the other hand, the passionate appeal to the two classes of men who had suffered from the Thirty—worked up with all the resources of a finished rhetoric. As

---

[1] Grote, vol. VIII. p. 402: Rauchenstein, *Introd.* p. 16: Blass, *Att. Ber.* p. 542. As to the number of men who supported Eratosthenes, see §§ 51, 56, 65, 87, 88, 91. As to the difficulty about witnesses, §§ 46, 47. See Or. X. (Against Theomnestus) § 31, and the remarks on it below.

regards the first, what may be called the private, division of the speech, it is very noticeable how little attempt Lysias makes to excite compassion; he contents himself with a bare recital of facts. He relies less on the atrocity of the wrong itself than on its significance as part of that system of organised crime which he sees personified in Eratosthenes. He therefore throws his whole weight upon the second, the public, division of his subject; and here he gives us, first, two political biographies, the lives of Eratosthenes and Theramenes—then, a retrospect of the government to which they belonged. In one sense this speech of Lysias may be compared with that of Demosthenes On the Crown. The question at issue involves a whole chapter of Athenian history, in which both the parties to the case were actors. But there is a difference. Demosthenes, the statesman, reviews the train of events with which he deals from the level of one who has helped to determine their course. Lysias stands on the lower ground of a private person; he sees the events of the Anarchy as they were seen by the masses who suffered, but were powerless to control; he does not discuss two rival lines of policy, but recalls, as a common man, experiences familiar to thousands. It is just because he speaks from among the crowd that he is so successful in denouncing Eratosthenes, and leaves the impression that in his attack upon the worst of close oligarchies he was the spokesman of an entire people.[1]

---

[1] Perhaps sceptical criticism has produced no greater marvel than an essay *De oratione in Eratosthenem Trigintavirum Lysiae falso tributa*, by A. Hecker (progr. Gymn. Leid. a. 1847-8). After proving to his own satisfaction the spuriousness of this speech, the author ends by regretting

2. *Against Agoratus.* [Or. XIII.]—Agoratus, son of a slave, had gained the Athenian citizenship by pretending to have had a hand in the assassination of Phrynichus in 411; a merit to which, according to his accuser, he had no claim (§ 76). For six years afterwards he had lived at Athens, exercising the trade of informer, and laying "all conceivable indictments" (τὰς ἐξ ἀνθρώπων γραφάς § 73) before the lawcourts. He is now charged with having slandered away the lives of several distinguished citizens just before the establishment of the Thirty.

It was in the spring of 404 that Theramenes came back from Sparta with the hard conditions of peace. Athens had been suffering for months the extreme of famine and misery; the mass of citizens were thankful for relief on any terms. But there were still a few men, influential by their position and service, who stood out against the bargain which the oligarchical party were about to strike with Sparta. The oligarchs, impatient to get rid of their opponents, had recourse to the aid of Agoratus. It was arranged that he should himself be charged with plotting to defeat the peace, and should then denounce a certain number of other persons as his accomplices. One Theocritus accused him before the Senate. A party of senators went to the Peiraeus to arrest him. Agoratus, feigning alarm, took sanctuary at the altar in the temple of Artemis at Munychia. Certain citizens

---

that he has spent some time in emending the speech Against Agoratus; "quam suppositam esse a Graeculo ludimagistro idoneis argumentis evincam. *Antiphonteae omnes et omnes pariter Andocideae orationes spuriae sunt. Quae brevi singula persecuturus sum.*" Literature has lost a curiosity by the non-fulfilment of this promise.

who suspected him to be the victim, or the agent, of a plot, gave bail for him, and offered to take him out of Attica to await quieter times. He declined this proposal, and appeared before the Senate to give information. He denounced, first, the men who had bailed him; then several of the Generals and taxiarchs (§ 13), among whom were the General Strombichides, Dionysiodôrus (kinsman of the accuser in this case), and probably Eucrates[1] the brother of Nicias; also a number of other citizens. These, with Agoratus himself, were imprisoned; and it was decreed that they should be tried both by the Senate and by a special court of Two Thousand. Immediately afterwards the peace with Sparta was ratified.[2]

---

[1] Eucrates is not named in this speech; but see § 5 of Or. XVIII., which refers to the confiscation of his property.

[2] That, according to Lysias, the informations of Agoratus were made *before* the acceptance of the peace and the surrender of the city, appears distinctly from § 17, εἵλοντο πρὶν τὴν ἐκκλησίαν τὴν περὶ τῆς εἰρήνης γενέσθαι τούτους (the popular leaders) εἰς διαβολὰς καὶ κινδύνους καταστῆσαι. It follows also from § 16.

Grote (VIII. p. 320) believes that Lysias has misdated the informations of Agoratus, placing them before the surrender, whereas they were, in fact, given *after* it. He remarks: (1) That it is difficult to suppose an interval sufficient for these accusations between the return of Theramenes and the ratification of the peace, for which the people were most impatient. (2) That the bailers of Agoratus could not have proposed to convey him away by sea from Munychia, when the harbour was blocked up. (3) That the expression "till quieter times" (ἕως κατασταίη τὰ πράγματα, *ib.*) would have been inappropriate at a moment just before the surrender.

Now, (1) all that Lysias relates about the informations need not have occupied more than one day; there is room for them, then, between the return of Theramenes and the ratification of the peace (on the day after his return, Xen. *Hellen.* II. ii. 22). Lysias describes the capitulation and entrance of Lysander into Athens as following *immediately* on the act of Agoratus, § 34. (2) We do not know how strict the blockade established in November 405 may have been in March 404: the "two boats" may have lain ready at some point in Munychia outside the harbour. (3) The third objection I do not understand. Surely the time just *before* the surrender—when Athens was full of misery and faction — might be called a troubled time.

No doubt Lysias had a motive for placing the informations of Agoratus

The government of the Thirty having been established, the prisoners were tried; but not by the Two Thousand; only by a new oligarchical Senate. They were all condemned to death, except Agoratus, who was banished. In 404 he joined the democratic exiles at Phylê, and afterwards returned to Athens with them; but appears to have been ill received (§ 77). He is now accused of murder by Dionysius, cousin and brother-in-law to Dionysiodôrus.

The procedure was not by an indictment before the Areiopagus or the Delphinion, but by an information (endeixis) laid before the archon, followed by a summary arrest (apagogê)—precisely as in the case of the Mitylenean charged with the murder of Herodes, for whom Antiphon wrote a defence; the case was therefore heard by an ordinary court under the presidency of the Eleven. There had, however, been a slight informality. Strictly speaking, endeixis and apagogê were applicable only in cases where the accused had been taken in the act; though, as appears from this and from the Herodes case, the limitation was not always observed. Here the accuser had left out the words ἐπ' αὐτοφώρῳ in drawing up the indictment; but had been compelled to add them by the

Mode of procedure.

---

before the capitulation, and thus representing him as responsible for it. On the other hand, it may be observed that the oligarchs would not have had the same motive for suborning Agoratus when the peace, which gave them the ascendency, had been ratified.

An ingenious attempt has been made (by Christian Renner, *Comment. Lysiac. cc. duo*, Göttingen 1869) to show that it is consistent with the narrative of Lysias to suppose that the peace had been *accepted*, and that the popular leaders, when denounced by Agoratus, were only agitating for a *revision* of it. But the words in § 17 bar this view. Renner can get over them only by supposing them corrupt. He proposes with Frohberg to strike out the words τὴν περὶ τῆς εἰρήνης after ἐκκλησίαν. This is to cut the knot.

Eleven, although in this instance they had no real meaning (§§ 84, 86).

Date. The trial took place "long after" the events to which it referred (§ 83); and the condemnation of Menestratus, who himself suffered on the same account "long after" his offence (§ 56), is mentioned as if it was not very recent. At least five or six years, then, must have elapsed since 404 B.C. The speech cannot be placed earlier than 400; probably it may be placed as late as 398.[1]

Analysis. The speaker begins by explaining that both on private and on public grounds he is entitled to be the accuser of Agoratus. On private grounds, since Dionysiodôrus was his cousin and brother-in-law; on public, because the crime of Agoratus affects the whole State (§§ 1–4).

The narrative of the facts (§§ 5–48) falls into four parts. (i) From the defeat at Aegospotami in 405 to the moment when Agoratus made his accusations, in the spring of 404: §§ 5–34. (ii) The trial and condemnation of the accused: §§ 35–38. (iii) Their last injunctions to their relatives: §§ 39–42. (iv) The sequel of their deaths—the reign of terror, which they had foreseen and endeavoured to avert: §§ 43–48.

The pleas which Agoratus may set up in his defence are next considered. He may deny the fact of having informed; but the decrees of the Senate and of the ecclesia will confute him. He may pretend that he informed in the interest of the State; but the events disprove that. He may say that he was forced to inform; but the circumstances of his arrest show that he did so willingly. He may throw the blame on Menestratus, who also informed. Nay, Menestratus was afterwards a victim of Agoratus, whose turn it is now to suffer

---

[1] Rauchenstein, *Introd.* p. 55; Blass, *Att. Ber.* p. 557.

himself. Compare the conduct of Agoratus with that of Aristophanes, who died rather than turn accuser (§§ 49–61).

The eminent men whom Agoratus destroyed may be contrasted with himself and with his family. His three brothers have all suffered death for base crimes; he himself obtained the citizenship by pretending to have assassinated Phrynichus. It is a dilemma; let him suffer for the murder or for the fraud (§§ 62–76).

He will perhaps claim sympathy as having joined the exiles at Phylê, and returned with them. The fact was that, when he appeared at Phylê, they would have put him to death, had not the general Anytus interfered; and when, at the entry into Athens, he presumed to bear arms in the procession, Aesimus, its leader, came and snatched away his shield (§§ 77–82).

Or he will raise technical objections. He will say that the time which has elapsed ought to exempt him from penalties; but there is no statute of limitations ($\pi\rho o\theta\epsilon\sigma\mu\iota a$, § 83) here. Or he will say that the words $\epsilon\pi$' $a\upsilon\tau o\phi\omega\rho\omega$ were omitted in the indictment; which is much the same thing as arguing that he is guilty, indeed, but was not caught in guilt. Or he will plead the Amnesty. This is in itself a confession. Moreover, the Amnesty was a covenant between the oligarchs in the city (§§ 83–90) and the democrats of the Peiraeus: it has no force as between two democrats.

The judges, the whole people, are bound by the solemn injunctions of the dead. To acquit Agoratus would be to confirm the sentence by which they perished. A democratic court must not be in unison with the courts of the Tyrants. By condemning Agoratus, the judges will mark the difference between them; will avenge their friends; and will have done right in the sight of all men (§§ 91–97).

In historical interest the speech Against Agoratus stands next, perhaps, to the speech Against Eratosthenes; but it is conceived in a totally different spirit. No transition from a private to a public character, like that which is so marked in the other case, occurs here. From beginning to end the accuser of Agoratus confines himself to his special task, that of demanding vengeance for the death of his kinsman. Much of the general history of the time is necessarily introduced, and the speaker of course avails himself of the great advantage which he possesses in being able to represent the slander of Agoratus as treason to the State. But there is no such large view of a whole period as is given in the speech Against Eratosthenes. The historical references are scattered, not concentrated, and, instead of forming pictures, are only picturesque; individual interests are in the foreground throughout. Lysias accusing Eratosthenes hardly attempts to excite a personal sympathy; he relies rather on the hatefulness of that system of crime to which this particular crime belonged; Dionysius accusing Agoratus describes the wives, mothers, sisters of the condemned visiting them in prison, and receiving their last messages of vengeance—a passage which strikingly resembles in conception and tone the prison-scene in the speech of Andocides On the Mysteries. The arrangement of the topics here, as usually with Lysias when he takes pains, is clear and good; though perhaps the speaker tries to make too many distinct points towards the end, and thereby rather impairs the breadth and strength of his argument. This is particularly the case in §§ 70–90; where the sophism about the Amnesty—that it was not meant to hold good be-

Character of the Speech as compared with Or. XII.

tween two men of the same party—is a curious exception to the usual tact of Lysias in argument.

3. *On the Death of Eratosthenes.* [Or. I.]— Euphilêtus, an Athenian citizen of the humbler sort, had slain one Eratosthenes of Oea (Οἴηθεν, § 16), whom he had taken in adultery with his wife. He is now prosecuted for murder by the relatives of Eratosthenes; and pleads in his defence the law which allowed the husband, in such cases, to kill the adulterer[1] (§§ 30, 31). As the law was clearly against them, the accusers were driven to allege that Euphilêtus had himself decoyed Eratosthenes into his house (§ 30); and that the real motive of the homicide was fear, enmity, or cupidity. This line of argument may have had some plausibility if Athenian husbands were in the habit of compromising such cases.[2] But the assertion of the accusers would be hard to prove; and Euphilêtus speaks throughout like a man confident of a verdict.

The cause would be tried, probably by heliastic judges,[3] at the Delphinion, the court for cases in which an admitted homicide was defended as justifiable. There is nothing to indicate the date.

The accused asks the judges to imagine themselves in his place: all Greece, he says, would recognise the justice of

---

[1] Dem. *in Aristocr.* § 53, ἐάν τις ἀποκτείνῃ ἐν ἄθλοις ἑκών...ἢ ἐπὶ δάμαρτι, κ.τ.λ....τούτων ἕνεκα μὴ φεύγειν κτείναντα.

[2] In one instance, at all events, we find that the injured husband λαμβάνει μοιχόν...καὶ εἰς φόβον καταστήσας πράττεται τριάκοντα μνᾶς —not an excessive sum: Dem. *in Neaer.* § 65. As Blass notices (*Att.*

Ber. p. 577), this case of Eratosthenes happens to be the only recorded example of that extreme and summary vengeance which the law allowed.

[3] After the year of Eucleides, heliastic judges sat at the Palladion: see Isocr. *adv. Callim.* § 54, Dem. *in Neaer.* § 90. Probably at the Delphinion also they had taken the place of the Ephetae.

his act. He had no motive for it but the dishonour done to his wife, his children and himself (§§ 1–4). Then comes the narrative (§§ 5–28), followed by the citation of witnesses and laws (§§ 29–36). He meets the suggestions of the defendants; as (i) that Eratosthenes was decoyed into the house, §§ 37–42; (ii) that the homicide was prompted by a former enmity, or by cupidity, §§ 43–46. In any of these cases, he would not have slain him before witnesses. The decision of the judges will have a good effect if it accords with the laws; if it does not, then these laws should be annulled, since citizens are only entrapped (ἐνεδρεύονται) by them. His life and property are at risk because he trusted to the laws of the city (§§ 47–50).

<small>Social interest of the Speech.</small> The first part of this speech (§§ 5–28) is curious as a vivid picture—vivid with almost Aristophanic life—of a small Athenian household;[1] especially as illustrating the position of a married woman of the lower class. The husband says that, at first, his wife gave him entire satisfaction as a housekeeper: on his part, he "watched her as far as possible, and gave all reasonable attention to the subject"; at length, however, at her mother's funeral, she for once left the house; and hence the intrigue. Lysias has been clever in making the defence homely and at the same time dignified; Euphilêtus, the plain citizen, feels strong in the law of the city.

<small>VI. 4. Defence Against Simon.</small> 4. *Defence Against Simon.* [Or. III.]—The accused, an elderly Athenian of good family and fortune (§§ 4, 47), is accused by one Simon of having wounded him in a quarrel about one Theodotus, a young Plataean. The indictment

---

[1] The passage §§ 6–18 may be noted as a locus classicus on the architecture of Athenian houses.

was for "Wounding with Intent" (τραύματος ἐκ προνοίας), a charge which, in this case, seems to have been made merely in the sense of "wounding deliberately."[1] But, as the accused justly says, the "intent" to which the law referred was not merely intent to wound, but intent to kill (§§ 40–43). It was for this reason that the Areiopagus had jurisdiction in such cases, as well as in those of actual murder.[2] The present trial took place before that court (§§ 1, 3); the penalty was banishment (§ 47), and further (as appears from Or. IV. § 18) confiscation of property. The battles of Corinth and of Coroneia had already been fought (§ 45); the speech is therefore later than 394 B.C.

Date.

After observing that Simon ought to be defendant rather than prosecutor, and requesting the indulgence of the court for the weakness which had involved him in so unpleasant a dispute (§§ 1–4), the accused gives his own account of the quarrel between himself and the prosecutor (§§ 5–20). He then refutes the account given by Simon (§§ 21–39). The formula, "wounding with intent," does not, he says, apply to this case (§§ 41–43). He wishes

Analysis.

---

[1] The τραύματος γραφή seems to have been notorious as an instrument of false accusation. Cf. Dem. *adv. Boeot.* II. § 32, ἐπιτεμὼν τὴν κεφαλὴν αὑτοῦ τραύματος εἰς Ἄρειον πάγον με προσεκαλέσατο, ὡς φυγαδεύσων ἐκ τῆς πόλεως. Aeschines charges Demosthenes with having brought a false γραφή of the same kind against one Demomeles (*De F. L.* § 93, *in Ctes.* § 51); indeed, he says, this was one of his habitual villainies—τὴν μιαρὰν ταύτην κεφαλὴν καὶ ὑπεύθυνον... μυριάκις κατατέτμηκε καὶ τούτων μισθοὺς εἴληφε τραύματος ἐκ προ-

νοίας γραφὰς γραφόμενος (*in Ctes.* § 212). Compare Lucian *Timon* § 46 ΓΝΑΘΩΝΙΔΗΣ. τί τοῦτο; παίεις, ὦ Τίμων· μαρτύρομαι. ὦ Ἡράκλεις, ἰοὺ ἰού. προσκαλοῦμαί σε τραύματος ἐς Ἄρειον πάγον.

[2] For the law see Dem. *in Aristocr.* § 22. In [Lys.] *in Andoc.* § 15 it is loosely said that "according to the laws of the Areiopagus" the penalty was banishment ἄν...τις ἀνδρὸς σῶμα τρώσῃ κεφαλὴν ἢ πρόσωπον ἢ χεῖρας ἢ πόδας—the mention of the πρόνοια being omitted.

that he was at liberty to give illustrations of Simon's character [the Areiopagus not allowing the introduction of irrelevant matter]. As it is, he will mention only one fact —that Simon was dismissed from the Athenian army at Corinth (§§ 44, 45). Simon, he concludes, is one of those informers "who force their way into our houses, who persecute us, who snatch us by force out of the street." He appeals to the services of his ancestors, and to his own: and says that compassion is due to him, not only in the event of being condemned, but for the very fact of having been brought to trial (§§ 46–48).

VI. 5. On Wounding with Intent.

5. *On Wounding with Intent.* [Or. IV.]—The first part of this speech has been lost,[1] and with it the original title. It is a defence before the Areiopagus on a charge of wounding with murderous intent in a quarrel for the possession of a slave girl. The defendant asserted that the slave was the joint property of himself and the accuser; the latter claimed sole ownership (§ 10). The penalty threatening the accused was banishment and confiscation of property (§ 18).

Analysis.

The speech, as now extant, begins at the point where the defendant is answering the assertion that a personal enmity of long standing accounts for the murderous character of the assault. It is not true, the defendant says, that they were at this time enemies: they had been reconciled. He had been called upon to perform a costly

---

[1] The loss must have taken place before the Palatine MS. was written. Sauppe (*O. A.* p. 73), regarding the speech as complete in its present shape, thinks that it was the last or at least the second ("epilogus vel deuterologia") made for the defence. In that case, as Blass says (*Att. Ber.* p. 590), the preceding speech or speeches can have contained little more than the narrative; since our speech deals with the proof. Francken (*Comment. Lys.* p. 37) and Scheibe (Blass *l.c.*) agree in thinking the speech imperfect.

leiturgia, and had challenged his present accuser either to undertake it himself or to exchange properties (ἀντίδοσις); and this had been cited by the accuser in proof of the alleged hostility. But it has been shown that this exchange was never actually made; friends mediated, and the defendant took the leiturgia. The accuser had, indeed, already received some property of his, with a view to the exchange; but had returned it when the reconciliation took place. Another proof is given that they were on good terms. The accuser had been nominated by the defendant as judge of the prizes at the Dionysia. Unfortunately, when lots were drawn, he was not among the judges elected. If he had been, his goodwill to the defendant would have been publicly shown: for he was prepared to give the prize to the defendant's tribe, and left a written memorandum of that resolve [1] (§§ 1–4).

Assuming, however, that this personal enmity did exist, yet the very circumstances of the assault exclude the idea of premeditation. The accuser had made the utmost of a black eye (ὑπώπια § 9), and had pretended illness. At the same time he has refused to allow the slave, who was the cause and the eyewitness of the quarrel, to be put to the question (§§ 5–11). After dwelling further on the

---

[1] § 3 ἐβουλόμην δ' ἂν μὴ ἀπολαχεῖν αὐτὸν κριτὴν Διονυσίοις, ἵν' ὑμῖν φανερὸς ἐγένετο ἐμοὶ διηλλαγμένος, κρίνας τὴν ἐμὴν φυλὴν νικᾶν· νῦν δὲ ἔγραψε μὲν ταῦτα εἰς τὸ γραμματεῖον, ἀπέλαχε δέ:—
"I could have wished that he had not missed the lot to be judge at the Dionysia, as then he would have proved to you that he was reconciled to me, by adjudging the victory to my tribe. As it was, he made a note of it in his tablets, but failed to draw the lot."

The reference is apparently to a private compact between the defendant and the accuser. The judges of the prizes at the Dionysia were nominated by the Senate; the names of all the nominees were put into an urn, and lots were then drawn (Isocr. *Trapez.* § 33). The defendant—being at the time a senator—had so nominated the accuser, under a compact that he should award the prize to the chorus furnished by the defendant's tribe. The accuser had registered this compact; but, in the end, his name was not drawn. This is Francken's explanation (*Comment. Lys.* p. 38); and no better has been offered. The shock which the candour of the defendant must have given to the Areiopagus is perhaps not a decisive objection.

refusal of this challenge (πρόκλησις) as presumptive evidence in his own favour (§§ 12–17), the defendant ends by contrasting the gravity of his danger with the worthlessness of its cause, and begs the court not to award so disproportionate a penalty to him, and so excessive a triumph to his unjust accuser (§§ 18–20).

<small>Special points illustrated by the Speech.</small>

This fragment has at least some antiquarian interest. It is curious to find from § 2 that the fact of having offered a man the antidosis could be quoted in court as presumptive evidence of ill-will towards him. The difficult passage in § 3 regarding the appointment of judges at the Dionysia has already been noticed. Section 4 illustrates a point in the peculiar procedure of the Areiopagus — that no witness could be examined who did not swear either to or against the guilt of the accused in regard to the particular facts before the court.

<small>Taylor's doubt of its genuineness.</small>

Taylor's suspicion that in this piece a sophistic writer has imitated the Defence against Simon seems gratuitous.[1] If the fragment which has been preserved is neither clear in arrangement nor strong in argument, it has at least the vigorous simplicity by which Lysias knew how to make the appeal of a commonplace man effective without making it rhetorical.

---

[1] "Multis modis mihi videtur haec declamatiuncula in umbra Scholae μελετᾶσθαι, ad imaginem superioris orationis elaborata, cui deinde ob argumenti affinitatem in scriptis codd., ut fieri solet, perpetuo adhaesit." Taylor ap. Reiske *Or. Att.* v. p. 164. Blass (p. 594) answers some objections raised by Falk to the arrangement of the speech; by Scheibe, to the weakness of the πίστεις and to some points of expression.

VII. Causes relating to Impiety (γραφαὶ ἀσεβείας, ἱεροσυλίας κ.τ.λ.)

1. *Against Andocides.* [Or. VI.] — This is certainly not the work of Lysias; but in any survey of his works its claim to be ranked with them must at least be examined. It is probable that it was really spoken against Andocides at his trial in 399 B.C. The occasion and the circumstances of that trial have already been discussed.[1] Of his three accusers — Cephisius, Epichares and Meletus — one, Cephisius, is mentioned by the speaker (§ 42): it is possible that the speaker himself may have been one of the other two.[2] Two lost pages of the Palatine MS. contained probably the latter part of the speech Against Callias, and the first part of this speech Against Andocides. But it is not likely that the part thus lost was so large as to include, besides the proem, a connected statement of the whole case. It remains to suppose that such a statement had been made by a previous speaker and is only supplemented here. This is what might have been expected; Cephisius, the chief accuser, would properly have made the leading speech.

VII. 1.
Against Andocides.

The fragment begins in the middle of a story told to show how surely the goddesses of Eleusis resent an insult. A certain man cheated them of an offering; and there came upon him this doom, that he starved amid plenty; for though good food was set before him, the goddesses made it

Analysis.

---

[1] pp. 112 ff.
[2] All that can be gathered from the speech about the speaker is that he was the grandson of one Diocles, whose father Zacorus had held the office of ἱεροφάντης, or initiating priest at Eleusis: § 54.

seem loathsome to him. Let the judges beware, then, of showing mercy to Andocides, whose punishment is claimed by these same deities (§§ 1–3). If he should be acquitted, and, as Archon Basileus, should some day conduct the festival of the Mysteries, what a scandal for comers from all parts of Greece! For he is known to them, not only by his deeds at Athens, but by his conduct during his exile in Sicily, in Italy, in the Peloponnesus, at the Hellespont, in Ionia, at Cyprus (§§ 4–8).

He will say that the decree banishing him from the agora and the temples has been cancelled. Let the advice of Pericles be remembered, that impious men should be liable not only to written laws, but to the unwritten laws of the Eumolpidae. Andocides has aggravated his offence against the gods by presuming to make himself their champion. Before he had been ten days at Athens, he accused Archippus of having defaced a Hermes, and withdrew the charge only on receiving money (§§ 9–12). He will say that it is hard if the informer is to suffer when the denounced have been pardoned. The court is not responsible for that pardon; besides, these men denied their guilt: he confesses it. A man is banished for injuring his fellow; shall he not be banished for injuring the gods? Diagoras of Melos mocked the religion of a strange land; Andocides outraged the religion of his own. It is a further proof of atheism that, not dreading his own crimes, he committed himself to the dangers of the sea. [A notable petitio principii.] But the gods were reserving him for a late reckoning. Let the judges consider what his life has been since his first great crime. Imprisoned, and escaping only by betraying kinsmen and friends; disfranchised and banished; rejected by oligarchy and by democracy at home, ill-treated by tyrants abroad; and now, in this same year, twice brought to trial! Men ought not to lose faith in the gods because they see Andocides surmount so many dangers: the life of pain thus spared to him is no life (§§ 13–32).

But he is not content to have escaped punishment; he dares to meddle in public affairs, even in the concerns of religion (§§ 33, 34). And now he will be ready with various pleas. That his informations relieved Athens from distress:—but who had first caused it? That the Amnesty shields him: but it was only political. That Cephisius is as bad as he is: perhaps so, but that is irrelevant. That no one will inform in future, if he suffers: nay, he has had his reward—he saved his life. He is now in danger because he has forced himself upon Athens—more shameless than Batrachus, the informer of the Thirty, who at least hid his infamy abroad (§§ 35–45).

Why should Andocides be acquitted? Not for his services in war, for he has never made a campaign. Not for services rendered by his boasted wealth; for at the citizens' sorest need he did not so much as buy them corn (§§ 46–49). [Here, after the ἀνταποδούς, follows a lacuna: see above, p. 196.]

The profanation of the Mysteries is an old story now, and men's horror of it is faded: but let them for a moment imagine Andocides mocking the awful rites of the Initiated, and then remember the priests standing with their faces to the west, and waving the crimson banners as they cursed him! The city must be purged and the gods appeased by his expulsion. Once, when it was proposed that a Megarian guilty of impiety should be put to death without trial, Diocles said that he ought to be tried indeed, but that every judge must come into court resolved to condemn. And now, let not the judges be moved by entreaty. Compassion is not for murderers but for their victims (§§ 50–55).

The doubt with which Harpocration twice [1] names

---

[1] s. vv. καταπλήξ, φαρμακός. It may be an accident that in a third citation, s.v. ῥόπτρον, the words εἰ γνήσιος are not added.

this speech is the only clue to the opinion of the ancients. Modern critics are all but unanimous in rejecting it.

The speech not by Lysias.

The diction shows many words and phrases which Lysias could hardly have used;[1] but it is not by the diction nor by the composition[2] that his authorship is disproved. The question is decided by broader characteristics. In arrangement Lysias was not faultless; but he would not have tolerated the chaotic disorder which is found here. Again, in several of those passages which dwell on the crimes of Andocides and on the vengeance of the gods there is a certain hollow pathos, a certain falseness and affected elevation, which are utterly remote from the style of Lysias. Further, the whole speech has what may be called (in the Greek sense) a *sycophantic* tone; it is rancorous, palpably unfair and prodigal of unproved assertion. Lastly, it is singularly deficient in the foremost general quality of Lysias—in tact; it is pre-eminently a blundering speech. The accuser makes at least four mistakes. First, he recites at length the sufferings which Andocides has been enduring without respite for the last sixteen years; intending thereby to prove the displeasure of the gods, but forgetting that he was more likely to move the compassion of men. Secondly, he

---

[1] *e.g.* §§ 4, 44 ἀθῷος: §§ 18, 48 κομπάζειν: § 30 ἀλώμενος: § 50 καταπλῆγες: § 49 ποῖα ἁμαρτήματα ἀνακαλεσάμενος, ποῖα τροφεῖα ἀποδιδούς. Blass further notes as non-Lysian such redundancies as § 53 τὴν πόλιν καθαίρειν καὶ ἀποδιοπομπεῖσθαι καὶ φαρμακὸν ἀποπέμπειν καὶ ἀλιτηρίου ἀπαλλάττεσθαι, etc. (*Att. Ber.* p. 574).

[2] The *composition*, indeed, is not very different from that of Lysias. It is free from the diffuse periods of the later rhetoric—such as those, for instance, of the speech Against Alcibiades attributed to Andocides—undoubtedly a late sophistic work.

observes that, strange to say, Andocides has always come safely through his perils; but that it would be wrong to suppose the gods capable of protecting him;—an awkward allusion to the natural inference, and almost a prophecy of acquittal. Thirdly, in noticing the charges brought by Andocides against Cephisius, he allows that there is something in them, and objects to them only as irrelevant; thus needlessly throwing over his own colleague, the leader of the prosecution. Fourthly, he ends by begging the court to remember a saying of his own grandfather—that, in certain cases, it was the duty of the judges to be prejudiced against the accused. Any one of these faults would have been striking: taken together, they make the authorship of Lysias inconceivable.

It is a further question whether this Accusation was written by a contemporary of Lysias, and was actually delivered in the Mysteries-trial, or is merely a rhetorical exercise of later date. Those who take the latter view lay stress upon the discrepancies between this speech and the speech of Andocides On the Mysteries. Two of these discrepancies are important. (1) Andocides complains of having been specially charged with denouncing his own father (*De Myst.* § 19): here, he is only accused generally of denouncing his kinsfolk (§ 23). Again (2) he speaks of having been charged with placing a suppliant's bough in the temple at Eleusis (*De Myst.* § 110); here nothing of the kind is mentioned. But in regard to such differences, it should be remembered that this speech, itself mutilated, was not the only one for the prosecution; and that, where the

Was the author a contemporary of Lysias or a later sophist?

subjects of accusation were so large and covered so many years, it would have been strange if every point had been touched by every accuser. On the other hand, a rhetorician who had prepared himself by studying the Speech On the Mysteries would have aimed at a more exact correspondence with it. He would probably have taken the charges against Andocides in the order set by his model, and have given paragraph for paragraph, or at least topic for topic. He must have been a subtle artist indeed, if with a general agreement he combined so many intentional differences of detail. It may be noticed that in § 46 Andocides is said to be "upwards of forty years old." This statement has been used as an argument for the late origin of the speech by those who identify the orator Andocides with the general named by Thucydides (I. 51) as holding a command in 435 B.C. But if, as is most probable, the general was the grandfather of the orator, and the age of the latter in 399 B.C. was really about forty, then the statement in § 46 is one reason the more for ascribing the speech to a contemporary of Andocides.[1] As regards the faults of expression, of method or of general tone, these help to disprove the authorship of Lysias; but they are not of a kind which help to prove that the author was a late sophist. Bad taste is of no age: and the fact of being contemporary with Lysias need not have given a good style to Epichares or Melétus.

---

[1] See above, p. 70. The inference is strengthened by the fact that the mistake which is *not* made by this speaker seems to have been a common mistake in later times. The author of the Plutarchic Life of Andocides, for instance, puts his birth in 468 B.C.

2. *For Callias.* [Or. v.]—The shortness of this speech does not necessarily prove it to be a fragment. It opens with an express statement that the case for the defence had already been fully argued by others; and it ends with a completed idea. Since, however, two pages of the Palatine MS. have been lost just at this place, comprising the first part of the speech Against Andocides, that For Callias has probably suffered also.[1] As it now stands, it gives no direct clue to the special nature of the case. The traditional title, "Defence on a Charge of Sacrilege," must therefore have been taken from the part now lost. The accused is a resident-alien (§ 2), an elderly man (§ 3), against whom his own slaves, in hope of being rewarded with liberty, have informed.

In the view of sacrilege taken by Attic law, its aspect as a robbery seems to have been more prominent than its aspect as an impiety. Thus it is mentioned in the same category with ordinary theft, housebreaking, kidnapping and like offences.[2] In this instance it appears from the address, ἄνδρες δικασταί (§ 1), that the trial was not before the Areiopagus. The cause must have been heard by

---

[1] Harpocration s.v. τίμημα has:—
τίμημα ἀντὶ τοῦ ἐνέχυρον καὶ οἷον ἀποτίμημα (*i.e.* "instead of *security*," or almost in the sense of "*mortgage*"), Λυσίας ἐν τῷ ὑπὲρ Καλλίου· οὗτοι δὲ φάσκοντες πλείονος μισθώσασθαι καὶ τίμημα καταστήσασθαι. Sauppe thinks that these words are a fragment from our speech; οὗτοι being the slaves of Callias, who accused their master of having agreed to rent some sacred land ("fundum sacrum") at a higher rate than he himself admitted (*O. A.* II. p. 192).

[2] Xen. *Mem.* I. ii. 62 ἐάν τις φανερὸς γένηται κλέπτων ἢ λωποδυτῶν ἢ βαλαντιοτομῶν ἢ τοιχωρυχῶν ἢ ἀνδραποδιζόμενος ἢ ἱεροσυλῶν, τούτοις θάνατός ἐστιν ἡ ζημία. Id. *Apol. Socr.* § 25 ἐφ' οἷς γέ μην ἔργοις κεῖται θάνατος ἢ ζημία, ἱεροσυλίᾳ, τοιχωρυχίᾳ, ἀνδραποδίσει, πόλεως προδοσίᾳ.

an ordinary heliastic court, under the presidency either of the Thesmothetae or of the Eleven.[1]

Analysis. The speaker says that, were it not a case of life or death, he would have forborne to come forward, considering the defence to be already complete; as it is, he desires to give a public proof of friendship for Callias (§§ 1, 2). He then refers very briefly, first, to the high character of the accused; secondly, to the worthless nature of the informations. It is the hope of winning freedom which has prompted the calumny of the slaves. If they are believed, servants who desire liberty will henceforth think, not how they are to oblige their masters, but what lie they can tell against them (§§ 3–5).

Conjecture suggested by § 4. The phrase used by the speaker in reference to Callias—"those who bring themselves into danger by lending their services to the Treasury" (τῷ δημοσίῳ βοηθοῦντες § 4)—is noticeable. It suggests that the "sacrilege" of which the title speaks may have been connected with the sacred treasury on the Acropolis. Callias may have had some employment under the Stewards of the sacred fund (ταμίαι τῆς θεοῦ, τῶν ἱερῶν χρημάτων) which gave him access to the inner chamber (ὀπισθόδομος) of the Parthenon; and may have been accused of profiting by that opportunity to commit a theft.

VII. 3. On the Sacred Olive. 3. *On the Sacred Olive.* [Or. VII.]—The man (VII. 2) for whom this defence was written—a rich Athenian citizen (§§ 21, 31)—had originally been

---

[1] Meier and Schömann suggest that ἱεροσυλίας γραφαί may have been tried (1) by the Areiopagus, when, besides the question of fact, there was a further question as to whether the fact, if established, would amount to sacrilege: (2) by heliasts with the Thesmothetae for presidents, when the question was of the fact only, the alleged act being clearly sacrilegious: (3) by heliasts with the Eleven for presidents, when the committer of sacrilege had been taken in the act (*Att. Proc.* pp. 306 ff.).

charged with destroying a *moria*, or sacred olive, on a farm which belonged to him. As to do this was a fraud upon the public Treasury, the form of the original accusation had been an apographê (ἀπεγράφην, § 2). But the charge was not supported by the persons who had rented from the State the produce of the moriae on this farm (οἱ ἐωνημένοι τοὺς καρποὺς τῶν μοριῶν, § 2). The accusers had therefore changed their ground. They now charge the defendant merely with uprooting the *fenced-in stump* (σηκός) of a moria; and they lay against him an indictment for impiety. The chief accuser is one Nicomachus.[1]

Throughout Attica, besides the olives which were private property (ἴδιαι ἐλαῖαι, § 10), there were others which, whether growing on public or on private lands, were considered as the property of the State. These were called *moriae* (μορίαι)—the legend being that they had been propagated (μεμορημέναι) from the original olive which Athena herself had caused to spring up on the Acropolis.[2] This theory was convenient for their conservation as State property; since, by giving them a sacred character, it placed them directly under the care of the Areiopagus, which caused them to be visited once a month by Inspectors (ἐπιμεληταί, § 29) and once a year by special Commissioners (γνώμονες, § 25). To uproot a *moria* was an offence punishable by banishment and confiscation of goods (§ 41).[3]

---

[1] Not the Nicomachus of Or. xxx, who had held public office in 411 B.C.; whereas this Nicomachus was a youth in 399 B.C. (§ 29).

[2] The μορίαι were under the special protection of Ζεὺς Μόριος (Soph. *O. C.* 705).

[3] In such cases the ἀγών was ἀτίμητος, and there was no fixed period (προθεσμία) after which the liability of the offender ceased: Meier and Schömann. *Att. Proc.* p. 307.

Technical terms.

The technical terms used in this speech need definition: see especially §§ 20, 24. Ἐλαία was the generic term. Common olive-trees were called, either ἐλαῖαι simply, or ἴδιαι ἐλαῖαι; sacred, either μορίαι ἐλαῖαι, or μορίαι simply. Σηκός properly meant the enclosure or fence intended to guard the stump (στέλεχος) of a moria which had been cut down or burnt down (πυρκαιά, § 24)—as often happened in the raids of the enemy during the Peloponnesian War[1] (§ 6). Then σηκός came to denote the fence with the stump itself; and this is the sense which it bears in this speech: see § 11, σηκὸν ἐκκεκόφθαι.[2] In §§ 2, 5 ἐλαία *as opposed to* σηκός means a full-grown moria.

Date.

The case is tried by the Areiopagus under the presidency of the Archon Basileus. The offence was alleged to have been committed in the archonship of Suniades (§ 11), Ol. 95. 4, 397 B.C. To judge from § 42 (τοσούτῳ χρόνῳ ὕστερον), the trial took place not earlier than 395; probably later.

Analysis.

A quiet life, the defendant had thought, was its own protection; but he has been taught that hired informers have a power which the unborn might dread (§§ 1–3). He will have done enough if he can show that there has been neither moria nor stump of moria on the farm since it came into his possession. This he proves by the evidence of tenants who had rented it from him (§§ 4–11).

After commenting on the unlikelihood of his having

---

[1] On the vitality of the olive, see Her. VIII. 55, Verg. G. II. 30, 181.

[2] It is true, of course, that as Rauchenstein says (Introd. to this speech, p. 171) σηκός was never a *mere* equivalent for the "stump" or "stock": on the other hand, an Athenian could say σηκὸν ἐκκόπτειν, thinking rather of the στέλεχος than of the fence itself. This is probably what Harpocration means when he says loosely σηκὸν δέ, ὡς ἔοικεν, καὶ μορίαν ὀνομάζουσι τὴν αὐτήν.

done a deed which could hardly have escaped detection (§§ 12–18), he observes that the accuser has failed to bring any witnesses (§§ 19–23). The defendant has several other farms, on which olive-trees abound; but, notwithstanding the strict watch kept by the Areiopagus, he has never been accused of any such offence as this. And here the risk would have been peculiarly great. It is strange if Nicomachus has discovered what escaped the regular Inspectors (§§ 24–29).

He then speaks of his own public services; of the accuser's refusal to give up his slaves for torture, and of the absence of witnesses for the prosecution. He describes the malice of his enemies who had bribed Nicomachus to bring this charge; and refers to the cruel sentence which hangs over him (§§ 30–41). He then concludes with a short review of the whole case. It depends upon an unproved assertion, which the accuser has refused to bring to the test (§§ 42, 43).

One attraction, which elsewhere seldom fails Lysias, is wanting in this speech:—there is no narrative, for there is no story to tell, except the former history of the farm. In this, one rather curious point may be noticed. The farm had belonged, it seems, to Peisander; had been confiscated; and had then been given as a public gift to Apollodôrus of Megara. Now Apollodôrus, as is known from the speech Against Agoratus (§ 71), was one of the two men who planned the assassination of Phrynichus; and so it appears that he had been rewarded for destroying one leader of the Four Hundred by receiving the property of another. As regards the character of the defendant, *Ethos of the speaker.* Lysias has described with a few touches the quiet citizen who shrinks from publicity (§ 1), but with whom, at the same time, it is a point of honour to discharge his public duties in the best way (§ 34); a man who, in Greek phrase, is at once ἀπράγμων and φιλότιμος. Photius says that some critics doubted the authenticity of this speech: and that the rhetorician Paulus of Mysia, in particular, absolutely denied its genuineness, for the unconvincing reason that *he* could not understand a word of it.[1]

[1] Phot. *Cod.* 262 ἀμφιβάλλεται παρ' ἐνίοις ὁ περὶ τοῦ σηκοῦ λόγος. Παῦλος δέ γε ὁ ἐκ Μυσίας τὸν περὶ τοῦ σηκοῦ λόγον, οὐδὲν τῶν εἰρημένων συνιείς, τῆς γνησιότητος τῶν Λυσιακῶν ἐκβάλλει λόγων.

CHAPTER XI

LYSIAS

WORKS

Forensic Speeches in Private Causes—Miscellaneous Writings—Fragments

OF the speeches of Lysias in private causes only four are extant; but each of these four represents a class.

I. ACTION FOR DEFAMATION (δίκη κακηγορίας)

Against Theomnêstus. [Or. x.]—The occasion of this action was as follows. (1) Theomnêstus, a young Athenian, had been indicted by one Lysitheus for throwing away his shield in battle, but had been acquitted. The present speaker had been among the witnesses of Lysitheus; and in the course of the trial had been called a parricide by Theomnêstus. (2) A certain Dionysius, also a witness of Lysitheus, was next prosecuted by Theomnêstus for perjury; and was sentenced to disfranchisement (§ 22). (3) The present speaker then brought his action against Theomnêstus —which was thus the third of a series.

The Athenian law against Defamation (κακηγορίας) punished with a fine of 500 drachmas (about £20)

<small>Law against Defamation.</small>

the utterance of certain reproaches classed as ἀπόρρητα (§ 2). To call a citizen a murderer, a striker of father or mother, or to charge him with having thrown away his shield in battle, were among these.[1] The present case had already been submitted to arbitrators (§ 6); it now came before an ordinary court, under the presidency of the Thsemothetae.[2]

<small>Date.</small>

From § 4 the date is certain. The speaker had been thirteen years old in the time of the Tyrants (404–3 B.C.), and was now thirty-three: the speech belongs therefore to 384–3.

<small>Analysis.</small>

Witnesses can scarcely be needed, since many of the judges themselves heard the libel when it was uttered in court. The prosecutor holds it mean and pettifogging (ἀνελεύθερον—φιλόδικον) to go to law about abusive words; but the taunt of *parricide* has driven him to it (§§ 1–3). He then proves by witnesses that he was only thirteen years old at the time of his father's death; and that he was directly a sufferer by it, since he became the ward of his father's elder brother, Pantaleon,[3] who has defrauded him (§§ 4, 5).

Theomnêstus owns that he used the taunt; and the taunt has been proved false. But Theomnêstus argues that it is not, in the view of the law, a libel. He said only "*slew*": not "murdered." Is it lawful, then, the speaker asks, to reproach a man with "flinging" away his shield?

---

[1] See the speech §§ 6–9: ἀνδροφόνος —πατραλοίας—μητραλοίας—ῥῖψαι τὴν ἀσπίδα. From Dem. *in Eubul.* § 30 it appears that to reproach a citizen with trading in the market-place (τὴν ἐκ τῆς ἀγορᾶς ἐργασίαν) came under this law.

[2] Meier and Schömann, *Att. Proc.* p. 67.

[3] The language in § 5 leaves it ambiguous whether Pantaleon was uncle or brother of the speaker; Sauppe assumes the former, which is more likely. The speech of Lysias κατὰ Πανταλέοντος (*Frag.* v.) may, he thinks, have had this man for its object. He conjectures that the father of the speaker—who is said in § 27 to have died for the democracy—may have been that Leon of Salamis who was put to death by the Thirty (*Or. Att.* II. 202).

The law speaks only of "throwing." He gives further instances; and then observes that, in the procedure of the Areiopagus, "slaying" is the term always used (§§ 6–14). Not content with this exposure of the quibble, he adds some illustrations from the old laws of Solon. These are full of obsolete words; but their meaning is the same now as ever (§§ 15–20).

If Theomnêstus got satisfaction for having been charged with cowardice, much more should the plaintiff get satisfaction for having been charged with parricide. Theomnêstus has had one favour done him already:—Dionysius, a brave man, has been his victim. For the plaintiff, what could be so shameful a reproach as to be accused of murdering his father—a man who, after serving the democracy all his life, died for it at the hands of the oligarchs? His bravery has to this day its memorials in the temples of Athens; even as the cowardice of Theomnêstus and of *his* father have their memorials—in the temples of the enemy (§§ 21–29). The plea that the libel was uttered in anger is no defence at law (§ 30). Let the court bear in mind that he, who is now accused of murdering his own father, had in his youth impeached the Tyrants before the Areiopagus. Remembering this, the laws and their oaths, let the judges stand by his father and him (§§ 31–32).

If not one of the most artistic or the most powerful, this is at least one of the most spirited of the speeches of Lysias;[1] and the doubt of its genuineness which seems to have existed in antiquity[2] must be explained—as in the case of the speech For the Invalid—by the slightness of the matter on which

The Speech suspected in antiquity but probably genuine.

---

[1] "Oratio prior in Theomnestum ad optimas Lysiae referenda," says Francken: which is true so far, certainly, that "indignationis et iusti plena doloris est oratio" (*Comment. Lys.* p. 72).

[2] Harpocration adds εἰ γνήσιος to his citation of the speech s. vv. ἀπίλλειν, ἀπόρρητα, πεφασμένης, ποδοκάκκη: but *not* s. vv. ἐπιορκήσαντα, οἰκέως.

the case turned. The verbal quibble of Theomnêstus is, indeed, treated at somewhat excessive length; but the absurdity of the defence was perhaps felt to be among the best supports of the complaint. The conclusion of the speech bears the sure stamp of genuineness. It was a characteristic of Lysias that he loved to end, not with a rhetorical appeal, but with a definite point, put in the fewest and plainest words. Just such an ending we have here. There are besides in the speech several passages quite worthy of Lysias :—for instance, the opening remarks (§§ 1–3);—the reference to the fate of Dionysius (§§ 24, 25);—and the speaker's tribute to his own father (§§ 26–28).

Reference in § 31 to "the Tyrants."

The reference in § 31 is of some interest. The speaker says that, immediately on reaching the age of eighteen—that is, in 399 or 398 B.C.—he had prosecuted "the Thirty" before the Areiopagus. Now when the Thirty Tyrants left Athens in 403 B.C., Pheidon and Eratosthenes alone of their number are known to have stayed at Athens. If the allusion here is to them, then we see that Eratosthenes escaped at least the penalty of death when impeached by Lysias in 403.

The "Second" Speech an Epitome.

The so-called Second Speech Against Theomnêstus [Or. XI.] is merely an epitome of the First, made by some grammarian later than Harpocration.[1] The epitome preserves for the most part the very words of its original, with which it corresponds as follows :—

---

[1] Who in no one of his six references to the speech Against Theomnêstus (see above) distinguishes it by α'.

Epitome §§ 1- 2 = Speech §§ 1- 5
,,   §§ 3- 6 =   ,,   §§ 6-20
,,   §§ 7-10 =   ,,   §§ 21-29
,,   §§ 11-12 = ,,   §§ 30-32.

II. ACTION BY A WARD AGAINST A GUARDIAN
(δίκη ἐπιτροπῆς)

Against Diogeiton. [Or. XXXII.]—After describing in detail the characteristics of Lysias, Dionysius illustrates his criticism by giving extracts from a Forensic, an Epideictic and a Deliberative Speech. The Olympiacus and the Defence of the Constitution (Or. XXXIV.) supply his examples of the two latter classes. The speech Against Diogeiton is chosen by him to represent the distinctive excellences of Lysias in the forensic style.[1] Photius, too, says expressly that it was among the most admired of all its author's works.[2] It belongs to a class of private speeches to which Dionysius gives a special title — the ἐπιτροπικοί, or those made in actions brought by wards against their guardians.[3]

II. Against Diogeiton.

Special prestige of this Speech.

Diodotus, an Athenian citizen, went to the coast of Asia as a hoplite under the command of Thrasyllus in 410 B.C.,[4]—the year of the battle at Cyzicus. In 408 he was killed at Ephesus, when the troops under

Occasion and Date.

---

[1] Dionys. *de Lys.* cc. 20-27.
[2] Phot. *Cod.* 262, θαυμάζονται μέντοι γε αὐτοῦ ἄλλοι τε πολλοὶ λόγοι καὶ δὴ καὶ ὁ πρὸς Διογείτονα ἐπιτροπῆς. After praising it in detail, he concludes—καὶ ἁπλῶς ὅλος ὁ λόγος ἄξιος θαυμάσαι κατά τε τὰ σχήματα καὶ τὰ νοήματα καὶ τὰ ὀνόματα καὶ τὴν ἐναργόνιον τούτων συνθήκην, καὶ τὴν εὕρεσίν τε καὶ τάξιν τῶν ἐνθυμημάτων τε καὶ ἐπιχειρημάτων.
[3] *De Lys.* c. 20, ἔστι δὲ ὁ λόγος ἐκ τῶν ἐπιτροπικῶν.
[4] Γλαυκίππου ἄρχοντος, Dionys. *Lys.* c. 21, in his ὑπόθεσις to the speech.

Thrasyllus were defeated by the allies of Sparta.[1] Before leaving Athens he had entrusted his two sons and his daughter to the care of Diogeiton, who was at once their uncle and their grandfather, since Diodotus had married his own niece, the daughter of Diogeiton. Eight years (§ 9) after his father's death — that is, in 400 B.C. — the eldest son attained his majority. Thereupon he was informed by Diogeiton that the property left by Diodotus was exhausted, and that he and his brother must shift for themselves.

This action was brought—probably in 400 B.C.— by the eldest son. It is contended that Diodotus had left altogether 15 talents and 26 minae. Diogeiton had at first represented the sum left as only 20 minae 30 staters, *i.e.* 26 minae altogether. But he had since confessed to 7 talents and 40 minae additional, *i.e.* 8 talents 6 minae in all. His accounts, however, made him out to have spent 8 talents 10 minae on his wards in eight years; so that, instead of having a balance to hand over to them, he was 4 minae out of pocket.

The speech is directed to showing, first, that the property left by Diodotus was about double of that to which Diogeiton owned; secondly, that his alleged outlay was incredible.

The speaker is husband of the daughter of

---

[1] Xenophon distinctly refers the battle at Ephesus, in which the troops of Thrasyllus were engaged, to the archonship of Euctemon in Ol. 93. 1, *i.e.* 408 B.C.: see *Hellen.* I. ii. 1 and 7. Blass (*Att. Ber.* p. 620) puts the battle in 410; Grote in 409 (vol. VIII. p. 174). But the statement of Xenophon, at least, is clear. I once thought that in § 7 of the speech we might read 'Ερέσῳ instead of 'Εφέσῳ: since Eresus in Lesbos was in fact attacked by Thrasyllus in 411 B.C. (Thuc. VIII. 100). But this, on the other hand, does not agree with the ἐπὶ Γλαυκίππου ἄρχοντος of Dionysius.

Diodotus and brother-in-law of the plaintiff. An action of this kind was τιμητή,—that is, the plaintiff named the sum which he claimed; as Demosthenes, for instance, claimed ten talents from his guardians. It does not appear what precise sum was claimed from Diogeiton. The case would come before an ordinary court; and, as a ward was suing his guardian, the president of the court would be the first Archon.

The speaker begins by explaining the necessity which forces him to appear against a relative. His brothers-in-law, cruelly wronged, have besought his aid. Their grandfather Diogeiton had rejected all attempts at mediation; they were therefore driven to seek a legal remedy for his flagrant abuse of his trust (§§ 1–3).

Analysis.

The narrative of facts falls into two parts:—(i) The circumstances under which Diogeiton was appointed guardian, and his assumption of the office on the death of Diodotus: §§ 4–8. (ii) The disclosure made by him to his eldest ward on the latter coming of age, and the interview which followed between the young man's mother and her father Diogeiton: §§ 9–18.

These facts having been proved by witnesses, the speaker turns to the case set up by the defence. The defendant (i) has denied receiving part of the property; and (ii) professes to account for the rest:—§ 20. This account is scrutinised in detail, and shown to be absurd. On the most liberal reckoning, a balance of six talents should have been forthcoming (§§ 19–29).

Here the extract given by Dionysius ends. The statement of the defendant as to the amount which he had originally received must have been the next topic; followed, probably, by the peroration.

The two-fold merit of the Speech.

This speech—or fragment—is admirable for two things: the compact marshalling of a mass of intricate details, so that the broad result is made triumphantly clear; and the artistic treatment of character. Nothing could be better fitted to disarm prejudice, or even to create one favourable to the speaker, than the simple opening words. They show no bitterness against Diogeiton,—on the contrary, annoyance at having to appear against him—a necessity for which no one but himself is to blame. But the rhetorical skill is highest in the dramatic passage where the plaintiff's mother is brought in upbraiding her father Diogeiton with his purpose of disinheriting her sons, and the effect of the pleading on those who heard it is described (§§ 12–18).

III. Trial of a Claim to Property (διαδικασία)

III. On the Property of Eraton.

On the Property of Eraton. [Or. XVII.[1]]—This is the only extant speech of Lysias in a diadikasia,—*i.e.* in a case of a disputed claim (διαδίκασμα, § 10) to property either between two private persons or between a private person and the State. Here the dispute lies between a private claimant and the State.

The speaker's grandfather had lent two talents

---

[1] The title in the MSS. is περὶ δημοσίων ἀδικημάτων. Reiske (*Or. Att.* v. 588) thinks that this title is common to our speech and to the next (περὶ δημεύσεως τῶν τοῦ Νικίου ἀδελφοῦ): and that it may have stood originally thus — ΛΥΣΙΟΥ ΠΕΡΙ ΤΩΝ ΠΡΟΣ ΤΟ ΔΗΜΟΣΙΟΝ ΑΔΙΚΗΜΑΤΩΝ ΛΟΓΟΙ. Dobree concurs in this view (*Adv.* I. p. 233).

Sauppe follows Schott (*O. A.* I. p. 110) in changing ἀδικημάτων to χρημάτων and so prints it in his edition; but this is unsatisfactory. Hoelscher (ap. Blass, *Att. Ber.* p. 628) suggests πρὸς τὸ δημόσιον περὶ τῶν Ἐράτωνος χρημάτων (better περὶ τῶν Ἐ. χρ. πρὸς τὸ δ.); and this would be a better title.

to Eraton, who died without having repaid them. Eraton's three sons, Erasiphon, Eraton, and Erasistratus, failed to pay the interest. The speaker's father therefore brought an action against Erasistratus, the only one of the three brothers who was at Athens; and obtained an order for the payment of the entire debt, principal and interest.

His father having died about this time, the speaker, in right of the verdict, took possession of certain lands of Erasistratus at Sphettus, and claimed at law certain other lands at Cicynna, which the representatives of Erasiphon, the eldest brother, refused to give up to him.

Meanwhile—for what reason is not stated—all the property which had belonged to the elder Eraton[1] was confiscated by the State. The speaker was obliged to give up the lands at Sphettus, which he had already for two years been letting to tenants (§ 5), and to withdraw his claim to the others.

He now brings an action against the Treasury for the partial satisfaction of his claim upon the property of Eraton. The whole of this property was (he says) insufficient to satisfy his claim. Yet he is ready to give up two-thirds of it to the State; and rates the remaining third, which he demands for himself, at 15 minae (§ 7);—*i.e.* one-eighth of the sum originally lent by his father to Eraton.

The case is heard by an ordinary court, of which the fiscal board of syndici (§ 10) were presidents. Since the action against Erasistratus fell in the

---

[1] In § 6 'Ερασιφῶντος must be altered to 'Εράτωνος (meaning the elder Eraton), as appears from §§ 4 f.

Date.	archonship of Xenaenetus (§ 3), *i.e.* in 400 B.C., and three years had elapsed since (§ 5), the date is 397 B.C., of which the winter months had already passed (*ib.*)
Analysis.	The plaintiff begins by expressing a fear that the judges give him credit for powers of speech which he does not possess—an exordium which suggests that he was at least in some way distinguished (§ 1). He then gives a narrative, in three parts, of the facts just stated, witnesses being called at the close of each part: (i) § 2: (ii) § 3: (iii) §§ 4–9. He ends by simply asking for a verdict (§ 10).
No ground for supposing this to be an epitome.	In this short speech there is no argument: the proofs are all "inartificial," ἄτεχνοι πίστεις: *i.e.* derived directly from witnesses and documents. But there is certainly no reason for suspecting that we have here merely an epitome of a longer oration, like the so-called "Second" speech against Theomnêstus.[1] Short as it is, the speech is in every respect complete and clear. There is nothing of that crowding which is generally apparent in a summary; the whole is on a small scale, but the symmetry of the parts is perfect. Besides, each section of the narrative is followed by a short recapitulation (§§ 3, 4, 10). An epitomist would have left out epitomes.

IV. ANSWER TO A SPECIAL PLEA (πρὸς παραγραφήν)

IV. Against Pancleon.	*Against Pancleon.* [Or. XXIII.]—The speaker had formerly indicted Pancleon, a fuller living at

---

[1] Francken (*Comment. Lys.* p. 123) says "probabile mihi videtur, esse hanc orationem commentarium, aut potius *excerptam* esse ex genuina Lysiaca"; and at p. 238 he describes it as "epitome."

Athens (§ 2), for some offence not specified; and believing him to be a resident-alien, had summoned him before the Polemarch, who heard cases in which foreigners were concerned. Pancleon thereupon put in a "plea to the jurisdiction," on the ground that he was a Plataean by birth, and, as such, entitled at Athens to the rights of an Athenian citizen: and that, therefore, the action ought not to have been brought before the Polemarch. This plea (παραγραφή) gave rise to a previous trial to decide whether the action, in its original form, could be brought into court (§ 5). In such a case the first speech was usually made by the maintainer of the special plea:[1] here it is evidently made by the opponent.[2] The date is uncertain.

With a promise that he will be brief, the speaker comes *Analysis.* to the facts. Pancleon, on being summoned before the Polemarch, stated himself to be a Plataean by birth, son of Hipparmodôrus, and enrolled in the Attic deme of Deceleia. On inquiry,[3] the speaker learned that Pancleon was in fact a runaway slave of a Plataean named Nicomêdes. A few days afterwards, Nicomêdes actually claimed Pancleon as his slave; but the latter was rescued by a gang of bullies (§§ 5—12). He had once before been brought before the Polem-

---

[1] See *e.g.* the speeches of Demosthenes For Phormio and Against Pantaenetus, and that of Isocrates Against Callimachus.

[2] Meier and Schömann, *Att. Proc.* p. 648. The speaker makes a full statement of the facts. He would have assumed a *general* knowledge of the case on the part of the judges, and would have addressed himself rather to particular points, if Pancleon had spoken before him.

[3] The particulars of the inquiry are curious. The speaker goes to look for the Deceleia men at a barber's shop in the Hermae street (leading from the Old to the New Market-place), a regular resort for the men of that deme—τὸ κουρεῖον τὸ παρὰ τοὺς Ἑρμᾶς ἵνα οἱ Δεκελεῖς προσφοιτῶσιν (§ 3). He seeks the Plataeans, again, at the cheesemarket in the Old Agora—hearing that on the first of every month ἐκεῖσε συλλέγονται οἱ Πλαταιεῖς (§ 6).

arch by a certain Aristodicus, and had blustered, but had eventually given in. Before doing so, he had withdrawn for a time to Thebes—a signal proof that he was no Plataean (§§ 13–15). If the judges bear in mind these plain facts the speaker is confident of a verdict (§ 16).

As in the last speech, so here, all is narrative; there is no argument but the logic of facts. These are not stated with the same conciseness and clearness as in the former case; but there is no better ground here than there for suspecting, with Francken, the work of an epitomist.[1]

Miscellaneous Writings

1. *To his Companions: a Complaint of Slanders.* [Or. VIII.]—A friend addresses friends who have wronged him—states his grievances—and formally renounces their acquaintance.

Analysis. The opportunity is favourable for approaching this painful but unavoidable subject. He has before him both those whom he wishes to accuse and those whom he wishes to witness the accusation (§§ 1–2). His so-called friends have spoken of him as having thrust his society upon them (§§ 3–8). They have also persuaded him to buy an unsound horse, and have since taken part with the seller (§§ 9–13). Lastly, they have charged him with inciting others to slander them (§§ 14–17). For all these reasons he renounces their friendship. He will be safe now—for they attack only their friends (§§ 18–20).

---

[1] *Comment. Lys.* p. 238 "*excerpta ex Lysiaca.*" At p. 164 he says only "*equidem spondere ausim, hanc Lysiacam esse; sed aut non satis ab auctore aut satis superque ab aliis relictam.*" Dobree notices, and appears to endorse, a doubt of its genuineness; but without assigning grounds (*Adv.* I. 245).

It is scarcely worth while to inquire how this curiously absurd composition first came among the works of Lysias. As it is too uniformly dreary to be mistaken for a joke, not even a grammarian's conception of his sportive style can explain the imputation. The person who could thus take leave of his friends is certainly hard to imagine; but it is perhaps equally difficult—notwithstanding the amplitude of fatuity conventionally supposed in "the late sophist"—to fancy any one taking such a subject for an exercise.[1]

2. *The Eroticus in Plato's Phaedrus* (pp. 230 E– 234 C).—Plato makes Phaedrus read to Socrates a speech of Lysias in which the claims of the non-lover are urged as against those of the lover. Even to ask whether this speech is or is not an actual work of Lysias might seem at first sight to argue a want of sympathy with the broad literary characteristics of the dialogues. This speech of Lysias, it might be assumed, is as much Plato's own creation as the funeral speech by Aspasia which Socrates repeats in the *Menexenus*,—or as the discourses put into the mouths of the sophists in the *Protagoras*,—or as those delivered by Aspasia, Agathon, Aristophanes and others in the *Symposium*. The gravity of the imitation is, of course, perfect; but only a matter-of-fact reader could be misled by it.

The Eroticus in the Phaedrus.

---

[1] Benseler—a very close observer of the style of Lysias—points out that in this Eighth Oration there are hardly any examples of *hiatus*, and that such as do occur can easily be removed—*e.g.* in § 7 by reading εὐνοοῦντες for εὖνοι ὄντες. Here, then—in this marked avoidance of hiatus—we have at least one definite mark of a post-Lysian style (Bens. *de hiatu*, pp. 182 f.). In § 17, again, one may recognise very distinctly the ring of the scholastic rhetoric—ᾤμην γὰρ ἀπόθετος ὑμῖν εἶναι φίλος, κ.τ.λ. Some phrases in §§ 2, 14 again—ἐναντίον τῆς ἐλπίδος—ὁ δὲ τοσοῦτον ὑπερεῖδε τὸ δι' ἐμέ—are not like the Attic of Lysias.

This is probably the light in which the question would appear at first to most readers of Plato. But a nearer examination of the *Phaedrus* brings out two points which seem to distinguish this case in an important way from cases apparently analogous.

1. Preparation for a verbally exact recital.

The first point is the elaborate dramatic preparation made for such a recital of the speech as shall be *verbally exact*. Phaedrus is asked to repeat it from memory—makes excuses—is pressed; and presently it turns out that he has the book with him. Now if the speech was merely Plato's imitation of Lysias, surely this preface would be somewhat heavy—inartistic, indeed, as forcing attention too strongly upon the illusion. It is perfectly fitting, on the other hand, as the dramatist's apology for bringing into his own work of art so large a piece of another's work.[1] There is surely a special emphasis here:—

Phaedr. What do you mean, Socrates? How can you imagine that I, who am quite unpractised, can remember or do justice to an elaborate work, which the greatest rhetorician of the day spent a long time in composing? Indeed, I cannot; I would give a great deal if I could.

Socr. I believe that I know Phaedrus about as well as I know myself, and I am very sure that he heard the words of Lysias, not once only, but again and again he made him say them, and Lysias was very willing to gratify him; at last, when nothing else would satisfy him, he got hold of the book, and saw what he wanted—this was his morning's occupation—and then when he was tired with sitting, he went

---

[1] *Phaedr.* p. 228. It may be noticed that at p. 243 c the speech of Lysias is designated, with the same emphasis which I recognise in the opening scene, as ὁ ἐκ τοῦ βιβλίου ῥηθείς.

out to take a walk, not until, as I believe, he had simply learned by heart the entire discourse, which may not have been very long...Therefore, Phaedrus, as he will soon speak in any case, beg him to speak at once.

Phaedr. As you don't seem very likely to let me off until I speak in some way, the best thing that I can do is to speak as I best may.

Socr. That is a very true observation of yours.

Phaedr. I will do my best, for believe me, Socrates, I did not learn the very words; O no, but I have a general notion of what he said, and will repeat concisely, and in order, the several arguments by which the case of the non-lover was proved to be superior to that of the lover: let me begin at the beginning.

Socr. Yes, my friend: but you must first of all show what you have got in your left hand under your cloak, for that roll, as I suspect, is the actual discourse. Now, much as I love you, I would not have you suppose that I am going to have your memory exercised upon me, if you have Lysias himself here.[1]

The second point to be observed is the closeness of the criticism made by Socrates on the speech— corresponding to the elaborateness of the contrivance for an accurate report of it. General criticism of expression or of moral drift would have been perfectly in place even if the speech had been fictitious. But detailed criticism—recognition, on the one hand, of "clearness," "roundness," "polish" in every phrase —on the other hand, ridicule of the chaos of topics, of the repetitions, and especially of the beginning which is no beginning—would this have much meaning or force if the satirist were merely analysing his own handiwork?

2. Character of the criticism.

[1] pp. 234 E-235 A. (From the Translation by Professor Jowett.)

Socr. Well, but are you and I expected to praise the sentiments of the author, or only the clearness, and roundness, and accuracy, and tournure of the language?...I thought, though I speak under correction, that he repeated himself two or three times, either from want of words or from want of pains.[1]

Again, further on :—

Socr. Read, that I may have his exact words.

Phaedr. (*reading*). "You know my views of our common interest ; and I do not think that I ought to fail in the object of my suit because I am not your lover, for lovers repent of the kindnesses which they have shown, when their love is over."

Socr. Here he appears to have done just the reverse of what he ought ; for he has begun at the end, and is swimming on his back through the flood of words to the place of starting...Then as to the other topics—are they not a mass of confusion ? Is there any principle in them ? Why should the next topic or any other topic follow in that order ? I cannot help fancying in my ignorance that he wrote freely off just what came into his head....[2]

Then comes the comparison of the speech to the epitaph on Midas, and Phaedrus can bear it no longer :—

You are making fun of that oration of ours.

Socr. Well, I will say no more about your friend, lest I should give offence to you....[3]

It is surely clear that the speech of Lysias is both so introduced and so handled by Plato as to stand on a wholly different ground from such dramatic fictions as those in the *Protagoras*, where the sophists are

[1] p. 235 E.   [2] p. 263 E.   [3] p. 264 D.

persons of the drama, imitated in their general method and style of discourse; or from the fiction of Aspasia's authorship in the *Menexenus*—a fiction, indeed, which Plato has taken so little trouble to keep up that he makes her allude to the Peace of Antalcidas.[1] It would not be much to the purpose to analyse the composition of the Eroticus, or to show that it bears the special marks of the style of Lysias.[2] This could prove nothing. Plato could have imitated Lysias, if he had chosen, without much danger of being found out by us. It is the evidence of the dialogue, not the evidence of the speech itself, which is important.

Lysias is the earliest known writer of Erotic discourses;[3] and he is in a twofold sense the object of Plato's attack in the *Phaedrus*. The primary subject of that dialogue is the antithesis between the false and the true Rhetoric. The true Rhetoric springs from Dialectic, and Dialectic from love of the ideas. Hence the secondary subject of the dialogue is the antithesis between false and true Love. Lysias is by his profession a representative for Plato of the false Rhetoric; by his Eroticus in particular he is the representative of the false Eros. Plato could have imitated well enough for his purpose the general rhetorical characteristics of Lysias; but he embodied

---

[1] *Menex.* p. 245 C.

[2] Blass (*Att. Ber.* p. 422) points out that, plain as the style of the Eroticus is on the whole, there is rather more rhetorical ornament of the type made popular by Gorgias than Lysias usually employed; see e.g. p. 233 E ἐκεῖνοι γὰρ καὶ ἀγαπήσουσι καὶ ἀκολουθήσουσι καὶ ἐπὶ τὰς θύρας ἥξουσι | καὶ μάλιστα ἠσθήσονται καὶ οὐκ ἐλαχίστην χάριν εἴσονται καὶ πολλὰ ἀγαθὰ αὐτοῖς εὔξονται. In such a piece as this—written very likely, as Grote suggests (*Plato* I. 254), simply for the amusement of friends—it was natural enough that Lysias should have drawn upon the ληκύθια of the Sicilian school rather more than he would have allowed himself to do in a graver performance.

[3] Dr. Thompson, *Phaedr.* p. 151, note 3.

the Eroticus in his dialogue, because, further, he wished Lysias to speak for himself upon a special subject.[1]

FRAGMENTS

Three hundred and thirty-five fragments of every kind, from speeches, letters or unknown works, are arranged and examined by Sauppe, *Oratores Attici*, vol. II. pp. 170–216. Of this number, 252 represent 127 speeches of known title. Six of the 127 are represented by fragments more considerable than the rest. These six demand a few words of notice.

In a Public Cause

Speeches. 1. Against Cinesias [LXXIII. LXXIV. Frag. 143 in Sauppe].

---

[1] In the foregoing discussion I have purposely abstained from attempting to examine several arguments, turning on more or less fine points of style, which have been brought forward on each side. The fact that we have to do with such a literary artist as Plato seems to minimise the value of any argument which might be founded on the internal evidence of the speech. As to external evidence, we know only (1) that Dionysius and the pseudo-Plutarch mention ἐρωτικοί among the works of Lysias; (2) that this particular ἐρωτικός was thought really his by Diogenes Laertius (III. 25), by Hermeias p. 63 (quoted in Spengel's συναγωγὴ τεχνῶν, p. 126); and (as Dr. Thompson points out, *Phaedr.* p. 184, Appendix III.) by Cornelius Fronto—who took it as one of his models in his extant ἐρωτικός to Marcus Aurelius. I would add that the reference of Hermogenes (περὶ ἰδ. I. 12, Sp. *Rh. Gr.* II. 331) makes it plain that he thought the ἐρωτικός authentic. The evidence of the dialogue in which the speech is set must decide the question. This is, to my mind, conclusive for the authenticity.

Modern critics have been much divided. Among those who believe the Eroticus genuine are Sauppe (*Or. Att.* II. p. 209), Spengel (συν. τεχνῶν, p. 126), Blass (*Att. Ber.* pp. 416–423—where L. Schmidt is quoted as agreeing)—and Dr. Thompson in his edition of the *Phaedrus:* see esp. Appendix I. Among those who regard the discourse as fictitious are Stallbaum (*Lysiaca ad illustrandas Phaedri Platonis origines*, Leipz. 1851); C. F. Hermann (*Gesammelte Abhandlungen*, pp. 1 ff.): K. O. Müller (*Hist. Gr. Lit.* c. 35, vol. II. p. 140 ed. Donaldson); and Professor Jowett, in his Introduction to the dialogue (Translation, vol. I. p. 553).

In Private Causes

2. Against Tisis [CXIX. 231, 232].
3. For Pherenicus [CXX. 233, 234].
4. Against the Sons of Hippocrates [LXII. 124].
5. Against Archebiades [XIX. 44, 45].
6. Against Aeschines [I. 1–4].

1. *Against Cinesias.*—Harpocration mentions two speeches of Lysias against Cinesias. One of these was probably identical with that speech of Lysias "For Phanius" from which Athenaeus (XIII. p. 551 D) gives an extract. Phanius had been accused by Cinesias of proposing an unconstitutional measure (παρανόμων). The short extract in question is a personal attack upon Cinesias, whose impiety, and unfitness, therefore, to be the champion of the laws, are set forth. He is described as having belonged to a club the members of which styled themselves κακοδαιμονισταί—"the Mephistophelians"—in ridicule of societies who chose carefully euphemistic names.[1] As the latter held their meetings on the first of the month, the seventh, or some such auspicious day, so this society made a point of meeting on one of the black days of the calendar (ἀποφράδες ἡμέραι). Cinesias is satirised by Aristophanes, partly for his dithyrambs, partly for his atheism;[2] and enjoyed the distinction of having a whole comedy written about him by Strattis.[3]

1. Against Cinesias.

---

[1] Such as the νουμηνιασταί mentioned in *Frag.* 143—ἀντὶ νουμηνιαστῶν κακοδαιμονιστὰς σφίσιν αὐτοῖς τοὔνομα θέμενοι.

[2] Ar. *Ran.* 366: *Eccl.* 330: *Lys.* 838, 852.

[3] Meineke, *Com. Graec.* I. pp. 227 f.

The next four fragments have all been preserved by Dionysius; who quotes the first of them in comparing Lysias with Demosthenes—the other three, in contrasting Lysias with Isaeus.

2. Against Tisis.

2. *Against Tisis.*—Tisis, a young Athenian, had quarrelled with one Archippus at the palaestra; had treacherously invited him to supper afterwards; and then tied him to a pillar and flogged him. Archippus brought an action for assault and battery (αἰκίας δίκη); and the present speech was written for him by Lysias. The extract given by Dionysius[1] contains the narrative of the facts, which he compares with the similar narrative in the speech of Demosthenes against Conon (§§ 3–9). The critic remarks that to other excellences Demosthenes joined those which distinguished the narrative style of Lysias—clearness and naturalness.

3. For Phereniens

3. *For Pherenicus.*—This fragment is concerned with historical names. Plutarch[2] mentions Pelopidas, Androcleidas, Pherenicus as the principal of the Thebans who fled to Athens when the Cadmeia was seized by Phoebidas in 382 B.C. It appears that Androcleidas had died soon after their arrival, and that Pherenicus had taken possession of his property. He was sued for it by a rival claimant, probably also a Theban; and the present speech was made in his defence by an Athenian citizen, who had been hospitably received at Thebes by Cephisodotus, father of Pherenicus, in the exile of 404 B.C. Dionysius expressly says that the speech was made for Pherenicus as for a ξένος—which is against the improbable

---

[1] *De Demosth.* c. 11.   [2] *Pelop.* c. 5.

statement of Aristeides[1] that the Athenian franchise had been given to the Theban exiles on this occasion. As the exiles were restored to Thebes in 379, this speech must belong to the year 381 or 380, and is therefore the latest known work of Lysias. Quoting a passage of the same kind from a lost oration of Isaeus[2]—in which the advocate explains the motives of gratitude which have prompted him to come forward—Dionysius compares it with this extract. In Isaeus, we hear the rhetorician; here it is the private friend who recounts in the simplest but most telling words the great services which Pherenicus and his father had rendered to the Athenian refugees.

4. *Against the Sons of Hippocrates.*—A guardian is here defending himself against a charge of malversation in his trust which had been brought against him by his wards. Dionysius[3] places an extract from the opening of this speech beside a defence written by Isaeus for a guardian; and remarks upon the difference between the styles in which they respectively resent the imputation. The client of Isaeus uses elaborate phrases; the client of Lysias speaks like a plain man, expressing a natural sense of hardship at the recompense which his wards are giving him.

5. *Against Archebiades.*—A young Athenian citizen who has lately succeeded to a fortune by his father's death is sued by Archebiades for a debt alleged to have been contracted by his father. The point of the contrast which Dionysius[4] illustrates by an ex-

---
[1] *Panath.* p. 300 c.
[2] ὑπὲρ Εὐμάθους, εἰς ἐλευθερίαν ἀφαίρεσις. Dionys. *de Isae.* c. 6. On this and the two next Fragments, see vol. II. pp. 279 f., 365 f.
[3] *De Isaeo*, c. 6.   [4] *Ib.* c. 10.

tract from this speech is the same as in the two last cases. Isaeus, too, had once occasion to write for a young client inexperienced in lawsuits. Yet even here he could not prevent his artificialism from showing itself. Lysias, on the contrary, has given to the life the character of a man who was never in a law-court before, who does not deserve to be there now, and who hopes never to be there again.

6. Against Aeschines.

6. *Against Aeschines.*—The Aeschines in question here is that disciple whom Socrates once advised "to borrow from himself by shortening his commons."[1] Athenaeus[2] quotes a curious passage from this speech by way of exemplifying the truth that philosophers are not always philosophers. "Who would have supposed," he says, "that Aeschines the Socratic had been such a character as Lysias makes him in one of his speeches on contracts?" (ἐν τοῖς τῶν συμβολαίων λόγοις). The "contract" to which the speech cited by Athenaeus referred was a debt, due from Aeschines to the speaker. It is not clear, as Blass remarks, how Aeschines came to be plaintiff instead of defendant in the action; that he was so, however, is plain from the opening words. Aeschines had applied for a loan to help him to set up in business as a distiller of perfumes (τέχνην μυρεψικὴν κατασκευάζεσθαι). The speaker had lent him the money, "reflecting that this Aeschines had been a disciple of Socrates, and was in the habit of discoursing impressively concern-

---

[1] Diog. Laert. II. 62, φασὶ δ' αὐτῷ λέγειν Σωκράτην, ἐπειδήπερ ἐπιέζετο ὑπὸ πενίας, παρ' ἑαυτοῦ δανείζεσθαι τῶν σιτίων ὑφαιροῦντα.

[2] XIII. p. 611 D.

ing Justice and Virtue." Then come some scandalous stories about Aeschines. The genuineness of the speech has been elaborately attacked by Welcker,[1] who takes it to be the work of a later rhetorician, inspired by hatred of philosophers generally. He thinks it too coarsely defamatory for Lysias. This kind of argument is scarcely satisfactory when not supported by particular evidence; and in this case there is none. Sauppe and Blass seem right, then, in holding the fragment to be genuine. The broad comedy of the latter part is remarkable.[2]

Letters are mentioned among the writings of Lysias by Dionysius, by the pseudo-Plutarch and by Suidas.[3] The last-named speaks of seven; one, "a business letter" ($\pi\rho\alpha\gamma\mu\alpha\tau\iota\kappa\acute{\eta}\nu$), is generally identified with the letter to Polycrates cited by Harpocration. In the other six may probably be included the letter (or address) in the *Phaedrus*; the Erôticus quoted by Harpocration; and the letters to Asybarus and Metaneira. A few short sentences are all that remain. But two of these are interesting; each belongs, apparently, to a letter written after some coolness or

Letters.

---

[1] The substance of his view, as explained in an essay, *Unächtheit der Rede des Lysias gegen den Sokratiker Aeschines*, is given by Sauppe, *O. A.* II. p. 170.

[2] Besides this fragment—to which Athenaeus (XIII. p. 611 D) gives the title, πρὸς Αἰσχίνην τὸν Σωκρατικὸν χρέως—two others are cited by the lexicographers: viz. (1) κατ' Αἰσχίνου περὶ τῆς δημεύσεως τῶν 'Αριστοφάνους χρημάτων : Harpocr. s.v. Χύτροι : and (2) πρὸς Αἰσχίνην βλάβης : Bekker *anecd.* p. 132, 23. Sauppe thinks that neither of the two latter was against the Socratic. Aeschines was one of the commonest names. Diogenes Laertius (II. 64) mentions eight bearers of the name who were all more or less distinguished. The speech περὶ συκοφαντίας which Diogenes notices in the same chapter as having been written by Lysias against the Socratic Aeschines is very likely that from which our fragment comes: see its opening words—νομίζω δ' οὐκ ἂν ῥᾳδίως αὐτὸν ἑτέραν ταύτης (δίκην) συκοφαντωδεστέραν ἐξευρεῖν.

[3] Dionys. *De Lys.* c. 3, cf. c. 1 : [Plut.] *Vit. Lys.* : Suidas *s.v.* Λυσίας.

misunderstanding with a friend; and each of them shows in the writer a characteristically eager warmth towards friends.[1]

[1] The two fragments are nos. 260, 261 in Sauppe, *O. A.* II. p. 210. In the second there is a striking phrase:—"I thought I was knitted to you by such friendship"—ὥστε μηδ' ἂν τὴν Ἐμπεδοκλέους ἔχθραν ἰσχῦσαι διαστῆσαι, *i.e.* "that not the Principle of Enmity itself could have parted us."

END OF VOL. I.

www.ingramcontent.com/pod-product-compliance
Lightning Source LLC
Chambersburg PA
CBHW022140300426
44115CB00006B/282